THE WHITE RIVER CHRONICLES
OF
S. C. TURNBO

The White River Chronicles of S. C. Turnbo

Man and Wildlife on the Ozarks Frontier

SELECTED AND EDITED BY

JAMES F. KEEFE AND LYNN MORROW

INTRODUCTION BY W. K. McNEIL

THE UNIVERSITY OF ARKANSAS PRESS   FAYETTEVILLE 1994

Copyright © 1994 by James F. Keefe and Lynn Morrow

All rights reserved

14 13 12 11 10   6 5 4 3 2
First paperback printing 1998

Designed by Ellen Beeler

The paper used in this publication meets the minimum requirements of the American National Standard for Permanence of Paper for Printed Library Materials Z39.48-1984. ∞

Library of Congress Cataloging-in-Publication Data

Turnbo, S. C. (Silas Claiborn), 1844-1925.
   The White River chronicles of S. C. Turnbo: man and wildlife on the Ozarks frontier / selected and edited by James F. Keefe and Lynn Morrow; introduction by W. K. McNeil.
      p. cm.
   Includes bibliographical references and index.
   ISBN 1-55728-307-9 (c)
   ISBN 1-55728-562-4 (p)
   1. White River Valley (Ark. and Mo.)—History. 2. Frontier and pioneer life—White River Valley (Ark. and Mo.) 3. Hunting—White River Valley (Ark. and Mo.)—History—19th century. I. Keefe, James F. II. Morrow, Lynn. III. Title.
F417.W5T87 1994
976.7′2—dc20   93-49518
                                                                                                 CIP

*Dedicated to the memory of
Elmo Ingenthron,
regional historian of the
White River Valley*

Contents

Editors' Note   ix
"I Am Nothing But a Poor Scribbler": A Foreword   xi
Introduction   xv

    I. Emigrant Indians and Plain Folk   1
    II. First Families   15
        The Coker Clan   16
        The Turnbo Neighborhood   24
    III. The County Seats and Outlying Settlements   41
    IV. Man and Wildlife   71
        Tales of Buffalo   71
        Tales of Bear   79
        Tales of Elk and Deer   111
        Tales of Wolves   135
        Tales of Panther   161
        Tales of Various Species   183
        Tales of Snakes and Centipedes   205
    V. "Hearts of Stone": The War at Home   223

Appendix: Selected Genealogies of the Coker
        and the Turnbo Families   255
Notes   261
Works Cited   323
Index   339

Editors' Note

The editors took 2,487 pages of typed material and selected 425 pages for inclusion in this book. We chose tales that seemed best to illustrate the times and events (primarily 1815–65) that Turnbo recorded and to represent his major themes. Those themes of pioneer settlement, sections I, II, and III; hunting and wildlife, section IV; and the Civil War, section V, are reflected in chapter divisions, although Turnbo constantly intertwined the themes throughout his chronicles. Hunting themes were, by far, the largest category; thus, hunting is the largest section. The collection contained more material about the Cokers and the Turnbos than any other families; thus, we chose those two families to represent archetypal settlers. The Civil War section is a selected chronological sequence of Turnbo's wartime incidents and represents a conclusion to the pioneers' relatively "easy life" of subsistence in the antebellum Ozarks.

The Turnbo Collection has 823 titled stories, but the titles often contain more than one incident. For example, "An Interesting Time Among Game and Finding Bee Trees During the Pioneer Days of Ozark County, Missouri," has multiple informants and eight different settings or events in Ozark County. These distinct tales bring the collection to some 936 separate stories. Turnbo often used in his titles terms like "Scenes . . . ," "Stories . . . ," "Encounters . . . ," "Accounts . . . ," "Incidents . . . ," etc. These generic categories are complemented by specific titles.

Turnbo's geographical references relied upon twentieth-century boundaries and so do ours. Fully 88 percent of all tales are set in Arkansas and Missouri counties whose drainage flows to the nearby White River. In fact, 69 percent of all tales are set in the four counties of Marion and Boone, Arkansas, and Taney and Ozark, Missouri. Thus, the collection, and this edition, are centered within those political boundaries—the heart of the upper White River region. The 12 percent of the collection not represented here are set in thirty-eight counties and nine states outside the White River hills.

Silas C. Turnbo's formal education embraced only a few months at subscription schools, that is, schools established by a group of neighbors, who pooled their scanty money to pay a teacher for a term of three to six months. The teachers themselves were often only a little more literate than their employers, and they tended to stay only for brief periods. Nevertheless, Turnbo acquired the skills to become a facile writer.

His writing tended to be direct and in the idiom of the Ozarks, although he occasionally attempted some literary flourish. He did not use the paragraph when he got rolling, his sentences tended to run on, his spelling was sometimes whimsical, and verb tenses often did not agree. The editors have kept as much of Turnbo's style as possible, changing spellings only when necessary for accuracy or identification. They have cut his long paragraphs into digestible portions and shortened some of his sentences. Any words in brackets are editorial insertions; clarifications and commentary are in footnotes. Citations for Turnbo's writings in our synthesis refer to the arrangement of his collection at the Springfield-Greene County Public Library, Springfield, Missouri.

"I Am Nothing But a Poor Scribbler": A Foreword

Silas Claiborne Turnbo was born in a log cabin on Beaver Creek, Taney County, Missouri, on May 26, 1844. It was almost the geographical center of the region that forms the basis of these chronicles. Although it was then a sparsely settled wilderness, the land around him already was undergoing great changes from that found by the very first white men to penetrate the upper White River region. These first-wave immigrants found bottom lands covered with cane and open forests with occasional tracts of pine trees, interspersed with broad prairies. It was a healthy land, relatively free from the malaria that haunted the Mississippi Valley and the lower White River. There were bear, buffalo, elk, deer, panther, and wolves without number. These were what the first families sought, for food and for hides, to clothe themselves with, and to sell to traders for the few necessities the land would not provide. The forests, prairies, and canebrakes—and their wild creatures—were the world of Turnbo's informants.

Turnbo's father, who came to the region in 1840, was among those who might be called the second wave of immigrants into the region. They came seeking land to farm and to settle. The first wave is typified by William "Buck" Coker and his relatives, who moved into the region between 1811 and 1815. They were hunters, gatherers, and stockmen first, settlers and farmers second. Many of the incidents in this chronicle involve some member of the Coker clan.

The White River region described by Turnbo is greatly different from what we find there today. The same natural laws hold sway, but the hand of man lies heavy on the land. Gone are the open woods and most of the glades with waving prairie grasses. The rich bottom lands covered with cane that the early settlers knew—those that have not been covered with the waters of giant reservoirs—have been altered almost beyond recognition.

The rich fauna that abounded in those forests, canebrakes, and glades is gone, the remaining creatures reduced to pitiful remnants compared to what the pioneers knew. Even the remaining forests have been altered. It is a closed, brushy forest today, having become so even in Turnbo's time during the late nineteenth century. The large stands of virgin pine were exploited almost out of existence. Reading Turnbo's accounts given him by the old-timers provides only tantalizing glimpses of what must once have been.

Turnbo, in his later years, traveled widely to interview old-timers about their experiences when the White River region was being settled by Euro-Americans. The region covered is roughly between the Arkansas towns of Mountain Home on the east, Eureka Springs on the west, Jasper on the south, and Springfield, Missouri, on the north. His aim was to support his old age by publishing and selling the accounts. A portion was published in the early 1900s in two paperback volumes entitled *Fireside Stories of the Early Days in the Ozarks* and sold for fifty cents a copy. They were not a financial success, and Turnbo divided his later years between sojourns in the Confederate Soldiers Home at Higginsville, Missouri, and with various offspring in Oklahoma, New Mexico, and Missouri.

He became acquainted with William E. Connelley, who published historical works in Kansas. Connelley toyed with the idea of publishing Turnbo's chronicles, keeping the old man's hopes alive for several years. Turnbo, in ill health and desperate for money, wrote Connelley in 1907 that "I am nothing but a poor scribbler without means and education" and eventually sold his entire output to Connelley for $27.50 in 1913. He lived on until 1925.

Connelley never published the manuscripts, and they later became the property of a Kansas City book dealer, from whom they were acquired by the Springfield Art Museum. The museum turned them over to the Springfield-Greene County Library in 1977. The library, upon the recommendation of its former director, Jewell Smith, consented to make them available to us for publication in this form.

Oral history is fraught with pitfalls for one trying to get at facts about the environment existing in the past and its flora and fauna. Hunters then, as do hunters now, remember the unusual, the brightest events of their lives. And they aren't above embellishing their yarns just a little. Turnbo "penned their incidents down as they were given," uncritically putting down their reminiscences, as old yarn spinners, glad for a willing ear, searched their memories for that world that once existed. Readers are warned that, taken in their entirety, the yarns will present a picture of what the White River region once was—but any single yarn must be taken *cum grano salis*.

Readers may ask, how truthful are these tales? We had several opportunities to check the veracity of the stories, and one, which is not a part of this book, illustrated how Turnbo's informant spoke the truth. A Frank

Stevens told Turnbo of four men from Cole County, Missouri, being taken by guerrillas and shot to death during the Civil War. Stevens told Turnbo that a stone had been erected over the grave of one of the slain with the words "Killed by Bushwhackers" carved thereon. The grave was supposed to be located in the Lucinda Amos graveyard, three miles west of Russellville, Missouri. Investigation revealed that the Lucinda Amos graveyard (now called Enon Cemetery) did indeed exist. The gravestone mentioned by Turnbo's informant was found, but the words carved on it read, "SAMUEL McCLURE/KILLED/by the rebels/Aug. 29, 1864/Aged 57 yrs, 4 mos, 20 days."

Close enough.

Our debts in research are voluminous. Institutionally, they include the Center for Ozarks Studies, Southwest Missouri State University, Springfield, Missouri; the Forsyth Public Library, Forsyth, Missouri; the Joint Collection, University of Missouri–Kansas City, especially Dave Boutrous; the Kansas City Public Library; the Kansas State Historical Society, Topeka, Kansas, especially Patricia Michaelis; the Marion County Library, Yellville, Arkansas; the Museum of Ozarks History, Springfield, Missouri; the North Arkansas Regional Library, Harrison, Arkansas; the Ottenheimer Library Archives, University of Arkansas, Little Rock; the Springfield–Greene County Public Library, Springfield, Missouri, especially archivist Michael Glenn; the State Historical Society of Missouri, Columbia; Special Collections, University of Arkansas, Fayetteville; and the White River Valley Historical Society, Point Lookout, Missouri, contributed papers, maps, and photographs.

Individuals who made specific contributions include Desmond Walls Allen, genealogist-publisher, Conway, Arkansas; Robert Anderson, librarian, College of the Ozarks, Point Lookout, Missouri; Emmit D. Acklin, Norfork, Arkansas; Rick Boland, computer consultant, Martinsville, Virginia; Robert Bounds, Wolf House Memorial Committee, Norfork, Arkansas; John Bradbury, Civil War specialist, Rolla, Missouri; Tom Burge, archaeologist, Mark Twain National Forest, Rolla, Missouri; Carolyn Earle Billingsley, researcher, Alexander, Arkansas; Chad Conyers, cartographer, Springfield, Missouri; Dennis E. Figg, wildlife ecologist, Missouri Department of Conservation; Greg Fox, Archaeological Survey of Missouri, University of Missouri–Columbia; Lee Good, Davis Gun Museum, Claremore, Oklahoma; Larry Grantham, archaeologist-draftsman, Missouri Department of Natural Resources, Jefferson City, Missouri; Ben Harris, photojournalist, Salina, Kansas; John Hartman, Jefferson City, Missouri; Leo Huff, retired professor of history, Springfield, Missouri; James Johnston, folklorist and historian, Fayetteville, Arkansas; Dr. Terry

Jordan, cultural geographer, University of Texas, Austin; Larry O'Neal, Jefferson City, Missouri; Dr. James E. Price, anthropologist, University of Missouri–Columbia; Suzanne Rogers, historian, National Park Service, Harrison, Arkansas; Penny Shepherd, computer supervisor, University of Missouri–Columbia; Kenneth Shuck, former director, Springfield Art Museum, Springfield, Missouri; Althea Smith, director, Carroll County Historical and Genealogical Society, Berryville, Arkansas; Dr. J. N. Smith, chair, Agricultural Department, Southwest Missouri State University, Springfield, Missouri; Ken Story, Arkansas Historic Preservation Program, Little Rock, Arkansas; Greg Thielen, curator, Springfield Art Museum, Springfield, Missouri; and the late Marvin Tong, Ozarks enthusiast and former director, Ralph Foster Museum, Point Lookout, Missouri.

Four members of the extended Turnbo family contributed in special ways. They were Leslie E. Breeding, Denair, California; Mr. and Mrs. Hillary Brightwell, Springfield, Missouri; Mrs. Stella Luna, Gainesville, Missouri; and Mrs. Lorene Necessary, Bixby, Oklahoma. And, of course, we thank Silas Turnbo, whose few terms of subscription school in the deep Ozarks allowed him to record a collective memory of White River folklore and history.

James F. Keefe and Lynn Morrow
Jefferson City, Missouri
July 1993

INTRODUCTION

Silas Claiborne Turnbo once described himself as "nothing but a poor scribbler."[1] Perhaps he was downgrading himself in an attempt to impress his correspondent, who he hoped would help him realize his dream of seeing the abundant materials he had collected in print, but it seems more likely that this was an honest opinion expressed by a man who prided himself on being truthful. But, regardless of Turnbo's intentions, the assessment was wrong, for he was much more than just a scribbler. He was a pioneer collector of Ozark folklore and oral history who amassed one of the most important collections of Ozark material ever assembled. That in itself is sufficient to make his name noteworthy in the history of Ozark studies, but even more impressive is the manner in which this collection was gathered. Turnbo acted on his own without funding, working intuitively without prior guidelines and, often, without much encouragement.

It would have mattered little if Turnbo had sought the help of professional scholars before starting his work because there was no succor for him in the works of most historians and folklorists active in the late nineteenth and early twentieth centuries. A leading influence on the historical scholarship of this era was Leopold von Ranke (1795–1886), the German master and pioneer of scientific history. Ranke's goal, and that of his followers, was to show what actually occurred, and he believed that the past could be totally recaptured by the scientific historian. But, his conception of the past had no place for rural dwellers in regions like the Ozarks; for him they were unimportant in the grand scheme of history. Furthermore, much of the material Silas Turnbo recorded would have been rejected outright by Ranke and his disciples as worthless, condemned as being mere hearsay. Finally, the Rankeans would have had little use for Turnbo's work because it wasn't focused primarily on politics, and for them the only worthwhile history was that of great political leaders.

True, the latter nineteenth century saw the idea that historians should tell the story of all of society, and not just of its great leaders, gain considerable popularity among professional historians. This concept, which goes back at least to the eighteenth-century Frenchman, Voltaire, was vigorously espoused by John Bach McMaster (1852–1932), who became the most notable nineteenth- and early twentieth-century American proponent of social and cultural history. Indeed, it is correctly asserted that McMaster's eight-volume *A History of the People of the United States from the Revolution to the Civil War* (written in the period 1883–1913) "awakened a vogue for social history that added a new dimension to the writing of man's past."[2] McMaster's like-minded colleague, Edward Eggleston (1837–1902), now better remembered as the author of the novel *The Hoosier School Master* (1883) than for his extensive historical work, promised to write a history of life in the United States that would treat "the life of the people, the sources of their ideas and habits, the course of their development from beginnings."[3] But McMaster's work and that of Eggleston and similar thinking historians were not to have their greatest impact until after Turnbo's collecting was virtually finished, and, in any case, his Ozark materials would have been disdained by them as much as it would have been disdained by the Rankeans. While the social historians did not maintain that history existed only among the famous, they relied almost exclusively on printed and written sources, as did the Rankean exponents of "scientific history."

Even as recently as 1955, many historians considered folk traditions worthless for historical purposes. In his book *Introduction to Research in American History* (1938), Homer C. Hockett argued that folk legends and traditions contain nothing "of any positive value" for the historian "for the simple reason that they cannot be traced to their origins. And without knowledge of origins the ordinary critical tests cannot be applied."[4] In his 1955 volume, *The Critical Method in Historical Research and Writing*, Hockett expanded his attack on oral traditions, maintaining that history was "the written record of past or current events."[5] Certainly, Hockett was not alone in his beliefs; the fact that his books were widely used as textbooks in college history courses is ample evidence that his views were held by many scholars.[6]

What about the folklorists of the nineteenth and early twentieth centuries? Surely here were kindred spirits, scholars who would be likely to be interested in the data Turnbo recorded and also in the people he collected them from. Folklorists were definitely not victims of a "great man" concept of history, but many of them were just as much prisoners of print as the historians. Indeed, one of the great folklore works of the nineteenth century was Francis Child's ten-volume *The English and Scottish Popular Ballads*, an important collection that is almost solely a library work. Child believed there was little value in field collecting since he was convinced that, for all practical purposes, traditional ballad singing was a thing of the past.

There were, of course, folklorists who were heavily engaged in field collecting, but few of them were interested in doing fieldwork among white men. Henry Rowe Schoolcraft (1793–1864), who is generally considered the father of American folklore studies, is remembered today primarily for his *Algic Researches* (1839), a collection of American Indian folk narratives. In the remaining six decades of the nineteenth century after the publication of *Algic Researches*, Schoolcraft's fellow American folklorists followed his lead and focused their attention primarily on American Indian traditions. The largest organized folklore collecting in nineteenth-century America was carried out by fieldworkers for the Bureau of American Ethnology. Beginning in 1879 under the leadership of John Wesley Powell (1834–1902) and, subsequently, of six other men until the organization was terminated in 1964, the Bureau of American Ethnology sponsored field researches solely among Native Americans. Much of this fieldwork dealt with aspects of folklore, and the results were published in *Annual Reports, Bulletins,* and *Anthropological Papers.* While much of the work conducted by the Bureau was important, few of the scholars involved had much interest in non–Indian materials. True, an occasional person who worked for the Bureau, like Walter James Hoffman (1846–1899), a physician and later a diplomat, produced some publications on the folklore of non-tribal groups, but they were very much exceptions to the general rule.[7]

Why did these fieldworkers concentrate so heavily on the American Indian? There is, of course, no single answer to this question; the reasons were many. One was that they were simply following the lead of their predecessors. American Indians were also fascinating to them because they were believed to be autochthonous. Not only were they the earliest known inhabitants of the American continent, they were also the only indigenous ones.

For many nineteenth-century scholars there was another motivation for their interest, and it was largely a result of their evolutionary views. Evolutionists, such as Lewis Henry Morgan (1818–1881), who was a great influence on Powell, maintained that all societies pass through three stages of development—savagery, barbarism, and civilization, all of which were already realized. Powell added a fourth rung to this ladder of culture—enlightenment, a stage that would be achieved in the future. To these men the Indian represented the lowest level of progress, that of savagery. Therefore, the study of these tribal cultures was very important because it was in effect examining civilized man in the beginning steps leading to civilization. Perhaps these evolutionists would have viewed Ozark backwoodsmen as examples of the savage stage of culture as well, but those people lacked the exotic appeal and lengthy history of the American Indian, and, of course, early collectors had paid little attention to them.

So, when Turnbo started intentionally gathering Ozark traditional lore in the late nineteenth century, he was breaking new ground, harvesting crops that few others even imagined were there. Moreover, in true pioneer spirit, he persisted in his work over many decades, often at the cost of great personal sacrifice. Possibly he hoped for some eventual monetary gain, but it is clear his main motivation was not financial. Instead, he was moved to action by a desire to preserve material that he thought might otherwise be lost. In short, he envisioned his task as providing an educational resource for future generations. One suspects, though, that his genuine love for this material was as compelling a reason why he entered on his life's work as any other.

Who was this man who compiled so much information, who undertook a generally thankless and financially unrewarding task that occupied much of his lifetime? Who was this person who characterized himself as a "poor scribbler" but amassed what is among the most important, if not *the* most important, manuscript collections dealing with Ozark culture? Silas Claiborne Turnbo was born on Beaver Creek, Taney County, Missouri, 26 May 1844.[8] The oldest of eleven children of James Coffee (1820–1870) and Elizabeth Onstott (1824–1868) Turnbo, Silas was probably named for an uncle, William Claiborne (1815–?). Although today the area of his birth is near a major Ozark tourist center, in 1844 it was a sparsely settled wilderness region. His father, a native of Tennessee, was among those numerous immigrants who moved into the Ozarks in search of farmland. Arriving in 1840, James Turnbo spent the remainder of his life, except for a brief period during the Civil War, in the Ozarks. During that thirty-year period he did his small part to help open the White River country to permanent settlement and trade.[9]

James Turnbo was an assiduous worker with some business and marketing sense, who, by the standards of that time and place, was prosperous. In 1853 he paid the rather lofty sum of $525 for a claim in southeast Taney County. Seven years later, in 1860, he purchased a female slave for $600. During the 1850s, when steamboats began arriving regularly in his neighborhood, James Turnbo bought staples and whiskey in bulk that he resold for cash or cattle. He also sold surplus products from his farm and regularly hired farm hands. Frequently, he gained additional income doing timber work or using his mechanical skills to build mills. James also sought ways to make his farm more profitable. Thus, on an 1858 trip to visit his relatives in middle Tennessee, he heard about sorghum seed and brought some back to try on his Ozark farm.

At a very early age, Silas Turnbo became interested in stories told by his neighbors in the White River country. While living at the famous Elbow Shoals of the White River (1849–53), he heard several stories about steamboating on the river and a very memorable account of an ambush that he found particularly horrifying. Over a half century later, however, he said, "the memory of those happy days from August, 1849 to October, 1853, is still fresh in my mind."[10] But Silas wasn't just interested in oral tales; at some point he acquired a love of books. Later, while serving in the Civil War as a member of the Twenty-seventh Arkansas Infantry, CSA, he used some of his sparse funds to buy books. Moreover, during this time he started keeping diaries in which he recorded his wartime experiences. Just how many diaries there were is unknown; if the volume of his later work is indicative of that of his Civil War diaries, there were probably a large number. No matter, because in 1868, a fire that destroyed the home of his parents also consumed the diaries. Although this was undoubtedly a minor loss in comparison with the destruction of James and Elizabeth Turnbo's home, it must have saddened Silas. If so, it did not totally discourage him, for he soon rewrote much of his wartime experiences and years later, in 1908, used them as the basis for his history of the Twenty-seventh Arkansas Infantry.[11]

Just when Turnbo began collecting the material for which he is now best remembered is uncertain. Possibly it was soon after he had rewritten his wartime experiences, that is, about 1870. By 1866 he was recording reminiscences from men a generation older than himself, because in his writings he referred to specific years as the time he heard a certain story. At that early date his recording of material was, as far as is now known, incidental. When he met someone with worthwhile information, he usually made notes and filed them away for later use. It was not until the 1890s that he started thinking in terms of a larger project, one in which he actively sought out old-time Ozarkers, many of whom were personal acquaintances, who would supply him with details about the past. His prior relationship with many of these people undoubtedly made his task easier, for he must have seemed a bit odd to those he interviewed. After all, he was a middle-aged man who was asking questions about schools, farming, hunting, and other backwoods activities that were commonplace to his informants. One can almost picture them asking, "Why would anyone want to ask about that? Everyone knows about that." But, no matter how silly Silas's questions seemed to these people, apparently, they answered them willingly.

Once Turnbo started full-scale collecting, he was not easily dissuaded from completing his task. Not even the loss in 1902 of his 160-acre farm in a foreclosure slowed down his collecting efforts. Although he was virtually penniless and was forced to move in with his daughter and son-in-law, Jess and Eliza Herd, in Pontiac, Missouri, he continued his interviews unabated. Indeed, his most extensive and intensive collecting seems to have been in the years 1902–08 while he and his wife, Mary Matilda, whom he called Tilda, were living at Pontiac. On many of his journeys in search of data, Turnbo traveled alone. But, on overnight travels in the Missouri-Arkansas border counties he was often accompanied by a man whom Turnbo never identified. Possibly, he was Andrew Turnbo (1863–1946), his youngest brother.

Probably from the very first of his intensive collecting efforts, Turnbo envisioned publication of his material in some format. His first opportunities came with small-town newspapers, which in the 1890s frequently ran nostalgic articles reminiscing about "old times." Turnbo's data, which dealt exclusively with "old times," were ideally suited for such a market, and from 1898 to 1907 he turned out numerous pieces for papers in Taneyville, Forsyth, Gainesville, and Kansas City, Missouri, and Lead Hill, Harrison, and Yellville, Arkansas. By 1904 he had decided to publish a volume of his stories. While he may have been motivated to take this step by a desire to see his name on a book, it seems likely that more than just ego was involved here. With the loss of his farm in 1902, he was impoverished, and it is likely that he saw a book as a means of helping him out of his financial straits.

In 1905 Turnbo published a book of 173 pages under the title *Fireside Stories of the Early Days in the Ozarks* and paid for the printing himself. At least three subsequent volumes were planned, but only one of those was printed. Turnbo sold the books for fifty cents, peddling them on his travels around the Ozarks. Favorable letters from well-wishers were plentiful, but sales were sparse. Still, the first volume either sold well enough to encourage publication of the second or Turnbo simply proceeded, hopeful that persistence would eventually pay off. Perhaps it was the latter, because the book that appeared under the same title in 1907 was only eighty-seven pages long, just about half the size of the previous collection. The few people who bought the two works were treated to a wealth of lore, good hunting stories, and stories about animals such as bear, buffalo, deer, eagles, elk, panther, snakes, turkeys, and wolves. Several of the tales deal with the Civil War in the Ozarks, including one interesting account of a young man executed in Searcy County, Arkansas, in 1862 for desertion.[12] Another intriguing entry concerned a meteor shower that occurred November 13, 1833. Some people thought it was the end of the world and sat up all night expecting to see the dead rise out of their graves.[13]

Whatever hopes Turnbo had of turning his massive collection into profitable books were weakened, but not totally erased, by the disappointing sales of the two volumes of *Fireside Stories*. The cost of printing them left him even more impoverished than before and, of course, he was still dependent on his family for support. A desire to change this situation and to become financially independent probably played a significant part in Turnbo's decision to continue seeking publication possibilities. Aware of his own deficiencies as a writer, he thought success more likely if he allied himself with an author who had an established reputation.

Such an opportunity presented itself when, in June 1905, he received a letter from William Elsey Connelley. Connelley was an author with broad-ranging interests, who at the time had published six volumes on American Indian folklore and Western history and would eventually produce eight other books, including five-volume histories of Kansas and Kentucky. Connelley (1855–1930), who spent the last sixteen years of his life as secretary of the Kansas State Historical Society, had an interest in Ozark history that had developed when he spent four years in the wholesale lumber business in Springfield, Missouri, in the years 1888–92. He read Turnbo's first volume of *Fireside Stories* and wrote, "I am interested in your stories, because I am a Kentuckian, and was brought up in the mountains of Kentucky, and always heard hunting stories just like yours from my grandfather and other old hunters."[14] This letter touched off a correspondence between the two men that lasted eight years and included more than just letters. Connelley sent Turnbo copies of his own books, some volumes written by Connelley's friends, issues of the *Kansas Historical Society Collections*, and the popular novel by Harold Bell Wright, *Shepherd of the Hills*. Small wonder, then, that Turnbo was encouraged to continue collecting and to believe that further publication was a distinct possibility.

Turnbo's hopes were further heightened when, in 1907, Connelley offered to find a publisher and to aid in preparing the manuscript for publication. Silas was agreeable to this end, fully aware of his own shortcomings as a writer, and was willing for Connelley to have a free hand in reworking the material. He asked only for joint copyright and a share of any money that might remain after expenses. Turnbo proceeded to send

Connelley drafts of his material along with testimonials about the value of his collection from Ozarkers still living in the region and from those who had moved farther west. One man not only lauded Turnbo's work but even made a lofty prediction concerning the future use of these narratives. "Turnbo is doing a real service to history ... his style is to be commended—simple, direct in his expressions, he puts plain, neat clothes on his homely stories ... When another century has left its foot prints upon the land of my boyhood home some Walter Scott will arise, search out from some musty garret these simple folklore tales and weave them into a romance."[15]

These unsolicited favorable comments undoubtedly were a subtle attempt on Turnbo's part to prod Connelley to quick action in getting his collection published. There were varied reasons why Silas felt that publication must proceed quickly if he was going to receive any benefit from it. Certainly, the likelihood that a book based on his collection would help alleviate his impoverished situation must have been on his mind. Even more important, though, seems to have been the fact that he was in failing health and feared that he might not live to see his work in printed form other than the two slim volumes he paid for himself. Beginning in 1907 he often included comments in his correspondence with Connelley about the possibility that he might not live long.

Silas's fears about his mortality must have increased following an incident that occurred in August 1907. One day near Oakland, Arkansas, in Marion County, he suffered a heat stroke and was discovered lying unconscious on a road near the Pace Ferry crossing on the White River. A local doctor was summoned and, after being revived, Turnbo was taken to Oakland. Later, he was moved to the house of his sister, Elizabeth, in Pontiac, Missouri, where he slowly recovered. Although he was soon able to get around, he suffered ill effects from the stroke for several months.

After losing his farm in 1902, Turnbo never again owned a house; instead, he lived with various relatives or in the Missouri Confederate Soldiers Home, in Higginsville, Missouri. Then, in fall 1908, Turnbo and his wife started spending short periods of time with his sister and three of their four other children, a pattern that continued for the rest of their lives. These moves took Turnbo to Protem, Missouri; Broken Arrow and Jenks, Oklahoma; and Montoya, New Mexico. Although it became increasingly clear to Silas that publication of his stories was an elusive dream, the desire remained strong for several years. Periodic letters from Connelley served to keep Silas's flickering hopes alive. In February 1909 Connelley wrote that he had visited several large publishing houses in the

Midwest and in the Northeast, some of which were interested in Turnbo's narratives. He noted, though, that acceptance depended on the manner "in which I sent the material to them," adding that he thought he could "send it in such form that it will be pleasing to them."[16]

Whatever hopes Turnbo had of realizing any profit from publication of his collection eventually faded, their end hastened by his desperate need for money and Connelley's failure to edit the stories and find a publisher. He turned to other sources of income, such as selling subscriptions for the *Kansas City Star* during a brief period in 1912, as a result. By April 1913 Silas's financial situation was so bad and the prospects for publication of his manuscripts so dim that he decided to get whatever he could from them by selling them to Connelley. To this offer Connelley replied, "I should like to have an idea of what the material is worth."[17] Turnbo responded that he had no idea what his collection was worth, but he considered Connelley "fair and reasonable" and was willing to accept his assessment concerning the value of the manuscripts.[18] Nineteen days later, on 13 May 1913, Connelley sent a money order for $27.50 as payment for the papers—all that Turnbo ever received for his monumental collection. If, as seems likely, he began recording the material in the 1870s, this means that he received approximately sixty cents per year for his efforts.

Apparently, Connelley did some editorial work on Turnbo's manuscript but never succeeded in getting it published. During the 1920s they were among items in his collections that were offered for sale. Evidently, there were no takers, for at Connelley's death in 1930 his widow held an estate sale—among the materials available for purchase were the Turnbo papers. Many different persons acquired portions of the manuscripts, but gradually over the years the collection made its way into several institutions. Sometime after World War II, J. N. Heiskell, editor of the *Arkansas Gazette* and a lifelong bibliophile, bought a copy of the Turnbo papers that in 1985 was given to the University of Arkansas at Little Rock. In 1947 or 1948 Edward Everett Dale, a noted frontier historian, bought a copy of Turnbo's history of the Twenty-seventh Arkansas Infantry that is now part of the Phillips Collection at the University of Oklahoma, Norman. In 1967 the Kansas State Historical Society purchased a copy of the Turnbo papers from a resident of Kansas City, Kansas. Marvin Tong, a one-time newspaper publisher and museum director, an amateur archaeologist, and an Ozark native, learned that a Kansas City bookstore had a handwritten copy of Turnbo's manuscripts and thought they should be in some Ozark institution, preferably one in the White River area. He was able to persuade Ken Shuck, then director of the Springfield Art Museum, of the significance of Turnbo's material, and the museum acquired the collection. Shuck had the original papers typed and put into twenty-eight notebooks of approximately ninety to one hundred pages each.

It was the Turnbo manuscripts in Springfield that got the greatest attention from Ozark journalists and researchers. Roscoe Stewart, owner and publisher of *The Ozarks Mountaineer,* the most widely circulated regional magazine, asked and was granted permission to publish some of Turnbo's material. In October 1955 the *Mountaineer* published the first of two dozen Turnbo stories that appeared in the magazine over the next four years. Genealogists and local historians also made use of the Springfield Art Museum's Turnbo collection. The obvious value of the material for such research led a number of people to suggest that the papers be moved to a public library where they would be more accessible. In 1977 this move was effected when the Art Museum presented its Turnbo materials to the Springfield–Greene County Library.

A partial collection of Turnbo's papers is housed in the Lyons Memorial Library, School of the Ozarks, Point Lookout, Missouri, and at the Arkansas History Commission, Little Rock; both were gifts from Marvin Tong. In 1987 many of Turnbo's stories were printed without contextual commentary by Desmond Walls Allen, a professional genealogist, who used the Heiskell Collection at the University of Arkansas, Little Rock. These paperbound volumes were issued under Allen's Arkansas Research imprint.[19] At the same time Allen was issuing these books, Lynn Morrow and James Keefe were doing the research that led to the present edition. So, at last the materials Turnbo hoped to see in print are being published, but, unfortunately, it has been over six decades since his death that this has come to pass.

After 1913 Turnbo continued his nomadic ways, moving from one relative's home to another and occasionally staying in the Confederate Home in Higginsville, Missouri. He also developed a reputation among his relatives for being somewhat eccentric. Many of them viewed him as someone who did no work and wasted his time talking about the old days before the Civil War. Some descendants later regarded him even more harshly and thought his writings were worthless. But, Silas Turnbo was not easily swayed by what others thought of him and his work, and he continued making notes and writing almost until his death in March 1925. His post-1913 efforts have disappeared and possibly were thrown away by unappreciative family members after his death.

What about William Elsey Connelley? Was he playing fair with Turnbo or was he merely taking advantage of him? Why didn't he edit the collection and find a publisher for the Turnbo materials? Did he really try? While the Connelley-Turnbo correspondence could incline one to a negative view of Connelley in regard to a potential book, there is no real reason to think that his intentions were anything but good. Therefore, one must seek other explanations for his failure to publish the collection. One obvious explanation is that he was simply so busy with his own projects that he was unable to devote sufficient time to the matter. After all, he was a prolific author who, during the years 1905–13 when he was corresponding with Turnbo, published eight books. Such productivity, combined with his regular job, left little time for other projects. It is certain that Turnbo's stories required reworking before publication because there were many narratives on each of several topics. Several accounts dealt with schools, methods of farming, hunting and outdoor craft, etc. While modern researchers find this multitude of corroborating accounts useful, it seems likely that a commercial publisher would have viewed them merely as unnecessary redundancies.

It is also likely that Turnbo's data were an embarrassment of riches. The collection now housed in the Springfield–Greene County Public Library consists of almost nine hundred stories ranging from one to ten pages each. Obviously, no commercial publisher was going to issue a manuscript that ran well over a thousand printed pages and had a limited buying audience. This realization posed the problem of how to cut the papers down to a publishable size, a difficulty that apparently proved insurmountable for Connelley. Then, there is also the likelihood that Connelley, whose books were mostly issued by historical societies or academic presses, insisted on a scholarly presentation of Turnbo's manuscripts that was rejected by commercial publishers. Whether for the reasons previously mentioned, or for other reasons, there is no evidence that Connelley's negotiations on behalf of Turnbo ever got beyond a wishful, talking state.

What is the significance for modern researchers of the collection compiled by Silas Turnbo? First, it is among the earliest collections of Ozark folklore and folklife so it has historical importance, but it has greater value because it is the largest such collection ever assembled. Beyond that, the data are very detailed and the documentation good—indeed, outstanding, when one considers that for much of the time while he was recording material, Turnbo acted on his own without advice or guidance from anyone. So, in effect, he realized almost intuitively the need for information about sources and supplied much useful commentary. For example, he not only names his informants and provides their addresses, he also often tells about individual collecting sessions. Few fieldworkers active in Turnbo's day were as attentive to such matters. In several instances, Turnbo even lists some of his informant's relatives, thereby making the collection of greater value to genealogists. In fact, one genealogist has characterized Turnbo's manuscripts as "a sort of 'Poorman's Goodspeed History of the Ozark Region.'"[20]

Possibly because he was unschooled in what to include and exclude, Turnbo literally collected everything that he thought might be useful in explicating the Ozark past. Of course, it is also likely that he adopted this holistic approach because he was very interested in anything and everything about traditional Ozark culture. Whatever the reason, Turnbo's willingness to record everything his informants told him meant that he obtained data on many aspects of folklore and folklife that other reporters might have overlooked because they seemed so commonplace. His discussion of a corn shucking in Madison County, Arkansas, is just one such example. The account of accidentally finding a madstone in a dish of cooked venison touches on a belief that was once widespread in the Ozarks and elsewhere, but is almost forgotten now. The same can be said for the experience of Calvin Clark and John Nipps, who believed that sighting an apparition of a deer was a warning to them for violating the taboo of hunting on Sunday. On the other hand, the hoop snake story from Ozark County, Missouri, deals with a belief that colonial travel writers in the eighteenth century frequently reported and which has not yet died.[21]

Turnbo's informants seemed to be especially interested in relating stories dealing with animals that were dangerous to men. Some of these narratives, such as Joe Hall's tale of numerous snakes drawn toward a fire made by his hunting party, are variations on widely told yarns. Typical versions of this tale have a young couple resting after a tiring day's travel in a long-deserted cabin. They build a fire and during the night the husband gets up and receives several snake bites from which he dies. Another early collector of Ozark folklore, Friedrich Gerstäcker, recorded a version of this well-known legend, and his informant, like Turnbo's, told it as a factual event; the main difference between the two reports is that in Joe Hall's text, as related by Turnbo, the story does not end tragically.[22] By contrast, the several accounts that Turnbo related that dealt with the ferocity of centipedes are rarely reported in American folk tradition. Still, John Bias's fear of being stung to death by a centipede and the discussion of Tom May's child, who was believed to be crippled for life as a result of being bitten by one of the creatures, are graphic reminders of the fear many hill folk had regarding the centipede.[23]

Some writers have asserted that Ozarkers paid little attention to the

Civil War, but Turnbo's manuscript provides ample evidence that such a view is erroneous.[24] Ozarkers were very much aware of the war, remembering it not so much for the famous battles but for the manner in which it most closely touched their lives. The remarkable prophecy of Every Milton, who predicted the war and its exact duration two years before battle started, was of more interest to many hillfolk than the machinations of famous generals and Washington politicians. Similarly, Elizabeth Terry's ability to save her property from guerrilla raiders by making loud noises and tricking them into believing she had a large force coming to her aid was a more memorable aspect of the war to her than battles at Pea Ridge, Wilson's Creek, or elsewhere. It is hardly surprising that prophecies like Milton's or tricks like Terry's are commonly encountered in the folk tradition of the western world.[25]

Many of the narratives recorded by Turnbo have a tall-tale quality about them, but there is no evidence that Silas, or his informants, had tongue in cheek when relating such stories. Bill Clark's account of killing six deer with three bullets is strongly reminiscent of a tale known throughout Europe and the United States as the Lucky Shot or the Wonderful Hunt.[26] Also, the report of Clark's phenomenal eyesight seems an exaggeration, but some bee hunters do have an ability to see small objects at great distances that those unfamiliar with the craft might find unbelievable. Of course, many of the narratives in Turnbo's manuscripts are intentionally humorous, several being variants of widely told funny yarns. Many are also variations on the theme of absurd ignorance, which has for centuries been a popular motif in the folk tradition of many countries throughout the world. The story of the two ladies who had never seen a mirror before visiting Alex Duggins's home is of this type.[27] Some of the humor, such as Zeke Eslick's description of his father's reaction to Dave McBride's encounter with a wildcat, is of a type that modern readers might find cruel. Such incidents, though, were typical of the humor in southwestern literature of the mid-nineteenth century and have lingered on in Ozark folk tradition; a similar yarn was recorded in 1979 from a Newton County, Arkansas, raconteur.[28]

Many early American folklore collectors sought examples of songs, games, and proverbs, aspects of the oral tradition that are sparsely represented in Turnbo's collection, possibly because he didn't specifically ask about such material. He did, however, note a few examples of these genres, and, as with most of the traditional lore he reported, put them in context. For example, a fragment of a derogatory song about Jeff Davis was given in the course of a story told by Lem Hollingsworth. Turnbo also reported proverbs and proverbial phrases in two ways: first, as used by his informants and second, included in his own commentaries as traditional sayings. Considering Turnbo's historical interest, it is hardly surprising that his manuscripts are heavily weighted in favor of folk history and historical legendry.

One of the major virtues of Turnbo's collection is that he provided each narrative in the informant's words, often also telling much about the manner in which each text was related. His recital of the place-name legend of Poor Joe Bald indicates that he didn't accept material literally just because someone told it. Instead, he tried to obtain the most complete account of the legend and then, if possible, to verify its accuracy. In the spirit of most historians of his day, he was seeking to find factual "truth" rather than psychological "truth," but even so, he was aware that what people believed happened (psychological "truth") was important. There are, of course, some shortcomings in Turnbo's work, one of the most notable being a certain nostalgia that permeates the collection. While Silas did record material dealing with then relatively recent times, the bulk of his collection is concerned with the antebellum Ozarks, an era that was for him a "golden age." Then, material is presented as if it were unique to the informants from which Turnbo collected, when in many cases the stories or lore are relatively widespread. But, in evaluating Turnbo's work, it is important to keep in mind that he did not see himself as a scholar, but rather as an individual passionately concerned with obtaining data on the history of the Ozarks, or at least one section of the Ozarks.

It is tempting to compare Silas Turnbo with another later collector of Ozark folk traditions, Vance Randolph. Admittedly, there are several similarities between the two men and their work. Both were enthusiastic about traditional Ozark culture and spent decades gathering information on the topic. Unlike most other fieldworkers, who spend an occasional day or two among their informants, both Turnbo and Randolph spent most of their lives among the people from whom they collected, Turnbo as a native and Randolph as an outsider from Pittsburg, Kansas. They did their work primarily in the field, interviewing old-time Ozarkers rather than just searching for information in libraries. Both men operated without the advantage of grants and other luxuries to which modern researchers have grown accustomed. Finally, both men were amateur fieldworkers in the best sense of that term. There the similarity ends, for Randolph was much more a comparativist than was Turnbo, one of the major reasons his work achieved more academic recognition during the years of his most intensive effort than did Turnbo's. Moreover, Randolph was a professional writer who used the folklore he collected in books and articles that provided him with a large portion of his annual income. Turnbo perhaps would have done the same but simply wasn't Randolph's equal as a writer. His two books were self-published and financial failures, and most of his articles were unpaid contributions to newspapers. But, the greatest difference between Randolph and Turnbo is that the former achieved acclaim during his lifetime for his work on Ozark folklore, while Turnbo has yet to be widely applauded for his efforts. It is certain, though, that without the "poor scribbler's" collection, our knowledge of Ozark history and culture would be considerably smaller.

> W. K. McNeil
> The Ozark Folk Center
> Mountain View, Arkansas

I

Emigrant Indians and Plain Folk

Editors' note: The Indians in the Turnbo Collection are primarily Shawnee, Delaware, and Cherokee. By 1780 bands of these groups had crossed the Mississippi River into the large New Madrid District of modern southeast Missouri and northeast Arkansas. Some Indians lived on lands near the great river, but others, especially as time passed and European-Americans immigrated to Missouri Territory, moved into the interior along the St. Francis River, the Whitewater River, and into the waters of the White and Arkansas rivers.

Commerce in the territorial Ozarks was profoundly influenced by the presence of Indians. They increasingly became wards of the federal government and as such received annual annuities, paid in specie, that regional traders sought for commercial profit.

Turnbo's stories, however, are not so much about trading as they are about daily social intercourse among these neighbors on the early Ozarks frontier. A number of Turnbo's subjects immigrated with Indian wives and married them in the territory or were mixed-ancestry offspring of former alliances in the East. The Turnbo stories communicate a relative ease of frontier association with the largely Anglicized southern and eastern emigrant Indians. He mentions several cemeteries in the White River Valley that were begun with Indian burials, but were succeeded by white burials. In characteristic fashion, Turnbo always tried to ease conflict with the soothing levity of storytelling.[1]

Chased by a Band of Indians [25:13]

ONE MILE WEST of Elbow Creek in Taney County, Mo., is a bald hill called "Poor Joe." There is nothing remarkable in the formation of this moundlike hill, but it possesses a name which it has borne since the early settlement of the country. Though while "Poor Joe" is not a tall eminence yet it is so situated that a pretty view from its top is obtainable and the common scenery of this part of the Ozarks are observed such as wooded hills, glades, bald knobs and prairie hollows. Looking southward and southwest and south of west many of the hills in Marion, Boone and Carroll Counties, Arkansas, are plainly visible.

There is an old time tradition in connection with this bald hill which the old settlers said was true. But the occurrence of it was so long ago that it is almost impossible at this late day to obtain an accurate account of it. But the story was told about this way.

Joe Coker had married in Alabama and his wife died in that state. The issue of that marriage was two sons and two daughters. William (Prairie Bill) and Herrod were the names of his two sons and Sally and Betsey were the names of his girls. Coker's wife was a daughter of Bob Brown, another old time settler on White River. [See chapter 2 introduction to Coker Clan.]

Soon after the death of his wife Joe married a Cherokee Indian woman named Aney (not Annie), but during the year previous to his marriage to this woman he sent his children and Negro slaves to White River in charge of his brother, Charles Coker, who reached the Sugar Loaf country in 1813 and as we have said before Joe Coker himself came here in 1814.

His father, William (Buck) Coker, pitched his tent on the north bank of White River January the 8th, 1815. The spot where he located is now the Dave McCord farm in Jake Nave Bend and is embraced in Boone County, Arkansas.

It was told by the settlers that after Joe took up his abode on White River he was not contented with one Indian wife and took unto himself another one of the name of Cynthiana. She was a daughter of John Rogers, a white man who had married a full blood Cherokee woman.

Many years after the occurrence of the story we have in mind Aney lived on the river and "Cyntha" lived in the Sugar Loaf Prairie. It was said that after Coker showed his affections for the second Indian woman the Indians, who were numerous here at that time but were friendly,[2] become greatly incensed at Joe's conduct for having one too many wives of their kindred and made up their minds to put him out of the way. But Coker understood the enmity they held against him and was constantly on the lookout for them to prevent them taking the advantage of him and thus it went on for some time when finally a bunch of the Indians got the drop on him and thought his scalp was in their grasp.

It is told that Coker and others had went to Elbow Creek to kill bear. The majority of the men were afoot. It appears that a small band of Indians were hunting here at the same time which was unknown to Coker and his friends. The Indians were all afoot and carried their bows and arrows and tommyhawks. One day while Uncle Joe was hunting alone on the west side of the creek the Indians discovered and recognized him. He in turn knew that they were his enemies. Joe had his rifle and hunting knife. The band of Indians raised the war whoop and charged toward him. Knowing he had no chance for his life in contending against so many Coker reserved his fire and fled.

The woods were open—that is it was divided into belts of trees and prairies without undergrowth or thickets or bresh. Coker was in the prime of life and stout and vigorous and he bounded along through the tall grass like a deer pursued by a pack of hounds. As he ran he looked back and perceived that the yelling band was gaining on him. This was not a good omen and he did his utmost to accelerate his speed. On came the noisy Indians who were thirsting for his blood and scalplock. Uncle Joe was not ready to surrender his life and he knew that his safety depended on his legs and he made good use of them. The pursuing Indians yelled like demons and let fly several arrows at the retreating form of Coker but they went wide of their mark.

The fast racing white man had no time to stop and exchange shots with the red men for his business lay rolling from there and that in a hurry. It was not long before the man drew near this bald hill. It lay directly in his course but he kept straight forward up the slope. Coker was afraid to turn to the right or left for fear the Indians might head him off. By this time the white man was becoming tired and his breath was coming and going at much shorter intervals than common and before reaching the summit the Indians gained on him rapidly and as the pursued and pursuers went rushing along over the top of the knob the latter came near overhauling their intended victim.

Thinking he would have to face death Joe thought he would stop and sell out to his enemies as dear as possible, but at this moment the red men thinking he was as good as theirs yelled the louder which put new life in Joe's system and without halting he renewed his running power to keep in advance of his foes. A few of the fleetest Indians had dashed forward ahead of their companions and were almost in the act of striking him with their tommyhawks, when Coker threw down his rifle which impeded his progress and cried out in a loud voice as he ran, "Poor Joe", "Poor Joe" a half a dozen times or more for he believed he was a goner this time sure.

By this time the white man and the foremost Indians had reached the slope on the opposite side from where he ran up and being relieved of his rifle he was now in better running order and he bounded along down the hillside like a rubber ball and soon outstripped the angry savages. Part of the Indians stopped to pick up Joe's rifle and exult over the possession of it. Of course when these Indians halted it gave the man some advantage and he made good use of it. When the other red men stopped the fleetest ones checked their speed and slowed up.

Very soon Coker looked back again and seen the Indians far in the rear. But he kept up the race when finally he lost sight of them. But on he went as fast as he could run over the rough ground and across glades, small prairies and wooded ridges. It was a desperate race. He looked back again but his pursuers if they were still following him were not in his sight. His strength was nearly exhausted and he could run but little further until he rested.

Seeing a fallen tree a few yards ahead which had been blown down by a windstorm during the summer and he sought its friendly shelter of limbs and dead foliage and lay in concealment until his almost exhausted organs of respiration could equalize the circulation of blood then he poked his head out of the tree top and finding the coast was clear left his hiding place and went on and escaped.

No doubt the Indians could have followed him to his place of refuge in the treetop for he had left a plain trail behind him in the rank grass, but fortunately for him they abandoned the chase and turned in another direction. This bald hill was called Poor Joe from that day and retains the name to the present time. More than likely this name will never be changed as long as the little brooklet which flows on the east side of it is called Elbow Creek. 🔖

GAMBLING WITH THE INDIANS [25:22]

ON THE RIGHT BANK of White River just below the mouth of Trimble's Creek in Franklin Township, Marion County, Arkansas, is the old farm once known as the Tom Brown place. Here on this land long before any white people lived in this bottom the Indians had a big village here and the fame of this Indian encampment traveled afar off. The camp extended from Trimble's Creek down to the mouth of Becca's Branch.

Allen Trimble was a little fellow while these [Cherokee] Indians lived here. His father, William Trimble, lived in the bottom on the north side of the river on the old George Fritts place that the writer's father bought of Mr. Fritts in the summer of 1859. Jess Yocum[3] lived on this same land above the sloo. Trimble lived below the sloo. Jess Yocum visited the Indian camp frequently and [would] gamble with the Indians and win deer hides, beads and moccasins from the red men at a game called chuckaluck.

Allen Trimble informed me that he would visit the Indian's village of nights with his uncle Jess Yocum and Yocum would remain and gamble with the red men until late at night before leaving.

"Mr. Yocum would go to the camp on horseback when the river was fordable and I would ride behind him. When the river was past fording we would cross in a dugout canoe and walk down to their camp," said Mr. Trimble. 🌿

Stories of the Shawnee Indians [25:23]

IT IS SAID that at the breaking out of the war between the United States and England in 1812 the Shawnee Indians were divided into two tribes. The majority favored Great Britain. The remainder favored the United States. If I am not misinformed the Shawnees formerly inhabited a strip of country reaching through Kentucky, Tennessee, Mississippi and Alabama.[4]

The part of the tribe friendly to the United States were headed by Chief Lewis. The famous Chief Tecumseh commanded those who took sides with England. I am told that many years ago the White River from a few miles above Batesville[5] to some distance up this stream was ceded to the Cherokee Indians. This was called the Cherokee Grant.[6] But it is told the tribe never occupied it. Whose fault it was I am not able to say.

Lewis' Indians were brought to it about 1819. There were about 2,000 of them of all sexes and ages. These Indians divided into three parties and each had a village on the river. One town was situated at the mouth of Livingston's Creek. Another village was somewhere near the mouth of Pine Bayou and the other a few miles below [the] mouth of Big North Fork. Finally several Indians located where Yellville, Arkansas, now stands on Crooked Creek.

Everyone acquainted with the history and nature of Indians understood their greed and love of whiskey. An incident of this kind which shows their ungovernable temper for fire water was told by old timers and occurred at the mouth of Livingston Creek near where Mount Olive is now.

Two white men of the name of McCoy and Bill Clifton brought a barrel of whiskey up the river in a large canoe. The Indians were on the alert and learned of the whiskey being aboard before the arrival of the canoe. As the men with their canoe hove in sight of the village the Indians began stirring around lively. The white men suspicioned that the red men were aware of the barrel of whiskey being in the canoe and they hovered as close to the opposite shore as the water would permit with the hope that they would not be molested.

In a short time a crowd of Indians had collected on the shore and gave the two white men a sign to bring the canoe to their side of the river, but they refused and pushed the canoe along as fast as they could. The Indians seeing that the white men had disobeyed their sign a lot of them ran along the bank ahead of the canoe then waded across the river and captured the canoe by superiority of numbers. Clifton was brave and stood in defense of his craft and bill of lading, but the other fellow leaped into the water and retreated to shore and ran into the forest.

Clifton did his utmost to prevent the surging crowd of Indians from taking the barrel of whiskey and fought them desperately with his canoe pole, but they were too many for him and he was compelled to yield. The Indians dragged the canoe to their side of the river where their village stood and rolled the barrel ashore and turned the man and his craft loose.

Clifton's temper was wrought up to a high pitch. He was angry enough to have cleaned out the whole crowd of Indians if it had lay in his power, but seeing now that further resistance was useless he left the shore silent and disgusted. A few of the wiser heads in the village saw what was coming for the whole village would soon be in a drunken row and they hurriedly collected all the arms in the village and put them together and stood guard over them with clubs. All the balance of the Indians, little, big, old and young, got drunk and kept up a terrible yell night and day for half a week.

During their drunken carousal a few whites visited them but they were careful to avoid trouble with them. Clifton visited them too and sought revenge for the loss of his barrel of whiskey. At the moment he would catch a drunken Indian away from camp he would knock him down and stomp him, then let him up and wait for another one to come along and he would treat him likewise.

When the Indians occupied Shawnee town [1820s] where the fine little city of Yellville was afterward built they were a lively crowd. White settlers visited them from far and near.[7] The Indians erected several small huts mostly of cedar logs. They covered [roofed] these with boards six feet long with about two courses to the side. It is told that the Indians notched their logs on top instead of the bottom like white people do.[8]

John H. Tabor, who died near Powell, Ark., in 1902, and Allen Trimble, who died in 1889, told some interesting stories concerning these Indians, especially about their green corn dances[9] which occurred annually about roasting ear time either at Shawnee town or at their village just below the mouth of Big North Fork. A noted Indian by the name of Bob lived at the latter village.[10]

Jake Wolf and [Tom] Stalling and Dearmond[11] had a trading post at [the] mouth of North Fork and when the Indians would arrange for a dance at the village below the trading post a goodly number of Indians would go down there from Shawnee town and have a gay time dancing and getting drunk. Trimble and Tabor said they were present on several occasions when these dances occurred. In describing the dancing floor they said the Indians would make a ring about one hundred fifty feet in circumference and clean the ground off nice in the circle similar to an old fashioned wheat yard that the settlers use to tromp their wheat out on with horses.

When all the arrangements for the dance was complete the performance began. One of the Indians beat a drum made of a hollow log that had been hollowed out until the walls were thin. The ends were covered with dry hide. As the drum would be beat the Indians would dance and half march around on the yard once, then face about and go back the other way. As they did so they would sing or chant. They would have their leggins filled loosely with small pebbles and mussel shells which rattled together as they danced and hopped around the circle. This combined with chants and noise made by beating the drum, including the action of the performance, was a scene of fun and curiosity. They would not dance long before they stopped and filled the bowls of their pipes that was fixed in their tommyhawks with tobacco or a substitute if they did not have tobacco, and sit down. After lighting their pipes [they] would take a puff then pass it around until every Indian took a draw from each pipe, then they would rise and go on with the dance. This was repeated several times before they become weary of their work.

If whites were present they would invite them onto the floor to dance with them. If they accepted the Indians would make sport of their awkwardness. If the whites smoked with them the Indians considered them friends. Allen Trimble said he was present one day while a green corn dance was going on at Shawnee town and one of the Indians got beastly drunk and was unruly and boisterous. Some of the other Indians tried to quiet him but failed. After enduring his recklessness a while longer they all quit dancing long enough, and with buckskin thongs they tied his hands and feet together like tieing a hog and picked him up and dumped him into the shade of a tree, where he was allowed to remain until he was sober enough to behave himself.

After the Indians vacated their huts some of the whites occupied them. It is told that Ben Woods lived in one of these cabins several months. The settlers called him Cedar Wood after that because the Indian hut he occupied was built of Cedar. Ben was a brother of William Woods, the first county judge of Marion County. The settlers called Judge Wood "Dancin Bill" because he was considered the best dancer in the county.

Mrs. Mary A. Holt, before her death at Lead Hill, Ark., told an amusing anecdote which is too good to be lost which occurred at Shawnee town, now Yellville, Ark., after the greater number of Indians had gone west. Mrs. Holt said that her grandfather, Jimmie Adams,[12] settled in the river bottom two and one-half miles above Big North [Fork River] at an early date.

"Some years after his arrival here he built a little mill on a small stream supplied with a fine spring of water. One of his sons named Matt usually attended the mill.[13]

"In 1838 the country was visited by a protracted drouth and corn crop was short. In the following year several settlers done without bread. My grandfather instructed Matt if a customer come to the mill with a small amount of corn in his sack and was without means to buy bread, not to toll it but put a tall dish full in his sack and grind it free of toll."

Mrs. Holt went on to say that before Mr. Adams built this mill Jess Everette built a little mill on Mill Creek just south of the Indian village where Daniel Wickersham built his mill afterward. Everette's mill was the first one built in what is now known as Marion County, Ark.

"One day," said Mrs. Holt, "grandfather and one of his black slaves named Jess went to Everette's mill on horseback. Jess the colored boy did not love Indians and did not appreciate the idea of being in their presence.

"As it was some distance to mill Mr. Adams was late in the day before arriving. While waiting for his grist grandfather took the Negro boy and rode into the Indian village. Some of the Indians were preparing a repast by broiling fresh meat on the fire and when they got ready to dine they invited grandfather to eat with them. The invitation was accepted. The

Indians also invited the young Negro to share their generosity. But he declined without saying anything.

"The Indians were kind and friendly and kept insisting on the colored boy to eat with them, but he shied off for he was afraid of them. The Indians told him that the meat was good and well cooked on the live coals of fire and that he was welcome to all that he could eat. But they could not prevail on him to speak much less to eat.

"At last the Indians grew impatient and offended at the stubborn boy and one of the Indians exclaimed in broken English, 'White man leetle better than injun. Injun leetle better than nigger. Nigger leetle better than dog.' The cutting remark cast toward the lad created a roar of laughter among the Indians and grandfather joined in with them and he took many merry laughs about it for years afterward.

"When Jess was grown he was a religious turn of mind and turned out to be a Baptist preacher and lived at Springfield, Mo., a few years after the war." 🗞

A Praying Indian Chief and Other Stories of the Red Men [25:31]

I AM REMINDED of another tale told me by Raleigh Austin, an early resident on Crooked Creek, who stated that one day in the early Fifties he was traveling over a trail on Bull Creek which flows into White River sixteen miles above Forsyth, Mo. By following the course of the river, [he] came to a large tree with the figure of an Indian armed with his bow and arrow carved in the bark of the tree. On the opposite side of the tree the figure of a bear had been cut in the bark.

Mr. Austin said these figures were a curiosity and he dismounted and examined them a half an hour without being able to solve them. Remounting again he rode on a few miles and met a settler and made inquiry of the man if he knew why the figures were cut on the tree. The settler informed him that many years before, an Indian warrior killed a bear at this same tree with his bow and arrows and the Indian cut the image of himself and bear on the tree to mark the spot where the bear was slain and to commemorate the deed.

Zeke Eslick, who died near Arno, Mo., several years ago said that when Art Eslick, his father, settled in Douglas Co., Mo., in 1839 there were bands of Indians passing through that section.[14] Mr. Eslick tells a short story of his father being out hunting one day near his house on Beaver Creek.

"It was in the month of March, a forest fire had swept through there a week previous, the fire had passed through a big hazle thicket and burned up the hazle bushes,[15] leaving the sharp stubs sticking out above the ground. As he walked along he heard the report of a rifle toward the burned over ground where the thicket had stood. A low hill lay between him and the ground mentioned. As the country then was so sparsely settled father thought a 'new comer' had settled there, and he went over to get acquainted with him and exchange hunting stories.

"On approaching the ground where the thicket had been destroyed he saw an Indian limping along like he was wounded in the foot. The man was carrying a rifle and father supposed he had accidently shot himself in the foot. Father hallooed to him to stop and he did.

"On getting up nearer the red man gave father a sign with his hand that he had snagged his foot and sat down and held up his foot for father to examine. The snag was a hazle stub. The Indian had shot and wounded a deer and while the Indian was running over the burned over spot where the thicket stood he leaped on one of these stubs and it perforated his moccasin and entered deep into the bottom of his foot and broke off.

"Father tried to pull the snag out but failed. Then the Indian made an effort to withdraw it but he was not successful. Neither man could understand each other's language but they made each other understand by motions and other signs.

"The snag stuck out a half an inch and it was causing the Indian much pain but he never evinced it by a groan or a frown. Father did all he could to pull it out of the man's foot but his efforts were fruitless. At last the Indian give father a sign how to get it out and that was to place the priming pan of his rifle under and up against the end of the snag where it protruded from the foot and he made father understand that the frissen[16] could be made to act as pincers and while father pressed the frissen hard against the snag which rested on the priming pan the Indian pulled back with his foot and the snag come out.

"The job of extracting the snag was rough and painful but not a murmur fell from the Indians lips. The length of the snag was one and one-quarter inches, which showed that it had run into the foot three-quarters of an inch. The wound bled and the Indian squeezed all the blood out he could and bound up the wound and with more signs he give father to understand that he felt very grateful to him for his timely aid in the rude surgical operation, then he started on the trail of the wounded deer again and soon discovered it lying down and shot it the second time and killed it.

"This Indian belonged to a band that was passing through and several of them had scattered through the woods to shoot deer."

Mr. Beden Eslick, who was also an early settler on [the] head of Beaver Creek in Douglas County and who come there five years earlier than Zeke Eslick, told me that one day soon after he come there a band of Cherokee Indians stopped a few days on Beaver Creek to hunt. The chief or head man of the party had a small son with him that he was teaching to be chief when he become older.

"One day during their stop here the chief and his little boy and a few other Indians come to our house to buy salt[17] which article was very scarce here then and high in price. The chief was an expert dancer, but he refused to dance unless he was payed for it.

"After father sold him a small quantity of salt and the Indian had paid for it in furs, father told him if he would dance awhile he would give him some salt extra. The Indian appeared to be pleased at the offer and fell to dancing at once and danced all over the yard before he let up.

"Then father invited all the Indians into his cabin. After they all got in the house the chief told the boy to beat on the back of a chair with an arrow, and while the boy was beating in a rough like way on the chair his father danced on the floor which was made of very rough puncheons.

"I was only a boy myself then," said Mr. Eslick, "and I remember how greatly I was amused at the big Indian's capers he cut while the boy beat on the chair. The Indian could beat a white man dancing two to one.

"Though we could not understand their dialect, but we understood their signs. They were all very friendly and peaceably disposed.

"A few days after this the men of this band went out in the hills to kill big game and was gone several days. My two brothers, John and Sam, were older than I and they requested father by signs to allow the boys to accompany them on the hunt. The boys wanted to go and father gave them permission. They said when they come back home they enjoyed being out with the red men, but they said that the religious fervor of the chief was more interesting to them than seeing the Indians go on the chase.

"The boys said that every night while they were in camp with the Indians the chief arose about midnight and devoted an hour in prayer. 'We did not know,' said they, 'who he prayed to but suppose it was to the Great Spirit. Anyway it was a mighty long prayer and was repeated about the same hour each night. When he brought his devotion to an end he would wake up his little boy from his slumbers and bid him to pray and while the little fellow was engaged in prayer the father would retire on his couch of skins again and was supposed to be in the dreamy land again.

The boy did not quit off short but he stayed up about as long as his father did, but finally after the religious devotion was ended he too lay down again and was soon apparently asleep once more.'"

SCARED BY THE INDIANS AND STUNG BY NETTLES [25:41]

SOME OF THE EARLY RESIDENTS of Greene County, Mo. was William Stacy, Joe Price, "Goody" (John) Wilkerson, Billy Fullbright, Joe Leeper, John Roberts, Beeze Hayden and Jess Bayles.[18] Stacy came from Jackson County, Tennessee in 1832 and settled on the north bank of the James River near where the old wooden bridge was built across this stream some seven miles from Springfield.[19]

Leeper Prairie derived its name from Joe Leeper. John Roberts built a little mill near four miles from Springfield and Beeze Hayden succeeded Roberts in the ownership of this mill. The man Bayles was a miner and worked on the same stream that Roberts built his mill on.

Away back in the early days of the James Fork of White River or soon after this stream began to be settled by the whites, the Indians would pass through on their way to the west and the white women and children were afraid of them.

On one occasion a large number of Indians gathered in the settlement on the James where it passed through Greene County[20] and scared the women and children into a hollow or deep ravine where the children got into a patch of nettles[21] and got their feet and legs stung. Some of them began to cry so loudly that their frightened mothers had to put their hands on the little ones mouths to prevent their cries reaching the quick ears of the red men. This scared the children so dreadfully that they thought they were going to be choked to death to save them from being tortured by the Aborigines and could not see much to recommend the maternal plan of salvation.

The settlers were uneasy for they expected an attack and they all congregated together with guns in hand and started and circled around through the woods and watched the Indians until [they] went on their way to the new lands.

The foregoing accounts was given me by Dr. Silas S. Stacy son of Bill Stacy while he lived at Isabella, Ozark Co. Mo. in 1869.

A Story of Hidden Gold and Silver in the Vicinity of Bee Creek [26:73]

THE FOLLOWING ACCOUNT was written to me from Arlington, Washington, by Mr. J. D. Row on the 11th of August 1907.

"When I got in Carroll County, Ark. on my way from Oklahoma territory to Boone County, Ark. in the year 1900, I stopped and visited with my cousin George W. Barnes of Maple Post Office.[22] He told me a story as follows. His brother Jasper Barnes had been over in the north part of Boone County, and in a conversation with Mat Boothe who lived on Bee Creek, he heard of a train of three wagons having been burned by the guerrillas in time of the war. He did not get many particulars about the occasion.

"Soon after this his step son come home from the Indian territory and he told Jasper a story he got from a Cherokee Indian, while he was in the Indian territory. The Indian said that during the war himself and three or four other Indians were coming through Missouri with three wagons, and they had a large amount of gold and silver coins that they were conveying from Southeast Missouri to their homes in the territory. They had been observed by some white men to have a lot of money and they had followed the Indians, presumably to rob them. They had observed the white men stealthily following them for two or three days.

"In the vicinity of Bee Creek the men had become more bold and the Indians feared an attack during the night while in camp. They held a consultation and decided to bury their treasure, burn their wagons, and ride their ponies home. Afterwards they would come back and secure their money.

"When the war was over and times were peaceable enough, the Indians were all dead but this one. He had made two trips back to Bee Creek to get the hidden money, but each time failed to find the place. The country had changed, farms had been opened up, houses built and he could not even locate the road they were on when they burned their wagons.

"This Indian and another one had taken the coins in two camp kettles a little ways from the road, to a sink hole and buried them in the sink hole while the rest of the crowd had run the wagons together and set them on fire, then they all jumped on their ponies and rode away in the darkness of early morning."[23]

II
First Families

Editors' note: By 1810 pioneers had settled intermittently along the upper White River. Trading depots at this early period developed at the mouths of Big North Fork River (Baxter County), Rocky Bayou (near Guion, Izard County), and Poke Bayou (Batesville). Traders ascended the river on keelboats to sell salt, powder, whiskey, lead, and other commodities in exchange for buffalo hides, bear skins, and pelts. Travel above the North Fork was considered hazardous, and few families lived in that area until the 1830s and later. Well known throughout the region in this group of hunter-stockmen were the Cokers.

William "Buck" Coker (1769–1855) and his large entourage of relatives exemplify a common type of immigration in the southern uplands. They left County Cork, Ireland, and were in Surry County, Virginia, by 1635. Apparently, they thrived in the colony, acquired a few slaves, and eventually exported tobacco to England. In the early 1770s some of the Cokers moved southward to the Carolinas and Georgia. Before long, some Cokers went west into Mississippi Territory, and other families remained in what became Montgomery County, Alabama. From 1811 to 1815 family members moved from northern Alabama to the upper White River. By 1816 newly arrived Paton Keesee reported that the families of Buck Coker, his son Joe (1787–1862), and his sons-in-law William Trimble and Girard Leiper Brown were the only white settlers on the White River in what are now northern Boone and Marion counties, Arkansas.

These "first families" gave several place-names to the land. Patriarch Buck Coker settled in a wide bottom, the Jake Nave Bend—ultimately named for a granddaughter's husband. Daughter Katie (1791–?, G. L. Brown's wife) gave her name to Katie's Prairie in Taney County, Missouri, and granddaughter Becca (Katie's child) is the source for Becca's Branch, Marion County, Arkansas. Poor Joe Bald in Taney County is a remembrance of son Joe Coker's narrow escape from angry Cherokees, and Trimble Creek in Marion County echoes son-in-law William Trimble. Buck Coker's wife became the first interment in Coker cemetery in Boone County's Jake Nave Bend. A listing of Buck Coker's large family and their intermarriages reads like a White River directory of first families: Anderson, Boatright, Brown, Friend, Hogan, Holt, Keesee, Magness, Manley, Nave, Trimble, Wood, Yocum, and Cherokee women. Many of the Coker descendants later became pioneers in Oklahoma and Texas.[1]

The first story in this section is a classic genealogical sketch by Turnbo.

✑ THE COKER CLAN ✒

A PART OF AN ACCOUNT OF THE COKER FAMILY BIOGRAPHICAL AND HISTORICAL [18:30]

THE FOLLOWING IS a biographical sketch of Buck Coker's children and grandchildren as far as we are able to obtain the information, nearly all of which was furnished me by Bill Trimble son of Allen Trimble, the last named was a child of Mrs. Sallie Trimble, daughter of Buck Coker.

The Coker family belongs to the oldest pioneer race of people in northwest Arkansas. We have mentioned elsewhere that Buck Coker settled at the lower end of the Jake Nave Bend of White River in what is now Boone County, Ark., in January, 1815. Joe Coker was Buck Coker's eldest child. He married a white woman in Alabama and two daughters, Betsey and Sallie, were born of this marriage. Soon after the death of this woman he married an Indian woman of the name of Ainey and the issue of this marriage were "Prairie" Bill, Herrod, "Little" Joe, Daniel the fiddler, Laferty Coon who was a confederate soldier and was killed at Port Hudson.[2] The daughters were Rebecca, Jane and Mary Ann. Joe Coker brought this Indian wife with him to White River in 1814 and as we have mentioned elsewhere he lived in the Sugar Loaf Country, Boone County, Ark.

After Mr. Coker come to northwest Arkansas he taken unto himself another Indian woman by the name of Cynthia. By this illegal marriage there were born John, George and Randolph. George was killed by Jake Nave in the Jake Nave Bend of White River and Randolph killed sheriff Billy Brown near the village of Dubuque.[3] Herrod married Miss Polly Orr. Sallie married John Carter. Betsey married "Squirrel" Bill Wood. Rebecca married Bill Daniels. Jane married George Hogan. Mary Ann married Bob Trimble.

Ned Coker, another son of Buck Coker, married Winnie Yocum, daughter of Solomon Yocum.[4] Their offsprings were "River" Bill whose first wife was Peggie, daughter of Wm. Holt, and Sallie who married Jake Nave. Among "River" Bill Coker's children by his first wife, for he was married the second time, are George who was born in 1850 and is one of the leading merchants of Lead Hill, Ark., and Winnie who married Bill Magness, son of Sam Magness, and Nina who married Eph Kelly, who was postmaster at Lead Hill many years.

William Coker, another son of Buck Coker, was also married and had several children but his wife's name is forgotten. His children were "Yellville" Bill, a noted fiddler and a confederate soldier and the first merchant of Lead Hill, Ark., and Ned who was a volunteer in the American army and fought through the war with Mexico and returned back home.

There was also another son named Charles. The daughters were Sallie who married Tom Brown and he died at the foot of bluff on the east side of the mouth of Trimble Creek, Marion County, Ark. Some years after the death of Brown she married Allen Trimble,[5] and Malinda who married Southfoot Bill (Will) Woods who built a mill on George's Creek six and one-half miles north of Yellville, and Nancy who married Lize Wood who settled the Arch Anderson farm near Dodd City, Ark., and Jane who married "Rosin" Bill Wood, and Abbie who married Jim Churchman and John Coker killed him and while sheriff Billy Brown made an attempt to arrest him [John Coker] for this crime Randolph Coker shot and killed Brown.[6]

Charles Coker, another son of Buck Coker, married a daughter of Shawnee Berry Jim Trimble. Her name is forgotten. Their children were "Wagoner" Bill, and Lenard who was another fiddler, and Ned who went to Texas in an early day, and Joe who was the youngest and also was a confederate soldier. After the death of Charles Coker's first wife he married Betsey Friend, daughter of Jake Friend, and a sister of Peter Friend. The issue of this marriage was Lucinda who married Henry Nipps, and after his death she married Tom Boatright and Mahala who married Dick Boatright, and Polly who married Henry Wiggins, and Betsey who married Bill Manley. Tom Boatright and his wife went from Marion County, Ark., to Missouri in time of the civil war and I was told that they both froze to death one bitter cold night. Henry Wiggins died in the cane bottom on White River a short distance above the mouth of Little North Fork [Marion County] during the war and was buried by women at the foot of the bluff and lies buried there in a lone grave. Three of Wiggin's children—Joe, Robert and Billie—[are] buried in the Asa Yocum graveyard opposite the Bull Bottom.[7]

Katie, daughter of Buck Coker, married Girard Leiper Brown who was killed on the Arkansas River. Their offsprings were Tom, Alex, Robert, Becca, and Catherine. The latter married Tom Magness, son of Joe Magness; after the death of Magness she married Pew C. Anderson and she died leaving little Tommy Anderson who was reared by his aunt Becca who lived at the mouth of Becca's Branch [Marion County] on White River just below the mouth of Trimble Creek. Little Tommy was a schoolmate of the writer in 1854. He died in 1867 and is buried in the graveyard opposite the Panther Bottom.[8] Katie, the widow of Girard Leiper Brown, died in the same house that stood at the foot of the bluff as mentioned where her son Tom Brown died.

Sallie, another daughter of Buck Coker's, married William Trimble in Alabama and they moved to White River in what is now Marion County, Ark., as early as 1814. The issue of this marriage were Dicy the oldest who married Jim Wood, and after his death she married John Nave. I am reliably informed that one day during a continued spell of sickness she sank so low that the family supposed that life was extinct and they laid her out for dead, but to their great joy she revived. Mary Jane who married Abe Nave, lies buried in the graveyard at the mouth of Bratton's Spring Creek, and Allen who we have mentioned so often in these sketches elsewhere will not be repeated here.

Soon after William Trimble was killed on White River Mrs. Sallie Trimble married Mike Yocum and the fruit of this marriage were Asa, Jake, Harve, William, Mike and Sallie. Asa was the oldest and was born in 1819 and was killed during the civil war and was buried in the cemetery on his old farm on White River opposite the Bull Bottom and three miles from Peel, Ark. The place is known now as the Bill Treadway land. The graveyard is on a beautiful low ridge-like formation of land between White River and a little shallow valley of a hollow, and is just across from where the lane was from the old Asa Yocum dwelling, the house and lane of which has been done away with many years ago.

Asa Yocum married Miss Elize Denison; the fruit of this marriage were Mike, Sallie, John, Harve, Nancy and William. I remember that Sallie married John Piland[9] in 1860 and lived on Little Creek in Ozark County, Mo., and both died there during the war. Nancy married H. H. Perkins who served two terms as sheriff of Marion County, Ark. A few years after the death of Asa Yocum his widow married Pew C. Anderson. She is dead now: on the 7th of November, 1907, I visited the graveyard at Peel, Ark., where she lies buried to read the inscription on her tombstone which reads "Eliza Anderson Born September 9, 1822, died March 2, 1906." She died in her 85th year. Mrs. Anderson is the oldest person that lies in that cemetery up to the present writing. The next oldest is Andrew J. Langford who was born September 22, 1814, and died July 17, 1894.

Referring to some more of Mike Yocum's children again, Sallie married Calvin Hogan, and William who was born January 12, 1829, and married Miss Nancy Keesee who was born November 11, 1834. They lived on White River in Marion County, Ark. William died one day in May, 1861, and lies buried in the Asa Yocum graveyard. His grave is boxed up and roofed with slabs of native stone.[10] Jane, the oldest daughter of Buck Coker, married Charley Sneed in 1824 which we have mentioned elsewhere.

An Incident of the Great Rise in White River in 1824 [25:43]

JUST BELOW THE RIVER BOTTOM known as the Jake Nave Bend, Boone County, Ark., is a tall bluff where a precipice reaches high up to the summit. Here one day recently I had a fine view of scenery along White River for several miles which includes a birds eye view of the Nave Bend. At the lower end of this bottom is where Buck Coker[11] pitched his tent January 8, 1815. Here on the bank of the river he and [his] family sheltered in this tent which stood in the midst of tall cane until he could build a small cabin to protect them from the cold wintry blast.

In the course of a few years Coker's wife sickened and died and she was buried nearby where the dwelling stood. This was the start for a graveyard there which we have referred to so often in other sketches. Among the old time residents who lie in this village of the dead is Billy Holt and his kind and industrious wife Mary L. or Aunt Polly Holt as she was commonly known. Here also lies their daughter Peggie wife of "River" Bill Coker, and their unmarried daughter Mary Ann. Here also lies Mary Coker Nave daughter of Ned Coker and the first wife of Jake Nave and also Aunt Winnie, wife of Ned Coker. This land is known now as the Dave McCord farm. A short distance above this land at a fine spring of water is where Jake Nave lived and died and lies buried in the cemetery at Protem.[12]

Just below where Buck Coker lived is the mouth of Pine Hollow at the head of which is a small pinery[13] where Ned Coker and "River" Bill Coker had their Negro men to fell pine trees and cut off logs of the desired length and haul them to the river at the mouth of this hollow with ox teams where the logs were made into rafts and floated down the river to Mike Yocum's saw mill in the mouth of Little North Fork [Marion County] where the logs were converted into lumber, and the Negroes hauled it back home on ox wagons.

The remarkable rise in White River in September, 1824, was probably the greatest flood in this stream during the 19th century.[14] The torrential rain storms that produced this freshet were so frequent that the hunters were driven from the forest and sought shelter in their cabins.

Allen Trimble, son of Bill Trimble, said that he was nine years old when this high water swept over the bottoms. At the time of its occurrence he was living with his grandfather Buck Coker. Also two other grandsons were staying with him at the time. These were "Prairie" Bill and Herrod Coker, sons of Joe Coker. Jesse Yocum, son-in-law of Coker's, was also there and when the waters began to threaten to reach the top of the bank Coker sent them all to higher ground, but Coker himself refused to go with them. The family thinking he would be willing to vacate the house when the water rose higher rested easy about him until the waters surrounded the cabin. There was no canoe available but Jess Yocum owned a fine horse he called Paddy that was a renowned swimmer. They owned other horses, but Paddy was the best swimmer in the bunch.

As the raging flood of water spread over the bottom Yocum swam his horse twice to the Coker dwelling and back to try to induce his father-in-law to leave the house, but he declined. The river continued to rise rapidly and was becoming deeper every hour between the house and the hill. The family was alarmed for the safety of him, and his son-in-law made the third trip back to the cabin to make a last effort to persuade Mr. Coker to vacate the dwelling. The raging waters had rose to the level of the floor. Driftwood was riding over the cane and lodging against the trees in the bottom.

This last trip for Yocum and his faithful animal was hazardous for the current was growing swifter and deeper. When Yocum reached the house he informed his obstinate father-in-law that this was his last trip to try to rescue him for the current was getting to be too swift and deep to make an attempt to come back again and if he intended to leave the house at all now was the time, and the old man looked at his son-in-law as he sat on his beautiful but wearied horse as he stood in the water over knee deep. He seemed to admire the man and appreciated his untiring energy in braving the strong and muddy current in an effort to save his life, then he cast his eyes over the great expanse of seething and foaming water that was spreading from hill to hill and then glancing his eyes once more toward his son-in-law he gave his consent to go, and Yocum took him up behind him and reining the horse's head around toward camp the horse started with his double weight and was soon in deep water and the true and ever faithful horse carried both men safely to shore. The highest stage of water reached the door head of the cabin before the flood began to subside.

After the great tide of water had spread over the field where there was a small crop of corn Mr. Coker's plucky grandsons "Prairie" Bill and his brother Herrod would ride their horses into the water where the corn was and gather the ears of corn to grate. It was interesting and certainly dangerous work for the boys to swim their horses around over the field and reach down into the water and feel for the corn and pull it off of the stock. The family used graters to make meal for bread.

Buck Coker lived in this bottom until after the big freshet in May, 1844,[15] when he went to West Sugar Loaf Creek [Boone County] where he died in 1855 at the extreme age of nearly 100 years. It is said that a year or more before his death he selected a spot of ground on the old Charles Coker farm for the burial of his body and his remains were the first interment in this small graveyard. According to accounts, the big freshet in the river in May, 1844, did not cover the bottom land where Buck Coker lived as deep as that of 1824.

Killing Three Bear in a Field of Corn [5:92]

JAKE NAVE, who was one among the pioneers of White River, said that when he come to Taney County, Mo., in 1832 the honey dew[16] in the river bottoms during dry weather was so excessive that it accumulated on the foliage of trees, weeds and cane and bushes so thick that he had known wild turkeys that were nearly grown get the feathers on their wings gummed so bad with it that they could not fly. Mr. Nave did not occupy his farm in the Jake Nave Bend in the northeast part of Boone County, Ark., until in 1840 or later.

When he had cleared land and raised a crop of corn on it the bears helped him gather it. These animals made frequent visits to his field and ate and wasted the corn to their hearts' content. Mr. Nave said that the havoc committed in a cornfield by a hungry bear was equal to the work of a big hog and was too much of a burden on a farmer to carry in peace.

"One night in the early fall," said Mr. Nave, "while the moon lit up the night with its brilliant light, I went to the field to make an investigation to find out if any bear were on the inside of the field. I stopped at the fence to listen for a noise in the field and my ears soon caught the sound of their work which seemed to be as much racket as if two or three head of cattle were in there destroying and eating corn. It was evident from the noise going on that there were more than one of the Bruins in there making themselves welcome. They appeared to be very busy breaking down the corn.

"Knowing that I could not do much with them alone I went across the river to Ned Coker [his brother-in-law] to get help and Coker sent his Negro man John with dogs[17] and gun with me. When we had crossed the river we made direct for the field and crossed the fence to the inside and the dogs rushed forward and attacked the bears which proved to be a mother bear and three large cubs. When the dogs closed in on the beasts there was a great stir. Corn and weeds were trampled down over a considerable space of land. As the fight went on I and the Negro man advanced up near where the battle was going on and I shot and killed the old one. Reloading the rifle I killed one of the cubs and while the dogs were baying the remaining two cubs I shot and killed one of them. The other cub escaped in spite of the dogs. I had three dead bear now on my hands and all of them killed in my field of corn. I and the Negro had plenty to do that night in removing the hides of the three animals and caring for the meat, and myself and wife and Coker and his family were not lacking for bear meat which had fattened on my corn."[18]

THE LAST HOURS OF MIKE YOCUM [1:21]

ONE OF THE EARLIEST SETTLERS in Marion County, Arkansas, is Mike Yocum whose name we have mentioned so frequently in these sketches.[19] Mr. Yocum had three brothers whose names were Jess, Solomon, and Jake. These four men had crossed the deep blue sea to America from Germany when they were little boys.

At the age of seventeen Mike was captured by the Indians and held a captive four years. At one time the Indians condemned him to suffer death by shooting him with arrows, but after the warriors had placed him on a block of wood to carry out his execution, the chief interfered in his behalf and saved him from the terrible death of shooting arrows into his body. These Indians had also captured a Negro man at the time Yocum was taken.

One day while Yocum and the Negro were prisoners but were foot-loose, the Negro and one of the Indian men got into a fight and the warrior bit off part of one of the Negro's ears.

Some years after Yocum and the Negro made their escape from the Indians, the latter finally fell in possession of Ewing Hogan, an early settler of Marion County, Arkansas. After the death of Ewing Hogan, Cal Hogan, son of Ewing Hogan, owned the Negro. As long as Mike Yocum lived he loved old Ben the Negro because they had been fellow prisoners and suffered together while in the hands of the red men. Ben lived until after the close of the civil war and died at an extreme old age.

In 1850, while Yocum lived at the mouth of Little North Fork and owned the mill there, he was a candidate for representative of Marion County. His opponent was Captain Henry[20] whose given name is forgotten. Both men were influential and had many friends which made the canvass hot.

Ned Coker, who espoused the cause of Yocum [Ned was Yocum's brother-in-law], was one day talking with one of Captain Henry's friends and during the conversation relating to the race between the two men, the latter remarked to Coker that "Captain Henry was a very nice man and ought to be elected."

"Yes," replied Mr. Coker, "Captain Henry looks nice enough, but he is a terrible liar."

Mr. Yocum succeeded in defeating Henry, and his friends rejoiced at the opportunity of sending him to Little Rock to represent [them] in the legislature. When the war between the states broke out, Mr. Yocum sympathized with the south, but he was too old and feeble to enlist in the army.[21]

❧ THE TURNBO NEIGHBORHOOD ❧

Editors' Note: The Turnbo westward migration and arrival in the White River Valley followed traditional routes. The name derives from Dornbach ("thorny creek") to Turnbach-Turnbaugh-Turnbo.[22] Palatinate German ancestors came to Pennsylvania ca. 1725, migrated south, and in 1774 lived in what became known as the Ninety-Six District in the South Carolina Piedmont. In the 1790s John Turnbough's family traveled westward into the French Broad Valley of East Tennessee and Knoxville. Two of his youngest sons, Andrew and James, went on to Maury County, Middle Tennessee, by 1811.

In 1811 James Turnbo married Felicia Coffee and the young Turnbo couple settled near Mt. Pleasant. In 1820 Silas's father, James Coffee Turnbo, was born in Tennessee.[23]

In 1840 James Turnbo and two neighbor friends, the Shipman brothers, traveled west to Memphis, Little Rock, and Ozark, and north to Carrollton, Arkansas. James continued north into Missouri where Dr. A. S. Layton hired him and others to cut pine logs in south Taney County in the "pineries."

James Turnbo was not a semi-nomadic southern hunter like many frontiersmen who had preceded him to the White River country; he was a frontiersman with a vision of opening the land to permanent settlement and trade. Thus, Turnbo often associated himself with men like Layton, who "did not hire them to hunt, but to work and they did not want to put in their time at hunting."

In 1842 James married Eliza Onstott, four years his junior. In 1844 their firstborn, Silas Turnbo, began life on Beaver Creek. The Turnbo family moved south to the mouth of Beaver Creek where they remained until 1849.

James and Eliza took their two children—Silas and Jasper Newton—further downriver to the mouth of Elbow Creek in 1849. Remembering life while living near the famous Elbow Shoals of the White River and near the Jake Nave Bend, Silas recounted stories involving small steamboats ascending the river.

In 1853, after four years at Elbow Shoals, James and Eliza gave $525 to Cage Hogan for a claim in southeast Taney County on the White River across from Panther Bottom. They built a new log house there, but by 1859 they had purchased George Fritts's farm further upriver.

James Turnbo did well by the standards of his day, and even paid six hundred dollars for a female slave in 1860. Indications are that he had a mechanic's skills and the desire to market them for mill building and timber work. He sold surplus products downriver and commonly hired farm hands. During the 1850s, after steamboats began to arrive regularly in the Turnbo neighborhood, James purchased bulk coffee, salt, sugar, and whiskey that he resold for cash or cattle.[24] Additionally, James had mature oxen which he rented to others for "breaking the land." He was quick to try the "new" sorghum seed in spring 1858 after acquiring the seed on a trip to visit his relatives in middle Tennessee.

James Turnbo was lucky to survive the Civil War. He had a short career as a lieutenant in Capt. Lewis Hudson's company of the Fourteenth Arkansas Infantry, CSA, and then resigned his commission. He spent most of the war at home raising crops, protecting his family of eight children, and providing money and clothes to son Silas, who spent three years in the Twenty-seventh Arkansas Infantry, CSA.

The literate Silas spent some of his meager funds to buy books during the war and was careful to keep a diary of his experiences. In one moment that would have been tragic for all, Silas was almost executed on false charges. At home, father James Turnbo, son J. N. (Newt), and neighbor men occasionally met to camp and hide out in the woods to avoid violent encounters with the Federals. James and Newt surrendered to Union officials, and in early 1865 the family vacated the White River and sought protection on Turkey Creek in southwest Ozark County among Union friends. In summer 1865, after Silas was paroled and found his family safe on Turkey Creek, all moved back to Marion County, Arkansas.

SOMETHING ABOUT THE WRITER'S PEOPLE [18:72]

THE WRITER'S PEOPLE on his father's side were Pennsylvania Dutch. They settled in the state of Pennsylvania many years before the breaking out of the revolutionary war. Some of them went from that section into

Virginia where my grandfather James Turnbo was born March 23, 1781. He left Virginia when he was quite young and made his way into east Tennessee and after living there several years he married Felicia Coffee, an English woman who lived at Knoxville and who was born February 3, 1787.

Soon after his marriage which occurred in 1811, the couple went to middle Tennessee and settled in Maury County. I am told that they lived on the Sugar Prong of Big Bigby Creek that runs into Duck River and some five miles from Mt. Pleasant. It is said that Sugar Creek derived its name from a wagon that was drawn along on the creek in an early [day] that was loaded with sugar and the wagon turned over here and part of the sugar was wasted in the dirt and hence the name.

Here on this farm on Sugar Creek my father James Coffee Turnbo was born February 13, 1820. There were nine children in all, four boys and five girls. The youngest child was Mary who was born in 1826. The names of the other seven children were Nathan, Margarette, Andrew J., Gracie M., Elizabeth, William Claiborne, and Nancy A.[25]

My grandfather died in 1827. He died begging for water. A fine spring of living water was in forty yards of the house but the attending physicians would not permit him to drink water for it was a custom then among the doctors not to allow their patients to drink water if they could help it. They supposed the use of water would kill them.[26] My grandmother died in 1865 at the age of seventy-eight years. They both rest side by side in the family graveyard on the old home farm. I am told that my uncle Andrew Turnbo set out a small cedar bush near grandfather's grave when he was a small boy and that an elm come up volunteer where the cedar was set out and both cedar and elm are large trees now.

My uncle Andrew Turnbo died in Tarrant County, Texas, in 1887 and lies buried in a graveyard at the White Chappel. His wife's maiden name was Miss Sarah Spain. She died in Green County, Oklahoma and is buried in a graveyard at Mangrum. There were eight children born to them equally divided between boys and girls. Nathan died in Decatur County, Tennessee, in 1884 at the age of seventy-one years.

Gracie M. who married Martin Johnson died in Parker County, Texas, November 4, 1890, at the age of seventy-one years. Her husband was a confederate soldier in a Texas regiment and died in the St. John College Hospital, Little Rock, Ark., in the summer of 1862. Nancy A. married John Baily. She survived all the other children until in 1900 when she too passed over the great dark river of death. She died in Maury County, Tennessee.

My uncle Clabe Turnbo paid my father a visit in the early Fifties while we lived at the mouth of Elbow Creek in Taney County, Mo., [1849–53] and remained with us three weeks. He had been to California where he worked in the mines and on arriving back at his father's old home in Tennessee he started to Taney County, Mo., to visit my father and come all the way a foot carrying his gold chain with him.

On his arrival at our house he took off his belt that contained his money and poured it on the table and counted it and there were $2060 in twenty dollar pieces beside some smaller pieces of gold and some silver that he carried in a purse to pay his expenses on the way to Missouri.

On his return back to Maury County, Tennessee he married Jane Mathis and they went to Texas where they lived a short time and then moved to Powhatan, Arkansas, where after a few years residence he died leaving four children. His wife had him buried in a metallic coffin and when she returned back to Maury County, Tenn., she had his body taken up and conveyed to his fathers old home farm on Sugar Creek and buried in the old Turnbo Graveyard there which I am told is five miles south of Mt. Pleasant.

OLD TIME RECOLLECTIONS OF ELBOW SHOALS [22:13]

JUST BELOW THE MOUTH OF ELBOW CREEK is a bluff which overlooks the John Yandell farm and Elbow Shoals. An observer here commands an excellent view of the neighborhood, and the usual variety of the scenery as found on White River is seen. One day recently [ca. 1905] the writer visited the summit of this bluff and viewed the old settled farm referred to above. Looking over the swift flowing waters of White River and the little brooklet of Elbow Creek, then at the bluffs, gulches, hills and the big shelving rock on the west side of the creek calls to mind incidents which occurred here in the long ago. On this farm I passed four years of my childhood. The memory of those happy days from August, 1849, to October, 1853, is still fresh in my mind.

Just below the shoals is Long's Ferry [White River], part of the shoals are in Boone County, Ark., and part in Taney County, Mo. The old channel is in Arkansas but the new cut is a ways in Missouri. Between the two channels is an island where, I am told, a man was assassinated in 1839.

A man by the name of Stephens was the first to settle in this bottom locating here in 1837. One morning in 1839 Mr. Stephens accompanied by his daughter started for Carrollton, Arkansas, for the purpose of prosecuting a maker of counterfeit money,[27] who was there awaiting trial, and while they were riding over this island Stephens was ambushed and shot. The horror of the murder and the death scene in the presence of his young daughter was sad and distressing. The screams of his helpless child as he fell from his horse into the cold embrace of death ought to have softened the heart of the cruel assassin, but with a boastful and exultant laugh he was seen to leave his concealment immediately after he had slain his victim.

Stephens' cabin stood in a small clearing near the mouth of the creek and after he was murdered his wife and children sold the claim to John Haddon and Mr. Haddon sold the improvements to my father and he entered forty acres of land in this bottom which was the first entry of land made on this farm.[28]

The channel and shoals here were once a dreaded place for the passage of flat boats,[29] two of which collided against the right bank and sank. The first of these occurred in 1835. This boat was loaded with iron vessels, such as wash kettles, pots, frying pans and other vessels of a like nature which the owner was selling or trading to the few settlers who lived along the river.

After the boat sank and before the proprietor could recover any of his wares, a big freshet come down the river and when the water subsided the boat and contents were entirely covered with sand and gravel. The boat had been built at the mouth of James River [Missouri] and the iron vessels had been brought from Saint Louis there in freight wagons.

The other boat that sank belonged to Ben Majors. His boat was loaded with corn and fat cattle that he was taking to New Orleans to market.[30] As the boat was passing the curve which the shoals and the creek takes its name from, the swift current forced the bow of the boat against the bank and tore away one bottom plank at the corner of the boat, and the water come into the boat in a sluice. Unfortunately the cattle which were five and six years old and large and fat had been tied with ropes to the boat and there were no hopes for their escape. The men realized their danger, and as the stern end of the boat was swinging around, Majors and his crew rushed to the bow of the boat and leaped for the shore. All landed safely except Bob Rains and he fell backwards into the water but was rescued by his companions. The sinking boat and drowning cattle were swept along rapidly until it reached deep water below the shoals where it sank from sight.

This was in the early spring of 1848, and during the succeeding summer and fall, a large number of fish collected at the sunken boat, and settlers visited the spot in "dug out" canoes and killed hundreds of them with harpoons, and during low stages of water, great flocks of buzzards gathered in the vicinity, but they were unable to get the carrion as a little water covered it. Mr. Majors was one of the first settlers of Taney County and was a prosperous man, but he never fully recovered from the loss suffered from the sinking of his flat boat.[31]

In those early days farmers did not plant their corn until after winter was broke or when the leaves on the trees were the size of squirrels' ears which calls to memory another incident. In the month of June, 1851, when the earliest corn was nearly knee high people along the river were surprised as well as delighted at seeing a steam boat shoving its way up the river. As the boat came in sight of each cabin it gave a loud whistle, and the people ran to the bank to see what made such a strange and fearful noise. The sight was wonderful to them, [but] cattle were terrified and stampeded and horses snorted and ran away.

The name of the boat was "Eureka" and it was the largest and finest boat ever came this far up White River. The day was sultry, the air calm suffocating, small cumulus clouds floated slowly along in the aerial regions. It was just such a day that knowing ones who tell you what the weather is "going to do", view the watery clouds and predict a thunderstorm.

As the boat approached the shoals the firemen were ordered to heave wood into the furnace that there might be plenty of steam to force the boat over the shoals. Great volumes of smoke ascended high in the air and slowly drifted away. Great jets of steam belched from the escape pipes and formed miniature white clouds that rested over the water until dissipated. The propelling wheel of the boat churned the water so rapid and strong as to dash water high up on the bank; grown people as well as we children looked on with wonder and amazement.

The steamer as she plowed her way through the swift current of water had attained good speed when she arrived at the foot of the shoals and entered the old channel, her intended destination was Forsyth [Missouri].[32] The captain and passengers were anxious to pass the shoals and as she was forced along against the strong current the water heaped and foamed against the bow. The beautiful steamer succeeded in reaching the curve where her speed was checked and she soon came to a standstill and the bow, in spite of the efforts of the pilot to prevent it, turned toward the south bank.

For a moment the pilot had lost control of the boat and there was imminent danger of a collision against the shore and the chimneys being swept off by the timber. The engines were instantly reversed and the boat was righted again by its being backed down stream a short distance, then another trial was made to stem the rolling tide of the swift flowing water with no better success than the first attempt. It was now evident that she could proceed no further up the river, the efforts of the captain and crew were unavailing and they had to drop back to the landing at Dubuque [Arkansas] two miles below the shoals. The captain and the passengers were sadly disappointed at not reaching Forsyth.

The village below the shoals was not yet named, and the few settlers asked the captain to name it. His home being Dubuque, Iowa, he named this village in honor of that city. The boat remained there that night and early the following morning a crowd of men, women and children had collected at the landing to see the boat, and just before her departure from here back down the river she gave a loud whistle which startled the entire assembly of people.

Among the crowd was a young man with red hair and red complexion who, when the steamer whistled, thought the boat was rent asunder and started away on a fast run and was soon lost from view. Those of the crowd that quickly recovered from the fright created by the blast from the whistle yelled and laughed at the panic stricken fellow. The "Eureka" was the first steam boat ever reaching this far up White River.

During the early summer of this same year work was began on the shoals to improve the navigation of them by cutting a channel just over the state line in Taney County, Mo.[33] "Hack" Snapp[34] who lived on the opposite side of the river from Forsyth was foreman of a large number of men who were employed to cut the new channel. The water was at a low stage and the men kept busy at work for several weeks. The labor was tedious and disagreeable on account of working in the gravel and water, but the new channel gradually widened and deepened and great banks of sand and gravel were heaped upon either side until a part of the river sought this route. The men then devoted their labor to build a dam of stone part of the way across the head of the old channel, thus throwing volumes of water through the new made chute.

The work to some extent was a success, the hands (men) were a merry and fun loving crowd. They camped on the south bank of the river just above the shoals and passed the time of evenings by debating, having literary work, or other pass time amusement. When the work was completed Mr. Snapp paid the men their wages in gold and silver coin and they all left camp for their respective homes rejoicing and jingling their money in their pockets.

The following spring or in 1852, the "Yaw Haw Ganey,"[35] a much smaller and older boat than the Eureka, came up the river and steamed into the mouth of the chute. She was heavily loaded with freight for the merchants of Forsyth. The crew of the boat worked hard all day trying to pass through the chute. A large number of the passengers disembarked and waited on the bank of the river at the mouth of Elbow Creek for the boat to pass over but she failed to pass over the shoals and late in the night the captain was compelled to back his boat out of the chute and landed at the lower part of the bottom on the north side of the river and put off 300 sacks of salt which belonged to the merchants of Forsyth.[36]

The following day was Sunday and just before noon she succeeded in passing through the chute and went on to Forsyth. The "Yaw Haw Ganey" was the first steam boat reaching that town. The salt was left in the care of the writer's father, [and] Jim and Tom Clarkstone, sons of Lewis Clarkstone who lived then on the old Buck Coker place at the lower end of the Jake Nave Bend of White River. [They] were employed to haul it on ox wagons to our house on Elbow Creek one half a mile above the mouth where the salt was stored in a new log house. Bob Williams hauled most of the salt to Forsyth during the summer following the spring that the "Yaw Haw Ganey" came up. Williams used a big stout wagon drawn by two yoke of oxen.

"Ben Lea," another fine boat less in size than the Eureka, but larger than the "Yaw Haw Ganey" came up in the spring of 1853. She was just five hours in passing the shoals, but on her second trip that same spring she lay in the chute two days before she succeeded in passing. In the evening of the first day after her cable had been made fast to a willow tree she pulled it up, and during the night following she jerked up another willow tree.

Other steam boats that visited Forsyth from 1854 to the beginning of the civil war were the "Mary L. Darity" [Daugherty], "Mississippi Belle," "Jesse Lazza R.," "Mary M. Patterson," and "Thomas P. Ray," the two last named made several trips.[37] Jesse Mooney[38] and George Pearson had charge of the "Ray," and in the spring of 1858 she steamed as far up as the mouth of James River which was the farthest point reached by a steam boat at that time. Mooney and Pearson had her upper deck elaborately decorated with flags to celebrate the occasion on their return trip, [and] this was her last trip. Her owners sold the machinery to a Mr. Long, who converted it to the running power of a saw mill at what is now known as the Boiler Spring just below where Dodd City, Ark., now stands; this mill was burned down during the war.

The "Mary M. Patterson" was owned by Morgan Bateman; this was a trading boat and made many trips to Forsyth. One night in the early part of 1859 after landing at the spring where George Fritts lived, in now what is Keesee Township, Marion County, Ark., the boat caught fire and barely escaped destruction and was saved by the heroic efforts of the crew and passengers.

During another trip which was in April, 1860, while she was anchored at Forsyth the water fell so rapidly and the weather remained dry so long that she was compelled to stay there until the following February [1861] when there was sufficient rainfall to raise the water in the river to allow her departure; but she traveled only as far as the Ned Coker farm, just below the mouth of East Sugar Loaf Creek, Marion County, where she had to remain until a higher stage of water which was just enough to float her down to Bull Bottom where she was compelled to stay until the latter part of March when the river rose several feet. Bateman went on his way rejoicing and swearing alternately, glad that he was able to get away and sorry he had to stay so long.

A Remarkable Period of Ice and Snow [25:53]

OVERLOOKING WHITE RIVER and vicinity from a tall bluff makes an interesting view especially if calling to memory old time scenes and incidents. On the north side of White River just above the Panther Bottom and over the line in Taney County, Mo., is a high bluff where an observer commands a good view some distance up and down the river. In the early Fifties the face of this bluff was covered with a thick growth of cedars, but in the month of April, 1854, while the weather was so dry, a forest fire swept over the face of this bluff and destroyed all the cedars in places. The great devouring flames as it ran through the rank grass would ignite the cedars and the flames of fire would dart up several feet above the top of the cedars and big volumes of black smoke would rise high above the summit of the bluff. The spots where this great fire reached is naked to the present day.

On the opposite side of the river in the southeast corner of Taney County, Mo., is the old farm where we lived from October, 1853, to February 13, 1859. When we first moved there the dwelling houses stood on the river bank just above the mouth of the hollow. Later on or in 1856 we built new houses further back from the river on the bank of the hollow. The corner of the porch stood in a few feet of the division line between Ozark and Taney County. My father bought this land from Cage Hogan in the month of June, 1853, for $525. Mr. Hogan remained here until the following spring after we moved here when he moved to Rock Bridge.[39]

A number of old timers lived here before Hogan did. Among them was old Billy Howard who it is claimed was the first settler here, then came Jess Journagan, Peter Snapp, and the Magness boys Bill and Joe, also John Fisher, and his brother Enoch Fisher,[40] and Martin Johnson lived here.

As I stood on the top of this bluff I call to mind the memorable cold weather and snow and ice during the months of January and February, 1856. The severe weather and lasting snow made it a remarkable period. On the 23rd day of January a heavy snow began falling which continued at intervals for several days. When it ended, twenty inches of snow on an average covered the ground. In places where it drifted the snow was much deeper. Men experienced great difficulty in traveling around either a foot or horseback. Women and children were compelled to remain indoors until the snow settled down a few inches.

In a few days after the snow ceased falling a warm wave set in followed by a light rain which materially lowered the depth of the snow, but on the 2nd of February a severe blizzard swept over the Ozark region from the northwest and the weather turned to icy cold. On the morning of the 3rd the temperature was eighteen degrees below zero and it was twelve degrees below on the morning of the 4th. Though the thermometer climb[ed] back to zero and above, the weather remained so cold for several days that a hard crust of ice formed on the snow. The water in the river was hid by thick ice. Wild animals including flocks of wild turkeys crossed at will, [but] the crust on the snow cut the deer's legs so bad that they were hardly able to keep out of the hunters way. Hundreds of them were slaughtered for their hides only.[41]

The men who hunted on horse back wrapped their horses legs with leather to prevent the ice from cutting them. Deer and turkeys were soon on starvation and became very poor before the snow and ice went off which did not occur until the middle days of February when the air warmed up with south wind and rain clouds formed and a heavy rain followed. This with the melting snow soon put the river on a boom and it rose twelve feet in a few hours which broke the ice to pieces. Some of the flakes were very large and thick. The river was choked with floating ice for three days. The noise of the ice crushing and grinding together, as the swift current carried it down was heard for miles. When the biggest flecks of ice would collide against the bank they would force away tons of dirt and sand and would crush down and ride over small trees. I never witnessed such a sight before or since that time.

A large number of skiffs and canoes were swept downstream by the ice and water. It was said that the majority of crafts along the river were carried away, part of which was crushed between the jamming together of ice. 🌿

An Old Fashioned Barbecued Dinner [20:45]

THE 4TH DAY OF JULY, 1855, was a memorable one to the writer. At that time my parents were living on the south bank of White River in the southeast corner of Taney County, Mo. My father had bought this land from Cage Hogan and we moved there from the mouth of Elbow Creek when I was less than ten years old. This land is known now as the Bill Dial place and is owned now by Baxter Brown.

On this farm there was a fine barbecued dinner eaten here on that day. The dinner came about in this way. The settlers from the mouth of Shoal Creek down to Bull Bottom devised a plan to get rid of some of the obnoxious birds and ravenous wild animals. They were determined to exterminate all they could. Crows, hawks, owls and eagles were on the list of destruction. The animals that were selected to go on the list of the dead were possums, coons, moles, skunks, squirrels, foxes, wild cats, catamounts, wolves and panthers. The arrangements were completed in the early spring.

The men were divided into two companies. The writer's father, J. C. Turnbo, headed the lower company which included all the settlers living along the river from our house down to Bull Bottom. George Fritts was foreman of the upper settlement who lived on the river from Allen Lucas's to the mouth of Shoal Creek. The dinner was to be eaten on our place on the 4th of July. Every member of the two organizations agreed to do their part in furnishing provision for the dinner and bring in the scalps to be counted by a committee appointed for the purpose.

Everyone including the women did their duty in making ample preparations for the feast. Plenty of beef, mutton, pork and wild meat was furnished which was barbecued by Martin Johnson, Rube Denton, and others. The wives and daughters prepared plenty of bread and nicknacks of all sorts, that were in common use in that day. It was understood that the side that was defeated would furnish two gallons of pure whiskey for the occasion.

When the day arrived a large crowd assembled on the ground for the celebration which was selected in a hickory grove. The people all proved to be quiet and orderly. There were no lemonade stands [or] dancing floors on the ground.

The scalps of birds and animals were all counted carefully which was done before noon and the number was found to be three thousand when the men completed the task of counting the scalps. They put them all into one heap and the pile of scalps of birds and animals were astonishing to look at. The bird's scalp consisted of the upper bill and the top part of the skin and feathers on the top of the head. The larger animals consisted of both ears attached together by the skin on the top of the head; the mole scalp was the nose including a strip of hide from the base of the nose to the top of the head.

Many favorable comments were made by the people as to the great number of scalps brought in to be numbered. The lower company showed up the most scalps and won the whiskey, but the committee deemed it advisable not to have whiskey on the ground so the upper company was informed that if they were willing to agree to it that they need not furnish the liquor that the people would get along better without it and so the two gallons was not on the ground.

At twelve o'clock the scrumptious dinner was placed on a long table that had been prepared in the hickory grove in the woodland pasture which is now in cultivation and men, women and children enjoyed themselves together eating an old fashioned barbecued dinner.

Recollections of the First Introduction of Sorghum Seed [22:39]

I REMEMBER DISTINCTLY when the seed of sorghum cane was first introduced into our neighborhood when we lived on the farm on the south bank of White River in the southeast corner of Taney County, Mo.

In the fall of 1857 my father went on a visit to Decatur and Maury Counties, Tennessee, to see his relatives and brought a few of the seed with him to Taney County. Later on in the fall of the same year John Jones moved here from Tennessee and he brought a few of the seed with him. The seed had been introduced in some localities in Tennessee in the early spring of 1857.[42]

My father had just enough seed to plant nine short rows in a small patch of land on the bank of the river just below a little hollow. The sorghum was planted between the river bank and the graveyard and was just over the line in Ozark County, Mo. Of course the seed was not planted until the spring of 1858 and when it had matured in August following, our first start at making syrup was ludicrous.

After stripping the blades from the stocks and cutting down the stocks and taking them where we wanted to make the syrup we cut the stocks into small bits and placed them into a trough and mashed them with a pestle like Indians beating corn. We now put the stuff in a pot and pouring water in we boiled the juice out and reduced it to a syrup and strained [it] through a coarse cloth. It did not take long to find out that this process of making molasses was a failure and other means had to be resorted to.

My father now hired John Anderson to make two wooden rollers to press the juice from the cane. Anderson tried to make them with draw knife and ax but they failed to work and then my father hired Martin Johnson to make a sorghum mill of wood, and he succeeded in doing it, and the cane was run through it and the juice squeezed out. This mill was the first of the kind made on this part of White River.[43] The cane juice was reduced to a syrup by boiling it in iron kettles. No one understood then how to make molasses without scorching them and they were as black as tar or stone coal which colored the lips, gums and teeth a deep black.

THE OLD HATTER SHOP [26:65]

JAMES W. JONES proprietor of the Jones' Ferry crossing of White River at the mouth of Music Creek[44] in Marion County, Ark., is a son of Hugh Jones and Hester (Hettie Bevins) Jones and was born in Madison County, Ark., in 1847. His father and his grandfather Jimmie Jones came to White River in 1849. Hugh Jones died at Benton Barracks in Missouri during the civil war. His wife Mrs. Hettie Jones lies buried in the graveyard in the southwest corner of Ozark County, Mo., opposite the Panther Bottom.

Soon after settling on White River Hugh Jones and his father Jimmie Jones built a log house of two rooms on the right bank of the river just over the line in Taney County, Mo., from Ozark County and opposite the upper end of the Panther Bottom where they manufactured hats out of fur and sheeps' wool. This house was standing there when the writer's father bought this land from Cage Hogan in 1853 and my father used it for a blacksmith shop and it was still standing when we left there on the 13th of February 1859. This building was known far and near as the "hatter shop."

We have mentioned elsewhere in another chapter that Jimmie Jones', father of Hugh Jones, built a mill on Big Creek [Taney County] which stood at the upper end of the John Pelham place known now as the Joe

Glass Haskins land. Here Mr. Jones ground corn into meal for the settlers and manufactured corn whiskey and made hats also. His son Hugh Jones also went to Big Creek and lived in the creek bottom known now as the Sam Holdt place which is just below the Joe Glass Haskins' land. Here Hugh Jones built another hatter shop where he manufactured a great number of hats.

I have sit and watched Mr. Jones many hours prepare the fur of animals' and sheeps' wool by mixing it together with a small machine made for the purpose. The making of home made hats was interesting to me.

There is an amusing incident connected with Jimmie Jones' mill which I will give.

In the summer of 1858 when the water in the creek was very low Jones could not grind but one half a bushel of corn or wheat a day. Jones' customers had to patronize a "far off" mill until the creek rose. Mr. Jones got tired sitting around the mill house doing nothing. He could not grind any grain to amount to anything and his tall corn run out and he could not make any more whiskey till the water rose so his customers could come back and bring him more corn to grind and he rented his mill to a fellow who had peculiar ways and of a boasting disposition. Among other things he said that Joe Womack's mill on Beaver Creek had ruined the now Keesee mill,[45] for Womack had built a mill dam sufficient to not let a drop of water leak through the dam and flow down from Womack's mill to the Keesee mill which would ruin the latter mill for it was operated by water also and that Womack was going to procure a patent on his invention, and then if he were a mind to he could construct dams across other streams and prevent the water from getting below it. This foolish man actually believed this.

One day during the summer of the year named [1858] this same fellow while he had the mill rented was seen with a water bucket dipping up the water from below the dam and pouring it back into the mill pond to get a head of water and [it] was laughable to see him do this. 🕮

A Few Thoughts of the Past [20:19]

DURING THE SPRING SEASON of 1860 a fruit agent, who represented a large nursery at Lock Port, New York, came into Marion County, Ark., soliciting subscribers and he sold a large amount of fruit trees. We were living then on the north bank of White River in Keesee Township.

My father bought seventy-two apple grafts at 25 cents each, nine pear at seventy-five cents each, three grape vines at twenty-five cents each and two peach at one dollar each, or a total of $25. The man was to deliver the trees in November of the same year, but when that time arrived, the war was being hotly agitated by many who sympathized with the South and the man experienced great difficulty in getting his steam boat load of fruit trees as far up White River as Buffalo City [Baxter County] and sent word to his patrons that it was impossible for him to deliver the trees as promised and that if they would come after them they could have them at a reduced price.[46]

Several parties who lived in the north part of the county that were subscribers refused to go themselves or send after the trees. They said it was Northern fruit and they would not have it if the agent were to make them a present of it all. My father and "River" Bill Coker who lived opposite Shoal Creek [Marion County] on the [White] river and M. P. (Mose) Ray who lived on East Sugar Loaf Creek near its mouth [Boone County] went down to Buffalo City and paid the man as they had promised to do and brought the trees home with them.

It was in the middle of January, 1861, when they returned back home and I and my father set ours out in a few days afterward. The trees had but little care while the war lasted but after the close of it my father gave the trees close attention until his death. These trees bore fine fruit and turned out to be what the agent represented it to be. A few of these trees are standing at the present day (June 1st, 1907).

I well recollect that in the month of November, 1865, I went to the top of the bluff opposite where the big log house stood on the bank of the river where we lived and dug up thirty five small cedar bushes and dug thirty five holes around the house and placed a flat rock in the bottom of each hole and placed the cedar's roots on these stones and filled in the dirt.[47] A number of them died out and when Jim Roselle the present owner of the farm removed the old house to cultivate the land he destroyed all the remaining trees except three which are standing now and these remind me of the lonely hours that I whiled away on this farm during that beautiful fall season after the close of the war. 🌿

SOMETHING ABOUT SCHOOLS IN THE EARLY DAYS [23:15]

WHEN MY MIND WANDERS back to the pioneer days when I was a little fellow, I wonder how it was that a few parents ever succeeded in giving their children some education in spite of all adverse circumstances. Hundreds of little fellows received no education at all. We have often met people of an advanced age that could not write their names or read print.[48] I have met some few old people that said they did not know their A. B. Cs. I have heard a number of men and women complain of a lack of education and I have always felt sorrow for those who wanted an education and was too late now to obtain one when they was standing on the brink of the grave.

Luckily a few old timers took an interest in the welfare of their little ones and would employ a teacher and have a small subscription school taught in their neighborhood.[49] Those who were in favor of their children learning something would patronize the school, while others would refuse to send them. They seemed to have opposed the teacher, discipline and education and kept their children at home, or send them into the woods to hunt rabbits or allow them to gossip about their neighbors' business rather than give them a chance to have the benefit and liberty of looking into a spelling book.

In some cases in those early days a teacher had to accept his pay "in chips and whet stones." A few of these teachers could not teach further than Baker in the Blue Back spelling book and their discipline was slack in the school room and therefore they deserved small pay, while others were better teachers and were given better pay.

I well remember the first school I ever attended. My parents were living at the mouth of Beaver Creek. In the early part of 1849 a few citizens employed Bill Wheeler who had a little education to teach a small subscription school in a little log hut near Bob Thurman. This was the first school in that vicinity and my parents sent me there five days in succession. I was too much astonished to think of anything except the noise made in the hut.

Though I was not five years old, I remember that school distinctly for three reasons: First because it was the first school I went to. Second because I did not learn my A. B. Cs. and the teacher accused me of "sucking the hind teat." That is, I lagged behind all the other scholars. Third because the students were allowed to spell as loud as their vocal organs would permit, thus making a mighty racket during school hours. Some of the scholars that I particularly recollect attending this term of school were James Harvey Laughlin and his two sisters Margarette and Elizabeth who were cousins to the writer.[50]

In the summer and fall of 1860, I attended a three months school which was taught in a dilapidated log house near this same spot by a man of the name of McDonald. But the custom in the school room had changed and there was no spelling aloud this time. McDonald taught under the free [public] school system which was in existence then.

As stated above a few settlers in the early days took an interest in school matters, but parents who did take action in having a school taught had nothing like the opportunity to school their children that they have now. When the public school system was ushered into existence citizens became interested in organizing school districts and the desire to form new school districts gradually increased. The incipient formation of some of the districts are worthy of mention and we will relate one incident here.

In one settlement in Taney County the settlers held quite an interesting school meeting in 1850 which is told of by William Thurman. Mr. Thurman said that "A few citizens, who lived on the south side of the river from Forsyth met one day for the purpose of organizing a school district. They assembled about two miles from Forsyth. I was only twelve years old then," said Mr. Thurman, "and of course did not count for a man, but I was present at that meeting and saw and heard all the proceedings. There were eleven men there and a peculiar and strange feature of this gathering to me was that the men had on their hunting garbs and all wore moccasins, boy, like I thought they ought to have on their Sunday clothes! Ten of them carried their rifles.

"The most amusing part of this assembly was the discussion the men had over the game they killed as they went to the designated place of meeting. Harrison (Hack) Snapp killed four squirrels; two of the Haworth boys, Absalom and Jim, killed two squirrels each; Z. P. Moore, Dave Wood, and Jim Phillips killed a turkey apiece; Elisha Thurman and Ward Stover each killed a deer; Ben Chenoworth and John Mitchell brought in a deer between them.

"When the settlers met they put the dead squirrels, turkeys and deer together, compared notes and counted their game and found that there were eight squirrels, three turkeys and three deer or an aggregate of fourteen. This showed that if the men could not succeed at one thing they could another. The name of the man who did not bring his gun was Harkness Ogle.

"Though this was the first school meeting held in that neighborhood, yet it was a lively one, from the fact that the men had a warm discussion over their game as well as a funny debate about school matters," said Thurman.

III

The County Seats and Outlying Settlements

Editors' Note: Early nineteenth-century travel accounts referred to the "settlements of White River," but following statehood and county formations, citizens commonly referred to county seats as immigrants rapidly moved into the Trans-Mississippi. Most of Turnbo's Ozark Highland was the District of Louisiana (1804–05), the Territory of Louisiana (1805–12), New Madrid County in Missouri Territory (1812–15), and Lawrence County in Missouri Territory (1815–19). By 1819 Arkansas Territory governed the region south of the Missouri border. In 1821 Missouri state government exercised hegemony north of the Arkansas line, and Arkansas remained a territory until statehood in 1836. The remote Great Bend of the White River, where so many of Turnbo's stories took place, continued as a vast government-owned open range. The Arkansas and Missouri boundaries remained contested after initial surveys, and the state line had to be resurveyed in the 1840s.

Repeated group migrations to the Ozarks frontier had a powerful impact on the development and social relationships of specific locales. Dramatic examples included the Adams-Wolf families at the mouth of Big North Fork River and the Coker relatives on upper White River. Turnbo recorded numerous such migrations that accounted for valley settlements having high concentrations of kith and kin from the east. Finally, Southerners and Ozarkers, known for their perpetual provincialism, became proud of their "blessing of being located." Turnbo's stories would leave the reader lost if it were not for repeated references to county seat villages.

"PITCHER" POTTS AND COL. WM. C. MITCHELL OR CARROLLTON ARK. IN EARLY TIMES [21:37]

THE FOLLOWING old time amusing anecdote was written to me by Hon. S. W. Peel[1] of Bentonville, Benton Co., Ark. The letter is dated July 19, 1904, and relates to the ways and manners of a saloon keeper and his customers at Carrollton, Carroll Co., Ark., in an early day. In giving an account of it Col. Peel who is so well known in Ark. and who served in Congress a number of years said that the incident occurred when he was a small boy and that he was present at the time. Here is how Col. Peel stated it.

"I knew personally well all the characters mentioned and the facts given are actually true," said he. "The village of Carrollton come into notice in the pioneer days and was among the oldest trading points in northwest Ark.[2]

"The first saloon—as called now but then by the most refined grocery store—stood on the north side of the public square. The house was fourteen feet square and built of round logs[3] and covered [roofed] with oak boards four feet in length. The boards were held down by round logs called weight poles, the door was in the south end of the building and the door shutter was made of oak slabs; at night this door was made fast after being closed by tying it with paw paw bark which answered in place of a lock. The floor was composed of native earth. A huge puncheon[4] which reached two thirds of the way across the house formed the counter. The fixtures and merchandise consisted of a barrel of cheap whiskey, one tin quart and one pint measure, a greasy deck of cards, a fiddle and a flint lock rifle.

"John Potts, better known as 'Pitcher' Potts, was sole owner of the building and outfit. In those days Mr. Potts was considered a shrewd business man and his customers lived far and near. Peltry, furs and bees wax were the principal articles of exchange. In one corner of the house was stacked the cakes of bees wax. In another corner was piled the peltry and furs consisting of deer skins, coon, catamount, wild cat, otter and fox skins. Around this noted establishment the male population gathered day after day bringing the above named commodities to exchange for whiskey. Sometimes trade was quite brisk, at other times exchanges dragged along slow.

"One gloomy rainy day customers did not come in very fast and business was rather dull until in the afternoon when those that had arrived in the forenoon had remained and the few coming in later on made up a fair crowd for a wet day but trade was slow. Though as stated several had collected but about all the exchange done for some time was talk.

"Among the party who lived in the neighborhood was Bill Mitchell afterward known as Col. Mitchell and who was the first commander of the 14th Ark. (Confederate) regiment.[5] This man was endowed with plenty of wit and humor and enjoyed all the fun loving jokes he could pass off on his friends. He was also one of Potts' regular customers. The crowd that day was not flush with money nor furs and peltry and soon exhausted their means in buying whiskey and drinking it. After their funds had run short trade dropped to a low stage and the conversation grew monotonous.

"Finally a hunter come in with a small deer hide and laid it down on the counter. 'Pitcher' who was rather a polite and courteous fellow and was always on the lookout for a good trade asked the hunter if the hide was for sale and the hunter replied in the affirmative. 'Well what do you want for it?' said the grocery man and the hunter who looked like his mouth was dry said that he wanted something to drink which the proprietor readily interpreted as meaning some of his rotten whiskey and 'Pitcher' promptly weighed the deer hide and told the hunter that it 'come to a quart'. And after tossing the skin in the corner where the other hides lay in a pile and drawing the amount of liquor equal to the price of the deer hide and handed it to the man who in turn passed the adulterated stuff around among the crowd until the contents of the cup was exhausted.

"But it was not enough and it was not long before the men were licking their lips and getting thirsty again for the want of more whiskey. To purchase more of the stuff was a puzzle for 'Pitcher' Potts abhorred the credit system and refused to trust his customers with a drink on time.

"But soon afterward Mitchell's fun and wit began to crop out and whispering to a few of his associates he stepped out of the building and passed around to the corner where the peltry and furs were deposited. The openings between the logs in the corner where these commodities lay was rather large, the owner being careless and not taking time to chink the cracks and Mitchell catching an opportunity while the proprietor was not looking toward that part of the house reached in and pulled the same deer hide out and stepping aside he carefully rolled the hide up and tied a cotton string round it without 'Pitcher' seeing him.

"Though a light rain was falling Mitchell did not enter the house until a newly arrived countryman came to Mitchell and after the latter explained how it was the man took charge of the deer hide and walked into the saloon and sold it to the proprietor. After the hide was weighed

Potts said it 'Just come to a quart' and threw the hide back in the same corner and drawing a quart of the liquid he gave it to the new arrival, who passed it around until the cup was emptied of its contents; of course Mitchell got in the house in time to share his part of it.

"By this time all the men but 'Pitcher' understood it and he was ignorant of the job put up on him. It was all some of the men could do to keep from laughing outright but they managed to keep quiet and after the expiration of a half an hour Mitchell went out again to the corner and pulled the same deer hide out the second time without being observed by the owner though the other men saw the trick but kept perfectly mum. Mitchell rolled the hide up again and tied it with another string that he had prepared himself with and gave it to a different man that was on the outside who went in and sold it to the dealer for another quart of whiskey and a division was made of it among the settlers immediately.

"This was repeated again and the crowd was nearly ready to give in with loud rejoicing, but a shake of Mitchell's head quieted them and soon after this Mitchell took the same deer skin out for the fourth time and sent it into the house and the man who took it in the house told 'Pitcher' he had brought him a deer hide. The proprietor took the hide in hands scanned it closely for he had become suspicious that a trick had been played on him. He looked at it keenly and turned it over and untied it and unrolled it and after a thorough examination and hesitating a little he remarked that it was very strange that all the deer hides brought in that day were of the same size and weighed just the same number of pounds and was worth each exactly one quart of whiskey.

"This was more than the crowd could stand and they all laughed outright like the roar of a lion. It was now that Potts caught onto the game that Mitchell and the other men were up to and he joined in the fun and amusement at his expense and told the men that they had beat him for once and that it was his treat and stepped to the barrel and drew an extra quart of whiskey and passed it around free of expense. After this was consumed 'Pitcher' informed his customers that he had better stop them cracks before he purchased any more deer hides."

STORIES OF PIONEER DAYS IN NORTHWEST ARKANSAS [22:28]

IN GIVING ACCOUNTS of other matter in the early history of northwest Arkansas Mr. [J. M.] Upton went on to say that after leaving Shawneetown that the family he was living with went on west and stopped on Osage Creek, Carroll County "and there we found Charley Sneed, James Fancher, old man Kenner and two or three other pioneers doing well after the fashion of those days.[6]

"From there we went on to War Eagle River eight miles south of the present site of Huntsville in Madison County and found that quite a little community had sprung up there also, including Tom and Will Jackson, Henry McElhaney, Bill Henderson, and John Martin. They were all farming without fences;[7] they didn't need them much for there was only about one cow, ox or horse to the family and they were kept at work most of the time, but there were plenty of bear, deer, turkey, coon and possum which we all feasted on plentifully. Our corn at first was carried from Cane Hill [Arkansas][8] some forty miles, on our backs in sacks, to make what little bread we had and furnish seed for the future crop.

"To get it into meal we would chop down a tree, build a fire on the stump and burn a large bowl. We then dressed it out by scraping out the charred wood and fixed over this a spring pole with a pestle on the end of it and beat our corn into meal quicker than you would think. In addition to this contrivance we would peel a large elm tree leaving the bark in the shape of a bucket, at one end of which a deer skin with small holes punched in it was stretched, and this made us an excellent sifter which held back a little of the coarser husks of our precious corn."

The contrast in the mode of travel and the manner how farming operations were carried on in the early days and the present time is wonderful and no doubt improvements will be developed on the present way as time goes on. Here is how it was done in the primitive days as told by Mr. Upton.

"As farming operations developed we all had to have some sort of a vehicle. Some made sleds[9] and others crude carts to haul their products in; some drove a cow, others an ox, and a few horses. Their harness was chiefly made of hickory bark, with collars and harness in a single piece cut from maple wood.

"As soon as we began to grow corn in any quantity we built big rail pens for it, and then we started corn shuckings. The whole neighborhood would turn out in the fall evenings and shuck corn, first for one man and then for another, after the corn shucking we would let all the furniture out of the house for a dance. This was no small job, for the bedstead had but one leg and for the other three were fastened to the wall.[10] The chairs were blocks sawed from a tree with pegs stuck in them and the table was a very heavy cumbersome affair, frequently too big to get through the door without being taken to pieces.

"Some had dirt floors, but the more aristocratic ones had puncheon. The puncheon floors were made from logs cut long enough to reach across the house, split open and then hewed somewhat flat on top. These floors were a little rough but we danced [on them] just the same, then as the night wore on and we mellowed to each other more we would bring in chairs for our girls and play one good long play [party].[11] Before starting home in the moonlight, in this play we would all join hands and sidle around singing that good old song:

> Ah Sister Phoebe how merry are we
> As we all sit under the juniper tree.
> Put my hat on your head to keep you warm
> And take a sweet kiss T'wil do you no harm.

And then we took several to wind up the evening fun."

The foregoing statement as given by Mr. Upton certainly portrays the ways and customs on the War Eagle River in those early periods which held good among the settlers all over northern Arkansas and other parts of the Ozark region. Going on with his letter Mr. Upton said that "Our clothes were all made of flax or tow in those days, and pure white—until they got dirty. Both boys and girls wore very long white skirts, the boys with gores in the sides and the girls with drawstrings around the waist. The girls wore white tow bonnets, scooped shaped, and the boys coonskin caps. All were bare footed up to the age of fourteen years old. Our young people today will find it interesting to contrast their present condition and advantages with their condition seventy years ago [1830s]."

AN EARLY PIONEER [18:80]

ONE OF THE PIONEER SETTLERS of Marion County, Ark., was John H. Tabor who died several years ago. Mr. Tabor was a son of Elijah and Sarah (Green) Tabor and was born in Rutherford County, North Carolina, December the 11th, 1809. He came with his parents to the mouth of Big North Fork River on White River in 1826.[12] They and others pushed a keel boat all the way up White River. His parents died many years ago and both lie buried on East Sugar Loaf Creek on what was once known as the Akins' land.

"The year I came to [the] mouth of Big North Fork" said Mr. Tabor,

"I made a crop with Jack Hurst and 'Snappin' Bill Woods on the river near the mouth of Big North Fork. In 1830 I made a crop where Buffalo City now stands just above the mouth of Buffalo. I remember that soon after our arrival at the mouth of Big North Fork in 1826 a band of Indians came there one day with several elksheads and horns. The length of the horns were astonishing for by standing them on the points a man of ordinary height could pass under the heads without stooping.[13] There were plenty of buffalo along White River then, and great numbers of buffalo bones and horns were found all over the country.

"I have lived at various places in Marion County until I took up my final location on Crooked Creek [Marion County] some two miles below Powell.[14] I bought this claim from an Indian of the name of Little Pumpkin in 1836. This Indian had settled this land two years previous. I built a small log cabin on the claim during the same year I bought it. Some three or four years thereafter I built another log house near a fine spring of water on this same land and removed the cabin that I built in 1836 and attached it to this last house and the logs are in a good state of preservation to the present day.

"I got acquainted with doctor Cowdrey[15] in 1829 and he was living in Batesville then. I recollect when de Armond shot and wounded John P. Houston, brother to the governor Sam Houston of Texas fame, a runner was sent to Batesville for doctor Cowdrey and he came and attended on Houston until he recovered from the wound.[16] Houston was at the mouth of Big North Fork River when he and de Armond got into trouble and was shot. Doctor Cowdrey was the only physician then on White River and came to Yellville in 1835. Cowdrey was one among the well educated and was a skillful physician and surgeon.

"Shortly after I came up White River I married Betsey Magness, daughter of Jimmie Magness."

In referring to the graveyard which is situated in the forks of Crooked and Clear Creeks, Mr. Tabor said that the dead bodies of some Indians were the first people buried there.

"These Indians were put away decently by being dressed in new calico that was bought from traders. The dead bodies were ornamented with pretty shells, beads, and rings.

"One night these graves were desecrated by grave robbers. The dead were taken out of the graves and stripped of their shrouds and ornaments. The Indians who lived on Crooked Creek lamented bitterly at the dastardly crime which they charged to two white men named Mose Mecks and Jerry Macks.[17]

"The first white person buried here was the dead body of a white man named John Wood," said Mr. Tabor. Going on with the account of the history of this graveyard, Mr. Tabor mentioned that Jimmie Magness, his father-in-law, is buried here and "also Betsey my first wife and a brother of hers whose given name was Jim lies buried here. Hugh Magness, once the popular merchant at Powell and son of Joe Magness, rests in this same cemetery."[18]

Mr. Tabor died on his old farm June the 26th, 1902, in his 93rd year. He had been living on this land sixty six years and in Marion County, Ark., seventy six years. He was buried in the graveyard in the forks of Crooked and Clear Creeks near where he resided so long.

A FEW ITEMS OF EARLY TIMES [21:30]

NEARLY ALL THE OLD TIMERS of Marion County, Ark., have passed over the great gulf of darkness that lies between life and death. It will only be a few years more when they will all be gone to the silent village where they will never more sit by their fire sides and entertain each other with pioneer reminiscences of the rock ribbed hills of northwest Arkansas. May the great ruler of heaven and earth pour out his blessings of mercy and permit their souls to enter the place of joy and peace in the other life. Let us hope that we will all meet together in the better world where sorrow and troubles are not known.

Among the early day pioneers of Marion County is John B. Hudson, son of Jesse and Matilda (Everette) Hudson, and was born on Crooked Creek four miles below the site of Powell on Christmas day in 1837. His parents died many years ago and they both rest in the cemetery at the mouth of George's Creek. This graveyard is an ancient one; the dead bodies of a few Indians were the first interments here. Near this graveyard is a church house and school building. The White River branch of the Missouri Pacific Railway passed near this spot also.[19] Mr. Hudson stated to the writer that his grand parents John and Agnes Hudson when they died were the first white people buried here.

"My grandfather John Hudson settled the creek bottom just below the mouth of George's Creek and cleared the first land there in 1833. He lived in the bottom opposite the Spout spring. This land is known now as the Davenport farm. Also 'Dancin' Bill Wood, John Overcan, and sheriff Billy Brown who were all very early settlers here are buried here. Several years ago a new graveyard was started some three hundred yards northeast of the old burial ground."

Continuing, Mr. Hudson said that his father Jesse Hudson settled the Joe Burleson farm one and one half miles above the mouth of George's Creek where he worked in a blacksmith shop and "shod" ponies for the Indians and also repaired rifles and done other work for the red men.

"When I was a little boy my father sold his claim and blacksmith shop on Crooked Creek and bought an improvement of Jesse Everette on George's Creek five and one fourth miles north of Yellville. George's Creek took its name from George Wood who built the mill at the Big Spring on East Sugar Loaf Creek [Marion County] in 1854.

"Soon after we moved to George's Creek my father was attacked with palsey which affected his hands and arms very seriously. It almost debarred him from labor of any kind and he never did recover from it. He had a wheel-like construction prepared in the house with small levers attached to a shaft or beam set up right, and by pushing against one of these levers and walking a circle afforded him relief and rest.[20]

"Just before he was attacked by the palsy he built a little cotton gin on the creek near the house. This gin was operated by water and was a small affair yet it ginned all the cotton that was grown for home use eight and ten miles distant from George's Creek."

The writer will say here that he has seen Mr. Jesse Hudson on many occasions walking around on the floor of his house holding to the levers to relieve his paralytic body and limbs as much as possible. We lived then on the north bank of White River twenty one miles north of Mr. Hudson's, but not withstanding this distance, my mother sent me on several occasions with a sack full of seed cotton to Hudson's gin to have the seed taken out for domestic use. Sometimes I would ride this distance on a horse bareback and carry the cotton before me. I give this to show how we did some things in the early days.

HOW THE MEMORABLE METEORIC DISPLAY WAS OBSERVED AT YELLVILLE, ARK. [25:71]

THE GREAT METEORIC DISPLAY spread terror among the few settlers of Marion County, Ark., as well as it did elsewhere in North America.[21] Let us go back to an early period of Yellville and relate a brief history of the display as it occurred here on the night of November 13th, 1833, which was witnessed here by a few settlers and spread terror and consternation among the inhabitants.

At that time Yellville was known as Shawneetown and only a few white people lived here then. The Indians had been leaving the village and Crooked Creek for more than a year[22] and at the time I speak of there were but few stationary Indians here. The account of the display was told me by John H. Tabor, who said that on that day he moved into a small hut that had been vacated by an Indian of the village. His brother Smith Tabor had assisted him to move from the Flippin Barrens on pack horses.

In giving the story of the display Mr. Tabor went on to say that his brother and Nimrod Teaf remained overnight with him and "We were so tired that we all lay down early and went to sleep," said he. "Just before midnight my brother woke up and was nearly paralyzed with fear at beholding the air filled with 'falling stars'. When he was able to speak he woke us all up and told us to hurry and get on our clothes for the world was coming to an end.

"I was almost stupefied with wonder and astonishment and hurriedly rose from my couch of bear skins and looked out at the door and saw that the whole heavens, as far as I could observe, was brilliantly illuminated with hundreds and thousands of 'stars' shooting swiftly down toward the earth. Apparently they would disappear or go out before reaching the ground. It was a grand but fearful sight.

"Like my brother, I and Nimrod Teaf thought it the last of earth, and we all concluded that it was too late to pray and submitted ourselves to await the approach of our destruction. I fully believed that we would have to give an account of our sins to God at once and we sit down and waited for the awful moment to appear. The suspense of waiting was dreadful. If I was condemned to be hung and were standing on the trap door with the noose around my neck waiting an hour for the trap to be sprung, I could feel no worse than I did that night. We waited and went on waiting for the coming of our doom. The grand display continued and our terror did not grow less. The night seemed a month long, and the end of the world had not come yet.

"When at last to our surprise we noticed that day was breaking in the east and it looked as natural as it ever did, as we discerned the approach of day and as it grew lighter we found to our joy that mother earth was still here and the end was not in sight. The flying meteors were gradually obscured by the light of day and we were left unharmed and as far as we knew the earth remained intact. God in his mercy and goodness kept the earth in its proper place and did not allow the great flying objects to harm us in the least or knock the earth from its hinges.

"Others who had viewed this remarkable phenomenon said that they were as bad scared as I was and believed that earth and all living creatures would succumb to the wrath of God that night. I was a wicked man then but after the date of the 'falling stars' I did not live so sinful toward God." ✍

THE KING AND EVERETTE WAR AT YELLVILLE, ARKANSAS [26:83]

WE HAVE WRITTEN several fragmentary accounts as furnished us by a number of parties relating to the King and Everette War, most of these are disconnected. Capt. A. S. (Bud) Wood who is one of the old pioneer residents of Marion County, Ark., was an eye witness to this fight and gives me a connected account of this memorable encounter between those old time people that took part in the battle. Capt. Wood furnished me the story of the fight at his home at Kingdom Springs[23] [Marion County] on Sunday evening the fourth of August, 1907. Here is how he told it.

"The Everettes were from the state of Tennessee and settled in Marion County in a very early day. Ewell Everett was the oldest. John Everette was the next oldest, Cimeron [Simmon] Everette was the next. Jess Everette was next to Cimeron, and Barton Everette was the youngest. A year or more after their arrival here Barton Everette was elected sheriff of Marion County and served out his term of office.

"When the Everettes first arrived here they had dealings with Hansford Tutt who was a 'one-horse' merchant in Yellville.[24] Soon after this Jefferson Tutt and Davis Casey Tutt was involved in the quarrel and it continued to grow worse until other men were drawn into it, but up to this time the quarrel had not culminated in a fight.

"Finally the Kings moved into Marion County from Alabama. There were Billy King, James King, Hosea King, and Solomon King. These were the old men and they had nothing to do with the battle, but some of their sons did. The quarrel continued to grow until Sam Burns and Silas Cowan took a part in it. These men were brothers-in-law. Cowan was on the Everette side and Burns was on the Kings' side.

"One day in 1847 a great crowd of men gathered at Yellville which was then a mere hamlet and a few of the men began to quarrel and it went on until the leaders of each side began forming two lines opposite each other and only a few yards apart. Sam Burns and Silas Cowan were the starters of the disturbance that day and while the lines were being formed for a fight about fifteen men on each side fell in line armed with rifles, shot guns, pistols, stones and clubs.

"Just as the enraged men were ready to strike each other a blow a violent whirl wind that resembled a small tornado suddenly formed just east of where the lines were standing and swept toward the men and passed between the two lines and jerked the caps and hats from the men's heads and passed on toward the west. The great whirl wind had collected a thick cloud of dust and when it struck the men it bewildered them and they all backed off, separated and scattered and the trouble ceased for the time.

"The quarrel was not renewed to amount to anything until one day in the early fall of 1848 when another big crowd of the settlers gathered at Yellville which included some of the Everettes and Kings and a number of their friends. Some of the men of both sides become very boisterous and it was evident that a fight was brewing. The most of the men were assembled around a small grocery store.

"I had went to the village that day on a young bay horse I called Tom. This horse had been pretty wild but I had him almost under control. When I arrived in town I tied the horse to the body of a small tree with a strong rope. This tree stood near the grocery store. The men of each side grew more war-like until I saw that it was going to be a bloody one. They were all around my horse and I started on a run to take him away, but before I had time to reach him the firing began and the fight was on and I hesitated and stopped and turned back for fear I might get shot accidently. My horse was greatly frightened at the yelling of the men and the reports of the guns and he reared up on his hind feet and it seemed as though he tried to climb up the tree. Though he plunged and pulled hard at the rope he was not able to break it and had to stand the racket until the fight was ended.

"The casualties of the fight were as follows. Francis Everette, son of Ewell Everette, shot Jack King with an old squirrel rifle and he died on the following day. Barton Everette was killed at a black locust tree and as the fatal bullet struck him he clasp his arms around this tree and sank down at the foot of the tree and died. He had a ribbon around his hat for a hat band and when his body was removed from the tree some of the men took the ribbon from his hat and tied it around the tree and it remained there several months before it rotted away. Martin Sinclair, a Missourian, killed Cimeron Everette. After Everette was shot he walked to the grocery and fell in the door with his head on the inside and his feet on the steps. Francis Everette after he had shot Jack King, a man of the name of Mears advanced on him as if to take his gun away from him, and Everette struck

Mears with his gun and broke his arm. Dick King shot a man of the name of Watkins at the edge of the hair in the forehead which cut a trench through the skin to the top of the head without fracturing the skull. But he fell to the ground as if dead but soon revived.

"Just after the bloody scene closed Sinclair mounted his horse and called out, 'Here is enough beef to feed all the hungry hounds of this town and neighborhood.' There were only four of the Kings engaged in the battle [and] these were Loomis and Richard, sons of Billy King, and Jack and Tom King, sons of Solomon King. None of the Burns or Cowans were in the fight nor none of the old set of Kings as we have stated.

"Near about one year after the big fight come off Hansford Tutt was waylaid and shot on the bluff near where Layton's hotel[25] stood. He was shot on Monday and he died on the following Thursday.

"Shortly after the battle Jess Everette and his family went to Texas and he and his sons came back to Arkansas several years before the beginning of the civil war and went to Springfield in Conway County [Arkansas] where some of the Kings were living then, and arrested Loomis King and his father Billy King and young Bill King, son of Solomon King, and brought them ten miles south of Yellville and shot them. Their dead bodies were brought to Yellville and given interment on the Jim Wickersham property."

As Capt. Wood ended his account of this bloody affair he said there were eleven men killed from first to last as the result of the King and Everette War. 🖎

Eloped with His Wife's Brother's Wife [21:34]

IN THE EARLY PART of the year 1858 a man who said his name was Ben Jacobs moved into the northwest part of Marion County, Ark., and lived for some time on the Frank Pumphrey[26] place on Shoal Creek. The house stood on the east side of the creek and on the south bank of the mouth of a hollow that empties into the creek. This house was one mile more or less above the mouth of the creek. Jacobs seemed to be flush with money—wore fine clothes and rather on the aristocratic order. He had a woman with him that was supposed to be his wife. They brought a wagon with them which was drawn by a span of horses. He also brought a buggy and a mule with him and two Negro men that were called Nelse and Haywood.

Jacobs had not been there long before he turned out to drinking and proved to be an inveterate drunkard. He drank so excessively that at times he felt "snakes in his boots" and would be raving mad and knash his teeth together and foam at the mouth. But when he was not under the influence of liquor he was quiet and courteous. When he was not drinking he would go fishing in the creek or hunt for wild turkey.

Time went on and in the course of a few months an infant was born to the woman. Nothing was thought of this until one afternoon when Mrs. Elizabeth Holt, wife of Feilden Holt, who lived at the mouth of the creek paid the woman a visit to render aid in caring for the infant. The woman told Mrs. Holt that she appreciated her kindness—that she was not accustomed to children and never had the pleasure of caring for them. This remark was overheard by one of the Negro men who afterward mentioned this to one of the neighbors and said "Missus need not say that she was not use to children for she had run away with Massa Jacobs and left several small children at home in South Carolina." The Negro also gave the name of the post office where they had formerly lived.

The story of the Negro created a sensation among the neighbors and they concluded to make an investigation and "River" Bill Coker addressed a letter of inquiry to the Postmaster at the post office the Negro had given the name of and in due time a reply to the letter was received at Dubuque Post Office. The contents of the letter sent by the Postmaster read something like this: "Jacobs had married into a wealthy family but he soon turned out to be a set drunkard and his father-in-law looked on him as an unworthy man and refused to recognize him any longer as a son-in-law. And Jacobs eloped with his wife's brother's wife. The false and fickle couple had deserted their children as well as companions and Jacobs brought one of the Negro men with him which belonged to him and the guilty woman brought another Negro that belonged to her." It seemed by the way the letter read that the people who lived in the neighborhood where the sinful pair came from did not consider them worthy of notice.

But the settlers on Shoal Creek and along White River did not need their presence and it was suggested that a committee wait on the man Jacobs and read the letter to him which was done. It was so plain that the guilty man made no denial and the committee including Mr. Coker informed Jacobs that it would be prudent for him to take the woman and depart for some other county which he agreed to do and the man loaded his household into the wagon forthwith and hitching his horses to it and taking the woman and infant and the two Negro men left the county. They were heard of again on the Arkansas River where a few months later Jacobs and the woman died.

FALL OF THE BOASTING YOUNG FELLOW [21:1]

AMONG THE ACCOUNTS of incidents of roving and drinking at Dubuque on White River in what is now Boone County, Ark., is the following which was told me by Mort Herron.[27]

"One day," says he, "while I was in Bob Trimble's grocery store at Dubuque, a big gawky overbearing young fellow was in there boasting of his bravery and wanted to fight somebody. The fellow had red complexion and was sandy or red headed. The man would dance back and forth across the floor. There were several men in there at the time but no one payed any attention to him for it seemed that he was not considered worthy of notice. I was standing against the counter and leaning against it.

"Directly the fellow danced up in a foot of where I was and all at once he stooped and blew and spit a mouth full of tobacco and amber into my face and eyes which blinded me in a moment. The fellow burst out into a merry laugh at my discomfiture for he supposed he done a brave act and I heard some of his friends join in with him in the laugh. It was useless for me to attempt to say anything for I was blind and helpless. I took my old cotton handkerchief from my pocket and rubbed the amber and bits of tobacco out of my eyes until I was able to discern objects. My eyes pained me severely and I pulled my hat over my face and twisted and squirmed, then I continued to rub them with the handkerchief until I could see how to go out of the house and went down to the river and washed and bathed my eyes until I had got them cleansed from the tobacco and I could see my way well, but they still hurt me some.

"While I was at the river some of my friends come to me and said that the young gentleman was still in the store room boasting, dancing and whistling very gay over the manner he had treated me. I says boys 'That fellow has treated me very rough as well as undermining, for a high minded and brave man would not treat another fellow being as he has treated me, and I am going to have revenge for it', and they all said 'Mort if you want to fix him we will keep the dogs off.'

"I looked about and picked up two smooth stones at the edge of the water. These rocks were the size of goose eggs and were oval in shape and I and the boys went back to the grocery store and went in. The fellow was still dancing and seemed to ignore my presence and I struck him on the side of the head with one of the stones and the brave young man fell to the floor in a lump. The men collected around him but no one seemed to want to take it up for him. I and my friends stayed there an hour before we left and he was still unconscious.

"I did not go back to Dubuque for several weeks after this but I learned that the fellow lay four days at Dubuque before he was able to be removed to his home by his friends."

The Hollinsworth Mill and Stories as Given by the Proprietor [20:29]

THE WELL KNOWN milling establishment situated on the Little North Fork in North Fork Township, Marion County, Ark., called the Hollinsworth Mill was built by the Hollinsworth Brothers, Robert and Lemuel.[28] On the opposite side of the creek from the mill house is a bluff which follows the course of the stream like a rainbow up near the top of this bluff and just below the mill is a precipice. The mill has been very popular since its completion in 1885.

Robert Hollinsworth died March 17, 1899, leaving his brother Lem sole proprietor of the mill and the farm there.

One day the writer had a pleasant interview with Lem Hollinsworth at his home and he related to me a few interesting sketches of his and brother "Bob's" trials before and during the building of the mill. Lem Hollinsworth was born in Howard County, Indiana, October 30, 1854. His brother "Bob" was nine years his senior.

The people of Taney County, Mo., remember Bob and Lem Hollinsworth when they took charge of the Keesee Mills on Beaver Creek in 1873 and rented it for a term of years. They had made two trips to lower White River on a small boat to hunt and trap in the bottoms, but finding it not a very lucrative business they began a correspondence with Capt. A. C. Keesee and Willis Keesee, proprietors of the Beaver (Keesee) Mill,[29] and rented the mill and leaving the sickly swamp they made haste to get into the hills of Taney County.

In speaking of their journey on foot to Beaver Creek, Lem said that they struck Big Creek at Jack Nance's and going on to Beaver they found only one family living between Nance's and Beaver Creek and that was Cornelius Johnson who lived on the ridge three miles from the mill.

"The whole country seemed so thinly settled that it was discouraging to take charge of the mill here. Isaac Brown lived on a joining farm to the Keesee land. There was also a small Sunday school organization in Tennison Hollow some three miles from the mill. We believed that our patrons would be scarce but the proprietors of the mill assured us that we would have plenty to do, and we did, for we had no lack of custom. Instead of having to sit down and do nothing we were soon crowded with customers from far and near. Occasionally we had no rest time during day or night for a week at a time."

Soon after the expiration of their time at the mill, Lem said that he and his brother Robert and Jim Everette[30] of Forsyth selected the situation on Little North Fork for the building of a mill. "We three contemplated erecting the mill in partnership but finally Everette declined to assist and I and Robert went it alone," said Lem. The undertaking to build a good mill with such small means as they possessed at the time presented a dark future to the boys but each was endowed with plenty of pluck and industry and they went to work with a will. They were compelled to cease work on their mill building at times and go and hunt a job of work somewhere else in order to obtain money to pay for the necessary machinery."

The first permanent start they made was to purchase an acre of land from Charley Hassell for the mill site for ten dollars. The farm where the mill stands was once known as the young Mike Yocum place. Yocum was a brother of Asa, Bill, Harve and Jake Yocum and was a son of old Uncle Mike Yocum who once lived at the mouth of Little North Fork.

Then they paid $200 for a Leffel wheel or double turbine water wheel[31] of the firm of Jennings and Goslin who had built a grist and saw mill on Bryant's Fork, but the entire establishment had been swept away by a great freshet in the stream. The wheel including the coupling knuckle is supposed to have weighed 7000 pounds or more. But the unprecedented rise of water and the current was so swift and strong that the wheel was pushed about one half of a mile down the creek and was found in the creek bottom where it was partly embedded in the sand and gravel. "We paid $200 for it as it lay in the dirt. The original owners claimed that they paid $1200 for the wheel including the cost of transportation. It took I and my brother Robert one week of busy work to dig the wheel out of its bed, unbolt and prepare it for transportation to Little North Fork on wagons, and it took more time and hard work to haul the outfit.

"We bought the corn burrs from Barney Parrish[32] of Forsyth who had bought them for his own use many years before, and had come to pieces before we contracted for them. Parrish had never used them. When we purchased them we cemented and rebanded them and put them to use. The burrs we use to grind wheat was used by Anderson Chapman at that beautiful East Sugar Loaf Creek [Marion County]. There he run a saw and grist mill from the latter Sixties to the early Seventies. One day at the Chapman Mill while the miller was running the burrs at a high speed they come apart at the cemented seams and the blocks 'flew off the handle' and wounded the miller. These burrs are thirty eight inches across, the corn burrs are four feet across. It is unnecessary to go into every detail in the building of the mill but I will state that we had a hard struggle in getting it ready for business.

"There is an amusing incident connected with it that I will tell you which will probably make a little past time reading for some fun-loving person. In the fall of 1880 we hewed out part of the timber intended for the mill in the vicinity of Forsyth and after hauling the pieces to town we put them together and launched them into the river and floated them down to the mouth of Little North Fork and tied them as we thought secure until we could take them out of the water. Unfortunately before we did so the hard winter of 1880–1 set in and froze the river over with thick ice. This lasted until the 20th of January [1881] when it come a thaw and rain which swelled the river four feet high, which broke up the ice and tore our timbers apart and carried the most of the pieces down the icy current of water.

"After the waters had went down we searched both shores and all the islands for twelve miles below the mouth of Little North Fork without finding a stick of it. We continued to hunt for the pieces some time after but without success. Why we lost so much time in looking for the lost timbers I am not able to state unless we were following the example of the old darky who had lost a copper cent and continually hunted for it but was never able to discover its whereabouts. One day several years after the old colored fellow had lost his piece of money a man came along and seeing the darky still hunting for the copper he said to him, 'Why do you hunt for the copper cent so much for you waste more time than you receive profit?'

"'That is all true,' replied the old colored friend, 'but Massa, I am so anxious to know where my copper went to.'

"And that was the way with I and Bob, we wanted to know where those pieces of hewed timber had went to. As our long search was fruitless we had to prepare new pieces, but we did not go back to Forsyth to procure them. Though I and Bob have met with plenty of ill luck, we deemed it useless to be always complaining for growling at misfortunes in financial matters is almost sure to make things worse than better.

"Among our mishaps is one that I remember distinctly. We had bought five hundred bushels of apples from Captain A. C. Keesee and hauled them to the bank of the river on the John E. Williams land[33] where we put them on a boat prepared for the purpose of carrying the fruit down the river to sell. This was in the fall of the year and we expected a rise in the river in the latter part of November, but there was not sufficient rain fall to raise the river until the last night of March.

"By this time a big lot of our apples had rotted and we assorted the entire lot and threw the defective ones away. Then Bob and Charley Yandell started down the river with the remainder. The water was still low, but the boat men had splendid luck until they arrived at the Bull Shoals in Marion County where in passing over the rough shoal water the boat was forced against a rock by the swift current and a hole was knocked in the bottom of the boat. The craft struck the rock in such a shape that it hung on the rock and partly filled with water and ruined part of the apples. Yandell and my brother went to work and took about one hundred bushels of apples to shore. On hearing of the mishap I went down to assist the boys and we were two weeks in patching the hole in the boat and bailing out the water and assorting the apples again. Then we made another start and succeeded in arriving at Batesville where we sold part of the apples we had left, then went on to Jacksonport and Newport[34] and sold the remainder; we averaged them off at ten cents per dozen and $1.00 per bushel.

"I do not know whether you admire Ku Klux tales or not," said Mr. Hollinsworth. "I never was mobbed nor threatened by them as far as I know, but the stories I had heard about them sounded frightful to me and of all things that I wanted to shun it was a Ku Klux. I tried to fix it up in mind what they looked like. I knew they were not insects, birds or animals, but I imagined they were something that resembled a human. I had heard that Arkansas was full of these monsters and I was constantly in dread of them.[35] I had done no wrong to deserve their anger, yet I believed they would destroy a fellow whether they liked him or not.

"In the fall of 1872 when we crossed the line over in Arkansas I and Bob bought lumber at Van Winkle's saw mill, which I think was in the northwest part of Carroll County and was five miles south of White River. After hauling our lumber to the river we built a small boat to go down the river on a hunting expedition, not taking time to build a strong boat but rather a rickety affair, we put aboard our guns, ammunition, bed clothes, wearing apparel, traps, and provision, and between Christmas and New Year's Day we started down the river. The channel that far up was narrow. The weather was cold with snow on the ground.

"After a day's run down the river one side corner of our boat struck an old stump in a shoal, or glanced it rather, and the boat shot around and lay cross ways in the shoal lodged midway against the stump—each end of the boat rested against an object. The upper side of the boat was forced under the water and ourselves as well as all our freight got soaked in the cold water. We managed to get to shore by wading and walking on a drift and went a mile below to Wash Roller's at the crossing of the river known as Roller's Ferry[36] where we dried our clothes and procured more provision and borrowed a cable rope and went back and prepared a Spanish windless[37] and pulled the boat to eddy water and saved part of our things and remodeled the boat and went on downstream.

"As I have said before, I was afraid of the Ku Klux for it was my first trip in Arkansas, and as we floated on down the river I kept a close watch out for their forms to suddenly appear on either shore. Bob was not afraid of them and laughed at my fears. In a day or two the weather warmed up and Bob grew gaily and sang lively political songs that made my hair almost push the hat off of my head to listen at. One of these songs were about John Brown and Jeff Davis. I did my best to persuade him to hush, but he went on with his singing the same as if he had been in the extreme north part of the United States. I can remember only a few words of the song but a line or two was similar to these words: 'John Brown with his knap sack strapped on his back, and we'll free the niggers without the least doubt. And we will hang Jeff Davis on a sour apple tree.'[38] I protested strongly against Bob singing such stuff for we were in the wrong country to sing in favor of John Brown and against Jeff Davis. The Ku Klux might hear him and catch us and make us look up something worse than a sour apple tree, but my arguments had no influence with Bob. He said this was a free country and he wanted to sing what he pleased.

"My fears proved to be groundless for if we met any Ku Klux I did not know it for instead of being mistreated by the people who lived along the river we received the kindest of treatment and there was nothing said about Arkansas being full of Ku Klux and I quit giving heed to any more Ku Klux stories and was troubled no more with frightful dreams of these much talked of imaginary demons," said Mr. Hollinsworth.

Forsyth in 1837 and the Early Settlement of Swan Creek [19:35]

AT THE MOUTH OF SWAN CREEK opposite Forsyth, Taney County, Mo., is a towering bluff the summit of which commands a magnificent view. The fine town of Forsyth with its substantial business houses and neat dwellings, the beautiful waters of Swan Creek and White River, and a combination of other scenery form a picture that is not easily forgotten. At a low stage the waters of both streams flow gently along and glisten in the bright sunlight.

From the top of this elevation the author enjoyed the pleasure of a view of the town of Forsyth and vicinity a short time ago. It was a lovely afternoon in the month of September and the sight was an interesting one. The beautiful scenery fairly thrilled me with delight as I contemplated its loveliness and let my mind wander back to the incidents of the years in the long ago.

Looking across the river at the farm opposite town I thought of Hack Snapp, the noted farmer and stock raiser who lived on this farm many years ago. Glancing my eyes to the top of the ridge along which the Kirbyville Road leads calls to mind McCajor Haworth[39] and Doctor Maynard, the latter of which manufactured the Cook's pills and Maynard's tonic pills which sold at twenty five cents and seventy five cents per box respectively.[40] These three men mentioned have passed beyond this life and their mouldering bones lie in graves widely separated.

Turning my eyes toward Forsyth and looking over the town the names of several old time residents loomed up before me, but I can mention only a few of them here. Among the early merchants I remember seeing were Jesse Jennings and John P. Vance.[41] Later on Jim Huddlestone, Tom Anderson, Jake Nave, George McDowell and Dick Moore engaged in merchandising in Forsyth. I well recollect Doctor Wilson, the noted physician and surgeon, and also Jake Grider, the popular blacksmith.

William C. Berry was a noted county official of Taney County. He served eight years in succession as county clerk. Mr. Berry was known as Uncle Campbell and was a brother of the merchant James C. Berry who died at Yellville, Ark.[42] Through honesty and courtesy Mr. Berry was held in great esteem by the people all over Taney County. At the breaking out of hostilities between the north and south Mr. Berry embraced the southern cause and served in the southern army where he rose to the position of major in the quartermasters department. After the close of the great conflict he made his home in Augusta [Arkansas] where he engaged in the mercantile trade and died there in 1875.

Forsyth is an old town; its existence as a white settlement dates back to 1837. Dave McCord said that when he came with his parents to [the] mouth of Swan Creek in the month of September, 1837, there were no Indians living there then, they had deserted their village several years before.[43]

"A white man named David Shannon lived in a new log house in the bottom where Forsyth now stands. This man was a trader and sold goods to the few white settlers along White River and the roving bands of Indians. Shannon had about $100 worth of goods in his house when we came there and from appearances this settlement was recently made and the cane in a small space around the house had been cleared off. With the exception of this the entire bottom was covered with a dense growth of cane some of which was twenty feet high."

Forsyth has been a prominent trading point since the year 1840.[44] In the olden time the pioneers of Taney County visited Forsyth to buy supplies of coffee, sugar, salt and "spun thread" and paid for it in gold, silver, furs and peltry. There were no trust companies or other devouring corporations then to be enriched by the laboring classes. Trusts, combines and monopolies were unknown then and the people did not feel themselves oppressed or bound down by the money power.[45]

As I sit on the top of this high eminence I noticed the substantial court house built of stone which I am told rests on the same spot where the brick court house formerly stood that was built several years before the civil war began. I well recollect seeing the workmen lay the foundation stones; this stone house when completed was said to have cost $5,500. Here on this same spot is where the old log court house once stood.[46]

Turning my eyes and looking up the beautiful valley of Swan Creek I was reminded of the old time settlers who once occupied the rich bottom lands on this stream. These old timers lie in neglected graves. As my thoughts went back to the first settlement of Swan Creek I wondered how many of us now living cherish the memory of those pioneer families. I am told that Bill Stacy camped a few days on Swan Creek just above its mouth in 1834 and he settled on the head of this stream in 1836. A year or two after this Lewis Clarkstone settled on this water course. Then John Pelham was another early settler and lived at the mouth of Lost Hollow. Joel Hall settled at the mouth of Elk Horn Branch and John Edwards lived between Mr. Pelham and Hall. These old pioneers were followed by Amos Edward and two other men of the name of Brown and Anderson.

By this time the few settlers along this pretty stream of water began to feel at home and wanted a house of worship and the settlers combined their work and built a small log house above Mr. Hall's for a church house and decided to have a meeting, but no preacher resided in the neighborhood. But there was a minister named Leven T. Green who lived on Little North Fork and they sent for him to pay them a visit on a certain Sunday and Mr. Green responded to the call and arrived on the designated day in the garb of a hunter and carried his old flint lock rifle with him. A small audience had collected at the little church house and Green gave them a lively discourse. This was the first religious service held on Swan Creek. A year after this a protracted meeting was held at this same house the result of which eight persons were baptized in the clear and beautiful water of Swan Creek. Among them was a Negro woman that belonged to old Jimmie Cook.[47]

The Fourth of July at Forsyth in 1848 [22:33]

IT HAS BEEN MANY YEARS since my first visit to Forsyth, Taney County, Mo. It was then quite a small village but it did not lack for lively and stirring scenes. The memory of that day has never faded from my mind—but time and humanity since then have wrought a great change—it was on the fourth of July, 1848.

The weather was warm and serene, there was not a cloud hardly visible. The citizens of the village and the surrounding country gave a big dinner. It was an old fashioned barbecue and good order prevailed throughout the day. Though the country was thinly settled yet the size of the crowd that collected there on that day was astonishing. They came from far and near and from every direction. Some of the men and women came over fifty miles. The number of people were estimated at fifteen hundred including children, [which] was remarkable when we take into consideration the manner of traveling. Some came on horse back; some in ox wagons and hundreds came on foot.

They were all patriotic and enthusiastic and took that occasion to celebrate the great victories gained by the daring and valor of the American troops in the Mexican war. Peace had already been declared but news could not fly over the world in a minute in those days and the people of Taney County had not learned of the fact, and so they organized a company of volunteers to send to the front, but news of the declaration of peace reached Forsyth soon afterward and the company was soon disbanded.[48]

I am not exaggerating when I say that Forsyth was honored on that fourth day of July by the presence of five hundred ladies. I was only four years old then but I never will forget as long as I live what a beautiful appearance the ladies presented as they marched to the table in proper order. Nearly all of them were neatly dressed in clothes of their own manufacture dyed with old fashioned indigo and madder and barks, roots and weeds gathered in the forest. Many of the men wore moccasins and had on garbs of dressed buck skins, but a majority of the men and boys wore garments spun and woven by the industrious housewives and daughters. Nearly all the women and girls wore paste board and cedar split bonnets.

There were no lemonade stands for speculation [money-making] nor dancing floors to mar the feeling of those religiously inclined, but was simply an old time gathering of the people with plenty to eat and free to all that was present. 🌿

How a Young Man Was Whipped for Stealing Sugar and Other Articles [22:67]

THE FOLLOWING ACCOUNT which relates to the whipping of a young man was furnished me by Mort Herron, son of Lewis Herron, an early settler on Big Creek in Taney County, Mo. Mr. Herron said that when his father settled on that stream in 1841, Arch Tabor, John Tabor, old Jimmie Tabor, Tom Tabor, John Herron and John Morris lived on the west prong of the creek from the main fork of the creek toward the head. He said that Dave Taylor, an early settler on Big Creek, bought the little mill that Russell Tabor built at the Pelham place and kept it a few months and sold it again. Mr. Herron says that old Billy Clark settled the Jack Nance place on Big Creek. "And my father", continued Mr. Herron, "settled two miles above the Jack Nance place and one mile below the foot of the hill where the main road leads up and over to Brushy Creek. In the mouth of a hollow near this hill" said Uncle Mort, "my father killed four bear one day soon after our arrival on Big Creek."

Mr. Herron says that he remembers the first school that was taught on Big Creek.

"In the early Fifties a few citizens built a small log hut for a school house on the first place below the old John Morris farm known now as the Dave Coiner land. This was a subscription school and William Adair was the teacher. Among Adair's children were Carroll, Dick, Bill, Jim and Mary, these all attended the school. Carroll Adair was nearly grown.

"Soon after we moved from Big Creek and settled on Shoal Creek one mile and a half south of where Protem now is, he [Carroll Adair] married a daughter of the widow Pettigrew and after one child was born to them his wife died and Mrs. Pettigrew took charge of the child.

"While we lived on Shoal Creek, Carroll Adair had no regular home and some said that he was a thief. During the winter seasons while we lived on Shoal Creek we made enough sugar from the sugar maple trees which stood in the creek bottom which we called Sugar Camp Bottom to do us a year. Sunday after we had made a lot of sugar we left it in the house and went on a visit to be gone all day and when we come back home part of our sugar was missing. As Carroll Adair had been strolling over the country and on learning from others that he had been at our house during the day we suspected him getting the sugar. On close inquiry we found that after he had devoured all the sugar his stomach would hold, he sold part of the remainder for a five cent silver piece or half dime and we soon learned that he had visited another house and stole a silk handkerchief and a lot of buttons and got away with them. The unobserved theft was discovered soon after he left, and on the same Sunday he had stolen an axe from another party.

"After learning all these facts, I and my brother Simon Herron followed him. We left home after night. I rode a gray mare we called Ribbon and Simon rode a bay horse. Soon after we started from home I stopped and dismounted and cut a long slender hickory withe for we had decided that if we found and captured him we would give him a spanking good whipping and after ordering him to leave the country we would release him and give him a fair chance to go.

"The first house we stopped at was Bill Cowan who lived near the river above the mouth of Elbow Creek. Bill told us that Adair was at old man Cowan's, father of Bill Cowan. Cowan caught his gray mare and rode with us to his father's house. When we arrived there the family had all retired to bed except John and Tom Cowan, and Carroll Adair, and they were pulling off their shoes to get ready to go to bed. When we got into the house Adair seemed to suspect that we were on the hunt for him and worked rapidly to put on his shoes again in order to run off. We told him to hurry up for we desired him to go with us for the sake of company. After he had put on his shoes I said, 'Let us go,' and when we got out to our horses Bill Cowan and Simon guarded him until I remounted my mare and they made him get up behind me, but thinking he might leap off of my mare and escape we stopped and Bill and Simon tied Adair's hands behind him with a rope.

"We did not say anything harsh to him, he submitted to our orders silently not even speaking a word until we had traveled a short distance after his hands had been bound and stopped where we ask him if he was willing to confess that he was guilty of stealing the sugar from us and the handkerchief, buttons and axe from other parties. He said that he did steal the things that we charged him with and if we would turn him loose he would not do wrong any more, but we were convinced that this assertion was not true and we told him that we were going to punish him according to Judge Linch [Lynch] if he did not want the civil law to take hold of him and we would give him his choice to either go to jail at Forsyth or take a whipping; he said that he did not mind the whipping if we would scatter the licks and not lash him too hard.

"I then said, 'Carroll how many licks do you really deserve from this hickory withe?' which I held in my hand.

"'Well,' said he, 'about three stripes if they are not too rough.'

"Then we rode on again, and leaving the road we went on through the woods until we were near the southwest edge of Katie's Prairie [Taney County] where we halted and dismounted and held a consultation in his presence whether to take him on to Forsyth and turn him over to the proper authorities or give him a whipping and we decided on the latter punishment. There was no moonlight but the weather was clear and the many stars afforded some light.

"We told Adair to make up his mind to receive a sound thrashing, but we would not beat him to death but would whip him in a way that he would not forget it. He was thinly clad even wearing a linen duster in winter time. We held to him and selected a post oak tree, then we untied his hands but did not take off his duster or shirt. We told him to hug the post oak tree which he did without a murmur then Cowan took hold of one hand and Simon the other and they pulled him hard up with his breast against the tree and they put one foot each against the tree to brace themselves and held him fast and with the hickory withe I began the work of whipping him.

"I struck him hard but he never groaned. He was a large fat chuffy fellow and was well able to bear a severe thrashing and he got it there. I struck him fifty licks which the back of his duster and shirt bore evidence. No doubt my hickory cut into the flesh for when I ceased whipping him, I felt on his back with my hands and his back was wet which I supposed was blood.

"We told him that he must leave the country but he never uttered a word. After we had turned him loose he stood still. We told him to get from there and that in a hurry and never come back again, but he never moved nor said a word. At this Simon jerked what was left of the withe out of my hands and struck him a hard blow with it on the back and he started off on a fast run without any more warning. We heard of him a few days afterward and I suppose he left the country to stay away for I never saw him anymore."

IT WAS WONDERFUL TO THEM [22:43]

"AWAY BACK IN THE PIONEER DAYS of what is now Cedar Creek Township, Marion County, Ark.," says Mr. Peter Keesee [Silas's brother-in-law], "Alex Duggins who was an uncle of Cage Duggins who died on Big Creek in Ozark County, Mo., in the month of April, 1872, lived on White River at the mouth of Big Creek.

"On one occasion he went down to the mouth of Big North Fork to purchase supplies from Major Wolf who kept a trading store there. While buying coffee, sugar and salt Mr. Wolf the proprietor offered to sell Mr. Duggins a large mirror. Looking glasses were so rarely seen on White River at that early date that many people had never heard of such an article much less seen one. When Mr. Duggins bought the glass and had brought it home he hung it up to the wall of the house near the doorway and the family took its turn about in reflecting their images in the glass until they grew weary of it.

"One Sunday two young ladies who had never been blessed in viewing a mirror paid Mr. Duggins and his family a visit. It was something wonderful to them. They would take it, turn about in standing before the glass, and take a long look at their reflections, then dart out of doors to see if they could find their image implanted on the outside wall of the cabin, and failing to do so they would appear perfectly astonished where their pictures had went to: they both repeated their foolishness until they were thoroughly convinced that they were unable to dodge out of the house quick enough to catch sight of their shadows, [seen] only through the glass. They both looked on the mirror as the greatest inventions they ever met before or expected to meet in the future. Mr. Duggins wife's maiden name was Dial—his mother's given name was Moriah."

HIS LAST DANCE [22:45]

IN A USUAL WAY a man in following the wicked ways of the world is inclined to reach out too far which has been the downfall of many men unless they repent in time and cease to do evil. Mr. Peter Keesee, son of Paton Keesee, was born and reared on Little North Fork, Ozark County, Mo. He said that his first wife was Miss Jane Johnson, daughter of Sam Johnson. "After our marriage," said Mr. Keesee, "we lived on what is now the Carroll Johnson place on the east bank of Little North Fork. Sam

Bevins married my sister Gennie Keesee and they lived on the same side of the creek I did and just below where Theodosia is now.

"One day Mr. Bevins invited a number of the settlers to a big log rolling in the creek bottom. It was winter time and the weather was cool and disagreeable.

"On the morning of the day set for the log rolling, I says to my wife, 'Jane do not go to the field and turn out the cattle, it is too hard on you to have to hunt all over the field and collect the stock and turn them out to water. Let them alone. I will come back before night and turn them out myself, you stay in the house and do not go out in the cold. You may look for me back in the evening for I will come sure.'

"Then I left the house and my trusting wife and went on to my brother-in-law's to take part in the log rolling. There was a big crowd there with plenty of whisky and hard work to do. But we got all the logs piled by night. The names of a few men who were present that day was Pete Jones, Jim Tabor, Ron Burdon and my brother Dick Keesee. At night just before supper time Sam Bevins, who was an excellent violinist, tuned up his fiddle and began playing on it.

"At this Mac Holmes and his daughter Sarah stepped onto the middle of the floor and commenced to dance. This was a great surprise to us for Mac and his daughter were members of the Freewill Baptist Church. In a little while others were induced to dance and from this others took it up until nearly every one present—men, women, boys and girls—joined in a general dance. I forgot I had a wife who I ought to have known was waiting for me at home. It was the most awfullest dance I ever attended. Part of us got dog drunk and the remainder of the men and boys were not far behind this. I wore a heavy pair of boots that I had bought of Henry Bratton[49] and I danced in them so long that night they give me the string halt.[50]

"On the following morning I come to my senses and, oh, how mean I felt for not returning back home as I had promised my wife. Some of the men proposed to take Mr. Holmes and his daughter down to the creek and rebaptize them for we blamed them with it. They were members of the church and they ought to have set us a better example than to be leaders in a dance. We all said that they had not been baptized deep enough in the water. But we did not take them.

"Soon after breakfast I started back home and limped all the way. My poor wife who had suffered uneasiness about me all night met me before I reached home. I acknowledged to her that I had treated her wrongfully and if she would forgive me I would not treat her so bad any more. She said she would forgive me if I would be a better man and I told her I would. I was so bad used up by the boots at the dance that I was not able to walk any more for two weeks. I repented of my folly and told my wife it was my last dance and this time I stayed with my word and never went to another one." 🍃

BRIEF ITEMS AS GIVEN BY AN EARLY RESIDENT ON FINLEY CREEK [21:44]

ON THE 30TH of August, 1906, I interviewed a man of the name of John H. Shipman at Springfield, Mo., who said that he was born three miles east of Ozark in Christian County, Mo., August 18, 1843. Mr. Shipman said that his father Nathaniel Shipman settled on Finley Creek in 1820.

"My father informed me", said Mr. Shipman, "that there were only three settlers on Finley Creek when he came there and their names were Bill Garrison, Bill Gardener, and his grandfather on his mother's side John Hoover.[51]

"My father," continued Mr. Shipman, "settled on a tract of land three miles east of where the town of Ozark now stands. I have lived on and own this same farm where my father first settled to the present time which is the same land I was born on. My father lived to be eighty five years old before he passed from this life and lies buried at Linden in Christian County. My mother was eighty four years old before death called her away and is buried in the cemetery at Sparta.

"Billy Friend[52] is said to be the first settler on the land where the village of Linden now is. There was an Indian village or camping place at Linden before the Indians moved from southern Missouri. There were numbers of tommyhawks, war clubs, arrow heads and other Indian relicts plowed up there by the early settlers after the land was put into cultivation.

"A village of the Delaware Indians stood in the forks of Finley and James where it is said that the Indians constructed huts out of bark which with their bark floors and bark bunks with other vegetable accumulations was a menace to the few white settlers in that locality who rose up in anger and kicked against the nuisance and demanded a stop be put to it. The white people claimed that the decomposing vegetable matter produced chills, malarial fevers and other kinds of sickness."[53]

Going on with his early reminiscences Mr. Shipman said, "There is a place on Finley Creek known to the early settlers as the rock house where John Young, a blacksmith, and Bill Stacy, father of Doctor Silas S. Stacy, and others were the first settlers in that immediate vicinity. The Cherokee Indians while moving to the territory used to camp under this shelving rock and chant their weird songs which put a move on the bats and screech owls and stirred them from their places of abode. It is said that several wagons could take shelter under this projecting cliff.

"My first recollection of Springfield is that there were only five business houses there. Among the merchants of that day who sold goods in Springfield were Gen. Holland[54] and Bill McElhaney.[55] A man of the name of McCracken[56] kept the post office then. The buildings were chiefly made of round logs.

"Mr. Calvin Johnson taught the first school in our neighborhood and was the first school I ever attended. The school house consisted of round logs seventeen by twenty feet with an open fire place ten feet wide. I was only a little shirt tail lad of a boy then but I distinctly recollect the rough log seats we had to sit on to learn our ABCs in the old blue back speller. This same house is standing to the present day and is now weather boarded on the outside and sealed on the inside. Every time I pass this building I think of my early school days there," said Mr. Shipman.

IV
Man and Wildlife

❦ TALES OF BUFFALO ❦

Editors' note: The largest wild mammal species inhabiting the White River country in settlement days were the buffalo, *Bison bison,* the black bear, *Ursus americanus,* the elk, *Cervus elaphus,* and the deer, *Odocoileus virginianus.* The elk and deer are treated elsewhere.

The buffalo was the largest mammal occurring in the region and, according to Charles W. and Elizabeth R. Schwartz, "only vague accounts are available concerning its former numbers and distribution here, but from these it is concluded that in the period immediately preceding the settlement by whites it occurred sporadically and was never abundant."[1] Indians from ancient time trapped buffalo in pits, perhaps encouraging pioneers to trap wolf and panther, as recorded by Turnbo, in the same manner. By 1840 only remnants of the magnificent buffalo were found in the northwestern and southeastern sections of Missouri, and these soon disappeared.

Turnbo has only a few tales about buffalo, indicating they were not abundant. By settlement times, the Osages were making long buffalo hunting trips to the western plains each year, further indicating the scarcity of buffalo in the White River region.[2] Schoolcraft recorded twenty species of game, from quail to passing mentions of buffalo.

Stories of Buffalo and How a Hunter's Wife and Three Children Were Saved by a Buffalo Calf [14:53]

DURING THE EARLY SETTLEMENT of Upper White River hundreds of buffalo were discovered grazing on the tender grass. Many of the calves were captured and a large number of the old ones were shot.

When Paton Keesee settled on Little North Fork in 1823 he met several small herds on this stream where he captured and killed a few. This man Keesee used to relate an amusing account of how he attempted to capture a buffalo calf once and was foiled by the little animal.

Keesee had gone up North Fork one and one-half miles above his cabin to hunt for a bear when he noticed a buffalo calf butting a bank and otherwise playing. The little fellow seemed quite frisky and frolicsome as it pushed its head against the dirt. The calf was standing in the bed of a hollow near the mouth. The little animal appeared to be near three months old and was fat.

"I looked in every direction," said Mr. Keesee, "to see if its mother or other buffalo were in sight, but seeing none I made up my mind to capture the calf alive and make a pet of it. I had two trained dogs with me, but I was afraid they would cripple it if I allowed them to catch it. So laying my gun down and leaving the dogs to guard it I crept around and approached the top of the bank where the young buffalo was standing and leaped down and caught it before it was aware of my presence.[3]

"The beast's strength surprised me. I found in a moment that I was not able to control it. The calf kicked, bellowed and butted me against the bank. Little nubs of horns were just putting out on its head and it used its head with such force against my body and legs that I was compelled to release it at once and the contrary little beast ran off out of sight as fast as it could go. It was lucky for me that the mother of the calf was not in hearing distance or there might have been a worse row than was.

"Sometime after this," continued Mr. Keesee, "I met a young buffalo calf near my residence which was younger than the one I failed to capture and after a scramble with it I overpowered and carried it to the house and made a pet of it. It thrived and became very docile. I kept it ten years and it made a big fine buffalo. I then sold it to Jake Wolf who lived at the mouth of Big North Fork."

Mr. Keesee also said that it was common among the early residents that after killing a buffalo they would pluck off the wool and carry it home and knit socks out of it.

In the early days when Crooked Creek [Boone and Marion counties] with its numerous bubbling springs of living water afforded excellent grazing grounds for the herds of buffalo that fed in the broken prairie hollows, hunters from other parts of the now famous Ozark hills passed many happy days in chasing and killing buffalo on this famed water course. But as the emigrants pushed their way up this stream seeking desirable locations, the buffalo were forced to retreat westward until there were none left here to crop the fine grass and drink of the pure flowing water, and the daring hunters had to seek elsewhere for their buffalo meat.

Paton Keesee was one of the numbers that made several incursions here among these animals and captured a few calves and shot a number of the old ones, but we will have to confine ourselves to only one account of his raids on these animals on Crooked Creek, the story of which was given me by Elias and Peter Keesee, sons of uncle Paton.

They said that one fine afternoon their father left home on Little North Fork and remained all night with a hunter who lived in the river bottom near the mouth of Little North Fork.

"They had arranged to go to Crooked Creek to capture buffalo calves. On the following morning with their usual camp equipage and a lariat rope each they mounted their horses and struck out through the then wild region of hills. As they were not seeking the fat bear nor fine bucks they took no dogs with them. They might interfere with their sport of catching the young calves, for capturing calves was the only object of their trip.

"This was about 1826 and we will pass over what father said about seeing herds of deer, a few bear and other wild animals as they rode along that day. It was nearing sunset when they pitched their camp on the bank of Crooked Creek at the mouth of a prairie hollow. A few scattering trees fringed the bank of the creek where the hunters camped and a few saplings stood here and there. The water in the creek bottom was as clear as crystal. Their camping place was a picturesque spot.

"They allowed their wearied horses to graze on the tender grass until bedtime, when they brought them to camp and tied them securely to the trees. Then the hunters retired to rest on a bed composed of the skins of wild beasts.

"Early the following morning they were up and turned their horses loose to fill up on grass while they prepared their morning fare. Soon after the sun had risen above the hilltops, the men had mounted and were ready to hunt for the buffalo and chase them.

"It was a warm morning. The stones were 'sweating,' the air was humid with a fresh southeast wind. A few scud clouds[4] flew with the wind as the day advanced the wind increased in velocity. It was not a good day to be out hunting for buffalo, but the hunters went on.

"In a short while they discovered fresh buffalo signs where a small herd had been feeding. The men followed the trail and soon overhauled them. Among the bunch were four or five cows with calves following them. It was a grand sight to view this little herd of buffalo with their heads down in the grass feeding. Two of the calves were playing while the others were quiet. The men were more than a quarter of a mile from the herd.

"As they sat on their horses and watched the old ones graze they saw one of them raise his head and look toward them and there was a commotion among them and the herd started off on a brisk run. The one that raised his head was one of those ever-watchful bulls and he had given the herd the signal of danger and his companions had heeded him and they were soon gone. The hunters urged their horses into a gallop and sped on after them.

"It was a lively race and grew more exciting as the herd was pursued across prairie hollows and over wooded hills until the men got in advance of two of the calves which, being very young, had given out on the chase. The herd seemed to be too much frightened to turn back and protect them but went on helter-skelter until they passed from view over a hill. The men soon captured the calves without injuring them and tied the ropes around their necks.

"As soon as the exhausted calves had rested a short spell the men fastened the ropes to their saddles and began training the little fellows to lead, which they stubbornly refused at first by jumping around, pulling backward and bellowing. The hunters now expected the herd to rush back to rescue the calves and were prepared to retreat, but the old ones, not even the cows made their appearance and finally after some hard struggles the calves gradually gave up and followed the horses, but they would sull at times and give the men trouble before arriving at camp.

"It was in the afternoon when the two men reached their stopping place on the creek. The almost worn out captives, horses and riders were glad of a rest. They tied the calves fast to a sapling that stood twenty yards or more from camp and after turning their horses out to graze the buffalo hunters partook of a cold lunch and laid down on their couches to rest.

"By sunset the scud clouds had disappeared and a bank of leaden colored clouds had risen above the western horizon. The men knew a storm was brewing and with a few forks and poles they erected a frame and covered it with the skins of animals they had brought with them. They now had a rude shelter to protect them from the drenching rain.[5]

"As darkness settled down bright flashes of lightning lit up the beautiful valley at short intervals. Low rumbling thunder was heard as frequent as the lightning was seen to flash. Later on the elements showed greater anger and the men realized that it was not an ordinary thunder storm. As the dark roaring cloud approached nearer the lightning grew brighter. The crashes of thunder were deafening. It was a fearful night. Then the storm broke. The rain poured down for a few moments and slacked up followed by a wind of almost hurricane force. The shelter was swept away. The storm was terrible. The men and horses were in imminent danger of being killed or wounded by the flying limbs wrenched off of the scattering trees along the bank of the creek.

"Father's companion was a come and go religious fellow who when there was no danger in sight was a wicked man. 'But when he thought there was a chance to lose his life he was the humblest man I ever saw,' said father. 'He would change at a moment's notice and went according to the danger existing at the present.

"'When the tempest was raging, the wind blowing with great force and peal after peal of thunder was following the flashes of lightning in quick succession, and the shelter gone, this man thought his time was up and began to pray. It was a frightful hour and the man was very humble. He did not stand and pray like some do now to save their pride and clothes but he got right down on his knees in the water and wet grass. His prayer was loud and it was undoubtedly an earnest one. His form could be seen dimly in the dark and very plain when a flash of lightning occurred. His voice was heard above the sound of the raging storm.

"'As the roaring wind continued to blow it seemed that we would be swept from the face of the earth, but as I held to a small bush I was amused at my companion praying so fervently while he was holding to a bunch of grass in two or three feet of me.

"'I did not make sport of the man for praying but I well knew his humble devotion would last no longer than the storm would. He begged the Lord to save him from the thunder and wind and went on with his prayer until the storm abated and, perceiving no further danger, he quit praying and rose to his feet and became interested about the safety of the buffalo calves. He was afraid they were killed.

"'He now started to the sapling where they were tied and soon came in contact with the head end of one of the calves and the next thing my companion knew he was lying down in the wet grass. He quickly rose up and swore at the calf. The calf which had plenty of slack rope did not give the man much time to utter but a few wicked words before it went for him again by butting him down the second time.

"'This put the man in an awful rage and he cursed the calf as long and loud as he had been praying. The calf was all right and it had proved it to him. The other calf was all right too, but the fellow did not bother them any more till daylight.

"'Soon after the calf had taught the praying and swearing man a lesson, the air became calm. The storm cloud passed eastward and left a clear sky and the beautiful stars showed their little light, but the man with his wet clothes on had to stand up and make the best of it during the balance of the night.'

"Soon after sunrise they left for home but it was nearly two days before they reached White River with their calves. 'My companion kept one of the calves' [my father said] 'and I the other. I taken mine home.

"'My companion where he lived on the river had a small clearing in the bottom that was fenced and also owned two milk cows and he soon taught the little buffalo calf to share the milk with the other calves, but the former did not seem anxious to take up with the other calves in a friendly way, but appeared to like its human friends the best and stayed in the yard.

"'One day during the following fall after its capture while the man was gone from home on a hunt and had left his wife and three children alone, a bear paid the family a visit. He was some twenty yards from the cabin when the woman saw him coming. She was milking at the time but lost no time in getting into the house.

"'Closing the door shutter she raised a puncheon and put the children into the cellar [under the floor]. Then she got down where the children were and put the puncheon in its place and waited. The poor woman trembled with fear and excitement. The children cried out and the mother was not able to quiet them until she made them understand the peril they were in and they hushed up.

"'It seemed that the bear paid no attention to the cows, calves, but went on to the cabin and the woman heard it press the door open and come into the cabin.

"'The woman when she rushed into the house put the milk pail down on the floor as it contained milk. Bruin concluded he would test it by first smelling in the vessel. The flavor of the milk seemed to suit him and he lapped his tongue in the milk and did not cease drinking until the vessel was empty. Then the beast began to walk around on the floor inspecting everything in sight. Then he lowered his head and thrust his nose in the opening between the puncheon directly over the cellar. He had treed the woman and children and sniffed and smelled several seconds.

"'The poor woman gave up for lost. She believed herself and darling babes would soon be destroyed by the merciless bear. Ah, that her man would return and save her and her helpless children. The beast would soon uncover her retreat by raising the puncheon with its claws and kill them all. Ah, if she had protection, but none were in sight. Her husband would not be apt to be at home until night. By that time she would need no help, for the mangled forms of herself and precious children would be found in the cellar or in the cabin or in the yard. These thoughts were horrible. The despairing woman was about to scream out in terror, but smothered it down and listened.

"'The bear had raised its head. Something had called its attention and it turned around and passed out of the cabin and the woman heard the bear catch and kill the buffalo calf which by this time was larger and stouter. The bear made a meal of the poor calf near the door. After his bearship had finished his meal, he was slow about leaving the premises, but finally walked back into the cane and disappeared.

"'An hour or so after it was gone the woman ventured out into the yard and found that all that was left of the calf was its hide and bones. The young buffalo had saved herself and children by showing itself to the bear.'"

Huge Buffaloes [4:72]

IN ALLUDING TO the wild beast that inhabited Washington County, Ark. in the early period of its history, Mr. Joshua Baker, an old pioneer of that section, said that he had been frightened many times at the herds of buffalo that fed on the spurs of the mountains and along Illinoise Creek.

"I remember," said he, "of seeing sixty buffalo in one bunch that was lead by a male buffalo that was estimated to have weighed 1,800 pounds. It is a remarkable truth but I have seen small herds of them get frightened in Washington County and while they were stampeding they would grunt so loud that they could be heard two miles. It was something interesting to me to see two buffalo bulls meet and engage in a savage fight. It was a worse fight than when our domesticated cattle engage in a combat.

"The hunters in Washington County had plenty of buffalo meat to eat before they were all killed or driven out. Some of them were very fat.

"One day my uncle Caleb Baker got up near a herd of buffalo and picked out a very large one and shot it down. The others took to flight and was soon beyond his view. He now went up to where the dead one lay to examine it and found that it was so big and fat that he was not able to turn it over and he come to my father's house for assistance and he went back with him and they removed the hide and dressed the meat. My brother Calvin Baker hauled the meat home on a big sled at three loads.

"The animal was killed near our house on the Illinoise Creek one mile above where Prairie Grove is now." 🕮

Several Stories of Interest as Told by an Old Veteran Hunter [15:27]

ALMOST ALL the old timers of Boone County, Ark. knew Peter Baughman.[6] He was one among the famed hunters of Crooked Creek and was born in Iron County, Mo., October 11, 1830. He is a son of Henry and Charity (Sutton) Baughman.

Mr. Baughman says that his parents arrived at Yellville, Ark. from Iron County, Mo., on the 11th of October, 1840, when he was just ten years old.

"Yellville was quite a small village then and I remember that circuit court was in session on the day of our arrival court was held under a brush arbor and a big crowd was in attendance. The citizens had their rifles stacked around the arbor.

"My parents lived in Yellville awhile, then went on up Crooked Creek where they made a permanent location. Here in the fall of 1842 a big bunch of buffalo were discovered traveling up Crooked Creek.

"My father and John Sutton followed them and shot and killed two grown ones on Terrapin Creek, which empties into Long Creek below Carrolton. They followed the herd several miles west of here and killed two more, one of which was full grown and the other a calf. They would have pursued them further but they were afraid the Indians might interfere with them and both turned back." 🕮

Sugar Loaf Prairie [23:50]

ON THIS PRAIRIE is a grove of small pine trees which mark the spot known to the present day as the "Buffalo Lick." It is supposed by some that the way these pines got started to grow here was by the buffalo bringing the seed from the pineries in the wooly hair that covers their heads.[7] Here on this ground in the midst of the beautiful wild flowers which then adorned this fine landscape, the buffalo would graze on the wild grass, tender herbage and taste of the saline dirt.

I was told by Sam Carpenter who was born in the hills of northwest Arkansas before the buffalo had been killed or driven out of this section that he has seen herds of buffalo that once inhabited north Arkansas. This was when only a hunter's hut stood here and there along White River and its larger tributarys. Mr. Carpenter said that when he was quite a young man John Hart, a negro man and himself, while passing through the prairie one day met three buffalo—a bull or "Surley"[8] as he called him, a cow and a small heifer. Each man carried the old style flint lock rifle.

"The animals were wild [Mr. Carpenter said], but we wanted 'to take them in out of the weather' and by being very careful we gained the advantage of them and managed to kill them all."

Said he, "I shot the cow, Hart shot the heifer and the negro the bull. The three buffalos furnished us a fine supply of meat which we had been wishing for many days."

TALES OF BEAR

Editors' note: The black bear, *Ursus americanus,* was the largest carnivore in the White River region. It was reported to be a common resident of both Missouri and Arkansas and was the premier game animal of settlement days. Because bear could be dangerous, bear hunters were esteemed over other hunters. Bear were sought for their meat, which was sold in urban markets; their skins, which were used in making rugs, blankets, and hats; and their grease and oil, which were used for softening leather, greasing wagon axles, supplying lamps with fuel, cooking and seasoning of food, and even for human hair dressing. Eating bear meat was considered a way to restore a man's sexual powers.

The bear trade in Arkansas flourished on the lower White River at Arkansas Post during the late eighteenth century. It moved upriver to Oil Trough, Arkansas, in the early 1800s and continued into the uplands, where bear hunters congregated at the mouth of the Big North Fork River and at the Coker family settlements at the mouth of Bear Creek in modern Boone

County. At these sites, hunters rendered bear oil and stored it in troughs made of hollowed logs, before sending it to downriver ports and on down to New Orleans. One observer wrote, "I have seen boats loaded till the guard rail was under water; dressed deer and bear meat topped the local freight, and wild turkeys hung from the upper deck."[9] Turnbo's bear hunters were important for the supply of meat markets in the towns and cities of the lower Mississippi Valley.

Along with deer hides and wild honey, bear provided trade items needed by the pioneers. By 1850 bear in Missouri were becoming rare, with the last survivors in the southeast lowlands; they were much more common in Arkansas throughout the late nineteenth century.[10] The state of Arkansas has released black bear in the northern part of the state in recent years, and they are once again reported reliably in Missouri, south of the Missouri River, probably from the Arkansas releases.

Beginning in 1834 Americans were reading of the famous bear hunter, Davy Crockett. By the late 1830s C. F. M. Noland began publishing the exploits of White River country bear hunters and frontiersmen in the *Spirit of the Times* in New York, and his character, Pete Whetstone, became a voice of traditional Arkansas culture. Later, Thomas Bangs Thorpe published "The Big Bear of Arkansas," ensuring the image of Arkansas in southwestern humorist literature. Turnbo's characters formed a significant backdrop to the folklore and history of bear hunting in Arkansas, which led to the reputation and naming of the Bear State and the creation of the "Arkansas legend," according to folklorist Otto Rayburn. Missouri, continuing the bear image, uses the bear on the Missouri state seal.[11]

HOW A BOASTING FELLOW WAS VANQUISHED BY A LITTLE BEAR [7:35]

WE HAVE SAID in other sketches that Paton Keesee come to Upper White River in 1816, and wishing to explore this stream further up toward its source, he and three others in the early fall of 1816, prepared a dugout canoe from a bur oak tree,[12] and put it into the river and loaded in provision, cooking vessels and hides of wild animals for bedding, and started up the river in this craft to examine the river bottom lands and scenery. Their starting point was five or six miles below where old Tolbert's ferry[13] was established, ten miles east of [where] Yellville, Ark., [was] fifteen years or more later.

Their voyage up the river was interesting. At that date as far as known, only four families of white people were living on White River above the starting point, and these were William Trimble, Buck Coker, Joe Coker and Girard Leiper Brown.[14]

The water in the river had swollen a foot or more above the ordinary stage of summertime and the men did not experience a great deal of trouble in getting the clumsy canoe over the shoals. The river bottoms and the face of the bluff were covered with tall cane. Flocks of wild turkey were seen frequently, and deer and other game was noticed along each shore. Hundreds of beautiful colored song birds were seen and heard in the timber bordering the shores. The dense growth of timber, cane and grapevines tangled together, and added to this the high craggy bluffs, made the scenery all along as far as they went up, seem like a great jungle of other climes. Though the scenery was wild yet it was beautiful, grand and enchanting and the journey up the stream was enjoyable and entertaining to the little band of explorers.

They did not push their craft up the river in a rush but went along slow and made frequent stops to examine the soil in the bottoms, the water in the mouth of the tributary streams, and the high overhanging cliff along the bluffs. They pushed their canoe as far up the river as the Elbow Shoals, where they stopped a few days and rested and hunted in the wild picturesque hills of Elbow Creek, and then they started back downstream and arrived at their starting point on the second day after leaving the mouth of Elbow.

The foregoing account was related to me by Elias Keesee, son of Paton Keesee, which he said that his father told him this repeatedly.

Continuing the account Mr. Keesee went on to say that one of the men that made this trip in the canoe with them was a big stout muscular man, who boasted of his great strength and valor. He said that he wanted to fight a bear single handed and without any weapons except his bare hands. He declared on the day that they started up the river that he intended to fight a bear the first opportunity offered. He claimed that he was able to whip a full grown bear.

"My father said that he had no idea that the man's intention was to put his threat into execution," [said Elias Keesee] "for it was not reasonable that a man was able to defeat a bear in a fair fight and it was certain that Bruin could whip a man in a few moments. They looked on the man as a boaster and that his words were idle and harmless fiction.

"'On the morning of the second day after we started up the river,' said my father, 'we hove in sight of the mouth of Little North Fork, and shortly before we reached the mouth of the creek or just below what is now called the Gar Shoals, we spied a small bear lying on the end of a log which extended from the bank straight out into the river. The log was near thirty feet in length and the underside of it was under the water.

"'This bear was what hunters call a fall bear, or a runt, was brown in color and a year old. Bruin was basking in the sun and was resting quiet.

"'We told our companion in a jocular way that now was the time to show his bravery for yonder was a bear waiting for the attack. The man replied that he did not desire to belittle himself by jumping on such a puny looking creature as that bear looked to be. "I want to fight a bear," said he, "that is more of an equal match for me. But," continued the man, "rather than miss a fight, I will slap it a few times to see it cut up to get out of my way."

"'We had no thought the man intended to attack the bear, but to see him back out as we supposed, we landed the canoe one-hundred-fifty yards below the log the bear was on, and believing that we would bluff him, we all went ashore. The little bear did not appear to notice us. Apparently it was asleep.

"'We now passed up the bank and made a circuit through the dense cane and approached that part of the shore where the log was. The bear did not move but from the manner it was breathing it was in a deep slumber.

"'To our surprise the man still showed his inclination to fight the bear. We told him that it was dangerous to do so for the beast might kill or cripple him, but he insisted so strong to be allowed to attack Bruin, and finally seeing that the man was in earnest, we give up persuading him and agreed to let him tackle it and told him to go.

"'As the fellow started into the water to wade out to the end of the log where the bear lay he said, "Now men don't show any foul play in my favor but you can help the bear if you feel like it."

"'As he waded along at the side of the log the water increased in depth but the deepest place was not over two and one-half feet. The noise and bluster the man made as he went along through the water roused little

Bruin from his nap and slowly raised up on his feet and turned around with his head toward his foe, and after eying him an instant, he started and walked along on the log to escape into the forest.

"'The man now halted and just as the bear was passing him, the man by a skillfull movement, jerked the bear from the log into the water and dealt it a blow with his clenched hand and the battle began. The man being robust and very stout and Bruin being so small in size and thin in flesh, it seemed that the man might overpower it.

"'While the fight progressed the combatants worked nearer to the shore where the water was eighteen inches deep. Here the belligerents settled down to desperate fighting. The water splashed and foamed. The young boaster struck the bear with his hands and kicked it with all his strength. Little Bruin returned the compliments by biting and striking the man with his paws. It was a busy contest as much as it was interesting and amusing. We cheered both man and beast.

"'As the battle went on we noticed that little Bruin was getting the better of the man but we continued to cheer both of them. Sometimes we would hurrah for the bear alone and then for the man, and at times we would halloo for man and beast together. In a few minutes more we saw plainly that the man was badly worsted. But knowing we could interfere before the man was severely injured and that he requested us not to show foul play for the bear, we let them continue the combat and went on with our cheering.

"'The bear, instead of giving out, seemed to gather more strength and hit the man vigorous blows with its paws. Not so with his human antagonist for he was loosing strength rapidly and we perceived that our friend the blower's resistance was growing weaker, when suddenly the bear caught the exhausted man in his embrace and would have soon hugged him to death but we quickly interfered and killed the bear and led the now thoroughly beaten boaster out of the water and he sit down on the shore for a breathing spell.

"'Though he was not seriously hurt yet he was the worst whipped man I ever saw and we enjoyed many hearty laughs at his expense. This incident put a quietus on his boasting as to his prowess as a bear fighter.

"'We saw more bear as we went on up the river and back again, and when we would catch sight of one we would tantalize him by saying, "There is another bear. Don't you want to fight it." And his invariable reply was, "No, I don't volunteer to fight any more bear.""'

A Hungry Bear Eats His Last Mess of Pork [5:6]

JUST OVER THE Missouri state line in the north part of Marion County, Ark., is the old Wilshire Magness place. This land lies on Big Creek at the mouth of Little Cedar Hollow. It is known now as the Steve Copelin farm. Just below the mouth of Little Cedar at the foot of the bluff is another spring of water which was well known to the old time settlers.

Many years before Wilshire Magness and his wife lived at the first named spring, it was the scene of an interesting encounter between a lot of dogs and a bear, the story of which was told by Mrs. Patsey Magness, widow of Joe Magness, who died in the old Magness bottom in the latter Forties. Two years before the death of Mrs. Magness I heard her relate the account of the bear and I give it in her own words as near as I can remember it.

"When I and Joe Magness, my husband, settled in this bottom, Joe cleared and fenced enough ground in three years to raise plenty to live on. The soil was so fertile that it produced big ears of corn and monster pumpkins. We located here in 1827, and by the time 1830 rolled around, Joe and the boys had a nice start of hogs, but it required close attention to prevent their destruction by wild beast.

"In the fall of 1830, Joe enclosed three acres of ground adjoining the yard fence with heavy poles and rails and put three of our best hogs in there to make bacon of them. The fence was so stout and high that my husband scouted[15] the idea of a bear climbing over the fence and attacking the porkers. They were fed on corn and pumpkins until they were exceedingly fat and were ready to be butchered.

"One morning early, Wilshire, who was a little fellow then, went out to feed them and found that one of the hogs was missing. The child hurried back to the house and told us about it and Joe went to the lot and found that a bear had entered the enclosure and killed the hog and had carried it to the fence and, after pushing off some of the top rails, threw the hog over the fence and climbed over and picked up the hog again and passed on through the cane and up the face of the bluff on the east side of the hollow opposite the house. I do not know how it happened that we never heard the bear kill the hog nor the dogs never found it out.

"After Joe followed the trail of the bear a short distance up the bluff he returned to the house and [after he] had ate breakfast, he sent one of the boys down to Alex Duggins[16] at the mouth of Big Creek, with a request for Duggins to come and bring his gun and bear dogs. As soon as Mr. Duggins arrived he and Joe rode across the bottom and, with their combined force of dogs, reached the foot of the bluff where they dismounted and lead their horses up the bluff where the bear had carried the fat porker. Some distance up on the bluff they found where the bear had stopped long enough to devour part of the dead hog and concealed the remainder with leaves and trash.

"The hunters did not tarry long here, but hurried on to overtake thieving Bruin. The trail lead straight toward Big Creek. Before arriving at the creek, they found where the animal had lay down to rest and had got up and went on. On following his trail three hundred yards further they overhauled him while he was lying down asleep. The dogs soon woke him up and Bruin prepared himself for battle, and while the fight was going on one of the men shot and wounded him, and the result was a running fight from there to the creek and across to the spring on Little Cedar Creek, one-quarter mile east of Big Creek. Here at this water, Bruin took his last stand and fought his last battle.

"My husband said that when the dogs closed around Bruin he knocked them right and left with his big paws. The fight did not continue long before some of the dogs were disabled. One of which was almost killed. As soon as the two men had approached near enough, they shot the bear down. By the time they had removed the hide from the bear and cared for the meat, the men thought the dog was dying and would not live more than three hours at least. They cut the bear's meat into chunks and loaded it onto their horses and started back home, leaving the dog lying at the spring nearly lifeless.

"Now comes in a mystery to me," said Mrs. Magness, "for just one week from that day we were all astonished and puzzled to the fullest measure to see that same dog return home. But he was so desperately hurt that he never did get entirely over it."

A Bear Finds Five Bee Trees [5:47]

JOHN FORD, who settled on the north bank of White River in what is now North Fork township in Marion County, Ark., in 1818, was a famed hunter. His principal hunting grounds were in the hills between the river and Little North Fork. Mr. Elijah Ford, son of John Ford, related to the writer some accounts of his father's experience with the wild beast that then infested the wild forest. Among other things he told of a bear that was a skillful bee hunter.

Mr. Ford said that one day in the early part of December, 1830, while a deep snow lay on the ground, his father went out into the woods to hunt for a bear and kill it.

"I was too young at that time to remember the incident but I learned the story from my father after I was old enough to understand and remember anything told me. My father said that he owned two well trained dogs and, with his rifle and accompanied by the two dogs, he left home and waded through the snow in search of Bruin.

"During that period of the settlement of the country bear were so plentiful that it took only a short time to strike a trail of one, especially in a snow, and as usual while hunting for bear in the snow, he soon struck a trail of one that had passed along the day previous. The weather after the snow had fell turned warm enough for the snow to settle down and melt a little.

"After following the trail of the bear a short distance he found where the beast had discovered a bee tree and had climbed up to dine on wild honey, but after Bruin had knawed off the bark he found that the wood was solid and he could make but small headway in getting at the honey and gave up in disgust and descended the tree and went on. After traveling a mile further his bearship had discovered another bee tree but he was not any more successful in reaching the abode of the bees than before and quit his labor and went down the tree and traveled on.

"It was not long before he found a third bee tree and up he went, to try for the honey, but his luck was as bad as ever and he went on again. By this time his trail was fresh, for the animal had delayed a great deal of time at the three bee trees. A mile or more further and his bearship found the fourth tree, but like the other trees, he failed entirely to knaw into the storeroom of honey.

"The trail from this tree indicated that his bearship was only a short distance in advance and my father said that [he] kept his dogs nearby him and used a vigilant eye on the lookout for the bear and overhauled him very soon after leaving the fourth tree, where he was at work on the fifth tree. This time his success was better but he did not have time to feast on honey.

"He had just reached the honey when my father and the dogs interrupted him and he was not a bit pleased at being disturbed so abruptly. He did not have time to remain angry very long before my father shot him and he fell at the foot of the tree. I suppose his death was sweet to him for he died with a mouth full of honey.

"After removing the hide and hanging the meat up on a limb, my father said he returned back home over the same trail and marked each tree the bear had found, so that he could locate them after the snow disappeared. On arriving home he mounted a horse and went back and took the bear hide and meat home.

"The bear in traveling through the snow had noticed small bits of honeycomb, bee bread,[17] and dead bees lying on the snow under the trees, which the bees had thrown out during the warmer hours of day. The bear had learned these signs of a bee tree from natural instinct and this explains why Mr. Bruin was such an expert bee hunter."

A Terrific Combat between a Boar and Bear [7:50]

JAMES KNIGHT furnishes the following sketch through a letter written by him at Bruno, Marion County, Ark.

"My father, Jonathan Knight, was a Virginian and emigrated to Tennessee where he lived eight years and then went to Greene County, Mo., where he lived four years. In 1837 he left Missouri and settled on Buffalo Fork of White River, where he lived until his death. There were only a few settlers on this stream when he come here. My father said that on his arrival here in 1837, the mountainsides as well as the creek bottoms were covered with cane.[18]

"When emigrants began settling along Buffalo [River] they usually cleared a small piece of land to plant in corn. But bear was so plentiful that it was hard work to prevent them from destroying the crop. The men would go out of nights to their field and whoop and yell and discharge their rifles to frighten the bear out of the fields.

"Father killed a goodly number of bear on Buffalo. Him and Sam Parks and Oliver Taffer hunted together and kept a pack of well trained dogs. A fearless educated dog was worth more than a horse then."

In relating an encounter between the boar and bear on Buffalo [River] Mr. Knight said that he witnessed it from a tree.

"It occurred when I was just large enough to carry a rifle. One late afternoon I took the rifle and went up to the field to kill some squirrels. About the time I reached the fence I heard hogs rallying on a hillside above me. At first I thought they were wild hogs and were preparing to attack me, and throwing my gun down I went up a tree as fast as a coon could climb.

"Getting up high enough in the tree where I could obtain a plain view, I saw at once that the hogs were tame ones and I knew their owner. The hogs were all bunched close together and I saw a big bear walking around them.

"All at once the bear rushed at the hogs and struck some of them with his paw, which made them all scatter except a four years old boar, which stood his ground and squared himself for battle, which was followed by one of the most fiercest struggles between animals I ever heard of. They closed together like two savage dogs and fought terrible. As I witnessed the fight from the tree my blood almost chilled while watching them.

"As the two infuriated animals fought they gradually worked down the hillside to a white oak tree that was swelled near the ground. Here they separated for the time and each beast appeared to want to shelter himself behind this tree, and for a half hour or more they kept up a duel game by springing at each other from behind the tree, but each would dodge in turn and resume their respective positions.

"As they would catch at each other with their teeth they would wrench pieces of bark off of the white oak. At the expiration of the time stated above the bear seemed to grow tired of this sort of maneuvers and changed tactics and left the tree and walked around the hog with the intention of seeking the advantage of his antagonist. As he passed around, the boar turned and stood on the defensive.

"At this the bear halted and rose on his haunches seemingly intending to grasp the hog in his embrace. But just as Bruin rose, the boar made a furious rush for his adversary and knashed him with his tusks just under the foreleg. It was now his bearship's turn, and before the boar could do him further harm, he instantly dropped down on the hog and caught it at the back of the neck with its teeth. Then ensued another fierce struggle.

"The bear lay on the boar's back. The latter made violent efforts to hurl the bear off, but his frantic attempts were in vain. The bear had the advantage and he appeared to be determined to retain his hold. Both animals were badly wounded and their strength was much weaker now than it was when the fight began, but both were still game and ferocious.

"The struggle went on, but the advantage was all on the side of the bear now for he held the boar in such a shape that he was powerless to use his tusk again on Bruin. The furious bear held him as if in a vice. The boar struggled, but that was all he was able to do. At last his efforts to extricate himself from the power of the bear seemed fruitless and he gave up and began to squeal. He evidently had hallooed enough and sank down.

"I thought the bear had killed him, but after holding him a short time longer Bruin let go his hold and backed off a few yards. As soon as Bruin had left him, he began showing signs of life and scrambled to his feet with great difficulty and staggered off. The bear stood and looked at him a moment, apparently saying, 'Now, don't go off and say you whipped me, for you know I got the best of you.' Then he turned around and walked away in an opposite direction.

"It was now after sunset and I slid down the tree and picked up the gun and went back to the house. Next morning we found the boar lying dead near the scene of the fight, and with dogs we followed the bloody trail of the bear and soon overhauled him and finished his life."

A Lively Fight with a Bear [5:80]

A WORTHY AND MUCH ESTEEMED citizen who died on Crooked Creek in Marion County, Ark., several years ago was John H. Tabor [who] also was among the earliest settlers on the upper White River. In referring to the game that existed in the White River hills when he came there in 1826 and for many years thereafter, Mr. Tabor said that it was astonishing to think about it. One could hardly pass through the forest without being in sight of deer and turkeys.

"I have seen as many as twenty bucks in one bunch and from one-hundred-fifty to two hundred wild turkeys in one flock. Bee trees were so plentiful that almost every hollow tree was occupied by a swarm of bees," said he. Mr. Tabor has killed many fat bear. An account of his experience with these animals, if put into book form, would fill many pages. One of his most amusing stories of encountering Bruin was told by him to the writer in this manner.

"When I bought my claim here on Crooked Creek two miles below Powell in Marion County in 1836, I made a small clearing in the creek bottom and planted it in corn in the spring of 1837. The land was fertile and produced a fine crop of corn but as soon as it was in roasting ear, bear, deer, squirrels and everything else seemed to concentrate in my little field of corn. I guarded it all I could but the wild animals devoured nearly all the crop in spite of me. Bear invaded it day and night and so did the other animals.

"One afternoon I took my rifle and a favorite dog I called Blue, and started to the creek bottom as usual to drive out the wild beast. When I had got down at the foot of the bluff near the field fence, a large hawk flew and lit on the limb of a tree near where I was passing. I stopped and shot at the hawk but missed it. Squirrels were so numerous that I seen several of them running out of the field, and seeing no larger game, I thought I would kill enough squirrels for supper and reloaded my gun with squirrel shot.[19] But just before I had finished reloading it, the dog darted off up the side of the bluff and run beyond my view.

"Very soon after he was gone I heard him barking in a vigorous way, and before I could have counted ten, I seen the dog coming back in a fast run with a big bear in pursuit of him. The dog made no halt until he got to where I stood. The bear got in ten paces of me before it discovered me. Then it stopped.

"By this time I was ready to shoot again and, while Bruin was standing and gazing at me, I fired the load of squirrel shot into its body and down it tumbled and come rolling down the face of the bluff toward me. A short sycamore log lay a few feet below where the bear fell and the animal rolled against it and its weight started the log, and here come bear and log together, down to the foot of the bluff, where the log lodged against a sapling and stopped and the bear stopped against the log.

"I supposed the bear was dead and was puzzled to know where the squirrel shot had hit the bear to kill him so easily, but I was counting chickens before hatching time, for all at once Bruin got up, which surprised me no little, and the dog was equally as astonished as I was but he delayed no time before he sprang forward and made a vigorous attack on his bearship.

"But Bruin was so large and stout that he soon caught the dog by the throat with its teeth and held him like a vice. I had no time to reload my gun but I was determined to save the dog's life if I could, and so I dropped the gun on the ground, and snatching my hunting knife from the scabbard, I uttered a loud yell and rushing up to the bear I sank the blade of the knife into the bear's body.

"At this moment my other two dogs, which I had left at the house a few minutes before, hearing the racket come bounding down the bluff and attacked the bear, which compelled the beast to release the dog to defend himself. He only stood his ground for a moment for the reinforcement of dogs gave him a scare, and he seemed to think it best to retreat and away he went followed by the two dogs. The other dog was not able to go.

"I now reloaded my rifle with a bullet and went on after them. The bear run two hundred yards before it come to a halt, and when I come up the dogs were baying it and I shot it again, and down it fell once more and up it got again and fought the dogs as lively as ever.

"I reloaded my rifle and shot it the third time and killed it for good. My dog was so severely hurt by the bear that it was many days before he fully recovered. This was his last bear fight for I never could persuade him to tackle another bear. He had enough of Bruin and he had sense enough to know it."

How a Hunter Got His Back Scratched by a Bear [4:87]

"Though I never delighted in hunting for deer or other game, settlers all round me killed fine bucks and big bears," said Mr. George Trammel, an old pioneer of Crooked Creek in Boone County, Ark.

"Away back in 1842, when I was seven years old, Bill Freeman and a man of the name of Ross, who were accompanied by two other men, with several dogs, went out into the hills south of Crooked Creek to kill game and in a few hours the dogs discovered a fresh trail of a bear and followed after it in a lively manner until they overhauled him, and a sharp chase ensued when the bear took refuge in a cave.

"When the hunters come up to the mouth of the cave they agreed that one of them ought to go in and reach [search] for his bearship and, after a torch was made, one of the men took the light in one hand and a gun in the other and went into the cave, but made his exit in a few minutes and reported that he was not able to find bruin. Then one of the other men signified their intention of making a search for the animal and went in and come out without any better success. And the third man did not succeed any better.

"It was now Ross' turn to go in and he told the other men that he intended to locate the bear before he come back and, with the light in his left hand and his rifle in the other, he passed in and the light from his torch was soon lost to view.

"After the man was gone awhile they heard his hallooing in distress. The men on the outside believed that bruin had attacked their friend and was killing him. One of the men wanted to go to his assistance, but his companions objected. Their excuse was that there was nothing to prepare another torch, and it would be foolish to go in the cave without one. They said it was best to not send the dogs in for it would make matters worse for the man and in their fear and excitement they decided that it was best not [to] attempt to interfere in the dark.

"They did not know what was best to do unless it was to stay out and, while they were engaged in suggesting plans and discussing them pretty lively, bruin come out among them unexpected. He was in the midst of the men and dogs before they could think twice. The men jumped out of bruin's way and gave him all the room necessary but the dogs were fearless and showed fight.

"The three men, after running a few yards and seeing that the dogs had brought the bear to bay, they stopped and went back and fired three balls into the bear's body and the big black animal yielded up his life and sank down among the dogs.

"Just after the bear was dead, Mr. Ross made his appearance out of the cave with his clothes all torn and covered with dirt and his back gave evidence of bad treatment. The man was in a condition of excitement and his actions resembled a horse that was shieing at some object. After his nerves got in better shape for talking he said that he had a close call from bruin.

"After he had passed into the mouth of the cavern he examined every ledge and offshoot as he went along until the cave narrowed down, and after he had proceeded a few yards further he saw the bear by the light of the torch. The beast was lying down but when the light flashed on him he raised up and made a rush at him.

"'I had no time to shoot or turn round before it struck against me and knocked me down,' said Ross, 'and as it passed over me, it pressed me so hard against the floor of the cave that the beast nearly squeezed me to death and this accounts for the deep lines of gashes it made on my back with its rough claws as it went over me. It was then that I stood in need of help. However, I might have called for assistance until doomsday without you men offering to extend a helping hand to me.

"'When the bear struck me the torch was knocked from my hand and extinguished, and when it passed over me and went on I followed it out.'

"After Mr. Ross had got in a better humor they all removed the hide of the bear and dress[ed] the meat and cut it into chunks and put it into sacks and loaded it onto their ponies and carried it home that evening. This was on Saturday and on the following Sunday religious services were held in the neighborhood. Rosses wounds, though very sore from his contact with the bear, did not prevent him from attending meeting, which he seemed to enjoy much better than an encounter with an angry bear in a cave or elsewhere, and after services were dismissed, Mr. Ross told all his friends how bruin tickled his back with his claws."[20]

How Settlers on Horseback Chased the Bear [6:45]

THE FOLLOWING IS an account of two settlers on horseback, worrying a bear until it was completely exhausted. The story is related by Frank Woods, who was born on Crooked Creek below Yellville, in March, 1838.

Said Mr. Woods, "I will tell you the bear story, the occurrence of which dates back several years before I was born. My authors of the story were my father and grandfather.

"A good number of Indians were living in their village called Shawnee Town, where Yellville now stands. Grandfather was residing on the creek below the village.

"One day Grandfather and father rode into the hills south of the creek. Father was a young man then. They were not accompanied by a dog, though Grandfather carried his rifle. Father was mounted on a splendid mare. Two or three miles southwest of the village they spied a bear that was so fat that it was not able to travel fast. They said it was the clumsiest bear they ever saw. Here was an opportunity for fun, and they charged up near to compel it to run faster. There was no brush in the way to prevent close pursuit.[21]

"In those days there were many huckleberry patches,[22] and bears grew fat on the fruit. When the horsemen pushed the animal too close he would stop, turn round and charge at them. But he was so fat that his actions were slow, and the men could get out of his way before he could do them harm. They followed the fat beast some distance and laughed at its awkwardness in traveling.

"They kept on just behind it until it was so tired that it was hardly able to get out of a walk. Finally it entered a thick grove of timber, where they had some trouble in driving it out into the open again, and went into a prairie hollow. By this time his bearship was so exhausted that he could hardly walk. Thinking the animal was not able to afford them anymore sport, father dismounted and took grandfather's rifle to shoot it, but his mare was not willing to relinquish such amusements, and the moment he dropped the bridle reins she rushed up to Bruin and bit him hard.

"Though the bear was almost given out, he had a little strength and energy left, and managed to resent the insult by wheeling around and catching the mare by the hamstring with its teeth, after she had turned around to get out of its way.

"The astonished mare kicked the bear viciously, plunged forward and released herself. At this moment father took quick aim at the bear and shot it down.

"The mare's leg was so severely lacerated by the bear's teeth that she never recovered sufficiently to be of any more benefit. They had enjoyed the fun of chasing and killing a nice, plump bear, but it was small recompense for the maiming of the fine mare. Father had paid well for the chase and amusement."

A Mad Bear Runs over Two Hunters; Leaping Astride of a Bear's Back [6:99]

WE ARE REMINDED of another story as told me by Frank Woods who said that, "Away back in the early history of Marion County, hunters met with many perils with bear on the chase and in caves, but for all this," said Mr. Woods, "the old timers enjoyed much fun together. Camp hunting was a common practice among the famed hunters as well as among those of less prominence.

"It was nothing unusual for a lot of fellows to go into the hills or to some stream of water, with dogs and guns and camp equipage, and be absent a week or more, and as a rule when they returned home their pack horses were loaded with wild meat and hides.

"Ever now and then quite a lively stir would happen on a camp hunt, which the participants would never tire of telling. I recollect hearing my father tell repeatedly of being on a camp hunt with John Churchman and others on Music Creek once. Churchman was a son of old Jake Churchman and was known to court danger on the chase when it was not necessary. 'We were gone several days,' said father, 'and loaded our horses to "the gourds" with a fresh supply of bear meat.

"'While we were camping on this rough stream we shot and wounded a bear that the dogs soon chased into a sink hole or deep swag with steep banks. There were enough room in the bottom of the hole to give the dogs a little play while they were fighting the beast. When we reached the swag and looked into it the dogs were baying the bear.

"'Churchman wanted to shoot Bruin first, and passed down the steep bank which surrounded the sink hole and halted just over the bear's back, and rested against a small sapling and pushed the muzzle of his rifle down toward the bear to shoot it in the back. In doing so the man reached too far and over balanced his weight and was precipitated onto the enraged animal's back.

"'The man was stout and active and as he started to fall he let go his gun, and with a dextrous movement he alighted astride of Bruin and caught the beast's left ear with his left hand.

"'The sudden onslaught and the weight of Churchman's body made his bearship stagger for a few seconds. But after recovering from the shock he made a desperate resistance against being broke to ride and leaped, plunged and reared to rid himself of his human burden. Then he wriggled and twisted his body into different shapes and did his utmost to bite the hunter. But Churchman held on the tighter, for he knew if Bruin succeeded in throwing him off his back, the enraged brute would either kill or maim him for life.

"'The dogs were thick in the offray, but Bruin heeded them not for he was giving all his attention now to the man. No doubt this was the liveliest hunting scene that ever happened on this noted stream.

"'We horrified spectators stood dumbfounded while this was going on. We had lost our presence of mind, for when we saw the man fall we expected every moment to see him mangled by the infuriated beast. But recovering from our fright, we started to rush down to save the life of our friend. But before we could render him assistance, Churchman jerked his long keen bladed hunting knife from the scabbard with his right hand and buried the blade into the body of the bear and it sank down in the agony of death and Churchman left the struggling beast and without taking time to pick up his gun got out of that swag in a hurry.

"'When the excitement had quieted down and while we were taking the dead bear out of the sink, Churchman remarked, "Boys, I had much rather be mounted on the worst bucking mule I ever saw, than undertake to break another bear to ride."'"

Encountering a Lot of Bear in a Cave [6:9]

IN AN INTERVIEW with Taylor Frazier, an old time resident of Marion County, Ark., one day in the month of September, 1896, he told me this account.

"I was born in St. Clair County, Alabama, October 17, 1840. I am a son of James Frazier and my father died at the old homestead in Alabama. After the death of my father, my mother brought me to Arkansas in 1845, when I was less than five years old, and settled on Crooked Creek in Marion County. My mother entered the dark valley of death in the pioneer days and received interment in the old burial ground at the mouth of George's Creek."

When the writer interviewed Mr. Frazier, he was living in Pangle Hollow, which enters Crooked Creek a short distance above the mouth of George's Creek.

In relating a bear story Mr. Frazier said, "There were plenty of bear in Marion County when we come here in 1845, but I was too young to hunt then. On one occasion when I was nearly grown, I and Berry Wood, a brother-in-law of mine, and Ozz D. Dearman, one of my half-brothers, and a Mr. Paxton, went to Music Creek on a bear hunt. We took pack horses and a camping outfit with us. About two inches of snow lay on the ground and when we reached the head of Music Creek, we struck the trail of a bear in a rough hollow and followed it down the creek some distance where it had gone into a cave.

"Here we met Sam Howard, who was on a bear hunt also, and he stayed with us. We carried plenty of fuel with us for a torch and after igniting some of it, I took the torch and we all went into the cave together.

"After we had went into the cavern several yards the bear, as we supposed, heard us coming and started out. As soon as the animal approached us near enough for us to see the outlines of his form by the light of the torch, Howard shot at it but the man was excited and we supposed he missed the mark.

"At the report of the gun the bear rushed at us. We were all grouped together and as the animal was coming toward us, I says to Dearman, 'Shoot it,' and as the beast was climbing up a low ledge of rock just in front of us, he fired his gun at it intending to shoot it in the forehead but the ball took effect in the bear's nose and Bruin snorted and the blood spurted from his nostrils. Bruin increased his movements more lively and was among us in an instant, almost.

"This part of the cave was narrow and the wounded bear and we five men had a fast stir among us. We pressed our backs against the wall of the cave to allow his bearship all the room possible to pass us, which it did. As the bear went on toward the mouth of the cave, we heard it blowing the blood from its nose. Just on the inside of the entrance into the cavern was a sink hole four feet deep, and when his bearship reached it he fell into it and he proved to be so weak from the effects of the shot that he was not able to crawl out. And we found him in this hole when we followed him up.

"Just before we reached the sink, I got in behind the other men and let those carrying the guns go in advance. I supposed by falling in the rear I would not stand in danger of being hurt by the bear but I found, to my surprise, that there was danger behind me as well as in front, for it was now that I heard the footsteps of an animal at my heels and I wheeled about to ascertain what it was and discovered a small bear almost under my feet.

"Though I was struck with terror but I had strength enough left to raise my foot and kick the little black beast on the head and it nearly turned a summersault in getting back the way it had come.

"The bear in the sinkhole was using all the strength it had to get out. I says, 'Howard, shoot it.' He replied, 'I can't.' I asked him why and he answered again, 'I can't.' Then I asked Dearman to shoot it but he refused to do it, and I says, 'What is the matter, Oz, that you don't want to shoot it?' and he says, 'That bear is dangerous and I don't want to get close to it.'

"By this time the bear had lay down and I gave the torch to one of the men and he handed me his rifle and I aimed the gun at the bear's head and pulled the trigger and a flash followed.[23] The rifle failed to discharge its contents. At this the bear rose on its feet and we rushed back a few yards from the sink hole. But perceiving that the bear was still in the sink hole and not able to follow us, we returned back and I reprimed the gun and sent a ball crashing into the bear's brains.

"As soon as Bruin was dead we tied ropes to it and pulled it out of the sink hole and out of the cave and took off its hide and dressed the meat.

"We camped that night at the mouth of the cave and on the following morning we went back into the cave to hunt for the cub bear that gave me such a fright the evening before and found and killed three cubs instead of one. In the afternoon of that day we went back into the cave and discovered another grown bear and killed it.

"It was night when we had got through caring for the meat and we camped here the second night, but before we lay down we all agreed to go back into the cave and hunt for another bear and we did, and found and killed a two-year old cub and took it out and removed its hide and dressed the meat before midnight.

"We had took six bear from the same cave, which cleaned up the bunch that inhabited this cavern. An equal division of the meat was made among us all which gave a fine supply of it to each of us."

KILLING BEAR WITH AN AXE [6:1]

JAMES HELMS, a native of Monroe County, Mo., and who came to Marion County, Ark., in 1870, said that in 1872, John Clark, a nephew of the famed hunter Bill Clark, had been burning pine knots on head of Music Creek for tar.

"One day he visited the kiln to look after the tar and seen a black animal traveling across the ridge near the kiln.[24] At first he thought it was a black muly cow[25] which belonged to him and thought strange of her wandering from home so far. After due reflection however, he concluded that it was not his cow but some kind of a wild animal. He had never seen a bear before this but from the descriptions he had heard of this animal he reached the conclusion that this one might be a bear.

"While he was trying to identify the beast it had passed almost out of rifle range and was going along at a moderate gait. However he aimed his gun at the disappearing animal and shot and inflicted a slight wound. After Clark had shot at the beast he observed two other black animals that were much less in size than the other one which he pronounced to be cub bears. Still he had some doubts that they were bear. These last were the size of big dogs and were following the old one some distance behind her.

"Clark reloaded his rifle and followed them and the two least animals hurried up and soon overtaken the larger one. In a little while the foremost animal went very slow and the hunter soon got in rifle range again and shot at the big one but he aimed too high for the ball, as he learned afterward, pierced the tips of both ears.

"Some distance from the kiln was a thicket of dogwood bushes and the three animals went into it. Here Clark left them and come to my house one half a mile from the thicket and requested me to go with him and help him kill a lot of bears or devils, he did not know which. He said they were the ugliest creatures that he ever saw.

"It was after sunset when the three beasts entered the thicket and it was growing dusky dark when Clark reached my house. I had no gun but I called my dogs, and picking up the axe went on with the man.

"When we had arrived near the thicket where Clark said the animals had went in it was dark, and when we were in fifty yards of the edge of the thicket Clark stopped and said that no amount of money would induce him to go into that thicket of dogwood while them things were in there.

"My two dogs were trusty and not feeling much afraid, I encouraged the dogs and they darted into the thicket and I followed them. The dogs attacked the beasts at once and when I had advanced up near them I could discern their forms in the dark. The larger one was sitting on its haunches and the dogs were baying it. The bears were on a steep hillside.

"Directly the two smaller ones got up close to the bigger one and while the dogs were baying them, I felt my way slowly and cautiously around above them and crept up in reach of the largest one whose back was toward me, and hit her a hard blow on the head with the axe, which stunned the beast and she reeled over. But as she fell she turned and struck at me with her paw and glanced my leg, which came near tripping me over.

"When the bear fell she rose up again but before she could do me harm, I gave the beast another blow on the head with the axe and knocked her down the second time. She rose partly up again but another hard stroke from the axe finished her life. While she was dying Clark called out, 'Helms, is it dead?'

"The dogs chased the cubs a short distance when they went up a leaning black oak tree and we cut the tree down but the young Bruins escaped in the darkness."

HOW A WOMAN AND HER CHILDREN WERE SAVED FROM A BEAR [4:76]

THE MOUTH OF BEAR CREEK is one of the earliest settled places on the upper White River. The place I refer to is where the Missouri state line divides Taney County, Mo., and Boone County, Ark. The division line between Missouri and Arkansas crosses the river at the mouth of Bear Creek.

Girard Leiper Brown was the first settler here. Brown married Miss Katie Coker in Alabama. They left Alabama for the wild west soon after their marriage and arriving on White River above where Batesville now stands, they dug out a big canoe of black walnut and in the late summer of 1816 they started up the river with their household. Among their effects was a small barrel filled with salt. The weather was dry and the water in the shoals was shallow and they experienced great difficulty at times in pushing and pulling the craft over the shoals.

It was in the middle of October of the year 1816, when they reached the mouth of Bear Creek and unloaded their stuff from the canoe. They selected a spot of ground near the bank of the river and built a small cabin and covered it with long boards. Then they dug a cellar and shaped it up to store their provision in and, as cool weather advanced, Mr. Brown began laying in a supply of wild meat for winter use.

They had been living here several months among the wild beast, though the nights were made hideous by the howl of the wolves and the scream of the panther, and the wild cat poured forth its nocturnal plaint to the silent stars. They both realized they were living in the midst of a howling wilderness. Yet they were not discouraged and they had built a new pole house [i.e., round log] and floored it with puncheons, which they had made by felling common sized trees and cutting off in proper lengths and splitting open and dressing the faces with the ax.

There was a big thicket of blackberry vines[26] near the house which were loaded with berries on the following summer after their arrival here, and the family had visited the patch frequently to gather the berries. One day during that summer, or in 1817, Mr. Brown went off early in the morning on a day's hunt, leaving his wife and two children—Tom and Alex—alone. The last named child was just beginning to walk. The first named was just old enough to barely sit alone.

As we have stated the cluster of blackberry vines were loaded with nice ripe berries and after Mrs. Brown had finished her housework and the heavy dew had dried off, she took the children and a small vessel and went out to the vines to gather berries.

After Mrs. Brown put the children down on the ground she soon become busy picking off the wild fruit but, before she had filled the vessel, she noticed that some of the briars had just been wallowed down by a wild beast, and on investigation she found that it had been done by a bear. Its big tracks were imprinted in the soft dirt.

This alarmed her for she realized that the animal was close by. Throwing the partly filled vessel down, she ran to her children and snatched them up in her arms and ran to the house. When she reached the door she glanced back toward the briar thicket and to her consternation she saw the bear coming toward the house. Then she rushed into the house and, putting the children down in the middle of the floor, she closed the door and made [it] as fast as she could with the means at hand. Then she raised a puncheon and put the children down in the cellar.[27] The moment she turned them loose in there where it was dusky dark, they both began to cry. The barrel containing the salt, but only partly filled now, was sitting in the room and she put it endways on the puncheon she had raised. Then getting down in the cellar where her frightened children were, she carefully pulled and worked the puncheon back in its place.

She had worked in haste and had barely sit down on the floor of the cellar to quiet her children and listen for the approach of the beast when she heard it push against the door shutter, which he soon pushed open and she heard his bearship come into the house. Then she heard him walking on the puncheons. Directly it stopped and put its nose down to a narrow space between two puncheons and she could hear it sniffle and smell.

Not being satisfied with that part of the floor, it moved directly over the cellar and put its nose down again and repeated its smelling and sniffles and in a short space of time it located her and the children. Then it quit smelling and went to scratching at the puncheon to raise it up, and in doing this it turned the salt barrel over and Mrs. Brown heard the barrel roll across the floor.

The mother and children were in a fearful position. The hungry bear had only to raise the puncheon out of its way with its paws, then raise a second one, which would give it plenty of room to get down into the cellar where it would have a delightful time while destroying the woman and her precious babes. She screamed out in terror and gave up for lost and abandoned all hope of escaping with her life. If her children were safe she could face death more easy. But her poor innocent children, how sad the thought that they would be torn to pieces by the monster wild beast. Mother and children were all screaming and crying. In the meantime bruin did not let up in trying to get into the cellar.

After Mr. Brown had arrived there the fall previous and got settled down, he went back down the river to his father-in-law's, Buck Coker, who lived at the lower end of what is now called the Jake Nave Bend, and bought a cow of him and brought her home and kept her lassoed in the cane near the house until she dropped her calf. Then they kept the calf in the yard which was enclosed by a good fence.

When the bear attacked the house, the calf, which was quite young, was on the back side of the house, but while the bear was at work it was supposed that the calf had come around to the door where the bear could see it and the next thing the mother knew, her black enemy suddenly quit scratching at the puncheons and ran out of the house into the yard and she heard it catch the calf and kill it in front of the door.

The little calf bellowed pitiful as the black beast was slaying it. The sight of the calf caused bruin to leave its human victims for a mess of veal, but Mr. Bruin did not have the pleasure of enjoying his feast very long, for while he was devouring the calf, the husband and father made his appearance. Hearing the cries of his wife and children, he rushed up with gun in hand within plain view of the house and, seeing the bear in the yard devouring something which greatly alarmed him, and taking quick aim at a vital spot, he shot the bear down. While it was kicking and struggling in its dying moments he rushed into the house and found his wife and children safe in the cellar.

The report of the gun had given Mrs. Brown new life for she knew her husband had arrived and had killed or wounded the bear. But the fright had almost unnerved her and, when Mr. Brown lifted her out of the cellar, she was hardly able to stand. But realizing that her man had come in time to save her and the children from the black beast and seeing the bear as it lay dead in the yard, she nearly swooned with joy.

A Desperate Combat with a Bear [5:29]

BETWEEN THE EAST prong of Bratton's Spring Creek and Gooley's Spring Creek[28] is a small prairie hill known as the Salt Bald. This mound is three miles northeast of Pontiac, Ozark County, Mo. On the south and southwest slope of Salt Bald Hill it is rough, with low ledges of rock, and big stones lay promiscuously over the side of the hill. Rocky Branch has its source here, which forms a gulch, and part of it is lined with scrubby timber. This part of Ozark County was one of Paton Keesee's favorite hunting grounds for bear.

Elias Keesee, son of Paton Keesee, give me an interesting account of a bear fight that his father and his dogs had one day on the south side of this noted hill. Mr. Keesee said that it occurred in the month of April, 1830.

"I was nearly six years old when the fight occurred. One day my father took five bear dogs and rode up the right prong of Bratton's Spring Creek to the mouth of what is now Trace Hollow, and up to the source of it, where the dogs met a bear and after a hot chase, overhauled it near Bushy Knob. Father shot and killed it and, after taking off the hide, he cut the meat into four parts and loaded it and the hide onto his horse and lead the horse home with his load of wild meat.

"Having such excellent luck, he decided to return the following day in search of another Bruin and kill it, to increase his supply of meat. Instead of going up the creek as he did on the previous day, he followed the divide between the right prong of Spring Creek and Gooley's Creek, but neither one was known by any name at that early date. Near one-quarter mile south of Salt Bald, which bore no name either, he saw an enormous bear.

"The dogs were brave and eager for the chase and my father encouraged them and off they started on a lively race. The bear made in the direction of the Salt hill and stopped in the gulch at the base of the hill for a battle. The plucky dogs attacked him at once and bear and dogs fought in the gulch and all around on the south and southwest slope of the hill. The bear was in a terrible rage and fought the dogs furiously and was more than a match for them.

"When father galloped his horse up to the scene of the combat, he saw at a glance that the huge beast would soon whip his dogs and, hurriedly dismounting and turning his horse loose, he shot the bear and wounded him, which rendered his anger more desperate and, before he could reload his gun, the bear killed three of the dogs almost instantly.

"One of the other two dogs was named 'Doc' and he was a favorite and a trusty one, and as soon as the fearful beast had finished the life of the other three dogs, he snatched up the Doc dog in his hug. Without waiting to finish reloading his rifle, father rushed up to the infuriated animal as he sit on his haunches with the dog in his embrace and jabbed the muzzle of the rifle into the bear's mouth which relieved the dog from the bear's teeth but not from its hug. He then jerked the muzzle of the gun out of the bear's mouth and reversed ends of the gun and forced the breech of the gun into the beast's mouth.[29]

"At this the bear dropped the dog and nearly shivered the breech of the gun into splinters with its teeth and would have hit father with its paws but he avoided the stroke by leaping out of the way. There was only one dog left that was able to keep up the fight and he would not get in close quarters with the enraged animal but he kept it at bay until my father hurriedly reloaded what was left of his gun and shot the bear dead, which ended the bloody combat.

"Though my father and one dog had come out a little ahead but it was a dear bought victory. Three faithful dogs lay dead on the battleground and another one so desperately wounded that he had to be carried home and a new gunstock had to be made and it was a long time before the disabled dog had strength enough to take part in another fight with a bear, and in the meantime my father had to raise a new recruit of dogs to engage in the chase."

When Mr. Keesee had finished the account of this desperate encounter with the bear he suggested that this bald hill ought to be called "Dead Dogs Hill" instead of Salt Bald.

FOREST SCENES THAT WERE FUNNY [15:94]

JIMMIE JONES, of near Lutie, Ozark County, Mo., was born near the mouth of Barren Fork, August 8, 1843. Uncle Jim is a son of Dave Jones and a grandson of "Sugar" Jones, the Methodist preacher who located in Ozark County in the early Thirties. Mr. Jones narrates an amusing story of his father and "Chat" Sallee, father of Captain J. H. Sallee,[30] putting up a job on Noah Mahan[31] in 1839.

"Noah was a brother of Isaac Mahan, who was a native of the state of Indiana, but desiring to move to a new country where there was plenty of game, for the portion of Indiana where he lived was an old settled section and the game that once existed there had disappeared.

"Father said that him and Sallee wrote to Mahan that Ozark County, Mo., was the place to come to, to live an easy life and kill all the game he wanted. Mahan wrote back that they might look for him in the course of a few months, and sure enough, he arrived sooner than expected and brought a new gun with him.[32]

"He wanted to go hunting the following day after his arrival and my father and Sallee consented to go with him and the three men, with dogs and rifles, started out to kill a bear. A mile or so from Little North Fork the dogs chased a small bear, but it ran several miles before it went up a tree. In the hurry and flurry of the chase Mahan was left behind. When father and Sallee reached the tree the bear was up they shot bruin and, as the tree had low branches and Mahan was a tenderfoot, the two hunters thought it a fine opportunity to play a trick on him, so they pushed the little dead bear back up the tree and placed it on a limb in a shape that it looked like a live bear. The men now encouraged the dogs to bark at it and they stepped away from the tree some fifty yards and awaited the arrival of their friend.

"After the elapse of an hour he failed to put in an appearance and they discharged their guns to attract his attention and it was not long now before he showed up. He reported that he had got lost. The men pretended to Mahan that their guns was out of fix and pointed to the dead bear in the tree and told him that his rifle was all the dependence to kill bruin and they wanted him to shoot it.

"Mahan was eager for the trial, and resting his gun against the side of a tree, he shot. He was told that he never touched the bear. He reloaded and shot again. The two hunters insisted that his bullet went wide of the mark, that when he hit the bear it would drop to the ground. Mahan continued to reload his gun and shoot but bruin never dropped from the limb.

"Father and Sallee could hardly refrain from laughing outright, but they managed to control themselves until Mahan ventured up nearer, and seeing bruin's tongue hanging out of his mouth, he remarked that he would 'kill him next shot or make him take his tongue back,' and then he shot.

"Father and Sallee burst into a roar of laughter. Mahan, finding that he had been wasting ammunition on a dead bear and that his companions were poking fun at him, flew into a rage and father and Sallee were compelled to apologize to him to get him in a better humor to avoid a fight with him. The man had almost riddled the dead bear with lead."

Imprisoned in a Cave with a Bear [7:45]

H. E. UPTON furnishes the following narrative regarding a daring exploit of a noted bear hunter, who has passed over the Jordan of death many years ago where he will meet the wild beast no more. Here is the sketch as given by Mr. Upton.

"Jesse Upton was a son of Tom Upton and was a cousin of my father's and my uncle Ned Upton. He lived on Caney Creek, a tributary of Bryant's Fork. Jess was a famed hunter. One of his best friends and associates was Alex Huffman, who lived on Pine Creek, another branch of Bryant's Fork which flows in from the west side.

"One day while Aleck Huffman and Jess Upton were together relating their yarns to each other, the former told of a terrible experience he had in a cave once on Pine Creek. He said that he had shot and wounded a bear and his dogs chased it into a cave.

"After preparing a torch he made several attempts to enter the cavern without the dogs but they were as anxious to go in as he was. When he would start in they would follow him. He made them go back several times, but they seemed determined to follow him into the cave in spite of all his scolding at them.

"'Finally,' said Mr. Huffman, 'I flew into a rage and swore I would keep them out. Going up on the hillside I rolled a large pine chunk down to the mouth of the cave, which had a narrow entrance. The cavern had its beginning in a sink hole or rather a deep swag in the ground. After I got the big chunk in a proper position, I crawled into the mouth of the cave with torch and gun, and with hard labor I continued to draw the chunk endways into the mouth of the cave, and after watching the dogs a minute or two and seeing that they were cut off from following me, I turned my attention to the bear. As I went along in the passage way of the cavern I rejoiced that I had beat the dogs.

"'After getting into the cave some distance I discovered the bear and shot it again, but unfortunately the flash of my gun extinguished the torch. I was now in total darkness. Not a ray of light penetrated a crevice as far as I could see.

"'A moment after the light went out I heard the bear coming toward me, but the opening at that part of the cave was roomy and I crawled to the side wall to give the bear plenty of room to pass. I did not know whether my last shot had wounded the animal bad or not, but anyway I heard it pass me and go on toward the entrance. But the pine chunk prevented it from going out. I did not follow the bear but remained where the bear went by me.

"'In a few minutes I heard Bruin coming back and after passing me he went on toward the back part of the cavern. I now realized my peril, for if the bear could not get out how could I? These were dreadful thoughts, and I made my way through the dark cave to the entrance and made all the efforts in my power to push the chunk back, but failed. I was imprisoned in a dark hole with a wounded bear.

"'My position was desperate. I wished now that I had let the dogs alone. They would have rendered me aid in the cave. But they were powerless to help me now. What would I do if the bear come back? I felt greatly troubled. Reflections were sad and heavy. At this moment I heard the footsteps of the bear returning back.

"'As stated above this part of the cave was small and I turned in an effort to try to gain a spot where the opening was larger, but having no torch I was too late and I met the bear in the narrow part.

"'I lay down with my face to the floor of the cavern and the bear tried to crawl over me. It was the worst squeeze I ever had. I thought it would smother me to death. I soon discovered that Bruin could not pass me and unless something happened in my favor I would not be able to tell this story.

"'My long keen bladed hunting knife was in my scabbard and I thought if I could kill the bear, it might be possible I could crawl from under it, so with a great effort I managed to turn on my back and reached for my knife, and drawing it from the scabbard I sank the blade into the bear's body once, twice and two more times. Then I felt the weight of the animal sink down on me.

"'I kept my left hand over my eyes to protect them from the bear's paws in its death struggle, but its dying agony was of short duration and then it lay still. I and that dead bear was wedged together. Talk about hunters being in close places, I was certainly in that fix. But I had noticed that while Bruin was pressing so hard against me in its efforts to pass over, that it did not try to bite me, and I wondered why it did not.

"'Bruin though dead was bleeding freely and I could feel the warm blood saturating my clothes and flowing over my body. But I must get from under it, and with this end in view I made a trial and slowly worked myself from under the dead bear, toward the opening and crawled back and labored a long time trying to push the chunk back but did not succeed.

"'I gave up in despair and let my mind rest awhile on my terrible doom that seemed in store for me. True, the dogs after starving a few days would return home, or it might be that my family would become alarmed at my prolonged absence and hunt for me and find my prison before the dogs left. Then again wife and friends might search for days in these wild woods and never discover my whereabouts. Oh, to be shut up in a dark cave with a dead bear and starve to death for food and water was a horrible thought.

"'But I did not lay there idle long without making another effort to move the log and to my joy I got it started into the inside. I worked with a vim, for I was encouraged and kept drawing the chunk on the inside, inch by inch, until there was just room for me to crawl out and I felt a glow of happiness spread over me. The sun was just setting and I had went into the cave in the early forenoon. Though I had beat the dogs by not letting them in the cave but I had come nigher beating myself and come nigh not getting out at all. I had a long walk in getting home that night.

"'Going back with help next day I found that my shot in the cave had broke the bear's under jaw which accounted for its not biting me.'"

HE HAD LOADED THE GUN THREE TIMES WITHOUT THINKING WHAT HE WAS DOING [5:62]

AMONG A NUMBER of amusing bear chases that occurred in Ozark County, Mo., is an account given me by Elias Keesee, son of Paton Keesee, who said his father and Mose Lantz, while hunting together one day on the left prong of Bratton's Spring Creek, met a big bear at the west end of Bald Jess which resulted in an amusing chase.

[Said Mr. Keesee], "The dogs were as anxious for the chase as the men were and the moment the bear was sighted, men and dogs went for it in a lively way. His bearship took shelter in a shallow cave where he was not able to hide himself entirely. When the men reached the cave they could see the bear's nose sticking out and the dogs were baying and barking at Bruin's smeller but was afraid to take hold, for fear he might use them up. The hunters shot at the protruding nose and struck it once and out come the bear in a rage. He snorted and the blood flew out of his nostrils. The dogs surrounded him and let on like they were going to take hold at once, but after scattering them with his paws, he started off on a run and the dogs followed him.

"The race was exciting and amusing. After Bruin had went some distance he halted. My father and Lantz were both afoot and the former outrun the latter and had reloaded his rifle and shot the bear once before it had stopped, but failed to knock it down.

"The fury of the bear had went up to fever heat and the wounded animal, when it stopped, had put on its fighting humor, and it caught one of the dogs in its hug. My father, seeing the danger to his dog's life and desiring to save the animal, he darted up and punched the bear hard behind the shoulder with the muzzle of his gun, for he had not time to reload it again after he had shot. Bear, dogs and hunter were in a confused mess in a hand to hand battle.

"At this time, Mr. Lantz come up on a fast run. Bruin went on with his work of crushing the life out of the dog. When father saw Lantz make his appearance, he stepped back from the bear and dogs and says, 'Mose, shoot it before it kills my dog,' and Mr. Lantz replied, 'Oh, I can't, I'm out of breath,' and handing father his gun said, 'Keesee, you shoot it.'

"My father not suspecting anything wrong with the rifle took it and shot the bear in the region of the heart, and it relaxed its hold on the now nearly lifeless dog and sank down with the dog in its arms. The report of the rifle resembled the sound of a small cannon, and father fell before the bear did, for at the report of the gun a blank come over him. He was unconscious and down he went to the ground and lay there senseless and helpless for a minute or more, before he was able to speak.

"Mr. Lantz was bad scared, for when he saw father drop to the ground so sudden, he supposed he was killed or severely injured and went to work to revive him, and was greatly pleased to see his old friend get on his feet again.

"When father had come to himself again he says, 'Lantz, did I faint or what was the matter with me? Is there anything wrong with your gun?'

"At this Mr. Lantz remembered what he had done, and explained to father that he had loaded his rifle three times after they had shot at the bear's nose in the cave and there were three charges of powder and three balls in the barrel and it come near getting the life of father as well as that of Bruin.[33]

"The dog did not revive and they left the dead form of the faithful animal where the bear had hugged it to death."

How Two Women Killed a Bear [7:32]

IN A FEW CASES the brave and noble women of the pioneer days of the Ozarks have been known to kill bear. Though not going out on the chase or on a camp hunt like the men, nor entering into caves with torchlight and rifle and shooting Bruin as he lay on his winter bed asleep, but when one of these animals put itself in the way, there were a few women that were not afraid to tackle it with a gun. Such a case is reported to have occurred in Taney County, Mo., in the bygone days, which is told by Mrs. Lucy Vance, wife of Calvin Vance.

"Well, you want to know about the women killing the bear," said Mrs. Vance. "My recollection is that I was twelve years old and I remember the circumstance as told by a number of people soon after its occurrence and they all said it was true. A man of the name of Hiram Collier lived on a small stream called Bear Creek which runs into Bull Creek. Collier lived near ten miles north of Forsyth. It was said that Mrs. Collier, his wife, was not afraid of anything in the shape of wild beast. The thought of wild animals attacking the house never bothered her mind in the least for she knew how to protect herself and children as well as her man did.

"One day while her husband was absent, she and her daughter, Ellen, who was nearly grown, went into the cornfield to see if stock had broke in and damaged the crop. In the middle of the field was a log house with log joist, with a few four feet boards lying on them. The building had been occupied by a family but was vacant at the time I speak of. Mr. Collier used it to store fodder[34] in, but at that time the house was empty.

"Finding no stock in the field they turned and started back home and went by the house in the field and, for the sake of curiosity, they both stopped and went in. There was a door shutter but it was standing open. When they stepped into the building they heard a noise up on a joist.

"Looking up to see the cause of it their eyes met the gaze of a bear, which was sitting on its haunches on a joist and boards. The sudden appearance of the women did not seem to disturb it one bit. He was a large fellow and docile and in a splendid humor.

"Though it was reported that Mrs. Collier did not fear a bear or other wild beast, but when her and her daughter saw his bearship had possession of the house, they got out of the building faster than they went in. They were aware that numbers of bears infested the hills, but they did not expect to meet one in the cabin.

"Neither one of the women swooned or screamed but set about to devise a plan to slay him. Mr. Collier had left his gun at home when he started on his trip that morning, and Mrs. Collier says, 'Ellen, we can shoot him, and you go to the house and bring the gun and shot pouch and I will stay and guard the bear to prevent him from leaving the house.'

"Ellen done as she was bid and run nearly all the way to the house and back and when she brought the gun it was empty. Mrs. Collier was an expert at loading a rifle and soon had it charged heavily with powder and ball.

"In the meantime the bear appeared to be careless of his safety, and made no move to get out, but composed himself very quietly. He did not suspect danger from a woman and did not permit the sight of one to break his rest.

"Mrs. Collier looked carefully to the priming of the gun, then stepped into the house, and without the least nervousness, took deliberate aim at the burr of the ear and pulled the trigger. A flash, a report and a dull thud on the puncheon floor, the bear lay broadside in a quiver, then he was quiet and dead."

Pulling a Dead Bear out of a Cave with Oxen [6:72]

THE FOLLOWING STORIES was given by E. J. (Jackson) Shields, who was born where the town of Lexington in Perry County, Ohio, now stands, June 28, 1829. Mr. Shields come to Taney County, Mo., and lived several years on Dry Caney Creek, a tributary of Beaver Creek. Caney Creek was his hunting grounds.

"The only encounter I had with a bear worth relating occurred on this same stream," said Mr. Shields. "The bear was an exceedingly large one and very fat and was killed in a cave which one of my dogs had discovered in there.

"I had no desire to tackle it alone and went after John Ingram, John Bryant and Tom Ellison to come and assist me to take him out which they did, but it taken us from Friday evening late until the following Sunday afternoon before we accomplished the death of his bearship and took him out.

"We at first tried to smoke him out by building a slow fire in the mouth of the cavern. Apparently the entire opening was filled with smoke but it failed to bring the bear out. Then we heaved rags and several pads of strong red pepper on the fire and gave it a fair trial of several hours, but if the smoke from the rags and pepper had any impression on Bruin he did not let us know it. Then we quit the smoking business and extinguished the fire and, after waiting some time for the cavern to clear of smoke, we sent the dogs in and a terrific fight ensued between them and Bruin.

"A grey hound which belonged to John Ingram was killed and one of my dogs was severely wounded. This ended the battle for the enraged beast forced the other dogs out of the cave.

"We dare not go in while the bear's temper was so high but after waiting a few hours until we thought his temper was more cooler, we filled a big cup with melted tallow. This cup was attached to the end of a long pole, and after putting a large wick in the tallow, we ignited it and we all started into the cave to hunt for his bearship, which we soon discovered and we shot nine bullets into his body before he lay dead. We would have not killed him then but as good luck would have it, the last ball took effect in the right eye.

"After he was dead we had a tedious job pulling him out of the cave. We first tried to drag the bear out ourselves but he was too heavy for us. We then all went home and brought over our women folks to the cave to assist us, but the combined strength of both men [and] women was not sufficient to pull the bear along the rough floor of the cave, only halfway out when we were unable to drag him any further.

"We increased our strength with the addition of a stout yoke of oxen. The mouth of the cave being large, we backed the oxen to the dead bear, and with a lug pole and log chain we hitched the oxen to the bear and pulled him to the outside. But owing to the indentations and rough stones along the floor of the cavern the oxen taken three hard pulls before we finally reached the mouth of the entrance.

"None of our party had ever seen as large a bear as this one. He was a monster indeed. We had no way of weighing him whole, but we sent after a pair of steel yards,[35] and after removing his hide we cut the meat into chunks and weighed each piece and the total weight of him net was six-hundred-sixty-seven pounds.[36]

"We made an equal division of the meat among us and we all fared sumptuously on fat bear meat for many days. The *middlings,* after they were well cured, averaged six inches thick.

"A few months after we killed the bear we taken the hide to Springfield, Mo., and several citizens of the town pronounced it the largest bear hide ever brought to the city during its history."

TALES OF ELK AND DEER

Editors' note: Elk, or more properly, wapiti, *Cervus elaphus,* probably ranged over the entire Ozarks region before the coming of the Europeans. Despite their great size—from five hundred to nine hundred pounds—elk are shy creatures and more difficult to hunt than deer. Yet by 1830 elk were becoming scarce, and after that date large herds were reported only in the northwestern and southeastern parts of Missouri.[37]

Turnbo has few accounts of elk hunting, indicating that elk were already uncommon in the region by the time Europeans began to occupy the White River country.

Exterminating a Small Bunch of Elk [8:56]

IN THE EARLY HISTORY of southern Missouri it was common to meet a small bunch of elks but this was when the settler's cabins were few and stood far apart. The intrusion of the hunters in Missouri soon forced these animals to disappear.

Elk were shy and not so easily approached by hunters as deer were. I have collected a few brief accounts relating to these interesting and beautiful creatures as they were observed in the forests of the southern part of Missouri. One of these accounts which was furnished by an original settler is as follows.

But we will first state that in the southeast part of Taney County, Mo., is a bald hill which was known by the old timers as the Five Oak Bald Hill.[38] This low prairie hill or glade is on the west side of the head of Big Buck Creek and took its name from five post oak trees[39] that stood near together on the southeast slope of the hill in the edge of the timber. As time went on two of these trees were prostrated by a wind storm from the north. One was sawed down for wild bees. The remaining two trees are combined together from the ground to a few feet above the surface where they become separate and are the only ones left intact at the present writing.

East of this bald hill is the bald ridge that was once called the Big Bald and it divides the head of Buck Creek and the Joe Eslick Hollow, the last named of which flows into Big Creek. The main wagon road leading from Protem to Dugginsville passes over the Five Oak Bald and by the Hester school house.

One day in 1859 a buffalo's horn was picked up on the head of Buck Creek. This horn had escaped the great forest fires that had swept over this section for many years since the buffalo had been driven from this region.[40] Now to our story that we started out to tell.

During the early history of Taney County, Arch Tabor who lived on Big Creek and Leven T. Green who settled on Pond Fork near where Igo Post Office,[41] Mo., is now, while hunting together one day in this section discovered a bunch of six elk feeding on the Five Oak Bald Hill. Two of them were bull elk and both carried great expanding horns.

It was an interesting sight to view these proud and wary animals while they were nipping the tender herbage that then grew so luxuriant on this low eminence. The hunters were not in gunshot range. The busy animals had not discovered the hunters or they would have run.

The two men concealed themselves in the tall grass and crawled inch by inch toward the unsuspecting creatures until they had approached within shooting distance of the elk and they both stopped where the elk were in full view by parting the grass with their hands. One of the men took aim at one of the elk with his rifle and fired, which was followed instantly by the entire bunch springing away and ran toward the Big Bald Hill. As the elk were darting off the other man rose to his feet and fired his rifle at them as they ran.

The hunters went to the spot where the elk were feeding and following their trail a few yards they found blood stains on the grass and saw briars[42] which indicated that one of the beasts was wounded and after following the trail across the Gilbert Hollow to the crest of the Big Bald and to a long sink hole lined with timber and which is just over the rise toward the north where the two men were much elated at finding one of the elk lying dead on the solid rocks.

After removing the hide and entrails of the dead beast, they taken the hide and meat to Arch Tabor's and returned back on the following morning and followed the trail of the remaining elk to head of Pond Fork where the two hunters contrived in a few days to exterminate the bunch. I am told that this bunch of elk was the last wild elk seen in this part of Taney County.

Editors' note: The white-tailed deer, *Odocoileus virginianus*, sometimes named *Dama virginiana* by some authorities, was the most common big-game animal in the White River region at the time of settlement.

Traffic in deer hides was even greater than that in fur trading. During Bienville's first administration (1718–24), the Alabama, Choctaw, and Chickasaw were trading an estimated fifty thousand deer hides, taken annually from the greater Mississippi River

Valley region, to the French. As early as 1715 the southeastern tribes of Alabama, Choctaw, and Chickasaw Indians were trading an estimated seventy thousand deer hides annually to the French.[43] In 1804, shortly before settlement began in the White River region, it is reported that at St. Louis deer skins were the basis of trade, a good one worth forty cents a pound. Deer skins glutted America's markets, and the various prices paid depended heavily upon foreign markets. In 1813 John Jacob Astor asked fur trader Charles Gratiot in St. Louis to purchase twenty-five thousand pounds of deer skins at twenty-five cents per pound. In 1841 he told Ramsay Crooks to buy shaved deer skins at prices up to thirty cents per pound.[44] In frontier Missouri and Arkansas, in the absence or scarcity of money, the deer hide became for a time an article of currency.

The earliest settlers in the region were essentially hunters, who sought deer, bear, wild honey, and more for their livelihood, raising only small crops of corn to supplement their diet of meat, honey, and greens. Deer hides and meat, bear hides, meat, and oil, plus wild honey and wax were used to buy those items they needed.

Prices paid for items in the Lawrence District of Arkansas (including the White River Country) in 1819 were:

Bear's meat $10/cwt	Buffalo beef $4/cwt
Cow's beef $3/cwt	Pork in the hog $3.50/cwt
Venison hams 24 cents each	Wild Turkies [sic] 25 cents each
Wild honey $1/gallon	Beaver fur $2/lb.
Bear skins $1.50 each	Otter skins $2 each
Raccoon [skins] 25 cents each	Deer skins 25 cents/lb.

Prices of items bought by market hunters and settlers:

Three point Mackinaw blankets $8	Butcher knives $2 each
Rifle locks $8 each	Common coarse blue cloth $6/yard
Coffee 75 cents/lb.	Salt $5/bushel
Lead 25 cents/lb.	Gunpowder $2/lb.
Axes $6 each	Horse shoe nails $3/set[45]

Deer are not herd animals, although in late winter feeding groups ranging up to one hundred or more deer may occur in local places. These are temporary groups and not a herd. Turnbo's chronicles are full of tales of deer being seen in large numbers.

While deer are forest creatures, they utilize the forest edges rather than dense forest stands. The reason for this is that their preferred foods occur in greater variety on the margins of timbered areas or in forest clearings.[46]

Hunting in the Early Days [22:35]

IN RECOUNTING STORIES of the times when Lick Creek was sparsely settled, Mr. Henry Sanders tells the following.

"When my father Allen Sanders came to Ozark County, Mo. in 1841 he give Tom Jones two good horses for a government claim[47] that Jones owned on Lick Creek three miles below where Gainsville is now. This was the first start he made in opening up our old home place on this stream.

"There were only three other families living on Lick Creek when my father located there. They were Jess Teverball, Bill Bridges and Matthew Shriver. Henry Sanders married Miss Rhoda Rice daughter of Thomas Rice in 1853."

Mr. Sanders says that his father was a deer hunter and he has known him to have as many as forty dead deer in his smoke house in winter time when snow covered the ground. His main time to kill deer was when it was cold weather with plenty of snow. When he would start out to hunt deer while snow was on the ground he would have us children to follow him with horses and ropes and when he would kill a deer we would tie a knot in the hair of the horse's tail, then tie one end of a rope around the dead deer's neck and fasten the other end to the horse's tail above the knot and drag the deer home. The snow would prevent the hair on the deer from being rubbed off and not spoil the hide.

"This was our daily work as long as snow lay on the ground. I have brought many dead deer home in this way as father would kill them. When a big lot of furs, pelts and deer horns were accumulated my father would load them into an ox wagon and take them to St. Louis and exchange them for salt, coffee and other needed supplies."[48]

Received a Good Price for the Hide and Horns of the Buck [8:54]

"ONE COLD FROSTY MORNING," said John Mahan, son of Isaac Mahan, "I was hunting on the bluff on the west side of Little North Fork just east of the mouth of Cowpen Hollow. I saw a buck which carried eight points on each beam. I shot the buck in the neck and it dropped as if dead, but he rose to his feet again and started off down the point of the bluff toward Cowpen Hollow and as he went on he fell a few times but would rise and go on.

"I was afraid he would escape and being a little excited I pushed a bullet down my gun without any powder and followed the wounded buck and snapped my gun at him several times before I thought what I had done.[49] By this time the deer was getting very weak and would fall and get up again and stagger along.

"I laid the gun down and caught the buck by the horns and attempted to cut its throat with an old case knife that I used to cut bullet patching with. But not succeeding in this I picked up a jagged stone and broke his skull bone with it. I sold this buck's hide for $1.50 and the horns for $2," said Mr. Mahan.

THE OLD ALLEN TRIMBLE FARM AND HOW ALLEN TRIMBLE AND OTHERS KILLED DEER [9:24]

ON THE RIGHT BANK of White River in Franklin township in Marion County, Ark., and just above the mouth of Trimble's Creek is the old Allen Trimble farm where he settled in 1842. William Trimble, father of Allen Trimble, had marked a sycamore tree which stood at the spring twenty-five years before his son, Allen Trimble, settled here.

Mr. [Allen] Trimble first built a small hut on the point of the hill above the spring and he employed a man by the name of Campbell Stacy to clear the cane off of six acres of land in the bottom. The cane stood very thick on the ground and was so tough that Campbell had to use a heavy homemade hoe to cut the cane with.

Mr. Trimble had ten acres of land in cultivation when the big overflow in the river come down in May, 1844, and swept over the field and washed away his fencing and young corn.

Allen Trimble was a great hunter and hunted part of the time from the day he was old enough to carry a rifle until he was feeble with age. Many fat deer yielded up their lives to his unerring aim with his favorite rifle but we can mention only two incidents of his deer killing here.

"One morning before breakfast," said he, "soon after I had settled in the river bottom in 1842, I met a herd of deer in a swag on a ridge just west of Trimble's Creek. They were mostly bucks and while they were frisking and playing I stood behind a tree and shot five times with my old muzzle loading gun and five big fat bucks lay dead in a few feet of each other. The deer was so busy at play that they paid but little attention to the reports of the gun. I could have killed more of them but I had as many as I could take care of for one breakfast spell.

"One night in August, 1845, I and another hunter run a race with two other hunters to see how many deer we could kill and see which party killed the greatest number of deer while fire hunting[50] from the mouth of Big Beach Hollow down to the Buck Shoals ford. Great numbers of deer would visit the river of nights in July and August to drink water and eat moss. We had two canoes and each craft carried a big torchlight which revealed the objects of deer on the shore as well as in the water.

"The race was exciting and merry, and many shots from the guns sounded out as the two canoes drifted down the river. When either party killed a deer it was marked to distinguish them apart and sunk in the water with stones. When we all had reached the Buck Shoals my companion and myself had killed ten deer and the other two men had killed nine. It was an interesting fire hunt and we all enjoyed it.

"We stayed at the shoals until the following morning when we pushed the two canoes back up stream and took the dead deer out of the water and removed the hides and left the carcasses of the deer along the shore to be consumed by the wild animals and buzzards."

Crooked Creek and Its Tributaries and Incidents of Old Time Hunting in This Valley [7:82]

Mr. Peter Baughman, an early resident on Crooked Creek in Marion County, Arkansas, told of killing several deer from the same tree which he related in this way. "One day I went out on the south side of Crooked Creek and seated myself at the foot of a tree which stood near where a trail had been made by deer as they traveled to and fro. I knew this to be a regular passway and I would wait for game to come to me which would save me from a long tramp in hunting for it.

"I had been here an hour almost when I observed four deer coming along the path in single file. The front one was a doe. Just behind her was a yearling doe and the other two were bucks. One had two prongs on each beam or what we hunters called forked horned. The other carried a spike or single horn.

"Very soon the two bucks stopped. The other two deer come up in thirty yards of me and stopped and stood side and side with broadsides toward me. I aimed at them and shot and both deer fell on their tracks. By the time I had reloaded my gun the two bucks had walked up to where the two dead deer were lying and stopped and I shot one down. The other buck seemed to be bewildered and stood still until I reloaded my gun again and I killed him also.[51]

"There four deer lay in a heap. In a minute or more after my last shot I saw three more bucks coming slowly along the same trail. Each one of them carried a big set of horns. I reloaded my gun in a hurry but by the time I had finished priming my rifle they had got to where the other deer lay and stopped and another dead one was added to the pile.

"At the report of the gun the other two ran off a short distance and stopped and turned around and come back to where the five deer lay dead. I was soon ready for another shot and the number of dead ones was increased to one more. The remaining buck took fright and away he went as fast as he could go. I supposed he was gone for good, but just before he passed beyond my view he stopped.

"My supply of powder was nearly exhausted. I emptied my powder horn and found there was not enough for a full load. I was so anxious to get him too that I only kept three grans[52] of powder back to drop in the priming pan to touch the load off with.

"As I finished loading the gun I saw the buck start back but after he had got a few steps he turned and did not come straight forward, but in a half circle until he got in one hundred yards of me, then he advanced up toward me straight until he was in twenty steps of me and then stopped and looked at me in a peculiar way. I aimed at him and fired and heard the bullet hit him. He turned and run a few yards and fell.

"I had shot and killed seven deer from the same tree, six of which lay in a heap. This was late in the fall of 1853 and the weather being cool I went to work and took the entrails out of all of them and went to George Ridinger's for assistance in taking the deer home. Mr. Ridinger hitched a yoke of his cattle to his wagon and went back with me and hauled the deer to my house," said the old timer and hunter.

A Night Scene at a Deer Lick [14:95]

AMONG STORIES GATHERED, is one given me by William Brown, stepson of Allen Trimble. Mr. Brown, in furnishing the other story, told it in the following amusing way:

"When I was nearly sixteen years old, Abe Perkins and I thought we would make a deer lick for our own particular use and kill deer mostly for their pelts. It would also be a nice past-time, staying there of nights watching deer come up to the lick, and then shoot them down. In our imagination we would have a merry time.

"We proposed to establish the lick on the north side of the river between Bull Bottom and mouth of Music Creek in what is now North Fork Township, Marion County, Ark., and did begin by boring a few holes with an augur at the roots of a stooping post oak tree, and filled the augur holes with salt. We then prepared a resting place in a tree, which was made of one or two pieces of plank and a few poles. The scaffold was constructed about ten feet above the ground. Deer were so numerous that they required only a day or two to find it [the salt lick] out.

"After waiting long enough we went there one evening to get a supply of venison and pelts. We imagined that all we had to do was to shoot, remove hides and carry them home. Arriving there we saw that deer had been there and had licked most of the salt out of the augur holes. We refilled them again with salt and when twilight settled down into dusk of the evening, we ascended the tree and seated ourselves for the night's watch and the slaying of deer.

"It was in the early fall season—the air was just cool enough to feel pleasant and the night was lit up by the moon. We watched and waited for an hour, but the deer declined to make their appearance and taste of the new supply of salt. After awhile Perkins began to nod and he told me to watch while he slept and then he laid down on the plank and was soon in the land of dreams.

"Before going to sleep he instructed me that if a small deer approached not to fool away time or waste ammunition on it. These instructions were strange to me for it was my understanding that we were to kill all the deer that came to the lick, big, little, old or young. He told me to let the little deer alone if they came and wait for a large one. I told him that I would obey him.

"I sat still for a long time and every now and then I could hear something drop on the ground at the root of the lick tree, which resembled small fragments of bark striking the leaves. I thought it was a ground squirrel up the tree pinching off bits of bark or wood. Of course, I did not think anything serious about it.

"As I sat and watched I saw a small deer walk to the lick and lower its head and begin tasting the salt. As I had told Perkins I would obey his advice because he was a good hunter, I refrained from shooting the little deer, though for all he had advised me against it, I found it was all I could do to restrain myself to keep from shooting at it. I looked at the deer and then listened to Perkins' loud snoring and thought certainly the little animal would take fright and run off. I expected to see a large deer come up to the little one, but none came in sight and my imagination began to dwindle down in regard to the load of deer hides and deer hams I would help Perkins carry off in the morning.

"I was somewhat discouraged, too, because Abe would not allow me to shoot at a little deer as well as a big one, when all at once something happened, for I was startled suddenly by seeing a long animal leap from the tree on the deer's back. I knew from a moment's thought that it was a panther. The poor deer jumped as far as it could with its unwelcome burden hanging on. The deer kicked, bucked and plunged but the ferocious beast still held on. The racket created by the struggling animals awoke Perkins, and forgetting the narrow bed he occupied, he raised up quickly, overbalanced, and went tumbling down to the ground.

"About the moment Perkins was aroused from his slumber the little deer was bleating piteously and was pulling the panther under the tree we were in and Perkins struck the ground, just in front of them, and before the man had time to think what caused him to fall from his roosting place, both animals ran over him.

"Perkins was as much surprised as he was scared and yelled for mercy while the beasts were passing over his prostrate form. I could not help laughing at Abe's terror and his hallooing in such a prayerful way. When the two animals had passed over Abe and from under the tree, I shot at the panther and it released the deer, and they both ran in different directions.

"After they were out of sight I spoke to Abe, who was yet lying on the ground, and said, 'Perkins, was that a big panther?' He quickly replied, 'Oh, Lord, yes, Bill, if you call twenty feet long a big one, it was.'

"Perkins, in his excitement and terror, was wallowing on the ground, trying to get up when he saw it, and of course, was not in a condition to answer as to the length of the animal and he just made a guess and it was a very lengthy estimation, too. With the exception of a few bruises Abe did not sustain injury in the fall from the tree.

"It is useless for me to inform you that we vacated that lick immediately and made for home, but by the following day we took courage and went back to the lick and following the direction the panther had gone, we found blood sprinkled along the way it went, which was unmistakable evidence that my bullet had inflicted a wound. We trailed it to a cave in the face of the Bull Bottom bluff. But we made no attempt to enter it or force the panther out.

"How the panther got up in the tree without us seeing it, I am not able to say, but my impression is that it was in the tree when we went there and was concealed among the limbs of the tree. Our anticipation of killing such a vast number of deer here fell so short that we did not visit this lick anymore for the purpose of killing deer. We should never count chickens before they hatch and hunters ought not to count deer hides before they kill the deer."

LITTLE ITEMS OF HUNTING [8:84]

MR. SIMON HERRON related the following little items of hunting to me one day in May, 1895.

"The biggest bunch of deer I ever saw was fifty, in the hills between Little North Fork and Big Creek. I also saw twenty deer together on two occasions. One of these bunches was in the glade where the Protem and Long's Ferry [road] passes through, before going down the hill into the hollow that leads to Elbow Creek in Taney County, Mo. The other bunch was in the creek bottom of Shoal Creek and just above where the town of Protem now is.

"The biggest deer hide I ever sold in market I took it off of a buck that I shot on the top of the McVey Bald Hill east of Big Creek in Ozark County, Mo. I sold this hide at Rolla, Mo.,[53] and received twenty cents per pound for it. The hide weighed fourteen and three-quarters pounds and brought me $2.95," said Mr. Herron.

Isaac Tabor lived on Big Creek in Taney County. "Deer was so numerous and gentle," said Mr. Tabor, "that they would venture close to the house. While I lived on the right prong of the creek I saw two deer feeding near the cabin. Taking my rifle down, I put it in shooting order. By this time the deer were side by side and close together, broadside toward the house. I blazed away at them both. They ran and I thought I had missed them but one of them got only thirty yards and fell. The other ran fifty yards and tumbled over, and I rejoiced at my lucky shot.

"One day while I was hunting stock on the head of the creek I met a fine lot of deer in one bunch. They were passing over an open ridge. I was afoot and had no gun with me. When I discovered the deer, I stopped and stood as still as a statue and watched them as they passed me. Some of them passed in thirty paces of me. I was so interested in taking items of their action as they went along that I never took time to count them accurately, but there was not less than fifty, if not more.

"On one occasion, while I was in the hills with gun and plenty of powder and balls, I stood behind a post oak tree and killed four fat bucks as fast as I could load and shoot. I was in the head of a gulch, and noticing a buck I shot it down. I thought it was alone but by the time I reloaded, another one walked up to the dead one. When I fired at it, it sprang away a few yards and fell.

"I thought that there were certainly no more deer nearby but when I finished reloading, two more advanced and I shot one of them. It jumped twice and fell. The other one darted away but seemingly it changed its mind after running a short distance, and came back to one of the dead ones and began smelling over it. I hurriedly reloaded and shot it and away it went and I thought I had missed, but it fell in a hundred yards of where the others lay.

"This was the greatest deer killing I ever got into. It seemed that the gulch had turned to bucks and I waited for others to show up, but not seeing anymore, I went to work and had a busy time dressing and carrying the hides and venison home."

Stories as Gleaned from an Early Resident [16:11]

"THE LARGEST NUMBER of deer I ever killed while standing at one spot is four," said Sam Carpenter. "This was on the head of Lower Caney Creek of Beaver. There were several deer in the bunch. The ones shot were a doe and three bucks. One of the bucks run a hundred yards before it fell.

"I remember shooting a deer on Elbow Creek that weighed one-hundred and forty pounds after it was dressed.[54] It was winter time and I took the deer to Springfield, Mo., and sold it and the hide for ten dollars. This was the largest deer I ever seen."

Forest Scenes That Were Funny [15:96]

PETER BAUGHMAN gives a funny story. "In the early Fifties," said he, "me and John Sutton, Isaac Carter and a man of the name of Napier, went on a camp hunt on Sugar Orchard Creek in Boone Co., Ark.

"One morning I and Napier left camp in one direction while the other two went an opposite way. Shortly after I and my partner left camp, we shot a deer. Just for fun we decided to wait until the animal had become rigid (the weather was cool) and then prop it up on its feet for our friends to shoot at it, if they came around that way. With this end in view we took a big laugh together and thought how bad our friends would feel when they found they were pumping lead into a dead deer. But it turned out different to our anticipations and it was well that we enjoyed a laugh before hand.

"After preparing the dead deer in a shape we wanted it, we went on and hunted all day without seeing another live deer. Near sunset, as we were walking along, we got bewildered.[55] We aimed to reach camp on the opposite side from the course we had left in the morning, but we came in on the same side without knowing it until afterward. As we went along we spied a deer standing perfectly still and we both shot at it, but the animal never moved.

"Napier says, 'Pete, what's the matter with our guns. Something's wrong with them or us.' Of course I agreed with him and we decided to reload the guns and aim more careful, and we took as accurate aim as our eyes would allow and fired simultaneously at the deer. The deer never flinched. We were astonished beyond measure. Directly Napier says, 'Pete, ain't that the same deer we propped up this morning to fool them other fellows?' and it flashed over me that what Napier said was true and I replied, 'Yes, it is.'

"We set a trap to catch the other boys and have walked into it ourselves. We promised each other that we would keep it to ourselves, but that night Napier said that it was too good to keep, and told it to the other fellows and we never like to have heard the last of shooting at the dead deer."

"One day in the early Fifties," said Sam Carpenter, "I and Tom Morrow were employed by Tom Scott to build a raft of cedar logs in the Horseshoe Bend of White River.[56] We depended on our rifles for meat and would hunt time about. One afternoon it was my turn to go out and lay in a supply of wild meat. After I had gone a short distance from camp I discovered two deer standing broadside to me. One was just on the opposite side from me. I shot at the nearest one to me and they both ran in opposite directions.

"Going up to where they stood, I found plenty of blood on the ground. I followed the trail of the one I shot at and found it dead seventy yards distant. For the sake of curiosity I went back to where the two deer had stood and discovered another deer lying dead a few yards away, and exactly on a line from where I shot from. I did not see but the two deer when I shot, and I did not see this one when I looked for blood stains. I had hit the deer I shot at just under the backbone and the bullet had sped on just over the other deer's back and struck the deer that I did not see when I shot."

A Hunter's Wife Saves Him from a Wounded Buck [9:19]

WE HAVE SAID elsewhere that Jimmie Tabor settled on Big Creek in Taney County, Mo., in 1835 and that he died December 22, 1895. In an interview with him a short while before his death and in relating reminiscences of the early days he said in answer to a question, "Did I ever get into a fight with a wounded buck?"

"No, I never did," said he, "I have had chances, but I was too careful for that. I never allowed a wounded buck an opportunity to fight me. I always refused to run to a buck after shooting it down unless I was perfectly satisfied it was not able to injure me, but I have known of a few fierce encounters between them and hunters. The worst one I remember now occurred on Pond Fork.

"Jimmie Friend was living on Pond Fork Creek in an early day. Friend's wife was named Jane but she was always known as 'Aunt Jennie.' Mr. Friend was a noted hunter and almost every settler in Ozark County, Mo., knew him. On one occasion while he lived on Pond Fork he went out to hunt and when he had went a quarter of a mile from his cabin he saw a fine buck and shot it. The deer fell but struggled and Friend ran to it with knife in hand to cut its throat.

"When he got in a few feet of it the buck attempted to get up and to prevent it rising he caught it by the beam of one horn with one hand and tried to stab it with the knife but the deer in its endeavors to rise on its feet kicked the knife from his hand and it fell several feet distant.

"The buck was reviving rapidly and a desperate struggle commenced and the enraged brute did all in its power to gore the hunter with its sharp horns. Mr. Friend exerted all his strength to prevent it. It was a furious battle. Though the buck was wounded and loosing blood, but Friend was growing weak from his exertions in contending against the deer faster than his forelegged adversary. Very soon after the knife fell from his hands he grabbed the beam of the other horn and held it with all his strength.

"Mr. Friend and the deer were both on their feet, but the angry animal surged and pawed so desperately that the hunter come near falling several times. At last he was about to give up for he realized that he could not hold out much longer. He was convinced that the furious animal would soon overcome him. With these serious thoughts looming up before him he thought of his wife, the dear good girl that he married in the southeast part of the state and both of which started to Little North Fork in a few days after they were married to locate them a home. He had just left her at the house. He would never see her again on earth. They had lived together many years and now to be parted in such an awful manner was appalling to think of.

"Then the thought came into his mind. Let me call for Jennie and she will hear me and come to my aid and kill the buck, and with a loud voice he called once for his faithful wife. She heard his despairing voice and knew something was wrong, and hardly knowing what she was doing she ran out of the house and snatched up the ax and sped off in the direction she heard him hollow. Before she had time to go more than a hundred yards she heard him call again and she answered and increased her speed and was soon on the scene.

"The buck was in the act of goring him for the man's strength was nearly gone. She took in the situation at once and needed no one to tell her what she ought to do, but with a strength and will saved her husband from death. She dealt it blow after blow with the ax until it fell and kept up the work until it was dead.

"The old hunter was overcome with joy and exhaustion and fell, but soon recovering he looked at the resistless form of the deer as it lay dead before him, then at his loving and affectionate wife as she stood and held the bloody ax in her hand and says, 'God bless you, Jennie. How grateful I feel for your timely aid. I never knew how well I loved you until this moment.'"

Encountering an Enraged Bear in a Cave and a Battle with a Wounded Buck [15:92]

UNCLE ABE [Abraham Cole],[57] in a reminiscent mood, says, "I will tell you now about a serious fight I had with a buck one day on Big Creek, where I lived at the next place below the John Morris land, where Dave Coiner now lives. This was away back in 1859.

"On the day mentioned, I shouldered my rifle and went into the forest in quest of game. I had proceeded only a short distance from my cabin when I noticed a big buck with large horns. He was standing still in the shade of a tree. I stopped and looked about for more deer but there were no other ones in sight.

"The animal, though seemingly on the alert, appeared to have not observed me. I pulled down on it and shot. When the bullet struck the beast it flew into a terrible fury, and seeing me now, it came toward me on a charge. The buck had a look of murder in his eyes. The angry deer was so near me that I had no opportunity to reload the rifle or scramble up a tree and felt like any other man when getting into a bad predicament.

"I well knew I was not able to outrun it and I clubbed my rifle and stood still. When within reach I struck it a hard blow, but did not stagger it. I was very stout and active then and contrived to dodge its sharp horns, and as I leaped about to avoid its sharp points, I kept hitting it sharp blows on the head with my gun. It was not long until the gun stock was shattered and the splinters flew in every direction. The combat lasted over fifteen minutes and we fought over twenty yards square.

"After the gun stock was broken I used the barrel. The barrel alone was much handier than with the stock attached to it, in a hand to hand fight.[58] After I had dealt the buck several blows it began to weaken, but it kept pitching at me and I had to jump around pretty lively to prevent it striking me with its sharp prongs of horns.

"I had worked so fast in defense that I was getting greatly wearied, but I never stopped hitting it blow after blow on its head and body until it sank down and was not able to give me further trouble. I cut its throat with a small pocket knife and watched it kick until its life was gone.

"After I knew it was dead, I sat down for a long resting spell, for I felt that I was in need of it. The flesh was so badly bruised where I struck it with the gun that it was not fit for use. This was the only hard fight I ever had with a buck and I do not relish the thought of coming in contact with another one," said Mr. Cole as he finished his account of the battle.

CROOKED CREEK AND INCIDENTS OF OLD TIME HUNTING IN THIS VALLEY [7:82]

THE VALLEY OF CROOKED CREEK [Marion County, Arkansas] in the early settlement of it was a famous rendevous for the old time hunter. Numbers of exciting scenes of chasing wild game have been witnessed on this stream and its tributary branches. Here as elsewhere in the Ozarks the wild bucks met each other, fought and locked horns and either died in that condition or was found and killed by the hunter.

Mr. Peter Baughman, an early resident on this water course, gave me two accounts of finding two pair of bucks locked by their horns in the old time hunting days of this locality. He said that the Tom Young Hollow was one of his favorite places to find deer.

"In this hollow," said he, "I discovered two pair of bucks with their horns locked together. The first set was found one morning at break of day. I had went into the hollow to watch for deer when I heard a noise a short distance off which I was at a loss to understand what caused it. I could hear something crash together which was repeated frequently. Though it was not yet daylight but I become so interested to find out the cause of it that I went toward where the racket emanated from and found that it was two bucks engaged in a desperate fight.

"But just before I got to them their horns become interlocked and then they both exerted their strength to get separated. Their struggles were frightful but they were not able to force themselves apart.

"I was more interested in the hides and meat of the two animals than I was to watch them fight and I cut their struggles short by shooting one of the bucks down and reloading my gun I shot the other one and saved the meat and hides of both. Each deer had five points on each beam.

"The other bucks were found nearly three-quarters of a mile from where I discovered the other pair. A snow an inch deep lay on the ground and as I went up this same hollow I found where a heavy object had just been dragged across the hollow. I knew in a moment what it meant. A battle had been fought between two bucks. Their horns were locked. One was dead and the live one had been dragging the dead one in the snow.

"On looking in the direction the dead buck had been pulled along I seen a deer standing with its head down and hung to the dead deer and I started on toward it and when I approached within a few paces of it I shot it down and as the hide on the other buck was not spoiled I saved the hides of both. A few days after this I went back into this hollow and carried the two pair of heads and horns home and kept them several years."

Ferocity of the Antlered Monarchs While Fighting [8:12]

THE FRIEND BROTHERS, Steve and Jim, sons of Peter Friend, give an account of seeing two bucks engaged in a desperate combat on Cedar

Creek one mile below the present site of Dugginsville in Ozark County, Mo.

"They made a terrible noise clashing their horns together. There were other deer standing near the fighting bucks which seemed surprised as the battle went on and reminded the men of human spectators when they were viewing anything interesting to their eyes.

"But when we advanced up nearer the fighting animals these deer ran away. But the two buck were too busy to pay any attention to us and went on with the fight several minutes more, when they separated and ran beyond our view.

"While they were battling together they would temporarily separate at times seven or eight yards distant, then clash together again. They were active and fought rapidly. One was much larger than the other. The large one whipped the smaller one and when he wheeled to run the big one gave pursuit. We did not follow them. This occurred in 1871."

"Many years ago," says Mike Yocum, son of Asa Yocum, "I saw two savage bucks on the river bluff below the Panther Bottom. I was afoot horse hunting and heard a terrible racket on the bluff mentioned and on approaching the spot where I heard the noise I discovered two bucks engaged in a mighty conflict. I stood and watched them intently.

"Very soon their horns become locked fast together. The animals exerted all the strength in their power in trying to get apart. They would surge, pull, twist, rear and plunge, run up against trees, run over saplings and would have run over me if I had stood in their way.

"After I viewed them for about an hour they continued to force themselves apart. Each buck now seemed willing to quit and when they found they were free, away they both went in opposite directions. This occurred in 1867. The scene was just over the line in what is now Cedar Creek township in Marion County," said Mr. Yocum.

George Billings gives the following account. "One day," said he, "while I and Eli Welch were hunting on Sister Creek south of White River and as we went on over the rough ground we separated to get together again before night.

"While I was alone my attention was called to a loud noise up on a steep hillside above me. The sound resembled two bulls fighting, but I was satisfied it was bucks. I soon got in sight of them and sure enough it proved to be bucks. The combat was desperate. Their ferocity astonished me, and I viewed them as they put forth their great strength with much interest. The clashing of their horns together sounded loud. As they fought they worked down the hillside.

"At times one would get the advantage and would turn his adversary almost a summersault but he would up and come again as lively as before. After a while one of the bucks backed up against a small tree and braced himself and the efforts of his enemy to push him away were fruitless. The buck seemed determined to hold the ground here at this tree.

"I shot one of the bucks down and after he fell the other seemed highly delighted for from his actions he thought he had vanquished his enemy and acted more like a rooster exulting over his fallen antagonist. After I reloaded my gun I shot at him but missed. But a second shot brought him down by the side of the other buck.

"By this time my companion joined me and we dressed the deer and carried them home. Both were in splendid order and each carried five points on each beam. One deer weighed one-hundred-five [pounds] and the other one-hundred-six net." This occurred in Marion County, Arkansas.

John Mosely,[59] the old timer of Taney County, Mo., furnished an account of seeing two bucks fight during the Civil War which he told in the following way.

"I and Bill Teague were out on the Bald Hills of Cedar Creek which flows into the river below Beaver [Creek]. We had separated and had just passed out of sight of each other when I spied two bucks fighting on a bald hill over a quarter of a mile distant from me. Their actions indicated that they were trying to kill each other. I could distinctly hear the clashing of their horns when they would run together after separating a moment or so.

"After I had watched their fast maneuvers and listened at the noise they made for a short while I concluded to approach nearer and kill them both for a good fat buck was worth a great deal in the way of food in war times. The meat was worth more to me and my family than the curiosity of seeing them fight.

"When I got in shooting distance I aimed at one and fired but the animals were in such a terrible motion and as the battle went on I supposed my bullet never touched the buck or he would have been apt to have shown some effect of it. I shot the second time but the fight went on for it appeared that they dodged this bullet, too. A third shot was fired on them but the result was the same as before. Of course, I was excited and liable to make a miss shot if they had been the size of elephants.

"During the fight the bucks changed around so much that it kept me on the run to keep in rifle range of them. After two more shots I could tell no difference in their movements. I was wasting too much ammunition for nothing, for powder and lead was then worth something too. But I decided that if they were able to continue the fight I could furnish ammunition in shooting at them so I reloaded my gun again but when I reached down in the shot pouch for the cap box it was gone.[60] I had lost it since I had reloaded the last time.

"I laid my gun down in the grass and commenced crawling around on my hands and knees in search of the percussion caps. At this moment the bucks quit fighting and one of them seeing me crawling in the grass come up in ten paces of me to see what I resembled. He stopped and took a long look at me. His hair was ruffled and the beast seemed mad.

"I was not mad but I was scared. I thought he meant to attack me. I wanted to be a way off somewhere else but I had no hope of getting away without permission from that buck. I would have climbed a tree but there were no trees near me. I dared not run for I knew if he gave pursuit he would overhaul me in a few moments.

"The suspense was trying on my nerves. If an artist could have happened along then with his camera and took our pictures the scene would have been amusing but it was not funny to me then. I kept my position and waited to see what the deer was going to do and wondered how long before he would pitch at me and gore me to death.

"Just imagine yourself in my place and you have an idea how I felt. But the fierce looking beast did not move any closer to me, but he was a furious looking animal and had fight in his eyes. I remained as motionless as possible and kept my eyes on him all the time, but it was not long before I heard the footsteps of some other animal approaching and I glanced my eyes toward the direction of the noise and peered through the opening in the grass and my blood almost froze at the sight of the other buck coming toward me. I thought now if one did not do me up the other would be sure to. I give up for lost, all hope of life was gone.

"As the seconds flitted away I could hear my heart throbs. It was heart trouble brought on through fear of an attack from one or both of those horned beasts. But to my joy when the other buck had walked up close to me the other attacked him and they engaged in another fierce conflict.

"Now was my time and I made good use of it by quickly rising on my feet and fleeing away from there. But when I reached a safe distance I halted and viewed the animals fight again.

"While the combat was going on my companion joined me again and after I had related to him the ill luck I had in shooting at them and the amusing adventure I had with them he intimated that it would be no trouble to him to kill them both so advancing up in fifty yards of the fighting animals he blazed away at one with the same success I had. After reloading he shot again with no better luck.

"This was seven shots in all and not a scrap of venison in our possession. After the bucks had fought a short while longer they separated and both ran off. After a close and tedious search we found my cap box.

"Then Bill Teague says, 'John, I am bound to have a taste of one of them bucks,' and he put his dog on the trail of one of them and the dog run it into Beaver Creek and Joe Mosely, a son of mine, shot and killed the deer and we all feasted on venison while it lasted. If I ever witness another encounter between bucks I want to be up a tree and not on the ground," said Uncle John as he ended his story.

FINDING A MAD STONE IN A CHUNK OF COOKED VENISON [7:78]

THE AUTHOR DOES NOT claim to know anything about the virtue of the so called mad stone.[61] Many people believe that it possesses the power to neutralize the poison introduced into the system when bitten by a mad dog if properly applied to the wounds.

It is possible that if the stone is applied immediately after the wound was inflicted some of the poison might be sucked out but it is not reasonable to think that a case affected with genuine hydrophobia can be cured by means of an application of the mad stone after the poison had absorbed into the circulation.

But we did not start out to discuss the curative properties of the mad stone if it had any but to state how one was found once, the story of which was told me by Ira J. David, who said that Sam Baty, while hunting one day in a hollow that leads into the Eleven Points Creek in Oregon County, Mo., five miles above Thomasville,[62] he saw a large deer that was between one and two years old and of the common color which he shot at eight times with a rifle that carried a half ounce ball before he killed it.

He carried the deer home and after removing the hide he cut the meat into chunks and his wife cooked some of it in a big pot without cutting up the venison any finer. After it was cooked his wife placed the meat on a big dish on the table and while they were at supper Mr. Baty found a hard substance in one of the chunks of meat that was two and one-half inches in length and near an inch thick. There were small pimples or cells all over it.

Not understanding the nature of it Mr. Baty carried it to Thomasville and showed it to three physicians there of the name of Lorants, Griffy and Cantrel and they all pronounced it a mad stone and offered him $200 for it. But Baty refused to sell it at that price and let Newel Baty have it and he carried it to the Indian Territory with him." 🕮

Reminiscences of a Pioneer of Big Creek, Taney County, Mo. [15:4]

"I HAD HEARD hunters talk of seeing white deer in the woods, but I never seen one until one day I and John Herron went over to the head of Shoal Creek to hunt a few days," said Isaac Tabor.

"We camped at a spring where Nelson Southworth settled later on. Some two-hundred yards from the spring I saw a white deer and shot it. After carrying it to the spring we removed its hide and entrails and cut the latter open to attract wild bees and found a hard substance in the stomach, which proved to be a stone-like formation, nearly two inches in length, one inch broad and one-half inch thick. One end of it [was] slightly tapering and very fine cells or pimples were all over it. It was a peculiar formation to be found on the inside of an animal.

"Thinking it of no value, we tossed it aside. Sometime afterward I gave a description of it to Peter Marsh and he told me that it was a mad stone and offered me $5.00 for it, if I could find it again. My energies were so stimulated by the price offered me for the stone that I visited this same spring on several occasions and searched carefully for it but never recovered it.[63] The deer was a doe and quite a small one. 🕮

How a Buck Deer Slayed a Rattlesnake [7:75]

MANY ARE THE STORIES told by hunters of seeing deer destroy serpents. In some cases there was only one deer present which took longer time to end the life of the writhing reptile, but in every case as far as I have obtained information bearing on this subject the deer whether alone or in groups never left the victim until it was dead, or so near it that it was not possible for it to revive.

The sight of witnessing these beautiful creatures killing serpents was an interesting forest scene to the old time settler and hunter. The impression made on the mind of the observer was never forgot until his eyes were closed in death.

An incident of this kind was told me by Mr. Alf Hampton, son of Zeke Hampton, who lived many years on George's Creek, five miles north of Yellville, Ark. He said that his grandfather, Dave Hampton, went out into the hills of George's Creek one day alone to kill a deer, when he noticed a buck acting like he was deranged.

"It would run and close its feet together and jump onto something in the grass. When the deer would light on the ground it would bound off like a rubber ball. Grandfather said that he was at a loss to understand what the deer was doing.

"After watching it some time the buck at last seemed to have completed the job he was working at and run off, and my grandfather said that he went to the spot where the deer had been so busily engaged to see whether it was really crazy or had killed something and found a common sized rattlesnake[64] with the hide peeled off nearly all over it by the deer's hoofs and was just able to wriggle its tail and was soon entirely dead. My grandfather said that he was so deeply impressed in watching the deer that he made no attempt to shoot it."

DEER KILLING SNAKES [9:47]

JERRY HUNT, a resident on Big Creek in Taney County, Mo., informed me that one day while he was hunting in the John Morris hollow that flows into Big Creek from the east side he saw a spike buck running back and forth with its feet closed together and jumping stiff legged.

"At a certain spot the deer would leap high and after alighting would leap as far as it could then stop and wheel around and repeat. I stood still and watched the deer's movements a few minutes and I pronounced it a crazy buck, and I shot it down. On going to where it lay I discovered a black snake[65] lying in the grass badly disabled. The mystery of the deer's foolish actions were now explained for it was killing the snake. I finished what life was left in the snake with a stick."

Old Uncle Jim Barnette said that on one occasion while he was hunting on the west side of Little North Fork he saw four deer kill a rattlesnake on a ridge one and one-half miles above the mouth of Pond Fork. The deer just before leaping on the snake would close their legs together and after alighting they would instantly spring away. Only one deer at a time would hit the snake. The reptile was cut nearly to pieces with the deer's feet.

"Just up on the point of the hill between the main hollow of Cedar Creek and the hollow that the main road passes up from Dugginsville to Pontiac in Ozark County, Mo., and in sight of the former named hamlet," says Henry Grace, "I seen a deer kill a rattlesnake.

"I did not understand what the deer was doing until I heard the serpent singing.[66] The deer would stomp its forefeet against the ground, then leap on the snake and jump away as far as it could, then turn and repeat. Finally the deer quit and walked off a few yards and stopped and I shot it down, and when I walked up to where it did the work with the snake which was entirely dead. The deer had cut the middle part of the serpent's body into mincemeat with its hoofs."

"In the year 1856," said William C. Patton (who afterwards went blind and is dead now), "I was hunting horses in the hills of Hampton Creek, a tributary of Crooked Creek in Marion County, Ark. I was horseback and as I rode along I saw three deer acting queer. They would run one at a time stiff legged with hair turned up and leap on something in the grass and then spring off. Then they would return and repeat.

"I was much interested to know what the deer were up to and stopped and sat on my horse until the three deer had become quiet and started off. I then rode to the spot and was astonished to find a big rattlesnake beat to pieces almost by the deers' hoofs. Though there was a little life about the snake but it was too nigh gone to ever bother any more deer," said this old timer.

Just over the line in Ozark County, Mo., between Big Creek and the Panther Bottom was once a small pinery where in the latter Fifties Martin Johnson and others camped and sawed a lot of pine lumber with a whip saw.[67] About twenty-five years after the close of the Civil War some parties erected a saw mill at a spring in Pine Hollow and used up all the available pine timber here.

Pew C. Anderson said that one day in 1852 while he was hunting in this same pinery, he noticed a deer acting in a singular way. The animal would run and jump high with its hair standing straight out. When it alighted it would stamp its forefeet hard against the ground, jump forward a few yards, stop and look back, then it would wheel around and repeat which was done several times. At last the deer left and Mr. Anderson said to satisfy his curiosity he went to the spot to investigate as to the cause of the deer's strange actions "and there lay the largest rattlesnake dead I ever saw," said he.

⚹ TALES OF WOLVES ⚹

Editors' note: At the time of settlement there were three species of "wolves" in the White River country. These were the gray, or timber, wolf, *Canis lupus;* the red wolf, *Canis rufus;* and the coyote, *Canis latrans.* To the layman, the red wolf is practically indistinguishable from the coyote. Both are similar in color, although the red wolf typically has a more reddish cast, and there is a black color phase in red wolves that is rare in the coyote. Today, it is likely that only the coyote inhabits the Ozarks. The last authentic specimen of a red wolf was a small female taken in Taney County in 1950. Turnbo's tales of wolves seem to be entirely about the gray wolf, which is now extinct in the region. Turnbo sometimes stressed the color of wolves, as though that might indicate a different type. Such is not the case; what he described was the gray wolf or timber wolf.

NARROW ESCAPE FROM A SAVAGE PACK OF WOLVES [11:1]

ONE OF THE NOTED SETTLERS of Ozark County, Mo., was Leven T. Green, who located on the east bank of Little North Fork one half a mile above the mouth of Little Creek in 1837. I am told that two years after this Noah Mahan settled the land where Thornfield now is. Mr. Green had several grown sons, the names of which were George, Jesse, Phillip, Tom (Pleasant Thomas) and Ben.

Green and his sons were famed hunters and always kept on hand a supply of bear meat, jerked venison[68] and wild honey for the use of themselves and families. Though bread was scarce yet these old timers endured all the hardships subject to frontier life and fared as sumptuously as the wild woods afforded and were happy.

Leven Green was a Methodist preacher and used his influence among sinners and prevailed on them to repent. He would plead with them in an earnest tone to turn from their evil ways. His exhortations were as strong among the wicked as his ambition was in attacking and slaying a fat bear. On his arrival here the country was so thinly settled then that there were no schoolhouses or other public buildings where the people could meet for worship, but Green would hold meetings at the settlers' houses.

If he had an appointment to preach at a cabin some distance off to be filled at 11 a.m. of a Sunday he would rise early on Sunday morning and after partaking his morning meal of wild meat and honey he would take his rifle down from the rack and examine it well to see if it was in good shape for killing game. If so he would shoulder it up and with his family Bible and the old fashioned hymn book under his arm he would start through the wild woods to the place where [he] had announced he would preach that day. If he met any deer on the way he would kill them if he could and remove the hides and carry the hides with him. Sometimes it was late before his arrival but the audience knew he would make his appearance sooner or later if nothing occurred to prevent him and would wait patiently for the hour of his coming. On reaching the place of appointment, he would leave the rifle and deer hides in the chimney corner, then go into the cabin and prepare himself to deliver an exhortation to the congregation and persuade sinners to turn to the Lord and lead a better life. At the conclusion of his discourse he was ready to pick up his gun again and return back home through the woods and kill more deer and add more hides to his Sunday forenoon killing. Mr. Green's sons were as equally skilled in killing game as their father was.

The Greens were as expert in killing wolves as they were in slaying deer and bear and hunting bee trees. They shot them, caught them in pen traps, steel traps, and poisoned them and destroyed whelps until it would seem that there was not a live wolf left to tell the doleful tale of their destruction, but instead of being exterminated they appeared to increase in numbers as fast as they were thinned out.

Phillip Green [a grandson of Leven T. Green] relates the following account of an encounter his father had one day with wolves while he was out searching for young wolves and came near losing his life among them. Mr. Green says that he has heard his father tell the story repeatedly and "I will give it to you like he told it to me," said he.

"One day while my grandfather Leven T. Green lived on the old farm that he settled in Ozark County in 1837, my father and three of his brothers, George, Jesse and Ben Green, agreed to go out together on a raid against the wolves and kill as many young ones and old ones as they could find. They all left one morning with eight dogs. Each man carried his trusty rifle, plenty of ammunition and a hunting knife.

"After they had traveled a few miles from home the party divided in order to make a wide search for the wolves. Two dogs followed each man.

Sometime after the men had separated and while my father was looking among some shelving rocks for wolf beds, his attention was aroused by a disturbance in front of him and on looking in that direction he was almost struck dumb with astonishment at seeing the two dogs bounding toward him closely pursued by a pack of wolves which proved to be twenty in number.

"Father stood with his gun on his shoulder forgetting everything but the sight of the rushing wolves and when the dogs reached the spot where he was standing, the wolves overhauled the dogs and caught one of them at his feet. The other dog never halted but passed on as fast as he could go and made his escape. The whole pack stopped here and while the poor dog was yelling with pain and distress it seemed that every wolf in the bunch tried to get at him, and with piteous cries [the dog] was soon torn to pieces.

"'I was so terror stricken,' said my father, 'that I seemed to be stuck fast to the ground and as I stood there in the midst of the savage pack with my gun on my shoulder and my hunting knife in the scabbard the wolves fought desperately over the remnants of the dog. They fought all around me and some of them in their frenzy pushed others against my legs. What prevented them from taking hold of me and rending me in pieces like they did the dog I have never been able to account for, but they appeared to be so crazy for the dog's blood that they apparently gave me no attention for the time.

"'When they had fought one another so hard and gulped down the last bit of the dog I came to my senses and realized my dreadful peril. A tree stood in a few feet of me and I dropped my gun and sprang to it and pulled myself up it as hurriedly as lay in my power.

"'My movements attracted their attention and part of the wolves with fearful growls and angry snarls rushed to the foot of the tree in an instant and before I was out of reach of them one of the wolves leaped up and caught me by the foot, but fortunately my moccasins were large and fitted my feet loosely. When the wolf grabbed my foot with its teeth I had reached the first limb of the tree and I held to it with all the strength I possessed, but for all this the stout beast pulled my leg so hard that my body give down a few inches, but I still held fast to the limb.

"'Others of the pack were leaping up trying to get hold of my legs. I was frantic with fear and dread of being jerked down and torn to pieces. I kicked and hallooed and did not quit kicking until I freed my foot from the wolf's mouth, but the desperate animal pulled the moccasin off of my foot. Then followed a fight over the moccasin which they tore into shoe strings before they ceased to fight over it. My foot was not hurt bad for the wolf had took hold of the moccasin in a shape that the beast's teeth did not penetrate my foot.

"'The tree was of fair size but when I kicked loose from the wolf I did not quit climbing until I reached the topmost limbs. The wolves seeing that they were beat out of a taste of human flesh and blood set up a direful yelping and howling and I kept up a continual shouting for help. As it happened, my brothers were in hearing distance when the racket began and they hurried to me as fast as they could run and soon were together and they said they were nearly out of breath when they came in sight and seeing me up a tree with a big pack of wolves under it almost paralized them.

"'But knowing I was safe they took time for a short rest and keeping the six dogs with them, they now ventured up in rifle shot of the wolves and began pouring the lead in among them. Several of them were shot down and the remaining ones would leap on them and fight over the dead and dying wolves until their bodies were torn into mincemeat. It was a scene that only old settlers can describe.

"'When my three brothers had materially decreased the number in the pack they encouraged the dogs and they dashed at the remaining wolves and they took fright and scampered away.

"'When the men and dogs reached the foot of the tree I descended to the ground and picked up my rifle which was covered with blood from the wolves that had been shot and torn into fragments by the others. We were almost positive that there were young wolves nearby and after we had searched for them a short while we found a bed full of very small ones in the hollow of a large white oak tree, which we soon disposed of. This was the worst trouble I ever got into with wolves,' said my father as he told this story with a shudder."

Catching Wolves in Steel Traps [14:81]

MR. FIE SNOW, who was among the earliest residents of Little North Fork and who was a stepson of Jimmie Forrest, tells this about wolves in this section during the early days.

"Jimmie Forrest caught great numbers of wolves in steel traps and pen traps.[69] Wolves were noisy and troublesome all over Ozark County. I recollect on one occasion in 1844, I and Bob Forrest rode to Pine Creek, which flows into Bryant Fork, and stopped at sunset and camped in a rough hollow. We tied our horses to trees. The weather was cold and we soon made a rousing fire and began preparing our supper, and while we were broiling meat, wolves collected all around us and did some terrible howling. A few of them approached in a hundred yards of camp. We had no dog with us or no doubt they would have given us a closer interview.

"In a few yards of our fire was a small sink hole in the ground that had been caused by a forest fire burning down a dead tree and burning out the roots of it and we had our fire built against this log. After supper we fed our horses and spread our bearskin down in the sink hole and covered our bodies with our home woven blankets made of sheep's wool, but the wolves annoyed us so that we could only catch a few short naps. Some of them crept up during the night to where we had eaten our supper and stole the remnants we had left.

"On the following morning I and Bob reached the conclusion that there were too many wolves on Pine Creek for our comfort and we returned back home without killing a deer.

"Going back to the time when we caught so many wolves in traps, I want to tell you of an incident of how a single wolf became so famous," said Mr. Snow.

"One night in 1834, my stepfather set a steel trap on Barren Fork, one-half of a mile above the mouth of the creek. Sometime during the night a wolf got in to it and was caught by the middle toe of one forefoot. The wolf was gone but the toe was found in the jaws of the trap. The toe was either pinched off by the trap or the wolf had jerked it off. This wolf's tracks were afterward seen here and there all over the country between Little North Fork and Beaver Creeks, and from the former named stream to Bryant's Fork. The imprint of its feet in the mud or snow showed that the middle toe of the right forefoot was missing. No other wolf's track, as far as known, suited this description.

"The animal was of common size but it was an uncommon mean wolf and killed large numbers of hogs and sheep, but it was several years after it had lost its toe before it began to prove so destructive to domesticated animals. Almost every settler made some effort to kill it but failed so far. Then someone wrote a contract that if anyone succeeded in destroying the life of this wolf after the date of this writing, to a certain date in the future, and all signed their names to the document. It was so worded that each man agreed to pay the slayer of the wolf one dollar in silver or gold, provided he produced unquestionable evidence that it was the identical wolf sought for, but the tormenting beast remained monarch of the forest and survived the expiration of the writing several years. But he finally had to give in, which came about in this way.

"One day in 1857, while Bill Lord was hunting in a valley known then as Bryant's Fork Hollow, that leads into Barren Fork, he saw a big black wolf standing in range of his rifle and he shot and killed it. The animal proved to be the hated wolf. At least the middle toe of the right foot was missing and no more wolf tracks of this description was seen after the death of this wolf. Mr. Lord did not receive any reward except the scalp which he sold for a good price. The wolf met his death in a few miles of where he had lost his toe twenty-three years previous."[70]

An Amusing Scene While Husband and Wife Are Escaping from Wolves [10:58]

ONE OF THE MOST amusing accounts of an experience with wolves is the following, the story of which was furnished me by an old settler of Ozark County, Mo., who has been dead a number of years. This old pioneer said that it was true and that the incident occurred when wolves were more plentiful in southern Missouri than people. He said that a man of the name of Owen Kersey lived on the opposite side of Little North Fork from the mouth of Otter Creek which empties into Little North Fork three miles above the present town of Thornfield.

Mr. Owen Kersey's wife was a tall, slender woman and very active and was not so easy excited as her husband was. At least she was able to control her presence of mind while Kersey would entirely lose himself in a close place.

One day soon after they had settled on their claim, they had an experience with some wolves that was so amusing and ended so funny that Owen Kersey's wife grew weary in telling the story of it so often and laughed about it until she said her sides ached. "Here is the way it occurred," said the old timer. "Kersey owned one horse which he plowed and went to mill on. When he was not using the horse he would put a bell on him and turn him out on the range until he needed him. As the wild pasture was so fine on Otter Creek, Kersey would keep the horse on this stream where along the main creek the horse made his grazing grounds.

"One day in the spring of 1849 after the timber had donned its summer dress, Owen needed the horse to lay off corn rows with to plant his crop and he and wife went up Otter Creek to hunt for him. The man had no gun but they took their dog along for company. The tender grass was fine and nutritious and as the horse had been out several days he was getting fat and sleek.

"People did not break their ground then unless it was a new clearing and Kersey's land was second year's and the man did not need the horse until he wanted to go to mill or lay off corn ground and for this reason the horse had been allowed to run out a long time on the range, and Owen Kersey and his wife rejoiced that their horse was good and stout to pull the plow along in the rooty land and that his provender was no expense to them.

"The couple were glad they possessed a little home in the Ozark hills where they could breathe the balmy air and drink of the cool bubbling water and kill the fat bucks and big turkey gobblers. They were enjoying themselves among the beautiful hills, dales and clear running streams. As they passed on up the creek the dog appeared to enjoy himself too, by running and playing ahead of them. When the man and his wife got in hearing of the horse bell the dog was one hundred and fifty yards in advance of them. They caught a glimpse of him every now and then as he trotted through the pretty green grass.

"The man was in no hurry and he and wife walked on slowly toward where the horse was feeding. Just at this moment they heard the dog yelping in distress. Stopping to ascertain the cause of their dog's trouble, they saw the dog running toward them, hotly pursued by three wolves. The dog did its utmost to outrace them and the vicious beasts were exerting their best running power to catch him. They were so near his heels that there was small space between the foremost wolf's nose and the dog's heels. If they caught him it was goodby poor canine.

"Kersey and his wife was terrified like the dog was and they both made for the nearest tree which was a slippery elm. The woman reached the tree first and clasping her arms around the body of the tree pulled herself up out of danger and seated herself on a small limb. The man was making all haste in climbing too but he was not as nimble as the woman was and not so lucky either for in his rush and excitement he grabbed at a dead limb which snapped off at the trunk of the tree and down went Kersey sprawling on the ground.

"The wolves reached the foot of the tree just as the man started to fall and at the moment the three bloodthirsty wolves caught the helpless dog to rend him to pieces, Mr. Kersey was precipitated on the wolves' backs.

"It was hard to distinguish now which was the worst scared, wolves, dog, or man. The wolves darted away, two of them ran off one way and the other in an opposite direction. The dog fled down the creek toward home. The man lost his presence of mind and did not notice the wolves disappear and imagined they were pulling him to pieces and he yelled lustily for his wife to drive them away and save his life from the ravenous animals.

"His wife was scared too but she kept her senses and saw the wolves run off and knowing her husband was in no danger now laughed outright until she came near falling out of the tree. Kersey continued to call loudly for his wife to come and save his flesh and bones from the teeth of the impudent beasts and she answered by laughing the louder. But very soon she told him to hush his mouth and quit acting the fool and get up for the wolves were gone.

"At this Kersey became more quiet and raised up and looked about him as if bewildered and seeing the coast was clear was overjoyed to find that the wolves were gone and he had made a miraculous escape as he termed it. After his wife had come down out of the tree Kersey told her they must not take time to catch the horse, but 'we must hurry back home to escape a second attack from these terrible animals.'

"His wife tried to persuade him to not go back until they had secured the horse but the man was bent on going at once and says, 'Let us go now,' and he started off and the woman followed. He led the way down the creek to his cabin at no slow gait and believed that he had avoided another charge from the daring wolves."

When the old timer closed his story he remarked that Kersey was always reluctant about alluding to this incident but his wife recited the account of it frequently and vouched for its truthfulness.

Battle Between Wolves and a Negro Man [11:41]

ABRAHAM COLE was a resident of Taney County, Mo., from 1858 until his death March 1, 1899. He lies buried in the cemetery at Protem. He was born in Meade County, Ky., in 1821 and was seventy-nine years old at his death.

He came to Missouri while a young man, and after rambling a few years he married and settled in Ozark County fifteen miles west of Rock Bridge. Here at the mouth of Barren Fork of Little North Fork he lived from 1855 to 1858, and then he settled a claim on Big Creek in Taney County where he was living when the war broke out. He enlisted in the U. S. Army and served until the end of the war. Mr. Cole was a conservative man in both political and religious matters.

In recounting old occurrences of settlers with the wild beasts of the forest, Mr. Cole tells the following details of a combat between a negro man and a lot of wolves.

In narrating the story, Mr. Cole said that John Miller lived a few miles west of Rock Bridge on a ridge or divide. He was an early settler in that locality and owned a negro man named Bill, who was a robust fellow, obedient and kind and well thought of by those who were acquainted with him.

One of Miller's neighbors by the name of Joe Piland lived two miles distant. Joe was a brother of William Piland, who during the turbulent days of the great war commanded a company of cavalry soldiers in the union service and was known as an honest man and a distinguished officer.

When "hog killing time" came around in 1857, Joe Piland requested Miller to allow his negro man to help him butcher his porkers; the request was kindly granted. There were several big fat hogs to kill, dress and salt, and Miller and the negro labored hard all day and until after night before the job was completed.

The negro had instructions from his master to return back home that night and he started on his way home. He carried in his hand a long, sharp butcher knife that he had been using that day. The night was dark and the trail dim, but the negro had traveled over it many times and knew it well and he managed to sing and whistle and stay in the trail, too.

He had gone a mile, when suddenly his merry music was cut short by hearing wolves howl just ahead of him. Then he thought, oh, what a plight. I am in my clothes all covered with hog's blood. He stopped and drew a deep breath and conjectured whether the wolves would attack him or not. In a few moments while he was standing there the wolves began to collect behind him and he would not go forward or retrace his steps, but decided to await developments. He did not have long to stand to find out their intentions, for the blood thirsty animals scented the blood on his clothes and surrounded him, and threatened to attack him at once.

He had never thought of ascending a tree until at this juncture and seeing several trees standing in a few yards of him he jumped for the smallest one and began to hustle up it, but before he got high enough for safety, two of the wolves caught him by his shoes and trousers and jerked him down to the ground. Fortunately he alighted on his feet.

Then a terrible struggle ensued between the wolves and terror stricken man. The negro after desperate work kicked his assailants loose, and with his back against the tree, went to work with the butcher knife. The wolves leaped at his legs, body and throat, snapping, snarling and growling, and he kicked them with his feet and stabbed them with his knife.

The battle was desperate and both man and beasts put on a lively stir. The negro did not know how many were in the pack—he was too busy to count their dim outlines in the dark. He cut and slashed until he saw two of them lying still at his feet. How many were wounded he was unable to ascertain, but there must have been several.

He was worsting the blood thirsty creatures for they commenced to give back and retreated twenty or more yards from him. Now was his opportunity, and with a glance of his eyes up the tree and back where the wolves were growling, and with a quick stout pull, sprung up the tree again, and succeeded in getting out of their reach. The wolves darted back to the foot of the tree in a moment. To his surprise when they dashed up he did not hear them fight over the two dead wolves.

The weather was moderately cool, and when the warmth of his exertions and excitement began to cool, he grew chilly and then cold. The wolves gave him colder comfort by remaining under the tree until daylight, and then they scampered away. The negro gave them plenty of time to get off some distance before he ventured down, and that was sunrise.

When he slid down to the ground and after a short examination of the dead wolves and the blood sprinkled on the dead grass and leaves from the wounded ones, he scalped the dead beasts and left and started the free circulation of blood in his system while he was running home.

Torturing Wolves by Flaying Them Alive [28:33]

THOUGH INHUMANE and cruel but a few settlers of Little North Fork resorted to removing the hides of wolves while the animals were alive. It was said that the depredations of wolves were so terrible on stock that the pioneers did the acts of savages and in some cases inflicted the most cruel treatment on the ravenous beast they could invent in payment (return) for the destruction of property.

Mr. Elias Keesee told of two incidents of this kind. He said: "We settlers of Little North Fork in Ozark County, Mo., did all in our power to destroy as many wolves as possible. These animals made awful inroads on sheep, hogs, calves and young colts and our temper was irritated to the highest pitch. Sometimes when we captured a wolf alive we confined it and took off its hide.

"On one occasion when I was a small boy my father [Paton Keesee] caught a big wolf in a steel trap. It would show the animal too much mercy to slay it out right and we determined to punish it with the most cruel torture I could think of. Leaving the wolf fast in the trap I sought the assistance of Ben Risley and Levi Graham which was willingly given. With chains, ropes and stout thongs of dressed buck hide we tied the animal so secure that it could neither bite, kick or hardly move and with sharp knives we proceeded to remove its hide. This was horrible and was more like the work of savages, but we had been annoyed so much by them that we showed as little mercy toward wolves as the wild Indians did to white people living on the frontiers in the years gone by.

"The beast lived through the terrible ordeal and when we loosed it and turned it free it got on its feet and actually ran off out of sight. This was the last seen or heard of it. It is not reasonable that it went far or lived but a short length of time.

"Several years afterward or when I was a good sized boy I and a lot of young fellows took a live wolf out of a pen [trap] which we had built on the ridge between Little North Fork and where Isabella Post Office is now and after tieing it securely we went to work with our knives and skinned its body neck and legs. Our barbarous treatment was too much for it died at the moment we completed the horrible work. I felt afterward that I had acted too wicked to repeat the operation on another wolf and refused to engage in such work again."

Phillip Green relates an account of a wolf being flayed alive on Pond Fork a tributary branch of Little North Fork. In giving the story Mr. Green went on to say that when his relatives—Leven T. Green and family—settled in Ozark County they in common with others tortured wolves similar to Indians torturing their captives.

"My grandfather and my father Tom Green built a wolf pen on Pond Fork and caught several in it [but] finally becoming busy at something else the pen was neglected a few days. At this time a settler happened to pass by the pen one day and for the sake of curiosity tied an old dry bone of a horse to the trigger which he found (the bone) close by and set the pen and went on. On the following day a hunter happened along by the pen and discovered a wolf in it. The animal was certainly hungry for it had entered the pen and while knawing on the bone was caught.

"The hunter knowing who built the pen notified father and he in turn notified others and they all met at the pen. Among the number was the man who tied the bone to the trigger and caught the wolf. The crowd was angry and thirsted for vengeance in payment for stock destroyed. The animal was doomed. It must be skinned alive. It was some time before the men were ready to begin the work of cruel punishment but they finally commenced and slowly did the work with keen edged butcher knives. The suffering animal did not utter a sound until after they had taken the hide from its body and legs and while they were stripping its tail by force it gave a moaning growl, the men now turned it loose and it struggled to its feet and ran about a hundred yards and staggered and fell and death soon relieved its horrible suffering."

Another account of flaying a wolf alive is given by "Fie" Snow who came to Ozark County, Mo. in 1833. Here is the way Mr. Snow told the story.

"Years ago when my step father Jimmie Forest lived on Little North Fork at mouth of Barren Fork a man of the name of Haney sold goods at our house for several years. While Haney was there I got hold of a pup that was equally mixed with bull and cur. It was about twice the size of a house cat. Haney called it 'Chew of Tobacco.' When it was grown it looked larger and fiercer than a chew of tobacco but the dog was looked on as a trifling good for nothing fellow, but I failed to give him up.

"Along about this time a number of men came down from St. Clair County, Mo. to hunt and look at the country. They brought about twenty-five dogs with them.[71] One night while these men were staying at our house I caught a wolf in a steel trap. The trap had three springs, two on one end and one on the other.

"Next morning we all followed the trail of the wolf on horse back and soon over hauled it. The wolf was a large gray one. 'Chew of Tobacco' and the other twenty-five dogs were along, but they all declined to take hold of the wolf except Chew of Tobacco and he caught it by the bur of the ear and held the wolf until Mr. Haney dismounted and caught the wolf by its hind legs.

"The other men were soon on the spot and they all stretched it broad side on the ground and after tieing its mouth in such a manner that it was not able to use its teeth they took the trap off its leg and held its head down by placing a pole across its neck and while some held the pole in place others held its legs and the other men began the work of flaying it alive. They not only removed the hide from its body but taken it from its head, legs and tail. The beast was alive when they finished. When they freed it, [it] rose up and ran to a pool of water forty yards distant and plunged in where it was about eighteen inches deep and howled twice when death came to its relief. The carcass lay in the pool several days.

"The men gave my step father the scalp and he used it as part payment of his taxes but they carried the hide to St. Clair County with them."[72]

Stories of Vicious Wolves and How Settlers Took Wolves out of Caves [11:49]

AMONG THE MANY wolf stories gathered from pioneer residents are a few that we give to show how wolves in some cases were taken out of caves.

Sammy Stone, who was born in McCann County, Tenn., May 17, 1831, and who is a son of William and Martha (Filpot) Stone, has lived in Ozark County, Mo., many years. Mr. Stone in speaking of the manner of hunting and killing young wolves gives an experience of his own.

He said that one time in 1860, him and three of the Piland boys, Bill, Sam and Joe, Goodman Daves, and Mike Holmes made a raid on a wolf den at head of Thompson hollow which empties into upper Turkey Creek. The wolves were in a cave, the entrance into of which was too small to admit the body of a man.

"We could have sent the dogs in but that would spoil part of our sport. We procured a green pole fifteen feet in length and, after forming a piece of iron into a sharp hook, we fastened it to the small end of the pole. With this we worked several hours pulling out five young wolves as large as grown foxes.[73]

"It was amusing when we got a good hold on one with the hook and began hauling him out. He would kick, scratch, growl, whine and bite at the hook and end of the pole. As we would pull each one out of the cave we would turn it over to the dogs which would soon dispatch it. The old wolves would dart up close to us at times while we were capturing their young but they would not stay long enough for us to take accurate aim at them with the guns before they were gone again."

An Expected Fight between a Dog and Wolf Did Not Pan Out [8:87]

BETWEEN THE BREAKS at the three hollows called the Mahan Pine Branch or Stillhouse and the Cowpen, which lead into Little North Fork, is a hill that was known among the settlers as Bald Mountain. A settlement road leads along the Nat Richmond place over this hill and intersects with the main road leading from Dugginsville to Pontiac.

"Many years ago," said John Mahan, "my father, Isaac Mahan, constructed a wolf pen trap on this hill but only caught one wolf in it which was half grown. I and my father had went to the pen and finding the young wolf in the pen we concluded to have some fun with it and a bobtailed dog we had with us we called Tripp. He was a yellow colored dog. We decided that we would enjoy a fight between this dog and the wolf.

"We poked the wolf until we got him irritated and restless, and while he was running around on the inside of the pen we got hold of his hind feet and pulled his hindlegs out under the lower log, then we took hold of the dog's hind legs and my father took off his yarn suspenders that my mother had knit and tied the wolf's and dog's hind legs together. Then raising the trap we taken the wolf out to witness a fierce fight between the little dog and young wolf, but we were disappointed in seeing the fun and sport as we expected.

"Both animals kept their heads as far apart as they could and showed their teeth and looked in opposite directions. We did our best to get them both angry enough to fight but instead of growing furious they both sulled and finding that we could not get a fight out of them, we killed the wolf and scalped it and we ought to have did likewise with the dog but we let him go free.

"In a few days afterward my father took the scalp to Rockbridge, the then county seat of Ozark County, and sold it for $5 which was some consolation in tieing the wolf's and dog's [legs] together with the yarn suspenders."

How Two Cattle Herders Fought Wolves [8:105]

MANY TIMES my thoughts wander back to the time when I was a little fellow and lived on Elbow Creek. This was from 1849 to 1853. I well remember how I followed my father along this stream and over the hills of this rough valley while he was caring for his cattle that thrived so well then on the fine range.

This calls to mind another story originating from this same little creek which we learned from John Cardwell and Sam Carpenter, two early settlers of Taney County and both of Cedar Creek Post Office.

Mr. Cardwell said Bob Rains related the story to him soon after its occurrence. Mr. Carpenter [also] gave the writer an account of it in June, 1895. The narrative as given by each man is combined to make the story more complete. The sketch gives the present generation of Taney County, or those who are interested, an idea of how wolves, on certain occasions, were so vicious and held in such dreadful fear by a few of the settlers.

In 1856 or three years after we left that part of Taney County, Lige Majors, son of Ben Majors, established a stock ranch on Elbow Creek where the residence of John Cardwell now is. The camp was made just above the pool of water in Cardwell's stock lot and it was the year previous to Cardwell's settling there. Lige Majors, like his father, was a prominent citizen and stock dealer, and at the time we speak of owned a large bunch of cattle.

After deciding to keep his cattle on Elbow Creek he employed Bob Rains and Sam Carpenter to herd them on the range.[74] It was a delightful spot to camp on. There was plenty of water and an abundance of luxuriant grass on which cattle did well winter and summer. There were plenty of deer that were seen in large and small groups, which fed on the tender herbs and the small undergrass. Numerous flocks of wild turkey rambled here and there and lived on wild onions, wild grapes and wild vegetable seeds. In the spring of the year the goblers would get so fat that they were not able to fly but a short distance and hunters would run them down on horses or catch them with hounds.[75] The myriads of song birds of various colors and sizes sang from daybreak until dusk of the evening and the music was sweet and pleasant to the ear.

The little valley of Elbow Creek was open then, that is it was divided into bald knobs, prairie hollows and wooded hills. There was no brush then for the great forest fires that raged through the woods in the early spring kept the small undergrowth destroyed. It was then that the Elbow hills were the stockman's paradise and the hunter's happy hunting grounds—for the stock dealer could raise all the cattle he wanted without expense of feeding them and the hunter could kill all the game he wanted without having to go elsewhere to find it.

The two herders employed by Mr. Majors cooked in the open air but they built a small cabin of poles and roofed it with long boards to sleep in and store away their provisions. The men had a gay time, were happy and enjoyed their employment. They had nothing to do but kill fat bucks, cook, eat and sleep and prevent the cattle from wandering off. Wolves would approach of nights and set up a lively howling but the men slept in their huts and they had met with no danger so far.

There was no enclosure to drive the cattle into of nights and they would lay down to rest in scattering bunches and were not liable to be stampeded in this way by the wolves like they would be while penned up in a lot, but the two men were not let off free until a serious racket happened between the varmints and the herders which come about in this way.

One evening after sunset while they were collecting some of the cattle on the creek above camp, they noticed a big flock of wild turkeys flying up into the timber to roost. Not that they needed a turkey for food but they both agreed that it would be fun to shoot at them after night and they decided to return after nightfall and kill a few of the flock merely for pasttime.

After supper was over, which was a short time after dark, both men started to have a merry time with the turkeys. They concluded to take only one gun and use it time about between them and that would give each man an equal chance, for if one made two or three miss shots he could not say that he had the worst gun. They kept a large yellow dog with them that they called "Watch," and as the two herders and sportsmen left camp they called Watch to accompany them on their turkey hunt to share the enjoyment with them.

It was not a dark night and the moon was not full though it afforded light enough to see the turkeys sitting on the limbs of the trees, and they wondered how many turkeys each of them would kill before the remainder of the flock flew and sought safety from the leaden messengers that they intended to let fly toward them. But they were counting too fast, for it so happened on that occasion that man proposed and God disposed. For soon after leaving camp while walking through the tall grass near the bed of the creek where there was a little narrow creek bottom, they heard a peculiar noise behind them to which they gave hardly a moment's notice until they heard it the second time.

The dog showed signs of restlessness. He appeared to be uneasy and stayed near the two men and made a noise of whining and half growling. The men looked at each other in a doubtful way. They believed it was something but thought it might not amount to anything. Again the same noise was wafted to their ears and they wondered what it meant. They stood still and waited to ascertain the cause of it. They did not have long to wait before the cause of the fuss was solved, for they heard a rustling in the rank grass and a bunch of wolves began snapping their teeth together, and at the same time they saw the forms of wolves by the light of the moon, advancing at a lively gait toward them. The noises of the wolves and the sight of them alarmed the men and they rushed out of the tall grass and halted on the hillside.

The men, when they stopped, noticed the terrified dog cower at their feet. All but two of the wolves stopped; these seemed more bold and sprang forward to attack the men and dog. But Rains, who carried the gun, leveled it and took quick aim and shot one of the wolves before it had time to reach them. The other took warning at this and turned and fled back to the main bunch, which was in plain view a few yards distant. As the men saw the impudent beast fall and the other turn and flee they went off on a fast run in an opposite direction. They cared nothing for the kind of order they retreated. They considered it best to do their best. It was the quickest way to get away on quick time and they put it into execution, and away they went.

After a run of fifty or sixty yards up the hillside they halted where a tree had fallen, to reconnoitre. They heard the wolves coming and Bob Rains guessed at a charge of powder by pouring it from the powder horn into the palm of his hand and hastily pouring it into the rifle. He then rammed down a naked ball on top of it.[76]

He was none too soon for at the moment he primed the gun[77] four other daring wolves rushed up the hill at them, and when they got within a few yards there was another report of the rifle, but the men did not stay long enough to note the effect of the shot, but turned their course toward camp and ran in haste with the hungry wolves in hot pursuit.

How many of the gaunt beasts were following them they were not able to tell. There may have been only a few more than they saw, but the way they were pressing forward in the direction of camp it would seem there were a hundred. It not only seemed there were a hundred but the men were scared as bad as if there had been a thousand.

It was not far to camp but the race was none the less lively for they made steps fast. The wolves knew their enemies were panic stricken. It was more of a route than a retreat. The wolves snapped at the men's heels to urge them on faster. They needed no spurring for they were using their best speed and made good use of the time.

When the two terrified herders reached the door of their hut the wolves halted just a few yards away and set up a direful howling. The men did not take time to listen to the serenade until after they dashed into the hut, let the dog in and barricaded the door. The herders were in no mood to enjoy the unwelcome and lonesome music though they were forced to listen until near midnight when the wolves took their departure and allowed the men to rest.

Next morning soon after daylight they ventured back with dog and a gun each to the scene of trouble. The live wolves had disappeared but there were two dead ones lying stretched on the grass. As hunting turkeys on their roost were not as enticing as they supposed it was they declined to venture out anymore after night.

Mr. Cardwell said that Bob Rains informed him that the night they were attacked by the wolves he felt like he could run faster than he ever did in his life, and according to the account given by Mr. Carpenter we suppose that Rains and Carpenter certainly did some fast running.

Humans Killed by Wolves

> *Editors' note:* Conservationists say that there are no authentic accounts of humans being killed and eaten by wolves in North America. The following two accounts would seem to indicate otherwise. It may be significant that both accounts involve negro women and children, leading one to wonder if the two tales do not reflect a single incident. This may be unlikely because both the Clapp and Coker families were so well known and lived in different counties. The actual evidence that wolves were the *cause* of death in both cases is speculative: the dead could have been killed by another agency, such as bushwhackers, and the victims eaten by wolves.

Wiped out of Existence by Wolves [11:34]

THIS SAD STORY was furnished me by Mr. Lafayette Abbotte, son of William and Matilda Abbotte, who lived in southwest Missouri in the pioneer days.

"Well," said Mr. Abbotte, "you want to know if I ever knew of wolves destroying a human being in Christian County, Mo. I certainly do know a case of this kind. This sad and pathetic incident is so well authenticated that there is no question as to the truth of it.

"The Clapp boys who rebuilt the Beaver Kissee mills in 1857 were industrious men. There were Irving Clapp and Patterson Clapp, who did the most work in putting the mill in good shape, but I was told in a reliable way that David Clapp furnished the principal part of the means to rebuild the mill. These men owned a few slaves but during the war, they with others, lost nearly all their property.[78]

"Irving Clapp was living in Christian County, Mo., when the war broke out and he went south and served a while in the Confederate army. In the fall of 1864 Irving Clapp's wife, who still lived at the old home in Christian County, wanted to go back where she had formerly lived in Taney County and she hired me to move her and her children to Forsyth in an ox wagon.

"Soon after I had returned back home from moving Mrs. Clapp into Taney County, a negro woman with three children, the eldest of which was a girl twelve years old, came to our house where we lived near Sparta and begged for food. They belonged to one of the Clapp brothers and were in a starving condition.

"My mother gave them something to eat and also gave them permission to stay at our house two days, when the woman taken the three children and went on their way toward Forsyth where Mrs. Clapp had stopped a few days. On the first day after they left our house they traveled some ten or twelve miles south of Sparta when night overtook them and they stopped to camp among some pine trees.

"During the night they were attacked by a gang of wolves and the entire family of negroes was wiped out of existence. I was thirteen years old at the time of its occurrence and I remember distinctly the sorrowful feeling it created in our neighborhood when the news of their destruction reached us. Their bones and pieces of their garments were found scattered around under the pine trees. Also a stout billet of wood was lying on the scene of slaughter that the unfortunate woman had used in an effort to beat back the vicious and snarling pack."

Devoured by Wolves [11:60]

ONE MILE AND A QUARTER northwest of the little hamlet of Cedar Creek and one quarter of a mile southwest of Bald Knob schoolhouse in Taney County, Mo., is a prairie hill known among the early settlers as Miliken's Bald Hill.

This bald knob derived its name from John Miliken, who built a log hut here during the early settlement of Taney County. He resided here a few years and feasted on fat bucks, bear meat and wild honey. His neighbors were the fat bear, the howling wolf, the vicious catamount and stealthy panther, yet this old time hunter and settler said he enjoyed living in this then wild region of Missouri. This was long ago when the tall grass covered the hills and numerous wild flowers emitted their sweet smelling flavors.

But we are digressing from our story and must return to the subject we commenced to narrate. It is a sad tale to relate, and is in connection with this bald hill, the occurrence of which happened during the bloody days of the war of the Sixties and is supposed to have taken place in the night time. The scene where it occurred was sad to look upon by the one that made the discovery. The awful circumstance was in the shape of three human beings slain and eaten by wolves.

There was scarcely any traveling through this section at the time and no one knew of the terrible tragedy until several weeks had elapsed. To make the story more complete, we will state that when the war broke out, Ned Coker and his son William—"River Bill" they called him, to distinguish him from "Wagoner Bill", "Yellville Bill" and "Prairie Bill" Coker—lived on the south bank of White River in Marion County, Ark.

The former's named residence was on the farm on the right bank of the river just below the mouth of East Sugar Loaf Creek. The latter lived on the farm opposite the mouth of Shoal Creek. Both these men were slave holders and possessed about fifteen negroes each. As the war progressed, father and son sought safety in Greene County, Mo., where they both died, eight miles north of Springfield.

A few of the slaves left before their masters but others remained until later before they went off. A few stayed until the summer of 1864, when the ravages of war forced them to vacate their old homes. Among the latter was a negro woman and her two small boys.

They were almost famished for food when they waded across the river at the Fish Trap Shoals Ford, where Bradley's Ferry is now, and stopped at John Jones who lived on the Mat Hoodenpile place, and Mrs. Elizabeth Jones gave them food. They were in such starving condition that Mrs. Jones and family kept them a few days and divided such food with them as they had. The woman's name was Delilah, the children were known as Sambo and Mugginhead. The woman wanted to go to Greene County, Mo., where Ned and Bill Coker resided, in order to procure food and raiment. Early one morning the mother and children departed on their long walk. Mrs. Jones gave them food sufficient to last them to Kissee Mills on Beaver Creek. As it was summertime they could use the soft grass for a bed at night, and the foliage of a tree for shelter.

It is told that they got on the Yellville and Forsyth wagon road at the John Yandell farm on Elbow Creek. This was the last heard of them until their bleached bones and bits of clothing were found near the foot of this bald knob. An investigation proved that the remnant apparel belonged to these three unfortunate negroes.

It was supposed they reached near the base of this hill the first day where they stopped in the timber for the night and were attacked by a pack of wolves during the night and destroyed.

Their awful doom and destruction can never be accurately described, but let us imagine the heart rending shrieks and dying moans of the unfortunate family. This, mixed with the noise made by the wolves snapping and snarling, was certainly direful.

It was told by those who discovered their remains that the evidence on the ground showed that the woman made a desperate effort to defend herself and children. She had fought the wolves over the space of half an acre. Stones, clubs and chunks of dead wood that she had used in resisting the attack lay scattered on the down trodden grass. They were the only weapons of defense, and she had made desperate use of them to the finish.

Probably she had beaten them back and kept them at bay some time before the ravenous beasts finally overcome her and gloated in the blood of the helpless human creatures. Their fate was simply awful. Who can imagine the consternation and terror of these poor beings when they were attacked by the vicious and hungry pack, and with loud screams and hard struggles were forced to yield their lives in such a horrible manner? Their destruction is sad to reflect upon.

GREAT TENACITY OF LIFE IN SOME WOLVES [11:91]

AN ACCOUNT IS TOLD by Mart Herron, who said that he met a wolf once that was remarkably hard to end its life. In telling the story, Mr. Herron said that in 1865 he and his brother, Simon Herron, and Bill Clark, the famous hunter, were hunting one day on Big Creek in Taney County, Mo., and while riding up the right hand prong of the creek they separated.

"Soon after this, as I rode along through the tall grass with my dog trotting along near the horse, I saw two young wolves the size of grown foxes. One was black and the other gray.

"I sat on my horse and shot at the black one. At this moment a big gray wolf sprang up out of the grass in a few yards of me. The dog flew at it and there followed a hard fight between it and the dog. But they had not been engaged long before the wolf backed off and wheeled and ran about one-hundred-fifty yards, when it turned on the dog which was pursuing it closely, and the result was another battle.

"Dismounting, I quickly reloaded my gun and remounting my horse again, I galloped up near where the fight was going on and shot the wolf through the body but it seemed to pay no attention to the effect of the bullet. Pouring a big charge of powder into my rifle, I reached in the shot pouch for another bullet, but they were gone. I had lost them since I had last reloaded.

"Not desiring to be outdone by the loss of the bullets, I cut a slug of wood, two and one-half inches in length, from a post oak bush and rammed it down on the powder and shot the piece of wood into the animal's body, but the wolf showed no signs of weakening and it and the dog went on with the fight as lively as ever.

"I reloaded the gun with another slug of wood and shot the wolf with it and I saw the blood dripping from the wounds but it and the dog kept up the fight. The wounds inflicted by my shots of wood did not seem to disable the wolf in the least. I now tried a different plan by trying to load my gun with a slug one-half inch long, cut from one end of my gunstick,[79] but the wood, while I was trying to push it down, choked the rifle and I failed to ram it down.

"My gunstick was much longer than the gun barrel and I cut off about fifteen inches of the stick and, inserting one end into the barrel of the rifle and jabbing the other end against a tree, succeeded at last in dislodging the short piece and finally pushed both pieces down and walking up in eight feet of the wolf, I fired both pieces of the gunstick into the beast.

"One end of the long piece protruded from the wolf's side opposite from where the stick had entered. It was a desperate wound and the wolf weakened. The blood was dripping from every wound and the animal appeared to be sick. The dog was weary of the fight and he and the wolf seemed to separate by mutual consent. The wolf ran a hundred yards and lay down. The dog lay down on the spot where him and his adversary ceased the combat.

"I selected a few small pebbles that lay on the ground and poured them down the gun on a charge of powder and approached in a few yards of where the wolf lay in the grass and shot the pebbles at its head, which caused it to leap to its feet and ran about seventy-five yards and lay down the second time. By this time I was disgusted, for I had shot a bullet, two slugs of post oak wood, two pieces of my gunstick, and a lot of small pebbles at the wolf and there was plenty of life left in the animal yet. "I concluded now to stone it to death and I went up close and hurled a few at it but by some means I failed to hit it. Then I encouraged the dog and the brave fellow attacked the wolf again. The dog caught the wolf by the throat and the wolf caught the dog's shoulder. Each animal would not let go his hold. Dog and wolf struggled hard for several moments when I drew my butcher knife from the scabbard and stabbed the wolf to death.

"About the time it was dead, Simon rode up and we went back to the spot where I shot at the young wolf and found it lying dead. The grown wolf was a he and while it was fighting the dog it would bark frequently like a dog in order to attract other wolves to its assistance but none came."

Stories Told by an Old Hunter [15:32]

"As to wolves," said Uncle Peter Baughman, "they did not lack for numbers in the early days here on Crooked Creek. They committed terrible depradations on stock. Settlers made all sorts of efforts to shoot and poison them and laid all kinds of plans to entrap them. I have known deep pits to be dug and prepared with trap doors. The doors were baited with fresh meat and when a wolf came along he would be sure to go for the meat and when he would get on the door he would drop into the pit prepared for his reception. The pits were so deep and the walls so steep that Mr. Wolf was not able to scale the walls and escape and was held a prisoner until the owner of the pit came along and ended his life with a bullet.

"Occasionally more than one wolf was caught in a pit at one time. Sometimes a catamount, wild cat, coon or fox would fall in and it was nothing strange to find a runabout dog in there too. It so happened that when one of these pits were properly constructed, a mixture of wild animals would be entrapped during one night.

"It is something remarkable about the peaceable disposition of wild beasts here when several of them were huddled together in one of these pits. Each tried to seek safety for itself by trying to climb out of the hole. Just for the sport of it hunters would occasionally confine a wolf with a chain and thongs, and after choking the animal nearly to death, would knock out every tooth in its mouth and after it had fully revived from the choking it had received, the hunters would turn it loose among a lot of dogs and hurrah until the dogs worried the beast to death.

"I will tell you of an experience I had with wolves once in 1850, while we lived near the now beautiful town of Bellfonte, south of Crooked Creek. Father owned a distillery and made whiskey. It was not an adulterated stuff like some that is sold nowadays, a few drops of which is liable to poison a man to death, but it was pure corn whiskey. While father manufactured whiskey he raised a fine lot of hogs. Among them was a male which he kept in an enclosure. It so happened that about then we had no dogs worth anything in the way of watch dogs.

"One night a pack of wolves entered the lot where the hog was kept and killed him while we and the dogs slept. It would seem that a stout boar would be able to whip a lot of wolves but by some means they overcame him and made a meal of him. Only a few remnants of the hog was left to tell the tale of his fate.

"The following morning, while father was lamenting over the loss of the boar, I informed him that I was going to try and take in a few of the wolves as partial payment for the hog. I went to Loranzo Rush's and borrowed a trained dog. Joe Rush went with me in pursuit of the wolves. The trail was easily followed by the assistance of the dog, for there were so many of the wolves together that they partly beat down the grass and weeds as they went along and left a dim trail in their wake.

"We followed the trail across Crooked Creek and over hills and across hollows to the Oregon Flat and to the head of Sugar Orchard Creek and on into the head of the hollow in which is known now as Elixir Springs.[80] Here in this hollow the dog indicated that the game was not far off. We followed the trail down the hollow to a large hollow white oak tree which stood just above the springs. This tree had a big cavity at the ground and here in this tree we discovered nine young wolves. The old ones on hearing our approach had scattered.

"We did not molest the pups for awhile for we wanted to slay some of the old ones. We stood at the tree several minutes before they showed themselves. They approached us on the hillside but they all stopped before getting in shooting distance. I requested Rush to remain at the tree and keep the dog with him and make the wolf pups squall, while I sauntered around close by and made an effort to shoot some of the old ones.

Though Rush made the young wolves cry out like hound pups but the old ones made no attempt to attack us or the dog. But they would howl, whine and dodge around.

"At one time, while Rush was making the pups squall, they ran up close, but wheeled and loped away. They kept moving around so much that I could not shoot at one with any certainty of hitting it until finally I saw one standing still and I shot him down. Soon after I had reloaded my rifle I got an opportunity and killed another one. The others took the hint and left.

"We now gave our attention to the pups and put them to death and threw them back in their bed for the old ones to grieve over. We had slain eleven including the two old ones. We had exterminated one nest of young wolves at least which had afforded some revenge for the loss of the hog."

MRS. TERSEY FELLOWS AND THE WOLVES [8:90]

AMONG THE OLD PIONEER SETTLERS who lived many years in the Flippin Barrens was the Hon. W. B. Flippin,[81] son of Tom Flippin. William Flippin is dead now but during his life he was an honorable and useful citizen. I remember that he represented the people of Marion County in the legislature at Little Rock and served a term as County Surveyor and filled other useful offices and was also a prominent preacher and a noted writer.

During his lifetime Mr. Flippin delighted to relate stories of early life here among the wild animals. His narratives are reliable and entertaining. One among his amusing accounts which he told frequently is of a woman who had an adventure with a gang of wolves while on her way to a blacksmith shop. The story as was told by Mr. Flippin is as follows.

"There lived in the early settlement of White River Valley, five miles above old Tolbert's Ferry, a woman by the name of Tersey Fellows who had, from some cause, separated from her husband. She was of Yankee descent and had a fair English education. Added to this she possessed good common sense. She had some sons and daughters nearly grown when she and her husband separated. She was a large fleshy woman and a good manager on the farm. Among her horses was a big gray or white horse she called Boston—Boss she often called him.

"She was monarch of her own land and superintended the cultivation of it and, of course, had to provide the necessary farming tools, which then consisted of the bull tongued and single shovel plows.[82] She would take a dry beef hide and soak it in water until it was soft and turn up the edges and shape it into a kind of saddle bag to hold her plows. Her iron, when she had any, consisted of a piece of an old wagon tire. When ready to start to the shop she would saddle up Boss and throw the beef hide containing her plows across her saddle and go to the blacksmith shop at the mouth of Big North Fork, which was twenty miles or more below where she lived.

"Just think, now, if men had to go to a blacksmith shop at the present day that was twenty miles from their home, lots of horses would go unshod and many farming tools would go unsharpened. This woman was certainly a plucky one.

"In course of time, Allen Flippin, an uncle of mine, moved into the country and located on Fallen Ash Creek, and put up a blacksmith shop. I was told, on my arrival here in 1837, Fallen Ash Creek was named for an Indian who once lived at the mouth of this stream. Allen Flippin lived near where the old village of Flippin now stands near one fourth of a mile from Flippin Station on the railroad and near ten miles from the residence of Mrs. Fellows.

"The following spring, after my uncle began work in his shop, Mrs. Fellows' plows needed some necessary work and Boss needed shoeing, she had no dry beef hide on hand, so she killed a beef and used the green hide and prepared it in the usual way to hold the plows, and mounting Boston, her favorite horse, she went on her way to the new shop—it was ten miles nearer than the one at mouth of Big North Fork. The trip would not be so long and tedious.

"She felt safe while riding Boss and never hesitated to go far and near when business called her. She knew the nature and ways of the prowling wolf and the screaming panther. She did not fear an attack from a wild beast while on Boss's back, if a wild animal should attack her Boss would soon carry her out of danger. On that day she was unexpectedly annoyed which was beyond her anticipation, for while she was riding along a dim trail at the north end of Lee's Mountain a pack of hungry wolves, attracted by the fresh beef hide, came rushing up behind her—howling like mad fury.

"The attack from the vicious animals took her on surprise but she kept her presence of mind and as the pack rushed toward her she urged Boston into a gallop and continued to urge him until he went along the trail at his best speed and the woman kept in advance of the howling pack.

"Mrs. Fellows was not overly frightened but however as the horse ran along a few yards in front of the impudent creatures, the beef hide slipped off the saddle, and hide and plows fell to the ground.

"Probably no other woman, or even a man would have stopped at this critical moment, but would have urged their horse along the faster. Not so with Mrs. Fellows, however, for she halted at once, and dismounting quickly snatched up some stones and threw them at the wolves and caused them to stop where they stood and howled while she was replacing the plows back in the hide. Then lifting it from the ground, she put it across the saddle and led the horse to a log nearby and mounted again.

"While leading the horse to the log the wolves followed and were in a few yards of her and the restless and frightened horse when she remounted. The entire pack put up a direful howling. Their presence and dreadful noise was not comfortable, and when the woman seated herself in the saddle again, she made Boss spread himself running. The noisy wolves pursued.

"The race was interesting from the fact that the large fleshy woman on the big white horse was able to keep in the advance of her four-footed foes. The wolves wanted the fresh beef hide and stayed at Boss's heels. Tersey was determined they should not have it. Onward she urged the willing horse at breakneck speed until she hove in sight of a settler's cabin. Here, to the woman's great relief, the howling beasts stopped and went back into the forest.

"After her excitement calmed and Boss's scare was over the woman proceeded on to the shop at her leisure and the smith sharpened her plows and shod Boston. When my uncle had finished the work the woman sold him the beef hide in payment for the work in sharpening the plows and shoeing the horse, saying that she could manage to do other ways to carry her plows back home by pealing hickory bark and tying the plows together and hanging them to the saddle. This trip to the shop put a weaner[83] on the woman, for she learned to carry her plows to the shop other ways than wrapping them in a green or fresh hide."

TALES OF PANTHER

Editors' Note: The panther, which goes by a host of other names—mountain lion, cougar, puma, catamount, and, more properly, *Felis concolor*—was found over most of North America in pre-settlement days. Because of its predatory habits it was extensively hunted by man, who greatly feared it, as Turnbo's tales show. Panthers may have from one to six young, averaging two or three; hunters, of course, killed them at any age. Turnbo almost always remarks on the size of panthers. Schwartz and Schwartz in *The Wild Mammals of Missouri* list panther lengths, including tail, from 60 to 102 inches. Males may weigh up to 160 pounds, females to 110 pounds.

The panther was not combative, and seemed to be easily intimidated by even small dogs. The panther, unless pressed, ordinarily would flee from a dog, whereas wolves might attack a dog. Deer were a favorite food, but wild small mammals and domestic livestock might be taken. The last definite record of a panther in Missouri was one killed in 1927 in southeast Missouri, when that region still possessed large timbered swamplands. Arkansas still has resident panthers, and with the comeback of the deer herd in Missouri, it is likely that a few panthers may also live in the Missouri Ozarks.[84]

Watching a Bunch of Panthers Frolicking [13:7]

AN INTERESTING STORY of a bunch of panthers was furnished me by Mrs. Sallie Anderson, who died near Dodd City, Arkansas, several years ago. Mrs. Anderson had been married three times. Her last husband was Arch Anderson. She said that Gid Brown, her first husband, was the author of the story and he had repeated it to her on several occasions after they were married.

"He told me," said Mrs. Anderson, "that his father settled on White River near the mouth of Buffalo in 1809. 'I was only a small boy when my parents came to that part of Ark.,' said he. 'There was only a little hut scattered here and there on the bank of the river. We brought seed corn up White River with us. We had no bread until we cleared a few acres of the rich fertile soil in the river bottom and planted our seed corn and raised a crop. We beat this corn in a mortar with a pestle.'"

Mrs. Anderson said that her parents were Millers and they settled on the river near where her first husband's family lived and came there the same year they did.

"Going back to the story of Gid Brown, my first husband," said Mrs. Anderson, "he said that it was not strange to observe two and three panthers together playing on the river beach or gravel bar.

"'But late one afternoon, [said he], when the evening shade had spread over the gravel beach or sand bar, near where our hut stood on the bank of the river, we saw a bunch of panthers collect on the gravel bar in full view of our cabin and play and frisk about like cats. There were nine of them—three full grown ones and six not fully grown.

"'We had seen one and two of these animals playing on the beach previous to this, but we were not prepared to witness the sight of so many panthers together. We were accustomed to see almost all kinds of animals that were natives there and did not feel much afraid until we saw this bunch of panthers, and we were sure afraid of them, but they did not offer to molest us and when they grew tired of playing they went back into the thick cane in the river bottom.'"

FINDING A PANTHER GUARDING A DEAD BEAR [12:20]

IN THE CEMETERY at Lead Hill, Ark., is an unmarked grave in which the mortal remains of Joe Coker were deposited. We have made reference to him in several other sketches. Joe was the eldest child of Buck Coker and was a noted character. He had lived on the bank of White River and in the Sugar Loaf Prairie and on East Sugar Loaf Creek. He had lived to a great age and had lived in this country forty-eight years.

When Joe Coker came to White River in 1814, he would go up on the Sugar Loaf Knob and see buffalo, deer and elk all at the same time. A narrative of his encounters with wild beasts and other matter relating to the early history of this part of Arkansas would fill a book of many pages, one story of which we introduce here.

In the month of July, 1824, Jane Coker, Joe's eldest sister, married Charley Sneed. Neighbors lived far apart then but a few days before the wedding came off Buck Coker sent for his friends to come and be present when his daughter and Charley were united in the bonds of matrimony. Among Coker's most intimate friends was Paton Keesee and he was among the invited guests.

Elias Keesee informed me that he was two months old when this occurred and that his parent told him that it was a hot July day's ride through the wild woods from where they lived on Little North Fork to where Buck Coker lived at the lower end of the Jake Nave Bend on White River, to be present at that wedding on the following day.

Soon after the marriage, Sneed and his wife located on Osage Creek seven miles west of Carrollton. Sneed's residence stood on the road leading from Carrollton to Huntsville and near the mouth of a hollow called Jew's Harp. Sneed and the Cokers, in visiting each other, beat out a trailway. The country looked so wild then that it made the visitors feel lonely to pass through back and forth between the Sugar Loaf country and Osage Creek.

On a certain time Joe Coker paid his sister and brother-in-law a visit and as usual he had gone alone. Two years afterward he told the story of this journey through the wilds of Carroll County to Dave McCord,[85] and Mr. McCord related it to the writer and here is the way it was told me. Mr. Coker said that he did not take the precaution to carry a gun with him on that trip but he met nothing serious until on his way back home.

"While I was riding down Lead Mine Hollow which flows into West Sugar Loaf Creek on the west side," said Uncle Joe, "I saw a huge panther crouched down at the side of a dead bear which lay at the foot of a post oak tree that stood at the side of the pathway. The panther was guarding the bear. The two savage animals had met here and engaged in a terrific fight and the bear was killed. The scene of the encounter was in a small prairie bottom with a few scattering trees and nearly one-half a mile above the mouth of the hollow.

"I rode up as close as I dared to view the ferocious beast and its dead adversary and the spot where they had fought. The panther showed much anger at being disturbed and growled fiercely and rose on his feet and threatened to spring at me. I needed no second warning and gave the enraged beast plenty of room at once and it lay down again at the side of its dead victim. The grass under the tree was all mashed down and stained with blood and the hair on both animals was red with blood. It was evident that they had met here and fought only a few hours previous to my arrival. Part of the outside bark of the tree was raked off from about two feet above the ground to four and five feet up the tree trunk.

"Evidently when the bear found that he was receiving the worst end of the fight he had attempted to escape up the tree but his powerful antagonist had pulled him back and he had clawed the bark off with his paws in trying to hold to the tree while the panther was preventing him from going up the tree. Appearances indicated that the bear had made several efforts to climb the tree before his enemy finally killed him."

Mr. Coker said that when he left them and went on home he intended to return back with gun and dogs and try to kill the panther, but on his arrival at home something occurred which prevented him from going back. Mr. McCord said that Uncle Joe gave him this account in 1838. The combat between the wild beasts took place two years before or in 1835. [1836?]

"Coker's story aroused my curiosity," said Mr. McCord, "and in company with my brother, John McCord, I visited the spot where Coker told me the fight occurred and we found evidence of the combat was still visible. The marks on the tree made by the bear's claws showed very plain and the shattered bark which had escaped destruction from the forest fires since the fight, lay around the roots of the tree, and a few of the bear's bones were found in the grass under the tree. Doubtless if Coker had reached there sooner he would have witnessed a terrible scene of savagery, blood and war between these angered animals of the forest."

KILLING PANTHER IN THE BUFFALO MOUNTAINS [13:86]

"TALKING ABOUT PANTHER," remarked Peter Baughman, "reminds me of shooting one in these same mountains while I was on Buffalo [River] once on a camp hunt. One day, while I was passing through a narrow gorge just above the mouth of Big Creek which empties into Buffalo from the south side, I heard a noise above me and looking up to the top of a precipice I saw the head of a panther protruding over the edge of a cliff directly over me. The animal looked down at me very saucy.

"Elevating my rifle straight up I took a steady aim between its eyes and pulled the trigger and the dying beast slid over the edge of the precipice and fell with a thud. As I was standing under it, I had to get a quick move on me to prevent it from falling on me.

"It was a small panther measuring only about eight feet in length. But this was not all the experience I ever had with a panther on this same stream. Me and Isaac Carter had hunted together frequently on Crooked Creek, but in the course of time Carter moved to Buffalo and lived on Calf Creek. In December, 1851, Carter sent me word to come down and take an old time bear hunt with him. Of course I accepted the invitation, for we had always seen a good time hunting together on Crooked Creek and I thought we could enjoy life in killing game on Buffalo.

"When I reached his cabin he had everything in shape to start and we did not delay anytime but struck right out into the forest with dogs and guns. We were out several days and met with only fair luck in killing game. We returned back to Carter's on Christmas Eve day. I remained overnight with him intending to start home Christmas morning.

"We sat up late salting away our bear meat that we had brought in from the forest on our pack horses. Then we had to tell several hunting stories for past time before we retired to bed. That night Carter's children told that when they would go into the field for corn which was less than one-quarter mile from the cabin, 'a big thing' would run them out of the field. Carter made sport of their story and said they had got scared at nothing, but the children insisted that they saw something.

"Next morning he told the children to get up out of bed and take a sack and go to the field and fill it with corn for the horses. The children were slow about starting and Carter, after scolding them and saying he had never knew his children to be disobedient before, ordered them in a humorous way to take the dogs along to frighten the 'buggers' away. They were in no hurry about going but finally they took the dogs and went on to the field.

"When they had time to reach the field we heard the dogs yelping as if they were on a hot chase and we heard the children hallooing and directly they came running back to the house and reported that they saw the same thing in the field and the dogs had run it out. The dogs soon treed it and were now barking furiously.

"By this time Carter's wife had breakfast nearly prepared, but me and Carter were still lying in bed. But we both rose in haste now and put on our clothes and, with guns in hand, went to see what the dogs had treed and found that they were barking in the mouth of a small cave or opening in a cliff.

"The crevice in the rock was straight up and down. Part of the opening was narrow but large enough to admit a man's body edgeways. But in one place the opening was big enough for a large animal to enter in.

"Thinking a lot of coons or foxes were in there, we concluded to go in and have some sport. With guns in our hands we scrouged in edgeways. Carter went in ahead of me. After passing into the mouth of the cave a few feet we observed a much larger opening or pocket, but before we had time to enter into it we saw a half grown panther in eight feet of us. Plenty of daylight penetrated through the opening and crevice and we could see the form of the young animal plain and Carter aimed at it with his rifle and shot it dead. Then he gave me his empty gun with the remark that he would drag it, but at this moment a full grown panther made its appearance and sprang at Carter to force its way out of the cavern.

"The beast hurled itself against the man's legs and tore his clothes and flesh with its teeth and claws. Carter did not attempt to back out to the outside, but snatched his knife from the scabbard and went to work stabbing the panther with it.

"Owing to the narrowness of the passage I was helpless to assist him, but I begged him to back out and give room for the panther to make its exit. This he refused saying that as long as the panther wanted to fight he should have the chance. So I gave him all the encouragement I could. The man was greatly excited and furious and fought the enraged beast desperately. Every stroke with the knife was effective. The panther growled loud and lacerated his flesh with its teeth and claws. Carter grunted and groaned with pain, kicked and struck the panther vigorous blows with the keen pointed hunting knife.

"How long the struggle between man and wild beast lasted, I am not able to say exactly but it was only a few minutes. But it was fierce, bloody and ugly, while it was on. But the knife did its work well, for the panther sank down and lay dead. But Carter's excitement and temper was wrought up at such a pitch that he was not sensible of his victory and refused to quit using the knife on the dead beast, and sent the long blade into its lifeless form twenty times more, before I could persuade him to let up and quit fighting a dead enemy.

"After we both got out of the cave I found that Carter's clothes were nearly torn off of him. His legs were gashed and bleeding and the man groaned out loud. I tried to persuade him to go to the house, but he would not hear to it until we had pulled both dead panthers out of the cave. The grown one was a she and was nine feet in length, but Carter had cut it almost to pieces with his knife.

"Carter was too severely wounded for me to leave him and I postponed going home for several days or until the man was better.

"On the following morning after Carter got into the combat with the panther, Enock Vaughn happened along near this same cave with his gun and dogs and the dogs chased something away from the cave and compelled it to climb a tree. When Vaughn reached the tree the dogs were barking up the tree. It proved to be a panther. He yelled for someone to come and help him kill it. Carter was not able to go, but I took my gun and went to where Vaughn and the dogs were.

"The panther had climbed high up in the tree and looked fierce as he lay crouched on a limb. We both shot at it the same moment. One ball crashed through its head and the other through its body behind the shoulder. The animal turned its hold loose of the limb and was dead when it struck the ground. This one was a he and was nine feet and four inches long.

"This last killing broke up the nest of panther at the cave and Carter's children could go to the field now for a sack of corn without being bothered by 'some big thing.' It was many days before Carter's wounds healed sufficiently for him to get around, but he learned one lesson from his encounter with the panther and that was he was careful after this about poking fun at his children when they told him they had seen a 'bugger.'"

TERRIBLE EXPERIENCE WITH A PANTHER [12:48]

THE FOLLOWING ACCOUNT of an exciting adventure with a panther is given by Mrs. Dora Ross, wife of John C. Ross, whose present residence is Harrison, Ark. The incident occurred when she was a small girl. The recollections of the attack of the ugly creature are so vivid in her mind that she remembers every incident. Here is how Mrs. Ross told the story of her dreadful experience with the ugly beast.

"My parents came to Arkansas in 1853, and located in Newton County, where the town of Western Grove is now. I was just five years old when we arrived there. After living here nearly one year we removed to East Sugar Loaf Creek and settled a short distance above the present site of Lead Hill. Here we made our home a number of years and enjoyed ourselves in the then seemingly wild forest of hills and dales.

"Father owned one-hundred-fifty head of sheep for the use of the wool, mutton and to sell to other parties. Mother, like other housewives in the early days, manufactured our wearing apparel from sheep's wool and cotton. This she did by the use of the spinning wheel and hand loom. She also taught we girls when we were old enough how to make our own clothes. People at this late day in buying all their clothing in the stores may think it strange, but women in those days made themselves nice dresses from beginning to finish.

"When there was a gathering of the settlers and their families in the neighborhood such as meeting and so on, men, women and children wore their homemade clothes. The cloth as a rule proved to be durable and generally of pretty colors.

"Owing to the hungry wolves which infested Sugar Loaf in great numbers, we were compelled to keep a constant watch over the sheep to prevent the ravenous animals from destroying them. In this way father required us children to herd them during daytime and drive them into the lot at night. As there was plenty of good stock range near the house, it was not necessary to leave our cabin far, and it was seldom that we were bothered with a wild beast approaching the house in daytime.

"One day in 1857, I and my sister Florence and brother Ernest, while having charge of the sheep, wandered off nearly one-half a mile. I was nine years old, Florence seven and Ernest five. We were happy little folks and tripped along through the grass as gayly as larks in an old waste field. We had commenced to round up the flock to drive them back to the house. Childlike, I stopped by the way to gather some blooms from a cluster of spice wood bushes.[86] When I got as many blossoms as I wanted, the sheep and other children had gone on near a hundred yards in advance of me.

"I now started in a hurry to catch up with the other children to help them with the sheep. I had gone only a few steps when I saw, as I supposed at the time, a yellow dog cross the path a few yards in front of me. But a moment's thought told me it was no dog and I knew I was in the presence of a panther. My heart seemed to sink. I stopped and for a short while I felt like my feet were glued to the ground.

"In a moment or two the animal sprang for a tree that stood nearby and dodged behind it, then raised on its hind feet and put its forepaws against the tree and peeped at me. I did nothing then but stand and scream, and the stealthy creature kept looking at me from behind the tree. In a little while I thought of my little sister and brother and I recollect hallooing, 'Run home, for a panther is going to catch me.'

"When I hallooed I seemed to revive from a stupor and my feet seemed to come loose from the ground and I started to run, but the ferocious looking beast left the tree and sprang before me. I stopped and walked backward until I reached a tree which was only a few yards away. I leaned my back against the tree. The dreaded beast followed and stopped just a few feet in front and glared at me steadily a minute or more. I waited in awful suspense for I expected it would spring on me and rend me to pieces. As these agonizing thoughts rushed through my mind in the presence of it, I made another effort to escape, but the moment I tried to run around it in order to get to the children, it sprang in front of me again.

"Then I ran in an opposite direction, but it ran around me and stopped just ahead of me. Though badly frightened and screaming, I kept my presence of mind and watched and hoped for a chance to escape. When the panther cut me off the last time, I did my best to run away from it, but it would dash in front of me, and when I would turn in another direction, it would spring ahead of me in a moment.

"I ran and dodged here and there over a small space for fifteen minutes or more, beating down the grass and weeds. It was certainly a desperate peril for a child to be in. The panther would raise its upper lip and show its long, sharp pointed teeth. I could hear its teeth ring when it would clash them together. It would sway its tail and strike it against the ground. The end of its tail struck me twice. This ordeal was so horrifying to me and the work and worry to keep out of its way had nearly exhausted my strength. I gave up for lost and resigned myself for as I supposed my impending fate.

"Then it was that curious thoughts rose into my mind. I wondered whether it would kill me and eat me on the spot, or conceal my body with grass and leaves after I was dead. These were almost unbearable thoughts as they flashed into my mind. I waited. It was an awful wait. I could see the other children where they had stopped and were looking on, but I only glanced at them for I kept my eyes on the panther all the time, except an instant when I looked at the other children.

"Though as great as my danger was, I kept my thoughts on the safety of the children, and believed when it killed me it would slay them also. Then I screamed to them again to run home for the panther would kill them, too, if they did not get out of the way. I do not know how it happened but I knew there was a great ruler in heaven and I was old enough to understand that he loved children and all those that love him. I was too young to believe that he would intercede and save me from the ferocious beast. As I screamed at the other children I thought of the beautiful heavens and the great power of God, and at the instant I hallooed at the children the panther sprang away and left me.

"Though rejoicing at its sudden departure I was greatly surprised at seeing it leave. As soon as it darted off I made my way to the other children, but I was so weak from exhaustion that I would tremble and almost fall as I made my way there in such a feeble manner. We left the sheep and went on toward the house.

"Just as we were leaving I saw the panther again. It attacked the sheep and caught and killed a lamb. When we reached the field fence I was not able to climb over alone, and Florence and Ernest helped me over. After crossing the field and arriving at the yard fence I scrambled to the top, but my strength was so near give out that I fell off into the yard and could not get up.

"Bettie, another sister who was thirteen years old, took me up in her arms and carried me into the house. Father was at Yellville that day and mother was bedfast with paralysis. Florence and Ernest were too young and too scared to tell mother what was the matter, and mother and Bettie were frightened. It was an hour before I recovered sufficiently to talk and tell them of my awful peril.

"It was several days before I was fully at myself again from the effects of that terrible fright in encountering that ugly creature. When I grew older I could not help but believe and realize that the good Lord saved me from the teeth and claws of that frightful animal." 🌿

A MIDNIGHT ATTACK OF A PANTHER ON A BUNCH OF HOGS [12:41]

THE OLD PIONEER, Joseph Hall, whose father, Dave Hall,[87] settled on White River in Marion County, Ark., in 1819, furnished the writer with this account.

"There were numbers of panther on White River when my father arrived here and for many years afterward. The river land on which my father settled was just above the narrows and near three miles below where Joe Pace has a ferry now.

"Early one afternoon when I was a little lad of a boy we heard as we thought a woman scream on the flat of land beyond the crest of the bluff that stood opposite the house. My father was gone from home that day or we would have not been mistaken as to the cause of those loud cries. Mother said it was a woman that had got lost in the wild woods and she answered the cry. When mother hallooed she was answered immediately by a scream and mother continued to answer and the cry on the bluff was repeated as often as mother hallooed.

"Finally the cry on the bluff became louder and nearer and it seemed that the noise emanated just on the top of the bluff. But owing to the grass, cedar trees and other growth we were not able to see anything. But we expected to see a woman come to the house. Mother hushed hallooing, but the noise on the bluff was repeated a few minutes longer when it ceased also. We kept looking for the woman to come to the house, but she never came and we thought it strange that she did not make her appearance.

"It seems curious to me to the present day that we did not understand the cause of that cry, but we did not think. Father did not come back home until near sundown and after mother had recited to him about the noise on the bluff and that she thought it was the screams of a bewildered woman and that she did not come to the house, he told her that it was not a woman, but a panther and mother and we children got frightened after the danger had passed.

"Father told us that it was fortunate for ourselves that we did not venture up on the bluff to hunt for the 'lost woman' or we might have got into trouble with the beast.

"About two o'clock on the following morning we heard the hogs rallying and very soon one of them commenced squealing. The dogs leaped over the yard fence and ran to where the hogs were and commenced baying some animal. Father supposed it was a gang of wolves that had attacked the hogs and rising out of bed he hurriedly put on his clothes and taking his rifle and went to the assistance of the dogs. But on arriving on the scene he saw by the dim light of the moon that it was a panther and not wolves. The stealthy beast had hold of a fine sow that weighed two hundred pounds.

"The dogs were baying the panther and had not yet taken hold of it. The panther was too busy trying to kill the sow to give any attention to the dogs, but when father got there he encouraged the dogs and they all darted onto the panther and it was not able to go on with the murder of the sow and fight the dogs too and it released the sow and thought it would try the dogs awhile, but quickly changing its mind and sprang away. But its temper was hot and while the dogs were pressing it hard in the race it stopped in two-hundred-fifty yards from where it had caught the sow to give battle to the dogs.

"When father reached there the panther had its back against a low bank and was striking at the dogs with its paws without hitting them, for they were careful to not get in reach of it. And while its attention was called to the dogs father reached as far as he could and placed the muzzle of his rifle near the region of the panther's heart and shot the animal dead. It was not a large one but it was big enough to have killed the sow if father and the dogs had not interfered. We supposed that it was the same animal that we heard screaming on the bluff. Though the sow was seriously wounded, but by close attention from us she finally recovered from her wounds."

A Hard Struggle with a Panther [13:47]

EVERY PIONEER in northwest Arkansas has heard of Sammy Hudson.[88] Many knew him personally, as he was a noted hunter and a prominent citizen of Newton County, Arkansas. Hudson was a remarkable bee hunter and always had on hand an abundance of wild honey for home use. After the close of the Civil War he became much interested in bee keeping and owned a large number of bee hives,[89] and has been known to have as much as eight hundred pounds of honey on hand at a time. He lived eight miles above Jasper, the county seat, and was one of the earliest settlers on Little Buffalo Creek.

In 1854 he was attacked by a panther, the awful scars of which combat he carried to his grave. In the year named, accompanied by Johnnie, his little five year old boy, he went into the forest to cut a bee tree. Hudson carried his axe, butcher knife and a large bucket. Arriving at the tree the old hunter soon felled it, and after chopping off a block in order to reach the honey, his attention was called to a loud coarse growl on a steep hillside nearby. There crouched on the ground was a large panther seemingly in an awful rage. It had apparently seen an enemy or was looking for one.

Hudson had neither dog nor gun. Picking up a stone he hurled it at the beast. The missile struck the ground a few yards above the furious animal. The stone rolled down toward it and the beast caught it in its mouth. This seemed to increase its rage. It dropped the stone, and with a dreadful growl it sprang along the hillside toward the hunter.

A big log lay between the beast and Hudson, with the top end down the hill. The large end was within twenty feet of the stump of the bee tree. The panther ran along on top of the log, and when it reached the end, it gave a long leap toward the frightened man, who now realized that a battle was to be fought. Hudson braced himself to resist it. The terrible creature sprang forward and when within a few feet, the hunter hurled his axe at it but missed.

As the ferocious animal reached him, Hudson raised his left hand and arm to protect his breast and face. As he did so the panther caught his arm in its mouth, when the terrible struggle began. The beast held fast and commenced to lacerate his flesh with its long, sharp claws. The man was dealing heavy blows with his clenched right hand. His clothing was torn in shreds, streams of blood flowed freely from great wounds inflicted by the animals claws. The struggling man and desperate panther were red with human blood. Hudson was rapidly losing strength, yet he did not lose courage or presence of mind.

The little boy stood within a few feet of the battle, being too young to realize the perilous position his father was in, and looked on as an idle spectator. As the combat continued the little fellow called out, "Daddy, do you think you can whip it?", and the father was too busy to reply.

Dark thoughts rose before the man, as he realized that if the panther gained the battle it would destroy the child. This gave him renewed energy. The man fought with desperation to save the life of his child as well as his own life. The boy supposed it was a fight as if between man and man. The butcher knife was on the ground nearby the boy. Presently the little fellow seemed to realize that the beast would kill his father and he cried out, "Daddy, do you want your knife?"

The despairing man heard him and replied, "Yes, quick!" The boy advanced boldly and handed the knife to his father, who in turn thrust the keen blade in the panther's body. Withdrawing it, he again sank the bloody knife into the body of the beast and turned the blade in the wound. Then he swooned and fell from exhaustion; but the knife had done its work well, for as Hudson fell the panther reeled and fell dead on top of him.

After a short time the weak man managed to crawl from under his victim, and drag himself away from the bloody scene, and with the aid of his little boy he struggled to get home. As his life blood was ebbing away, his little boy covered some of the wounds with mud. It was many days before he was able to hunt bee trees. Ugly scars were left on his head, face, breast and arms.

Hudson was quite popular with the settlers before the incident, but now they loved him the more, and thought him worthy of a place in the legislature, and he was elected to represent them in that capacity. When he arrived at the capitol the members of the assembly were eager to shake hands with the man who had killed a panther in a combat.

Hudson engaged in the mercantile business a few years later. A part of his goods were hauled from Springfield, Mo. One day while in the town named, a lot of young fellows who had heard of his combat, collected around him and asked more questions than he desired to answer. Finally he told them, "Yes, I was the man who killed the panther and I can whip the whole crowd of you fellows."

The youngsters saw fight in his eyes and immediately apologized. As pioneers pass the spot where the struggle for life transpired, they are occasionally heard to say, "There is where Hudson fought so desperately to save the life of himself and little boy." ✍

Two Children Kill a Panther but Thought It Was a Wolf [12:63]

THE FOLLOWING ACCOUNT of an old time incident was given by John C. Ross, formerly of near Gaither Post Office [1891–1909], Boone County, Ark., but now of Harrison, the county seat of Boone.

"Many years ago, when our family lived in the state of Tennessee, a man named Bob Justus lived a neighbor to us. In 1850 this man moved from Tennessee and settled on Long Creek in Carroll County, Ark. He lived on the west side of the creek at the mouth of a small stream called Dry Creek. But after residing here six years, removed to Howell County, Mo., where his mind became deranged and he was sent to the insane asylum at Jefferson City, where he died in 1858.

"Justus was a farmer as well as an experienced hunter. His main hunting ground while living on Long Creek was among the hills of this stream and the rough hills and hollows of Bear Creek where bear, deer and wild turkeys were abundant, as well as panthers and wolves.

"One day in 1851, while hunting on Bear Creek, he went up a narrow, rugged, gorge-like form of a branch of that stream, called Barren Fork, where it is said the sun is seen only once a day and that is at twelve o'clock. As he passed on up this hollow he discovered three or four acres of fertile bottom land which he determined to clear up and put in cultivation. What his motive was in having a small field so far from his residence on Long Creek was known only to himself. Unless he thought he could collect deer pelts and furs while he was clearing the land and live among the big and little game while he was cultivating it. When he was ready to put in the crop of corn, the land did not require a fence, for settler's stock had not yet invaded that section.

"Mr. Justus cultivated the land two or three years but the crops never benefited him any for as soon as the corn had matured, deer visited the clearing and destroyed it every year.

"In the late spring of 1852, after Justus planted the little field in corn and beans and returned home, he sent two of his children there to cut out the bushes with hoes. The children were a boy and girl named Ives and Mary. The boy was eleven years old and the girl was younger. These children being reared in a wild country were used to wild ways and did not fear wild animals and were not afraid to go anywhere they knew, and had been to Barren Fork with their father several times and Mr. Justus did not feel uneasy in sending them. They were to camp there one night and finish the job of work by noon the following day and return the same evening.

"Taking plenty of jerked venison and bread and a rifle and dogs for protection against wild beasts, they set out afoot. It was a long walk for children but they were accustomed to that sort of travel and arrived in the Bear Creek hills all right. Just before they reached the clearing the dogs sprang at some wild animal in the high grass and, after a short and lively chase, ran it into a cave.

"The children, being much interested, dropped their hoes and provisions, [and] went to see what the dogs were after. Finding that it had gone into the cave, they sent the dogs in to bring it out. The dogs were well trained and needed no second order, and dashed into the opening. Soon after the dogs entered the cave, the children heard them attack something and a fierce fight went on a short time, when the dogs came rushing out. The children tried to persuade them to go in again but they seemed cowed and refused to obey.

"The boy grew impatient and threatened to kill the dogs for not going back, for he wanted to know what sort of an animal was in the cave, and was furious because the dogs refused to go back, but without putting his threat into execution. He made up his mind to go in the cave himself and bring the beast out. Requesting his little sister to stay with the 'trifling dogs' on the outside, he put down the rifle and began crawling into the opening.

"He had not got far on the inside before he heard some animal approach with loud coarse growls. He stopped and with a long keen butcher knife held in his right hand, intended to kill it when he got in reach, but the beast was too quick for him. For with a sudden bound the great long beast struck against the boy and knocked him over before he had time to strike a blow with the knife. The animal rushed over the prostrate boy and darted out and the brave dogs dashed at it and hurried it up a tree which stood in a few yards of the cave. Fortunately the boy was not seriously injured by the rough encounter and crawled back out of the cave more angry and wiser in some things than when he went in.

"When he looked up into the tree where the ugly creature lay crouched on a big limb, he remarked to the little girl that it was 'the biggest wolf he ever saw.' Then he picked up the gun and after taking accurate aim, pulled the trigger. As the report echoed against the steep hillsides, the 'wolf' fell and lay dead, surrounded by the dogs ready for the attack if it gave evidence of the least sign of life. It was a yellow colored animal with a long tail. Its body including the tail was about the length of a ten foot fence rail, and the boy was highly elated about killing such an enormous 'wolf,' and was not a bit irritated at the dogs now for not going back into the cave.

"After half an hour's examination of the dead animal, they left it where it fell and went on to work and were unmolested during the night, and returned home in the evening of the next day as Mr. Justus had told them to do, and it did not take the boy long to tell his father about the wolf going up the tree and that he could prove it by his little sister Mary.[90]

"Mr. Justus informed him that it was not a wolf, for those animals could not climb trees. Being convinced that the children had killed an animal of some importance, he on the following morning early, mounted a horse and taking the boy up behind him, he visited the cave to ascertain the identity of the beast. He supposed that it might be a wild cat or a catamount[91] and was more than surprised to find that it was a large panther. The old hunter congratulated the boy and girl on their skill as hunters."

CARRYING A DEAD PANTHER TO FORSYTH ON A MULE [10:90]

MR. A. BROWN, or Uncle Auss [Austin], as he is commonly known and who has been postmaster at Peel, Marion County, Ark., for many years, relates some items of the pioneer days of White River.

"In the olden time," said he, "it was very common to fire hunt for deer of nights during 'mossing' time.[92] I well recollect of nine deer being slain one night in 1844, and also how two panthers were killed during the early days of Taney County and I will give the stories as I remember them.

"When I was only three years old or in 1838, my parents came to Taney County, Mo., and located on Bee Creek just above the mouth. I was born April 23, 1835. You can see by this that my parents were among the early settlers. Father died in the southeast part of Missouri in 1845.

"What I tell you may not be very interesting to some people nowadays, because there is no big game and people have almost quit talking about hunting, except for squirrels, possums, coons and skunks and such like.[93] One afternoon in the month of August, 1844, my father and two other men pushed their dugout canoe a few miles above the mouth of Bee Creek, and after night, while floating down the river with a bright light in the bow of the canoe, they shot and killed nine deer.

"When they had killed a deer, they would remove the entrails and sink the carcass in the river by weighting with chunk rocks or gravel, and proceed on down the river. The big torch, which was produced by burning pine knots and pine splinters, cast a light sufficient to see several deer along each shore, but those they shot were feeding on the moss in the water.

"The following day they pushed the craft back up the river, collecting their game then to save hides and hams if they needed the latter for meat. They found all where they sank them except the first one killed; this one was missing. It had been pulled from the water and dragged away. There was a plain trail, and the men followed it for half a mile, where it led into the face of a bluff, and there they discovered a panther lying on a low ledge of rock. It did not seem to be the least alarmed.

"The hunters kept approaching it until in close range and still it appeared to be not a bit afraid. The three men now stopped and father fired his trusty rifle. At the report the long ugly creature sprang up several feet above the ledge and alighted on the ground below the ledge and leaped the second time, and after rolling down the face of the bluff a few yards it died.

"The carcass of the deer was found within fifteen feet of where the panther was lying; the beast had covered it with leaves and was guarding it. More than likely the animal was nearby when the deer was killed and soon after the hunters had passed on down it had approached the edge of the water and waded in and pulled the dead deer to the gravel bar and, after appeasing its appetite on fresh venison, dragged the remainder into the bluff as related.

"Now I will tell you a little of my own experience," said Mr. Brown. "One day when I was a young man I mounted a mule and with dog and gun I rode into the Layton Pineries some twelve miles south of Forsyth. I enjoyed the sport of hunting and hoped I would meet something worth shooting at. My hopes were more than realized as the sequel will show.

"As I rode through the tall pine trees, the dog struck a hot trail of some animal, and after a short but lively chase, he treed it. I urged my mule along as fast as he would go, for I was convinced the game was worth capturing. The mule, like most mules, was quite stubborn and did not want to be hurried and had rather jump over the fence into some man's corn field than be bossed by a man. But finally, after threshing him lively with a stout switch, I got him into a gallop and after considerable trouble in preventing my gun from being knocked out of my hands by the limbs and trees, I was soon approaching near where the dog was stationed.

"I slowed up and directly the mule came to a standstill. Then I cast my eyes toward the top of a tall pine tree that the dog was barking up and saw a monstrous panther. I never had killed a panther, and now was my chance. Hunters, like everyone else pursuing a certain occupation, desire to do something elevating and now was my opportunity to be elevated in my mind as a hunter.

"Dismounting, I made the mule secure to a sapling, and after a critical examination of my rifle, I nerved myself and ventured slowly to within thirty paces of the tree. The animal looked fierce and angry and grew restless at my intrusion. I was careful to take accurate aim with my gun, pulled the trigger and sent a leaden messenger into the tree to invite him to the ground. After the report of the shot had died away and the smoke cleared, I saw it totter, then reel over, and as it swung off the limb it turned its hold loose and come tumbling down and struck the ground with great force. A slight quiver of the body and legs showed that my shot was well directed. It needed no second shot for it soon made its last gasp for breath.

"As it lay stretched broadside with the blood flowing from the bullet hole I viewed it with pride. The dog was as well pleased as I was. We were both highly elated for we had something to brag on. I measured the panther and found that it was nine feet long.

"I was so well pleased that I wanted to take it to Forsyth to prove to the world my skill as a slayer of wild animals, but I doubted the docility of my mule in carrying it; but the animal proved all right. But I had a hard lift in placing it across my mule's back. I succeeded in scrambling up behind the dead panther and went on.

"The trip to town was found to be no easy task, but I would much rather try to carry a dead panther than a live one. The river was low, and after fording it I rode into the village and dumped the dead panther on the street in front of John Vance's store. It soon attracted the attention of a large crowd who happened to be in town that day, and several of the old timers told interesting stories about panther and other big game and refreshed each other's minds until everybody in town was ready to give in his experience as a hunter. I was congratulated on my skill in killing one panther at least.

"After the men had run out of hunting stories I gave a man a half dollar in silver to remove the hide, then it was stuffed and Mr. Vance gave me permission to place it in a crouching position in the second story of his store house where it remained for several weeks."

THREE PANTHER STORIES [13:34]

THE OLD TIMERS of Taney County, Mo. that are living, remember Dr. A. S. Layton of Forsyth. Layton built a saw mill in an early day in the pineries twelve miles south of Forsyth. This mill supplied a large scope of country with lumber. Dave McCord, in referring to this mill, said that it received a large custom and that he has known lumber from this mill to be hauled as far as Warsaw in Benton County, Mo.[94]

Uncle Dave said that he has seen as many as twenty wagons standing at this mill waiting for their turn to load. The heaviest trade was soon after crops were laid by, when it seemed that everybody came to the saw mill for a load of lumber.

"You talk about a man handling gold and silver," continued Uncle Dave, "it seemed like Layton coined it at this mill and did, as far as selling lumber for the yellow and bright metal was concerned."

"Dr. Layton had his ups and downs with the wild beasts as well as others. One day he went into a cave where he thought a bear was. He was armed with a shotgun and pistol and with a bright torch. He went into the cave to slay bruin, but there was not a bear to be found in there; but he met a panther instead, which threatened to attack him, and while it was crouching and growling to spring at him, he quickly leveled his shotgun toward it and fired one barrel then the other at it. The animal was not killed, but was desperately wounded.

"Before the panther recovered from the shock of receiving the contents of both barrels of the shotgun, he shot it again with his pistol and the beast sank down and soon died. The animal was nine feet in length and the doctor had hard work while dragging it out of the cave. After removing its hide he cut off the panther's forepaws and carried the hide and paws to Forsyth.

"Layton and others stuffed the hide until it resembled a live panther. With the permission of John P. Vance, they placed the stuffed hide in his wareroom, which was attached to his storehouse. The men so shaped the stuffed hide that when anyone stepped into the wareroom it looked like it was going to spring on them.

"The fun-loving settlers saw a great deal of sport when they persuaded a fellow that knew nothing of the stuffed hide in there, to go in and see some of Vance's wares, but when he would catch sight of the stuffed hide he would hustle out of there.

"One day Isaac Essex put a stop to the fun in quick order. Essex, after coming into town, began drinking very freely. He kept pouring whiskey down his throat until he did not know the difference between a stuffed panther hide and a real live panther. After a while Essex got very noisy and went into Vance's store. Vance and others invited him into the wareroom pretending to want to sell him something. The drunk man was willing to go into the room and promising to buy anything shown him.

"The man was staggering like a horse with the blind staggers when he entered the room. He did not notice the stuffed hide until the men got him in close contact with it, when they all wheeled and ran out of the room yelling as they went out, 'Look out, Essex, there is a panther ready to jump on you.'

"But Essex was too full of liquor to be afraid and turning, he caught sight of the stuffed hide, and thinking it was a real panther he snatched his hunting knife from the scabbard and rushed up to the hide and never stopped until he cut it to pieces with the knife before he recognized the mistake. The other fellows were beat worse than Essex was, for it put an end to anymore fun out of the hide." ✍

PANTHER BOTTOM STORIES AND HOW THE BOTTOM DERIVED ITS NAME [19:32]

ON THE NORTH SIDE of White River where the division line between Taney and Ozark Counties, Mo. crosses this stream is a long narrow bottom known as the Panther Bottom. The line between the two counties named passes through the upper end of the bottom and the state line between Missouri and Arkansas crosses the river at the lower half of the bottom.

A man by the name of Barrett was the first settler in this bottom. This man built a little log hut on the bank of the river at the extreme lower end of the bottom where Pine Hollow runs into the river. When Mr. Barrett left this cabin John Johnson and his son Joe lived here and kept their cattle on the cane which grew so abundantly in the bottom and on the face of the bluff.

Mr. Johnson and his sons removed the Barrett hut and built a little larger house on the same spot where the Barrett cabin stood. In the fall of 1857 Tom Carroll taught a subscription school in the Johnson cabin. I remember well how we children who lived on the south bank of the river crossed it morning and evening in a dug out canoe.

Allen Lucas lived on the bank of the river on the north side in the first bottom above here and used water out of a spring that gushed out of the river bank. Mr. Lucas sent his two boys Jesse and Jim and one daughter whose name was Lizzie to this school in a canoe. As the boys pushed their craft back of evenings they would chase and kill the big buffalo fish.[95]

Robert Case Balet who settled on Big Creek in 1844 was the first man who cultivated land here. Mr. Case Balet lived in the creek bottom known as the Ben Ginch farm now and he hauled the first load of his corn crop in a big box fastened on a large sled drawn by a team of gentle cattle.

In the early Fifties a man of the name of Jobe Davis lived in the upper end of the bottom near the bank of a ravine. Davis was a noted violinist and used a loud sounding fiddle which could be plainly heard across the river.

Soon after Mr. Carroll taught his school here Elias Anderson and Ben Pearce lived a short time in the same cabin that Carroll taught school in. Overlooking the bottom is a bluff that extends from the upper end to the lower part. The bluff is divided in places by deep gulches and ledges of rock extend along the face of the bluff with a high precipice here and there which form a beautiful picture of the art of nature.

Panther Bottom has been known by this name for many years. John Bias, son of Hiram Bias, informed the writer how this bottom took its name as told him by his father. It derived its name in the following way:

"It was several years before I was born and I first saw the light of day on Bee Creek in Taney County, Mo. in 1844," said he. "My father said that one day he and Jonathan Baker were hunting together in the hills near this bottom. When they got to the top of the bluff over looking the bottom the men separated. Baker went down the bluff from where a high bald point is to hunt in the bottom. My father was to keep on the crest of the ridge to the foot of the bluff where he and Mr. Baker were to meet at the mouth of Pine Branch. The hunters had no dog with them except a little 'fice' which belonged to Baker.[96]

"After Mr. Baker had made his way down the face of the bluff into the bottom and while making his way through the thick tall cane near the river bank he stumbled onto four panthers before he was aware of their presence. The panthers consisted of a mother and three one-third grown cubs. The old panther was in a fighting mood and would have sprang on Baker before he could aim and shoot, but the fice dog interfered by dashing at her and she wheeled and sprang up a tree. The young ones followed her.

"Baker was glad he escaped the teeth and claws of the dreaded beast, but without taking time to thank the little dog for its timely intervention began shooting at once. When he had shot four times there were four dead panthers lying at the foot of the tree.

"The reports of the rifle and the barking of the fice attracted father's attention and he went down into the bottom where Baker was and found him exulting over the dead panthers. While they were removing the hides from the animals they suggested to each other that this river bottom ought to be named the Panther Bottom and it has gone by this name to the present day.

"After this occurrence Baker would have refused the offer of a fine farm for his little dog."

❧ TALES OF VARIOUS SPECIES ☙

Editors' note: The bobcat, *Lynx rufus*, which Turnbo calls catamount to distinguish it from the mountain lion or panther, was fairly common in settler times, and is estimated to be present today in the Ozarks at about one bobcat per six square miles. It prefers heavy forest cover. It is a carnivore, feeding on rabbits, rodents, opossums, and birds, and is capable of killing adult deer occasionally and fawns often.[97]

A CATAMOUNT LEAPS ON A WOUNDED BUCK [14:8]

FROM THE WAGON ROAD that leads from Protem to Hercules in Taney County, Mo. [modern Rte. 125 corridor], we have a fine view of the west prong of Big Creek. From that part of the road that leads along the high timbered ridge, nine miles north of the first named town, bald hills with skirts of timber and deep hollows form an entertaining view. Beyond this to the east is the valley of the east fork of Big Creek. Further on is seen the high hills that divide that part of Big Creek and the Pond fork.

A short time before the death of Wes Henderson he told me the following account.

"I had heard of catamounts attacking deer but I never witnessed that sight until one day while I was hunting on the left prong of Big Creek, near where the wagon way passes along the divide between this prong and the breaks of Caney Creek.

"I was on the slope of a hill, and noticing a bunch of deer on the hillside above me, which attracted my attention in a manner that I stood and watched them without making an effort to kill one at the present. There were six bucks and six does and just as many big fawns as there were does. The fawns were almost as large as yearling deer and they were trying to suck the does, but they and the bucks would not let them. The does would kick at them and the bucks would butt them. The old deer were trying to wean the young deer but the youngsters were stubborn and refused to be weaned.

"It was a curiosity to watch all their actions—the young deer in trying to suck and the old ones in trying to prevent them. It was amusing as well as curious, but after a while I became weary of waiting and watching and shot at one of the bucks and wounded it and it ran down the hill into a hollow below me where I saw him stop and lay down. The other deer went in an opposite direction.

"I started on down the hill toward where the wounded buck had laid down. Before I had approached close enough to it to shoot it the second time, the buck got up and ran up the hollow. I now saw that it was hobbling along, for my bullet had broken the bone of one thigh.

"Soon after it had passed beyond my view I heard a racket up the hollow the way the buck had gone. Thinking that the deer had fallen and was floundering around in its death struggles, I went on down into the hollow and saw the buck come running back down the hollow toward me with a catamount on its back. The frightened deer did not notice me and came swiftly on and as it darted on down the hollow it knocked the hold of the cat partly loose and it was hanging down and clinging on with its claws.

"I had just reloaded my gun and when the deer and cat were in twenty-five feet of me I shot the buck down. The ball from my gun had took effect in the deer's neck and broken it. The buck as it fell turned a sommersault, which broke the cat's hold on the deer and it hit the ground in ten feet of me.

"The moment the cat recovered itself it looked at me and bushed up its hair and growled at me. I jerked my butcher knife from the scabbard and stood a moment with it in my hand. The cat was very angry and seemed to grow more furious. I now reloaded my gun in haste and held the knife in my hand while I was reloading. I expected it to attack me every moment. But just as I finished loading the gun and almost ready to shoot the vicious animal, it darted off and was soon out of my sight. Of course the buck was dead."

The Catamounts Mistook Them for a Turkey [14:15]

AMUSING AS WELL AS SERIOUS accounts have been told me by hunters of their encounters with catamounts while in the woods hunting.

William Brown, stepson of Allen Trimble, informed me that one day while he was hunting in Big Beach Hollow near the division line between Franklin and Crocket townships in Marion County, Ark., he went down near the mouth of the hollow and sat down on a log to rest. This log lay near the river bank and was close to the log chute.[98]

"I was very tired," said he, "and after I had sat down on the log I became drowsy and went to sleep, but was roused from slumber by a noise and when I opened my eyes a catamount was standing in a few feet of me with its hair bushed up. The vicious animal was growling and getting itself in shape to attack me. I leveled my rifle at it at once and sent a ball crashing through its brains which relieved my anxiety for it is useless for me to say that I was not scared."

An amusing incident similar to this occurred to Mr. Fate Jones, son of John Jones, who settled the Jim Dean farm on the top of the bluff in Keesee township in Marion County, Ark., and opposite Bradley's Ferry. Mr. Jones said that one day he got among a large flock of turkeys on the north side of the river, and after killing two of them, the remainder rose and flew across the river and lit in the face of the bluff just below the mouth of Little Beach Hollow at the log chute we have just mentioned.

Jones got in a canoe and followed the turkeys across the river, but by the time he got across, the turkeys had scattered in the face of the bluff and Jones seated himself between two cedar[99] logs that lay two and one-half feet apart, one of which rested on a rock and was three feet above the ground. These logs lay near a ledge of rock near six feet high. The two cedars had been cut down by someone and the limbs were trimmed off.[100]

"When I sat down I rested my back against a water oak tree.[101] Then I began yelping with my turkey caller that I manufactured out of the wing bone of a turkey. I was well concealed and nothing could see me until I was approached in a few feet of me, except in front. As I went on calling I was on the watch for an approaching turkey to come up in front.

"I had called some minutes when on sudden an animal came crashing over the dead cedar limbs and alighted in a few feet of me. Without taking time to look around to see what it was but thinking it was a panther, I vacated the spot instantly by sliding feet foremost down the bluff and under the cedar log that was resting on the rock. While I was crawfishing under the log my coat, which was of new homemade jeans that my mother had made me, hung to a snag by the tail and, thinking the beast had hold of it, I gave a deafening yell and lunged forward with all the strength I had and tore loose.

"Then I rolled down the cliff without injuring myself, then leaped as far as I could down the bluff, hallooing as loud as I could, and then I stopped and looked back up the bluff for my enemy and saw a huge catamount go sneaking up the bluff above from where I had retreated from. The beast seemed as bad surprised as I was.

"After it had gone beyond my view I went back and recovered my rifle that I had dropped in the exciting scramble of getting away."

Charley Smith, the Miller and the Maker of Whiskey [17:93]

WE HAVE ALLUDED to the Charley Smith mill on Big Creek which was built just over the line in Ozark County, Mo. on several occasions in these sketches. Mr. Smith was a giant in strength. His mill stones were large but when they needed sharpening he could handle them the same as if they were only grind stones. The mill stood on the west side of the creek a short distance below a bluff. Here at this mill Smith ground corn into meal for the settlers and manufactured whiskey. He loved to drink liquor himself.

It was told by those who was well acquainted with Smith that he was stout enough to lift a forty gallon barrel full of whiskey from the ground and drink out of the bung hole.[102] This was hearsay only but it come from trustworthy sources. Smith was a hunter as well as miller and a maker of whiskey.

One morning before day break he took his rifle gun and went up on the top of the McVey's bald hill to shoot a turkey. When he arrived at the crest of the hill, he rested himself on a stone and waited till early dawn when he heard a gobler down in McVey's Hollow and he took his caller out of his pocket and commenced calling the gobler and he would answer frequently and advanced closer to him and so was a hungry catamount approaching him from the opposite direction from where the turkey was coming. The cat supposed that Smith was a turkey and he wanted breakfast.

Smith was ignorant of the cat's presence until the animal leaped on his shoulders and back. Though the man was taken on surprise but he was equal to the occasion. Dropping his rifle he reached up and grabbed the catamount by the neck and jerked it over his head and slammed it against the stones with such force that it was stunned and he finished its career with stones and then went on with his turkey calling and finally about day light the gobler got in gun shot range and Smith shot and killed it.

The catamount had scratched the man's back enough to make it bleed but the wounds were so slight that they soon healed over.

Among the Coons [14:29]

SOME OF THE INTERESTING STORIES of catching coons is as follows:
The Jones boys—Fate and Frank, sons of John Jones—told about catching thirteen coons one morning before breakfast, while they lived on

the old Mat Hoodenpile farm below Bradley's Ferry on White River, in Marion County, Ark. The most of these coons were caught by the dogs in the cornfield and the remainder were caught along the sloo between the river and field. This was done in war times.[103]

Jake Hetherly said that while they lived in Douglas County, Mo., he and his father and Jake's brother, Jack, went out one day during the deep snow in the early part of 1856 and caught twelve coons before sundown. They were not accompanied by a dog but tracked the coons in the snow to where the animals had climbed trees and went into the hollow limbs or cavities in the stem of the trees for shelter, and they would chop the trees down and capture the coons before they could make their escape from their place of refuge from the cold weather. Mr. Hetherly said that he was only seven years old but "enjoyed himself well that bitter cold day while catching the coons."

The best coon story I ever heard as regards the number of coons caught in one day, was told me by William M. (Mort) Ingram, who was born in Scott County, Virginia, January 20, 1817, and came to Taney County, Mo., in 1860 and lived near the Five Oak Bald hill on the head of Big Buck Creek in the southeast part of the county. Mr. Ingram said that one day in 1871, while he was hunting in the hills on the east side of Shoal Creek, he located a lot of coons in hollow trees.

"I went home now and brought my ax and dog and hunted for coons instead of deer and caught fourteen that day. Also John Ingram, a grown son of mine, in company with John I. Smith, killed eleven coons the same day, and Jim Henderson, son of 'Chris' Henderson, in company with another man whose name I have forgotten, killed nine—all the same day, making a total of thirty-four coons slain the same day. Of course, the weather was cold with plenty of snow on the ground or none of us would have been so lucky at capturing so many of them in one day," said Mr. Ingram.[104]

MISTREATING TURTLES [28:44]

IN THE PIONEER DAYS during the settling up of the country a number of men as well as boys waded and played in the water along the streams which partly accounts for the chills and fevers that were so prevalent then.[105] A number of people who visited Bratton's Spring in Ozark County, Mo. and some of them who lived on this stream were no exception to this custom. Those that delighted to play in the water would catch fish and turtles along Spring Creek.

Mr. W. C. (Carroll) Johnson who has known this stream and the customs of the people here all his life furnished the writer with this account.

"I have seen Hiram Bias and Gus Barnum and others catch turtles of all sizes in Spring Creek and peel bark from paw paws and hickory and tie a stout piece around the turtles' necks. Barnum, who was a very large stout man, with a companion would climb up a big sapling and bend it down until the top was low enough to the ground for another man who was on the ground to reach up with his hands and take hold of the sapling and while the three men were holding it down another man would tie the other end of the bark that was attached to the turtle's neck to the top limb of the sapling and when this was completed the two men on the sapling would jump off to the ground and at the same time the other man who was holding it would turn it loose and the top would fly up and jerk the turtle up with it which would kick and struggle to free itself. They would let it hang there until it was dead and the shell and bones would fall to the ground after the flesh had decayed.

"At other times, I have seen these same men and others take turtles out of the water and bend down saplings and put the end of a limb in the turtle's mouth and let go the sapling and as the top of the young tree went up the turtle would be jerked up with such force that the twig would snap asunder or slip from the turtle's mouth and the turtle would be hurled several yards away. This kind of sport seemed to be excellent pass time to some people but it was none to me," said Mr. Johnson.[106]

STORIES OF TURTLES [28:46]

THE FOLLOWING STORIES relating to turtles might be of some interest to the reader. Mr. Bennette Tabor who is dead now informed me one day several years before his death that himself and Harve Smith killed a monster turtle one night in White River while they were fire hunting. They discovered the turtle in the shoals water where Mr. Tol Wood the stock dealer of Greene County Mo. was drowned a few years ago. These shoals is opposite midway of the Panther Bottom and just on the inside of Ozark County, Mo.

The turtle measured twenty-eight inches across the belly.[107] It was in water only two feet deep and as it crawled along on the river bed its back showed above the surface of the water. In capturing the monster Mr.

Tabor said that he struck it with his three pronged harpoon but it failed to penetrate the shell when he hit it on the neck and the beards on the harpoon held it. "But the turtle pulled the canoe forty yards before we were able to control its movements and haul it to shore and kill it," [said Mr. Tabor].

"On the following day we returned back there and weighed it and it tipped the steel yards at one-hundred-twenty-five pounds. Then we took the shell off of its belly and took all the flesh out of the upper shell and for the sake of curiosity I put the shell in the water to see it float then I got into the shell and it held up my weight without sinking." 🌿

AMONG THE SQUIRRELS [14:39]

RATHER AN AMUSING STORY of hunting squirrels is told by Mr. Isaac Copelin, son of John and Tyne (Keesee) Copelin. Mr. Copelin formerly lived on his father's old farm at the Buck Shoals Ford of White River in Marion County, Ark., but his present residence is on the Wagoner sheep ranch just over the line in Taney County, Mo.

In reciting the story, Mr. Copelin said that one day while living at the Buck Shoals Ford, he took his axe and dogs and went up on the hill to hunt for squirrels and saw a fox squirrel[108] run into a hollow tree and "After I had chopped the tree down," said he, "I saw eight grown fox squirrels run in. The squirrels made their exit one after the other, and as they ran out they scattered and the dogs stood and looked foolish, for they did not know which ones of the squirrels to pursue.

"In the excitement of the moment, while chasing the squirrels and throwing stones at them after they had got up trees, I lost my pocketbook which contained $40 and $30 worth of notes.[109] I then quit the squirrel business and searched diligently for my money and notes the remainder of the day, without succeeding in finding it. I offered a reward of $5 to any person who would find the pocketbook and return all the money and notes. But no one was lucky enough to find it except myself and I, as the finder of it on the following day, saved the reward."

This land near this ford of White River is certainly a lucky place for squirrels for Mr. Arch Anderson informed me one day that, while hunting in the river bottom near this same ford, he noticed a lot of squirrels playing on the ground and the dogs chased them all up one tree and he counted twenty-four squirrels up the same tree. Mr. Anderson said that he shot squirrels out of this tree until he became weary of the sport and quit.

"Talk about squirrel stories," said Ben McKinney, who is an old resident of Keesee Township in Marion County, Ark., "I remember that one day while I was hunting on Shoal Creek below where I live, I noticed five gray squirrels playing on a cedar log that lay in the face of the creek bluff. The top end of the log pointed down the bluff. Very soon the squirrels quit the log and joined an immense bunch of squirrels, which I now saw in a low swag in the face of the bluff, which was in plain view from where I stood. This swag or sink was near twenty feet square and it was fairly lined with squirrels and were all gray ones.

"I had my gun with me but no dog. I was so astonished at the sight of so many squirrels that I made no effort to shoot at any of them. It was the largest bunch of squirrels that I ever saw together before. They were all chattering and playing. After I had watched them nearly ten minutes, part of them left the swag and ran up a cedar tree and the tree seemed to be alive with them. In a short while longer the entire bunch disappeared from my view. I had no way of counting them but I made as accurate an estimate of the number as I could and I think there was not less than three hundred of them if not more."[110]

Jerry Hutchison informed me one day in 1895, that while his father lived near where Isabella Post Office[111] in Ozark County, Mo., is, his brother George Hutchison shot and killed eighty squirrels during two days in succession, or in other words killed forty each day. They were shot on the fence and in the trees around the field.

RUNNING RACES TOGETHER KILLING SQUIRRELS [14:42]

IT WAS NOT UNCOMMON in the pioneer days for women to shoot hawks, turkeys or squirrels. We give two short stories here to show that on a few occasions a wife would exceed her man in killing squirrels.

Lige Motley,[112] an old time resident of Marion County, Ark., said that one day he and wife went out into the forest together to kill squirrels. They used only one gun and agreed to shoot time about with it. Mr. Motley said that he killed six squirrels and his wife killed seven during the rounds that day. Mrs. Motley's name is Elizabeth and is a daughter of Jesse Hacket.

Jack Haggard[113] tells of a man of the name of Ben McKinney[114] and his wife hunting squirrels together. Mr. McKinney lived on the south side of White River in Taney County, Mo., and two miles above Forsyth. McKinney's wife was named Catherine and was a daughter of Levi Casey.[115] McKinney would often remark that Catherine was a better shot than he was, and would shoot hawks if they interrupted the chickens. This man and his wife would usually run races to see who would kill the most squirrels. Each would carry their own gun and as a rule she would bring more squirrels home than her husband would.

[According to Haggard], "She would sometimes in a jocular way say, 'Ben, I only take you along with me to turn the squirrels[116] on the trees for me while I do the shooting of them.'"

A Man and a Mink Have a Stirring Time with Each Other [14:46]

SOMETIMES A MAN will stir around more lively from the effects of a fright from a small animal than he will at the sight of a large one, and it usually turns out very funny. Mr. William Riddle, who lives on Long Creek in Carroll County, Ark., said that many years ago a man of the name of John Brummer lived in two and one-half miles of Denver in Boone County, Ark., who went crazy and shot himself dead in his own bed with a holster pistol. His body received burial on his own land and the pistol was put in the coffin and buried with him.

One night, long before his death, he heard a disturbance among his chickens which were roosting in the hen house, and rising up out of bed, he took a light and went to see what was bothering them. On reaching the door of the chicken house he held the light on the inside of the building and saw a mink squatted down on the floor just on the inside of the entrance. Picking up a board he intended to poke the little animal hard enough with it to cripple it, but the mink was too quick for him for the moment that Brummer touched it with the end of the board it "scooted" out and ran up the board to his hand and on up his arm.

The man's shirt collar was wide open and the cunning little creature seeing a place of refuge darted into the man's bosom. As it did so, the board and the light both dropped out of his hands and the scared man cut all kinds of didoes by dancing, running, jumping and screaming.

This frightened the mink and it ran around on his back, sides and bosom in trying to find a getting out place and Brummer grabbed and clawed manfully until he tore off his shirt before he got rid of the mink. The lively little animal bit and scratched the man at a lively rate before they became separated. Each one was glad to get rid of the other.

The Hunter Played off on His Friend [17:31]

IN THE YEAR 1867 while Mr. Abe Cole lived on the old Cain Smiley place on Big Buck Creek in Taney County, Mo., he knew of two bee courses that he was anxious to find the home of. He hunted in vain for them day after day but failed to locate them. Finally he come to the conclusion that he was not a bee hunter and sent for Bill Clark, the famed bee hunter and deer killer, to come and hunt bee trees for him.

In a few days the hunter made his appearance and he lost no time in getting to work to locate the hives. Mr. Cole knew that Clark could find the trees in a few hours and wanted to go with him, but the hunter said he could find the bees with the least trouble by being alone and Cole stayed at home and let the hunter have his way. In a day or two the hunter went to Mr. Cole's and told him he could not find the trees. Mr. Cole thought strange at this but still did not suspect anything wrong, thinking he had told the truth about it. He went on about his business until a week afterward when he found where two bee trees had been felled and all the honey taken out. He suspicioned Clark at once and it turned out that he had found the two trees and robbed them without letting Cole know anything about it.

Bill Clark, the Deer Slayer and Bee Hunter [16:19]

BILL CLARK was well known many miles along White River. Almost every pioneer settler in Taney and Ozark Counties, Mo., and Marion County, Ark., knew him or had heard of him, for his fame as a hunter went far and wide. As a deer and bee hunter he had but few rivals.

It is told of him that he never done but few days' work on a farm, entirely depending on hunting for a living. When he was hungry for bread he would approach a farmer and purchase a turn of corn on credit, promising to pay for it with a fat buck. It might be a month or a year before he fulfilled his promise, but it is said he hardly ever failed to bring the deer according to contract.[117]

He tramped the woods so frequently in search of game that the front part of his pant legs, unless they were made of tanned buck hide, were worn into tatters by the saw briars. To avoid the wear and tear on his pants he would often step high through the grass like a blind horse.

Referring to his renown as a bee hunter, a settler who lived on White River sent for him one day to find a bee tree that he and others failed to locate. When Clark arrived several men were sitting around watching the bees sip the bait. Some timber prevented the men from getting the proper direction the bees came and went. Bill seated himself to watch the bees for a few minutes, then he stationed himself on the bank of the river. He soon discovered that they flew across the river (his eyesight was so good he could see the flight of a bee a long distance).[118] After getting the direction the bees flew, he prepared to locate their home. Every man in the crowd had his eyes on Clark, for he was acknowledged to be a great bee hunter.

Soon he noticed a bee heavily laden, which flew very slow. Bill watched it intently and said to the men, "Look, boys, look, look, look, boys, look. Into a tree it went, by jacks." His eyes had followed the bee into the face of a bluff on the opposite side of the river and saw it go into a tree. The men crossed the river in a canoe and discovered the bees in the tree Bill had named. He had located the tree in less than half an hour, where others had hunted for days and failed to find.

I remember seeing great numbers of wild bees visit our spring on Elbow Creek in 1850. The direction they came and went indicated that there was more than one hive nearby. Father was not a bee hunter, but he enjoyed eating wild honey and he sent for Bill Clark, and when he made his appearance, which was in a day or two, father employed him to find bee trees. I was only six years old, but I recollect how Clark coursed the bees from the spring.

The hunter seated himself near where the bees were sipping the water and watched those that flew across the creek; then he ran and followed one to the creek and halted and waited for another one. In a few seconds another one appeared, which flew just over his head. Bill began to repeat the words, "There it goes; there it goes; there it goes; over the hill it went, by jacks." Then he climbed the bluff on a line the bee had went and stopped on the top of the bluff, where he saw the bee pass over.

In a little while another bee went buzzing just over him. His eyes quickly perceived it and I heard him sing out, "Yonder it goes! Yonder it goes! Yonder it goes into a post oak tree, by jacks." The man had located it in a few minutes.

Returning to the spring he proposed to find another swarm in less than an hour. Another course was followed west from the spring. Some timber intervened and so obstructed the course that Clark had some difficulty in finding the tree, but in about forty minutes he treed the bees in a large cedar tree a few hundred yards from the spring. The bees went into the tree near the ground.

In the early forenoon the weather was clear and bright, but soon after locating the swarm in the cedar tree the sun was hidden by clouds, which broke up the bee hunt.

Going to the house for ax and vessels, the hunter chopped a big block out of the tree and exposed to view a fine quantity of rich honey comb, which filled the cavity in the tree. Rain began falling while we were feasting on the honey.

In a day or two we felled the post oak tree on the creek bluff that Clark had found first, but it contained only a small amount of honey.

Many years ago, when the fine valley of Big Creek in Taney County, Mo., was wild, Bill and his brother, Calvin Clark, were hunting one day on the right hand prong of the creek. The weather was warm and the weary hunters had stopped at a spring of water to quench their thirst. Before either one had time to drink, a bee alighted and began sipping at the water. Bill remarked, "By jacks, Mr. Bee, I will find your house before I drink of this water."

Both men waited patiently until the bee filled itself and started. Bill watched it move off and followed it with his eye and saw it enter the cavity of a post oak tree just fifteen paces from the spring. This proved to be a rich tree and the comb had a peculiar formation. The tree was large with a big hollow. A column of honeycomb was on two sides of the cavity, from the ground to seven feet above where the hollow terminated. From the center of the termination of the cavity was a round column of rich comb three inches in diameter and two and one-half feet in length, which hung between the two columns of the main comb. It was held in place by a small neck—the lower part was not attached to anything. Both of the men said that the formation of the comb in this tree was strange to them. 🐝

PUT TO FLIGHT BY HONEYBEES [17:36]

ONE DAY in the month of August, 1873, I and Allen Trimble were sitting together at my father's spring that runs out of the river bank where we lived from September 6, 1859, to my father's death in 1870. This spring gushes out at the foot of the bank and only a few feet above the common stage of water in the river. This farm is known now as the Jim Roselle land.

As Uncle Allen was an old pioneer of that neighborhood he recounted to me a number of incidents which occurred there in the near vicinity. Among the accounts given me was one that he said had considerable fun attached to it. Pointing up the river he says it occurred up yonder. The year it happened was in 1852.

"One day in that year I and a man of the name of Masters who lived just on top of the bank from this spring went up on the bluff just above the mouth of Big Beach Hollow to hunt a bee tree. Bee trees in that day were numerous and were but little trouble to locate. We took plenty of bait with us and after placing it in several places convenient for the bees to find we sat down by one of the baits to wait for the bees to come and sip the bait.

"We were not there but a few minutes before the bait was covered with them and soon after we had a few courses we started out to hunt for their abodes and discovered four bee trees in less than an hour. These trees were not over one-quarter mile apart. One hive was in a small shelly cedar which stood in the face of the bluff.

"I pushed the point of my hunting knife into this tree two feet below where the bees went into the tree which was near seven feet above the foot of the tree and drawing it out the honey flowed out and dripped down the body of the tree. Not deeming the tree rich enough on account of its small size we went back on top of the bluff and selected a much larger tree which stood on the brink of the bluff one-quarter of mile from the mouth of Big Beach Hollow which we thought was the richest in honey of the four trees.

"We had taken plenty of vessels with us to hold the honey and having our axes with us we went to work to cut it down, but very soon after we commenced to chop on the tree the bees flew into a rage and swarmed out of the tree and swooped down on us and forced us to retire on fast gait until we had went a hundred yards when we stopped behind a tree where we got rid of the fighting bees.

"The infuriated colony had drove us away but we did not propose to leave without robbing the tree, but the odds were against us for if the bees kept up the fight we would experience the pain of numerous stings before we got through. After we had suggested a few plans to protect ourselves from the fury of the hive, none of which seemed feasible, Masters says, 'Allen, I've got it, all right. Now I will pull off my shirt and you take it and wrap your head up in it, leaving only an open space large enough for you to see through, then go and chop the tree down.'

"To which I agreed to do and Mr. Masters pulled off his shirt and handed it to me and I wrapped my head up with it in such a way that I knew it would give ample protection to my face and eyes and on returning to the tree I went to work again to fell it. The bees got into an uproar again immediately and swarmed all around to force me to retire.

"Mr. Masters was entirely naked from the waist up and remained behind the tree where he had give up his shirt to me. Though the colony had attacked me fiercely but I was so well protected from their stings that they were not able to hurt me except my hands.

"Very soon after I had felled the tree, Masters left the tree he was behind and ventured up in twenty yards of the stump of the fallen tree. The anger of the bees had rose to a high pitch and were flying in every direction when all of a sudden I heard Masters cry out in agony, 'Oh Lord, Oh Lordy, Oh Lord God Almighty, save me from their wrath,' and away he went down the point of the bluff toward the mouth of Beach Hollow as fast as his legs could take him.

"At first I thought the man had gone crazy but at the next thought I knew what was the matter. A lot of bees had attacked him and were tormenting the man with their stings. I left the tree at once and ran in pursuit of him. As I ran along I could hear Masters yell at the top of his voice, 'God, have mercy, these infernal bees are killing me.'

"Though I knew Masters was suffering with pain but his actions and noise was so ludicrous that I laughed as I ran along behind him. In a little while Masters turned to the left and went down the face of the bluff to the river and plunged into the water and pushing out to where it was over his head he made a dive for deep water, then rose to the surface to get his breath. He went under the second time and by the time he come to the surface of the water again the bees had give up the fight and left and the man swam back to shore. The bees had stung him severely on his breast and back.

"I pulled the stingers out and gave him back his shirt which he soon donned himself with and I says, 'Masters, let us go back now.'

"'Go back where,' says he.

"'To the bee tree,' says I.

"'Oh no, I am going home,' said he and he left me and went down to the shoal at the mouth of Beach where the water was shallow enough to wade and he crossed over and went home.

"I went back up the bluff and gathered a lot of dead sumach[119] and bunched it together and tied it at one end and attached it to the top end of a long pole and after setting the sumach on fire I held the burning faggots at the opening where the bees passed in and out until I burned more than half of them to death and the remainder were suffocated so bad they were almost harmless and I went to work and filled all the vessels with honey which exhausted all that was in the tree.

"Then I went home for help to take the honey home and after I had divided a portion of it with Masters and his family I strained nine and one-half gallons out of the remainder for the use of myself and family."

The author will add here that the river bluff mentioned as the scene of this story is situated between the mouth of Beach Hollow and Bradley's Ferry all of which are in Crocket Township, Marion County, Ark.

Made a Honey Case in the Woods [17:48]

ONE OF THE INCIDENTS of hunting as told by Elias Keesee is the following.

"Many years ago when there were plenty of bee trees in Ozark County, Mo., my father Paton Keesee, who lived on Little North Fork, and Mose Lantz who lived on Bratton's Spring Creek went out coon hunting one day in the early part of the month of September. They were on horseback and carried an ax and their guns with them and while riding along through the timber on the divide between the east and west prongs of Bratton's Spring Creek they discovered a bee tree which they both pronounced to be rich in honey.

"They had plenty of dogs along to tree coons but they had no vessels with them to put honey in. But not to be outdone my father told Lantz that he would make a vessel and, telling Lantz to remain at the tree until he returned, he rode off.

"In a little while Mr. Lantz heard the report of his gun and in an hour or more my father rode back carrying a deer hide which on his arrival he rubbed the bits of flesh off with a stone and they both rubbed the inside part of the hide against trees for some minutes, then spread the hide out on the ground in an open place where the sun could shine on it and let it lay there awhile, then took it up again and rubbed it against trees and with stones until it was dry. Then they trimmed off the ragged edges and sewed the edges together with dressed buckskin string (leaving an opening) and called it a 'honeycase'[120] and felled the tree and filled it with rich honeycomb."

Drinking Honey out of a Deer's Leg [17:50]

OLD SETTLERS used to tell of drinking honey out of deer's legs which I have heard disputed, but it was true. This was done by lacing up a deer's hide and fill[ing] it with wild honey.

The usual way of making the case was to take the hair off the hide and thoroughly tan it and sew it all up into a sack except the end of one leg which was left open. Sometimes though the hide was formed into a case without removing the hair. When the case contained honey and a hunter become hungry for a drink of honey he would suck it from the apperture in the leg and this was called drinking honey out of a deer's leg.

Brief Items of Hunting [16:1]

THE FOLLOWING is an account as told by John H. Tabor.

"Soon after I settled on Crooked Creek in Marion Co., Ark., in 1836," said he, "I discovered four bee trees that stood near my spring. One of the trees contained only a small amount of honey but the combined yield of the other three was eleven gallons.

"Of course, I could find a bee tree whenever I wished to, but me and John Billingsly found a bee tree one day a little out of the ordinary way. We were riding along about four miles north of my place when I saw a honey bee enter a hollow in a big limb of a low boughed, but large bodied black oak tree. I wanted a mess of honey and I told Billingsly I was going to climb that tree and knock for admittance into the abode of the bees.

"So, after dismounting and hitching our horses, I climbed up to the limb where the bees were, which was only a few feet above the ground, and told my companion to toss up a rock, which I caught with my hands and sounded the limb with it and found that the limb was shelly. But when I hit the limb with the stone the bees swarmed out, and while some catched in my hair others stung me on the face and ears. Of course I went back down the tree much faster than I went up.

"We had some rags with us to use if needed, and with a piece of flint rock and steel and punk[121] we soon struck fire, and after wrapping some of the rags around the end of a stick and waiting awhile longer for the bees to quiet down, I went back up the tree and Billingsly set the rags afire and

I held down the bees with the smoke while I broke into the hollow limb with another stone that my companion had tossed to me. It proved to be rich in honey.

"Billingsly spread a deer skin on the ground and I dropped a lot of the honeycomb down on it, and after I descended the tree I and my partner consumed honey until it failed to taste good. Then we got sick, but we rode back home and was all right by the following day, and went back and took out five gallons of honey from this same tree."

Capturing Cub Bears and Killing the Old One and Other Reminiscences [15:56]

THOMAS BARNETTE located on Little North Fork in December, 1848. He was from Tennessee. Among Tom Barnette's sons was Jim who was twenty-one years old when he come with his father to Little North Fork and worked at the blacksmith trade in the early days. He said he well remembered the fine growth of cane in the creek bottoms and the tall grass which grew in the hills.

"Pleas McCollough and I were going down where Henry Bratton had a store at that big spring of water on Bratton Spring Creek, where Dick Martin lives now," [said Mr. Barnette]. "While passing down a hollow that runs into the creek above the spring, we noticed a deer running around in a circle with an eagle sitting on its back. The deer was suffering severely for it was bleating in a pitiful manner, and its strength seemed to be nearly exhausted. McCollough, instead of shooting the eagle, shot the deer and killed it to end its suffering.

"To our surprise the eagle, which was a bald eagle, did not fly. As we approached the eagle tried to get away and made a loud noise flopping its wings and jerking its feet and pulling the dead deer along for a few yards and we saw now what was the matter. Its talons, which were large and sharp, were hooked in the deer's flesh and hide in such a way that, with all the efforts the big strong bird made, it was not able to extricate itself and I killed it with a club, then cut its claws loose with my pen knife.

"We took the deer and eagle to the store and showed them to a number of men gathered there. It proved to be of much interest and the result was more stories of eagles attacking deer. The eagle measured six feet across the spread."[122]

Interesting Tales of an Old Timer of Southern Missouri [14:89]

"I WILL NOW give you an account of seeing an eagle striking a deer which interested me no little," said Ira J. (Joseph) Davis. "One day in 1858, while I and Elbert Peace were hunting together on the west side of Swan Creek [in Christian County, Missouri] and near two miles above where my father lived, we saw a deer close to the creek coming toward us at full speed. Very soon after seeing the deer we saw a grey eagle[123] flying along just above it. It was evident that the big bird was following the deer, but owing to the thick growth of timber the eagle had considerable difficulty in attacking the fleeing animal, but the latter soon passed into an open space and the eagle darted down and struck the deer. The stroke did not knock the animal down but it bleated in a pitiful manner. As soon as the eagle struck the deer it rose upward and down it darted the second time and hit the deer with its talons again. Just after the eagle struck the deer the third time both passed out of our sight.

"Being much interested to know whether the eagle had killed its victim or not we followed the trail of the deer some distance and found the eagle eating on the deer in the creek bottom close to the foot of a hill. The bird had struck the deer so often that it had become too weak to escape its ferocious enemy and fell, and the eagle finished its life and was satisfying its appetite on the deer meat when we arrived. Mr. Peace shot and killed the eagle and we took it and the deer home with us. The deer was a doe and was a year old past."

Depriving an Eagle of a Nice Mess of Turkey [17:15]

JUST BELOW the mouth of the Mahan Hollow and on the west side of the old Isaac Mahan farm on Little North Fork is a bluff or steep hill which John Mahan, son of Isaac Mahan, says that he saw some eagles and a flock of wild turkeys have a lively time one cloudy morning in the month of February.

In describing the incident Mr. Mahan said that, "There were two bald eagles and a gray eagle attacked a flock of forty turkeys in the face of this bluff. When one of the eagles would strike at a turkey it would dodge the stroke and after the big birds with the big talons had struck at the turkey some time without securing one for a meal the two bald eagles become discouraged and flew off.

"The gray eagle stayed with the turkeys and struck at first one and then another of the flock until he hit a large gobbler with his claws and disabled it. Then it took the eagle a half an hour to finish killing the gobbler. When the turkey was dead and the eagle was preparing to feast on the meat I scared the eagle away and took the dead turkey to the house. Its beard was seven inches in length and the turkey before it was dressed weighed twenty-three pounds."

REMARKABLE ESCAPE OF A PIG FROM THE TALONS OF AN EAGLE [17:11]

AN INTERESTING ACCOUNT of an eagle catching a young pig was told me by Mrs. Rhoda Sanders, daughter of Tom Rice. Mrs. Sanders is the wife of Henry Sanders, a well known citizen of near Gainesville, Missouri.

Mrs. Sanders said that her father settled near Pease's Mill,[124] Richland Post Office, [Richville, 1870–1933] in Douglas County, Mo., in 1872.

"Among his stock was a bunch of pigs which were about one month old. One day the old sow and pigs were near the house. A grey eagle darted down among the pigs and picked up a spotted one with [its] claws and rose with the little squealing animal to the top of a tall pine tree and lit in the highest part of it.

"Just as the eagle lit it dropped the pig and as the pig was falling the eagle darted after it. A small bushy-top tree stood under the bows of the pine and when the pig struck in among the limbs of the small tree it checked its speed in falling so rapid and the eagle caught it again. But the little grunter freed itself and fell twenty feet to the ground. The pine tree was estimated to be three hundred feet tall.[125]

"When the pig dropped to the ground my father scared the eagle away and picked up the pig and found that it was severely wounded by the big bird's claws. My father brought the pig to the house and dressed its wounds and poured turpentine into the gashes and cared for the little animal until the wounds had healed and fully recovered from the effects of its remarkable escape from death. This same pig thrived until it made a fine hog and my father fattened it and killed it, converting the meat into a fine lot of bacon," said Mrs. Sanders.

Among the Hornets and Yellow Jackets [17:51]

WE HAVE SAID elsewhere that a man of the name of Tom Patterson, son-in-law of George Wood,[126] lived in the Locust Hollow of East Sugar Loaf Creek. This man lived on what is now the John (Jack) Trimble land. Mr. Patterson said he was born and reared in Weakly County, Tenn. He lived in Locust Hollow fifteen years or more before the beginning of the war between the states.

Mr. Patterson had a son-in-law of the name of Tom Keeton who lived in a hollow that mouths into Locust where Patterson lived and which is in Marion County, Ark. Mr. Keeton had two boys named John and George who were very mischievous and were constantly playing pranks and tricks of many sorts on each other.

One day while these young scions were both up in a wild cherry tree devouring cherries, John, who was higher up in the tree than George, called his brother's attention to look up quick. Forgetting himself for a moment George looked up and John blew and spit a mouth full of cherry seed, peeling, juice and spittle into George's face and eyes, which exasperated him to such a degree that he tried to kill him before John could get down out of the tree and make his escape. But in an hour or so they made friends again, but George said, "John, I intend to play a prank on you worth something the first opportunity that presents itself."

"All right," replied John, "the same back to you when you do that."

A few days after this while the two youngsters were at play on the hillside near the corncrib they discovered a large hornets' nest hanging to a limb of a sapling.[127] The nest was four or five feet above the ground. John became much interested in the formation of the nest and said he desired to examine it and as the hornets seemed disposed to be quiet he ventured up to the nest and scrutinized it closely without suspecting the nature of his brother George.

The hornets did not offer to sting him. In fact, there were only a few of them on the outside, but a large number was in the nest. John's face was in a few inches of the nest and as George saw his brother's nose nearly touching the nest he thought it time for revenge. He was standing a few yards from his brother and above him and while John's back was turned toward him he stooped down and picked up a rock and threw it at the nest, just missing his brother's head and knocked a hole in the nest. As he hurled the stone he darted up the hill to get out of the way of his brother and the hornets for he believed he would be compelled to war with them both.

It was a critical time for John for the hornets swarmed out of the now torn and rent nest and stung the boy desperately. Some got into the bosom of his shirt. Others got down on his back from his shirt collar at the back of his neck. Some stung his naked feet for he was barefooted and a few got up his pants and stung his legs. The awful pain and suffering produced from the stings was almost unbearable and John kicked, jumped and yelled in agony.

George was scared too for it was not his intention of carrying it so far as this and he thought the hornets would sting his brother to death and he ran toward him intending to help fight the hornets away. But at this moment John started off on a fast run toward Locust Creek and running to the bed of the creek he found it dry and turning down the hollow he ran down it a half a mile where there was a pool of water and leaped into it and rolled in it until he got rid of the hornets. During his battle with the stinging insects and the run down the hollow he had torn all his clothes into shreds and jerked them off of him and he went back to the house as naked as a new born babe and took his bed where he remained many days before he recovered from the effects of the stings of the busy hornets.

George had followed him to the pool of water and back to the house and begged his brother's forgiveness which his brother did not do until after he had got well and then he told him he would forgive him if he would never treat him so bad any more and George promised him that he would not.

Though George had come near causing his brother to die and was quite humble for he knew he had carried his revenge too far and yet he felt satisfied that it was a worse trick than John got on him by spitting in his face.

The great suffering that George caused his brother to undergo come back to him in a few weeks after John had recovered from the effects of the stings of the hornets which [had] come about in this way. The floor of Keeton's house was low to the ground for the sleepers rested on the dirt.[128] There was just room enough for a boy to crawl along under the floor between the sleepers. One day George crawled under the floor to hunt for a hen's nest that was supposed to be under there full of eggs.

While the boy was making his way along in the dusky darkness under the house he struck a yellow jackets'[129] nest near the sill on the opposite side of the building from where he started in. The boy was in his shirt tail and the moment he disturbed the nest the yellow jackets swarmed up and all over him and with a scream of terror and pain George lunged forward to get off of the nest but finding he could get only a few feet from the nest on account of the sill, he kicked, hallooed and slapped his body with his hands. The yellow jackets continued to sting him severely. He could not turn around because the sleepers were too close together and the only way to escape was to crawfish back over the nest, which was a horrible thought but it must be done and that immediately.

The little fellow was crying and moaning for the stings from the yellow jackets tortured him until he was almost crazed with suffering. The house floor was made of puncheons and were fastened to the sleepers with wooden pins. His father was gone, but his mother was at home and so was John and the former in her frantic efforts to relieve her son cried aloud and done all she could to raise one of the puncheons to pull her suffering child from under the floor, but all in vain for she was not able to get it loose.

The boy finding that his mother could not raise the puncheon over him began the terrible ordeal of backing over the den of yellow jackets which stirred the yellow beings into fury again and their stings were so numerous that it felt like forty gallons of hot water saturated with strong cayenne pepper[130] was being poured on him. George screamed, twisted and squirmed as he was backing through and soon passed from over the nest and continued to back away as fast as the terrible stingers would let him until he got near the going out place.

His sorrowing mother whose name was Dula ran where he was coming out from under the floor and when he got in reach of her she grabbed him by his feet and pulled him out. The boy was covered nearly all over with the stinging insects and she knocked them off as fast as she could work her hands and while she was engaged at this she got her hands badly stung. George was compelled to go to bed where he remained as long as his brother John did when the hornets stung him.

After George got well he and John agreed that they were even now and ought to play quits.

❧ TALES OF SNAKES ❧
AND CENTIPEDES

Editors' note: Probably no creatures are surrounded by as many absurdities in folklore as snakes. The layman's knowledge of centipedes is virtually nil. Turnbo recognized this, but accepted—for the most part uncritically—the tales of his informants, faithfully setting them down for his readers. Only a brief selection are recounted here, and the reader is cautioned to take most of them with a large dose of salt.

A Monster Diamond Rattlesnake [16:59]

IT IS NOTHING UNCOMMON when a snake story is written and is put in print, the author of the account is known as a snake liar or snake fiend. If a man knows an unusually big snake tale and keeps it out of the printing office, it does not appear so bad to some people. But if he sends it to the editor, and he puts it into the paper instead of the waste basket, he [the editor] is counted a liar as well as the author of the tale.

Without further foolish comments, we will now get to our story. There is no question in my mind but that once in time, unusually large serpents inhabited the Ozark region and I am going to relate an account of an enormous rattlesnake that was discovered and killed near White River, the story of which may sound to some more like imagination than reality, especially to those inclined to be skeptical. But nevertheless, according to worthy testimony, it is true. I have never doubted its authenticity from the time I remember hearing it told, for it was common talk among the earliest settlers at the time of its occurrence. The following is the account of it which I have heard repeated often in my childhood days.

A large black oak tree stands at the roadside on top of the bluff opposite the mouth of Bear Creek, which empties into White River. This tree has been notched and blazed around with an axe. Near this tree on the west side of the road is where a schoolhouse once stood. The foundation stones of this house mark the place where the building stood and the black oak tree marks the spot where the Missouri state line crosses the road. Near one hundred yards west of the road is a high bluff where the line passes down, and after crossing White River it enters Bear Creek a few yards above its mouth.

The elevation of the bluff is so high that the river seems so far below, and as the bright rays of the sun strikes the surface of the stream the water fairly glistens. Bear Creek can be traced some distance from the river by the numerous sycamore trees and other timber which line the banks.

As mentioned elsewhere, Girard Leiper Brown was the first settler at the mouth of Bear Creek locating here in 1816. After Mr. Brown was killed on the Arkansas River his brother-in-law, Lenard Coker, was the next man who lived here; he lived on the south bank of Bear Creek a quarter of a mile above its mouth. Coker lived here many years and died on this land.[131]

I am told that the division line between the state[s] of Missouri and Arkansas was surveyed twice. The first line was run in the winter season while snow was on the ground. It proved unsatisfactory and a new line was established nearly one half a mile south of the original one. It was while this second line was being surveyed in the month of August that the big rattler was found and killed on the bluff before mentioned.[132]

Many years have come and gone and nearly every one acquainted with the circumstance have departed this life. But there are, no doubt, some living who remember hearing the settlers speak of the incident frequently. The story was common talk when I was a little lad of a boy and I was greatly interested in hearing it told for I was afraid of big snakes.

Beside my own recollections I have gather[ed] an account of it from various other sources and have interviewed two men who said that they were well acquainted with the slaying of the big reptile, one of which saw it soon after it was dead. This man, "Thresher" Bill Yocum, is dead now, but was living with Len Coker at the time of the incident. The other man is Mr. A. Brown, who has been postmaster at Peel, Arkansas, for many years. I also received further information from John B. Wood, a former resident on White River and who died at Tulsa, Indian Territory. His father was in the employ of the surveyors and he heard his father tell the story repeatedly. Mr. Wood said that he also heard the surveyors give the same account. The surveyors' names I am told was Clark and Shields. These men owned a small black dog which was a great favorite among the surveyor party.

Owing to the great number of crooks and bends in the river the men composing the party of surveyors were much vexed and irritated by being compelled to cross the stream so often. They had crossed it twice in quick succession only a few days before. One of these places was at the Panther Bottom and was just east of where the line between Ozark and Taney

Counties crosses, and they crossed it again just west of this line. Their only means of crossing was by building a raft of logs.

True the stream was low and the water was warm, yet the men did not feel disposed to wade or swim across for there was plenty of malaria in existence on White River then. The party had enough of wet dewy grass and weeds to pull through of mornings without wading the river. It took time and trouble to make these rafts and they were heavy and ill convenient to manage in crossing on, and the temper of the men would run up to a high stage when they had the river to cross.

While they were "running" the line east of the bluff referred to above, one of the party was sent in the advance and when he reached the top of the bluff and found that the river had to be crossed again, he went back and informed his friends how it was and soon afterwards when they discovered the big rattler they were angry enough to tackle a herd of lions.

On the previous day they had crossed the river to the left bank and stopped near the residence of William M. Brown, where they roomed at the spring, then went on with their work, and as the party were surveying through the wild woods to the top of the bluff and when about one quarter mile east of the black oak tree mentioned, the little dog began barking furiously one hundred yards north of where the men were at work.

One of the men was sent to see what the dog had found and on advancing up near, he was almost stupefied with astonishment to find that the dog was baying an enormous diamond rattlesnake.[133] The terrible looking serpent was in an angry humor and would have struck the dog but it kept out of striking distance of the monster. After partially recovering from his fright the terror stricken man yelled in a frantic way until the whole party dropped their work and was soon on the scene of snakedom.

The surveyors as well as their hired help were greatly amazed at encountering such a large sized reptile, and having plenty of guns with them, they soon shot it to death. Three of William M. Brown's sons, Martin, Andrew and Daniel, were close by when the snake was shot and, hearing the report of the guns, they supposed that the surveyors had fell in among a bunch of wild beasts and rushed up to find out what kind they had encountered, and was nearly paralized with astonishment at seeing the great serpent in the throes of death.

The time of the occurrence was said to be in 1842 or 1843, consequently the country was sparsely settled, yet the news sped like wild fire and a number of men collected on the spot on the following day to view the remains of the big serpent. Its length was said to be ten feet and the middle part of its body was more than thirty inches in circumference. Its head was as large as a big dog's head and measured five inches between the eyes.

Len Coker and "Thresher" Bill Yocum heard the news in a few hours after the snake was dead and they forded the river and visited the spot where the monster reptile lay to view it. Coker received permission to remove its hide, which was done after much careful labor, and then he cut the serpent open and exposed to view a wild turkey that was fully half grown, which the reptile had caught and swallowed just before it was discovered and killed.

Mr. Coker said he had heard the snake sing (rattle) on the bluff from his home on several occasions, but never could account for the strange noise till that day, for he had never dreamed of its being a rattlesnake.

Coker carried the hide home and stuffed it with wheat bran, which required several bushels. The bran had been brought from a far away mill. Coker mounted the stuffed hide on the porch side of his house where many people came to see it. The reptile was killed just over the line in Taney County, Missouri.

STORIES OF FINDING AND KILLING UNUSUALLY LARGE RATTLESNAKES [16:48]

AMONG OTHER SNAKE STORIES, we present a few of the finding and killing of large rattlers, as related by hunters and others. Jerry Hutchison, an early settler of Ozark County, Mo., tells of Jim Loftis discovering and shooting a rattlesnake which Loftis reported to be ten feet long.

"As the man seemed to be over excited about the reptile, I and others went from Isaac Mahan's to view the monster and found that the serpent had crawled away from where Loftis had shot it. But we soon found it a short distance away barely able to crawl. The reptile was about seven and one-half feet long and measured ten inches around the middle part of its body. The snake carried only seven rattles but they were an inch broad."

Mr. Hutchison said that he cut out one of its fangs with his pen knife. The fang was in size according to the size of the serpent. The snake was killed in a glade at the foot of Bald Mountain, near the 'Nat' Richmond land and where the old wagon way leads up the hill towards Dugginsville, and near three miles west of the mouth of Bratton's Spring Creek.

Mrs. Elizabeth Clark says that during the Civil War, while she lived in Bear Hollow which empties into Little North Fork above the mouth of

Little Creek, she killed a rattlesnake which was seven feet long and carried fourteen rattles. Mrs. Clark says that when the snake was discovered it was in a coil. The bulk of it resembled the size of an ordinary homemade washtub.

The largest rattlesnake the writer ever saw was killed on what is now the Gum Smith farm on Elbow Creek in Taney County in 1850. This was before Josiah Bone, the first settler of this land, located there. The reptile was nearly six feet long and also carried fourteen rattles. Its body was large in proportion to its length. My father was stock hunting afoot on the creek and I was with him and was barefooted. We found the rattler in the tall grass by hearing it singing.[134]

Mr. A. (Aus) Brown says that his father, William M. Brown, killed a rattlesnake under his house floor when he lived on Bee Creek, which flows into White River in Taney County, Mo. Mr. Brown said that the snake was seven feet long and eighteen inches in circumference. "This was in 1841, and just before my father made his residence below the mouth of Bear Creek," said Mr. Brown.

A few years ago I was talking with old Uncle Sammy Stone, who lived near Thornfield in Ozark County, Mo., about incidents of old times.

"I never had much trouble with wild beasts," said he, "but I had a fearful time with a big rattlesnake once, which makes my flesh fairly crawl when ever I think of it. When I first come to the valley of Little North Fork, the settlers told me about meeting unusually large reptiles here in the Ozarks. I gave these snake tales but little attention except I laughed at those who were bold enough to tell such stories. I believed half of the accounts were imagination and the other half was coloring matter, spread on to make these stories sound big and smoother.

"I was not convinced to listen at stories of 'snakedom' until one day I was face to face with a diamond rattlesnake. After this I never refused to believe any sort of a snake story told me.

"On a certain time, I and a companion were hunting in the hills over the line in Fulton County, Ark. The country was thinly settled and rank grass and other vegetation was thick all over the woods. While I was making my way through the grass and weeds, I got within a few feet of the rattler before I knew it. I was so horrified at the sight of it that for a moment I seemed to be under the influence of its charm. The serpent lay in a coil just to my right, and struck at me immediately, barely missing my breast. As it made the stroke it lengthened out and dropped full length at my feet.

"I have heard some people talk about getting scared nearly to death at a snake. I was that time. The reptile recoiled itself and drew its ugly head back and struck at me again. But by some means I avoided the stroke by jumping out of the way. After striking at me the second time it recoiled again and lay quiet. When I stepped back out of reach of its fangs I recovered from the shock and shot it through the head and there was some terrible squirming of the serpent while it was in the throes of death.

"My friend and I were separated about two hundred yards at the time. When I shot the serpent I called him to me. After the monster quit moving, we took the measure of it and found that its length was eight feet and was twenty-one inches around the biggest part of its body. I cannot call to mind how many rattles it carried but recollect they were one and one half inches broad."

Death from the Bite of a Diamond Rattlesnake [16:43]

IN THE DAYS of diamond rattlesnakes it was dangerous to encounter one and almost sure death to be bitten by one. Mr. Ben Hager, an old time citizen and resident of Madison County, related to me this story.

"Holman's Creek in Madison County, Ark., is a small tributary of War Eagle River. My father lived on this same creek.

"When I was a small boy, a man of the name of John Clay lived six miles from our house. One day Mr. Clay come to our house and asked me to go squirrel hunting with him, and as I was doing nothing at the time, my father gave his consent for me to go. Clay wanted me to go along and 'turn' the squirrels for him when they went up a tree.

"When we got into the edge of a small pinery, which was near one mile from Holman's Creek, the dog treed a squirrel up a pine tree that had a cordon of wild currant vines entwined around it. I and Mr. Clay walked around the tree in opposite directions to find or locate the squirrel.

"As Clay passed around with his face turned up looking into the top of the tree for the squirrel, a diamond rattlesnake darted its head out of a hollow place in the ground where a dead pine tree had been burned out by the roots, [and] in time the space had grown full of weeds and wild grass. The reptile was coiled in this sunken place and it struck Clay in the groin and sank its fangs into the flesh.

"The man stepped back instantly and shot the snake while it was getting into a coil again. There was not a moment to lose to see if he had killed the serpent and we started back to our house. The man soon began to suffer excruciating pains of distress and anguish. Added to this he become very sick. He could hardly walk.

"I assisted him all I could and he struggled on until we were in a quarter mile of the house, when he could get no further. I let him down on the ground and ran with all the speed I could command up near the house and called my father and soon informed him of Clay being bitten by the rattler and where I had left him.

"My father ran with me back to him and my father, who was a stout man, picked Mr. Clay up and carried him to the house and started a messenger off on horseback to Huntsville for a doctor.

"In the meantime we all done what was in our power for the relief of the suffering man, but all in vain, for he sank into a semi comatose condition. When we tried to rouse him up the man would say, 'Please, let me sleep.'

"It was only two miles to town and the messenger got there as quick as his horse could carry him. The first physician he met was Doctor Ruth and he informed him what was wanted and the doctor hurried to our house, but Mr. Clay was dead when he arrived.

"It was shocking indeed. Just a few hours ago he was in good health and in nice spirits. Now he lay dead. He had died in less than two hours after he was bitten.

"On the following morning after he died, I and father and Doctor Ruth and others visited the place where Mr. Clay had been bit and we found the snake dead. The shot from Clay's gun had took effect in the reptile's back and killed it. We had no way to measure its length correct, but the men all estimated it to be eight feet long."

In Close Quarters with Venomous Reptiles [16:65]

THERE IS NO DENYING the fact that venomous reptiles frighten humanity. Most everyone is afraid of snakes. Even harmless serpents have been known to frighten people out of their wits. When an abundance of game existed in the Ozark hills it was common for hunters to camp in the forest all night, or leave their cabins before daybreak and take their station at a certain locality and wait until daylight, and kill a deer on its passway. In the latter case it was rare that the hunter and his family did not feast on fresh venison for breakfast.[135] This sort of hunting was attended with danger, if it was carried on during the spring and summer season and early fall, on account of poisonous serpents.

Joe Hall related a story one day to the writer in which he said that during the pioneer days of Marion County, Ark., Henderson Hall, himself and others hunted one day south of White River and camped one night in a small narrow hollow that leads into Sister Creek. It was in the month of September and the nights were cool and pleasant and the days were pretty with bright sunshine.

"Our camp," said he, "was just up on the side of the hill, a few feet below a ledge of rock, and a few yards below us was the bed of the branch. During the night one of our party was attacked by a light chill and he arose to try to relieve his aching bones by the warmth of the fire.

"While sitting in front of the fire groaning and shivering, he suddenly rose to his feet and uttered a loud scream and then yelled, 'Snakes! and millions of them.' The remainder of us leaped up from our couches and threw a big lot of pine knots on the fire, which soon ignited and made a bright light, and were greatly astonished at seeing several copperhead snakes crawling out of a hole under the ledge and coming toward the fire.

"And we all jumped around pretty lively to avoid them and snatching up clubs, stones or anything in reach and went to fighting them and killed forty-five before they quit coming out. It seemed there was a den of them under the ledge and they had collected in there during the warm day for winter quarters, and probably the warmth of the fire and light attracted them.

"Our escape from their fangs was narrow. We stood up the remainder of the night and watched for more snakes, but no more appeared. When daylight came we put all the dead serpents in one heap, and it was the biggest pile of copperheads I ever saw."[136]

"Thresher" Bill Yocum told me of a close call he had with serpents one morning before daybreak which, he said, gave him a worse scare than a wild animal ever did.

"Here is how it happened," said he. "In 1855, I was living on East Sugar Loaf Creek, a short distance below where Dodd City, Arkansas, now is. I was in the prime of life, robust, and enjoying the best of health. It was little trouble for me to keep a supply of wild meat. If a hunter felt too lazy to tramp the woods in quest of game, all he had to do was to sit down and wait long enough and a deer would be sure almost to come within gun shot range. Of course a hunter could not slay a vast amount of wild game in this way, but he could kill enough to live on and that was all we needed then.

"One morning before daybreak I went out into the edge of a grove of pine trees, one half mile from my cabin, and sat down and leaned my back against a white oak tree. It was rather risky to slip out into the woods before daylight and wait an hour or two, on account of the approach of a panther to interview a fellow or come in contact with a dreaded serpent. A snake might be laying coiled in a few feet, ready to sink his fangs into your flesh, but I had gone out before day frequently to kill deer and never had been bothered so far.

"The temperature that morning was pleasant and as I sat there and breathed the pure fresh morning air mixed with the flavor from the pine trees, I enjoyed the pleasure of contentment and happiness until a rattlesnake began singing in a few feet of me. The serpent was answered by others nearby. The mild and exhilerating temperature seemed to change suddenly to the cold blizzard. I was so cold now that I was froze to the spot. It was too dark to see them but there were several and the singing sounded dreadful. The cry of a panther would have been sweet music by the side of those terrible reptiles.

"I remained perfectly quiet until I got over my worst scare and then I thought I would leap up and try to jump over them and make my escape, but after due reflection I decided not to raise up and make the attempt to make my leap, for fear one or more of them might strike me before I could get out of their reach. Still I was afraid to remain quiet for fear some of them might crawl up in reach of me and strike.

"It was a terrible ordeal but I chose to sit still and sat as motionless as possible. I knew it was not long till daybreak but in my perilous trouble it seemed hours. When I first observed the tinge of daybreak in the eastern sky, I kept my eyes riveted on that part of the horizon and my ears open to the least noise made by the reptiles. At last it was light enough to view my surroundings and I beheld five rattlesnakes of medium size lying stretched in a few feet of me. Although they were peaceable I rose quickly and sprang away out of danger.

"Not finding a stout club handy, I shot one of the serpents and reloaded my rifle and shot and repeated it until I dispatched them all. The stench from their bodies was almost unbearable. My appetite for fresh venison that morning was gone and I returned to the house empty handed but a wiser man for from that [day] on I made a practice of waiting until daylight before I went out to shoot game."

A Swarm of Diamond Rattlesnakes [16:88]

MR. BEN HAGER, an old time resident of Madison County, Ark., is responsible for this snake story which he said was strictly true.

"Many years ago," said he, "while my parents lived two miles south of Huntsville, my father and myself and others went out into the mountains on several day's camp hunt. Our destination was thirty miles southeast of our home. We expected to make our central camp between the sources of two canyons, one of which emptied into War Eagle and the other into Kings River. It was known that plenty of bear abounded on the summit of the high ridges and the sides of the mountains in this locality and our intention was to spend a number of days here among the big game.

"The names of our neighbors who went with us were Eaph Gourd, Dave Russell, John Phelps, Ed Clark and the two Ledbetter boys, Hugh and Harve. We took four ox wagons with us to haul our camping outfits in and to bring back the wild meat hides, furs and honey. We had a big bunch of dogs with us to chase the game and keep the wild beast away from camp of nights.

"On the second day before we intended to reach our stopping place, we noticed a small spike buck loping down the hillside toward Kings River. We were not over anxious to kill a deer before reaching camp but one of the men remarked that the little deer would furnish us plenty of venison for supper, and we halted the ox teams to see if one of the men wanted to shoot it.

"Dave Russell was an excellent shot at long range and one of the men says, 'Dave, hit it,' and he took aim at the fleeing deer with 'Old Greasy Kate,' as he called his old flint lock rifle. But just before he was ready to pull the trigger the deer began to act in a queer manner by jumping high, then it would go sideways a few yards and leap up and kick, as if something had struck its legs.

"Phelps says, 'Dave, don't shoot. The deer might be snake bit.' And Mr. Russell lowered the muzzle of his gun and the little buck increased its speed to a fast run and was soon beyond our view down the mountainside.

"Our curiosity being aroused, we all went to the spot where the deer had jumped around so and was astonished at seeing a large number of diamond rattlesnakes crawling on the ground, and they all seemed to be traveling from War Eagle River toward Kings River. The length of the reptiles ranged from fifteen inches to nearly five feet in length. We picked up clubs and stones and killed rattlesnakes until we all become sick from inhaling the odor from them, and had to quit work and went back to the wagons and drove on.

"Meeting the rattlers caused us to change our program of hunting. There were no roads in that part of the country then and we picked our way through the timber and the best places of the ground for the wagons to pass over. We drove down to Kings River and crossed it and camped four miles that night from where we had met the bunch of rattlers.

"The serpents had changed our course almost in an opposite direction from where we intended to have stopped. We were so afraid of their deadly fangs that we thought it best to put Kings River between us and the snakes and so we did. Our big preparations for a mighty hunt did not turn out very successful."[137]

STORIES OF ENORMOUS BLACK SNAKES [16:77]

THERE IS NO QUESTION but that large black reptiles once inhabited the Ozarks as well as other kinds of snakes. Though while not the size of serpents we read of which live in warmer climates, yet uncommon sized black snakes[138] were seen and killed here in various places by the pioneers. Without further comments we will now proceed to give a few brief stories of the dark colored serpents as told me by hunters and others.

G. W. Thurman says that in 1850, while his father lived on the south bank of White River above the mouth of Beaver Creek in Taney Co., Mo., he and his two small brothers, Granville and Willie Thurman, and three of his uncle Bob Thurman's children, Jane, Martha and Tom Thurman, while playing together on a drift near the river's edge one warm Sunday, they encountered a very large black snake which lay in a coil on two logs which lay across an opening in the drift. Mr. Thurman said that the snake raised its head in a foot of his face before he was aware of its presence.

"I happened to have a stout stick of green wahoo wood[139] in my hand, and as the ugly reptile darted its tongue out almost in my face, I struck it a blow on its neck which paralized the snake long enough for me to pull it out of the drift and finish killing it. The serpent was eight feet in length and measured three inches across the head. I was just twelve years old when I killed that big snake," said Mr. Thurman.

Mr. Ned Upton, who lives four miles west of Gainesville, Mo., says that, while he lived on Lick Creek below Gainesville, he was out hunting one day in a hollow which empties into this stream, and heard a great commotion among the little song birds, and on approaching the spot, he was surprised at seeing a monster black snake nearly eleven feet long, lying on the limbs of a large plum tree.[140]

"The reptile had its mouth open and a dozen or more of birds were fluttering and flying a circle around its head. This was carried on by the birds for a few minutes when one of the little songsters ventured right up to the reptile's mouth and the snake caught the bird and swallowed it immediately. This broke up the charm and the remaining birds ceased their noise and all flew off in different directions.

"The serpent was entirely too large for me to tackle it with a club, even if I could reach it in the tree, and I shot it to death. This was in the latter Fifties," said Mr. Upton.

Jasper Casey, who lives at Lead Hill, Ark., informs me that after his father left the Buffalo Fork of White River and settled on Clear Creek, three miles above its mouth in Marion County, Ark., he and his brother, Jesse Casey, while passing a tree that stood near the yard gate (this tree was the chicken roost), seen an extremely large black snake starting to crawl up the tree.

"We called father," said he, "and he come and killed it. The snake measured eight feet and four inches long and was between four and five inches through the middle part of its body. This was in the early Fifties and I remember that I was quite a small boy at the time of this little incident."

A Squirrel Hawk in the Deadly Folds of a Coachwhip Snake [16:87]

A CURIOUS FIND in the woods was told me one day by Sam Pelham, son of Jim Pelham. When Mr. Pelham give me the account of it he was living near Lutie, Mo.

He said that on a certain time, while he was riding across Aaron Quick's salt yard in the McVey Hollow, where Mr. Quick salted his cattle, he noticed something lying on the ground that he at first took to be a small quantity of salt that had been wasted. But on riding up nearer he thought it was a sack that someone had dropped. When he rode up closer the object proved to be neither salt nor sack, but a squirrel hawk[141] with a large coachwhip snake[142] wrapped around the neck and body of the hawk.

"I stopped and viewed the hawk and reptile with much curiosity. The snake had put in its work well, for the hawk was almost dead. Its breathing was just perceptible. After looking at them a few minutes, I dismounted off of my horse and picked up a stick and unwrapped the snake from around the hawk and killed it, and by the time the serpent was dead the hawk was reviving, and I killed it with the same stick I killed the serpent with and hung them both up on a limb."

A Hoop Snake [28:58]

ONE AMONG ACCOUNTS TOLD of hoop snakes by the pioneer residents of Southwest Mo. is an account furnished me by Tom McCollough, son of Pleasant McCollough, who came to Ozark County Mo. in 1844. Tom McCollough died about the first day of July 1907.

In giving accounts of incidents of early times he said that while he was hunting one day on the head of Little North Fork and some six miles south of the Douglas County line and while passing along a hill side he heard a noise and looking in the direction from whence it came he seen something rolling like a hoop toward him and he darted out of its way, and it rolled on by him and just before reaching a black oak tree which stood twenty yards from him the hoop straightened itself all at once and struck the end of its tail against the tree and stuck fast to it. The stroke of its tail against the bark of the tree sounded like it had been struck with a hammer.

"The moment it hit the tree I saw that it was a snake and I walked up near the tree and watched the reptile wriggle and squirm in its efforts to free itself from the tree but it was not able to release itself and I picked up a stout stick and killed it but I did not knock it loose from the tree and after I had viewed the strange snake a while I went on and left the serpent hanging to the tree.

"I was certainly frightened when it rolled by me and there is no question in my mind that if I had not avoided it as I did it would have struck me with its horned tail instead of the tree. It seems unreasonable to relate it but it is an actual truth that when I went back to this same spot two weeks afterward I found the leaves on this tree had withered since the snake struck it. The bones of the serpent were still hanging to the tree," said Mr. McCollough.[143]

Brief Stories about Centipedes [16:70]

ONE READING THIS CHAPTER need not think the Ozarks are infested with swarms of centipedes as large as alligators, for such is not the case. Of course, centipedes are here and have been since the country has been known to the whites, and no doubt will be here as long as our earth exists. Yet, as to number they are nothing in comparison here like they are in warmer climates. We make no pretention to give a scientific description of centipedes, but give only such accounts about them as gathered here and there from early residents.[144]

Dave Coiner, who lived on Big Creek in Taney County, informed me that one day, Jim Wood and a man by the name of Johnson, while in the hills salting cattle on the head of Little Creek that puts into Lick Creek below Gainesville, noticed a centipede eight inches long crawl out from under a rock. Having a large empty bottle with them they managed to induce it to crawl into the bottle, and corking it quickly carried the bottle to Gainesville, Mo., and presented it to Dr. Arnold, who placed the centipede in a glass jar filled with alcohol and kept it in his drug store.

A similar account is given by John Bias, who said on a certain time he had to attend a circuit court at Gainesville, Mo., and while on his way there from Dugginsville, he saw a centipede lying on a flat rock. He had an empty pint bottle with him and he wanted to capture the centipede alive and take it to Gainesville where he supposed he could sell it for something to help defray his expenses.

Dismounting, he took a stick and held it down on the centipede until he placed the mouth of the bottle before it, and kept at work until it started into the mouth of the bottle, and raising the stick off of it, it ran in.

"After corking the bottle," said John, "I put the bottle in the side pocket of my coat and rode on to Gainesville. I found that the market in town was too dull to sell centipedes, for there was no demand for them, and I gave the dangerous thing to an old settler, who managed to sell it to someone for a half pint of whiskey.

"I have often thought it was reckless of me—catching that centipede and carrying it in my coat pocket or anywhere about my person. Suppose the bottle should have happened to come uncorked. The centipede might have crawled out and stung me to death.[145] It was between seven and eight inches in length."

Many years ago the writer was reliably informed that an early resident of Stone County, Mo., by the name of Tom May and who lived on Railey's

Creek, a tributary of James River, came near losing one of his little boys, who was supposed to have been stung by a centipede. The child was barefooted, and while playing at the foot of a low hill near the house, he screamed out in agony and ran toward the dwelling. Some of the family ran and met the child and saw that it had been stung on the foot. Going to the spot that the boy indicated, they discovered a centipede seven and one-half inches long and killed it. It is said the child lay a year before he recovered. All the flesh surrounding the wound sloughed off. When the sore healed the child remained a cripple.[146]

Mr. G. W. Thurman tells about himself and Mose Lathrop dissecting a centipede one Sunday in 1859. They were in a glade on top of the river bluff on the north side of the river, three miles below Forsyth. The centipede was eight inches long.

"And after killing it," said Mr. Thurman, "we proceeded to take it to pieces for the sake of curiosity, and to examine its stingers. It was a rough dissection, for the instruments used were sticks and sharp stones. We had no microscope but our eyes were good, and we were able to distinguish all its parts.

"I do not suppose our examination is of much importance to the scientific world, yet we learned something for ourselves. Its pincers or teeth resembled a hook-like form or tongs, and were of a dark brown color. Evidently there was a stinger in each leg. The greatest curiosity was found in three pointers at the end of the tail. Each pointer contained a large stinger. The middle one was much the largest and the stinger was flat shaped, resembling a disk knife, and about one-sixteenth of an inch in length.[147] This was my first and only dissection of a centipede, and I don't want anymore of it for my part."

R. M. Jones, of near Protem, Mo., tells of finding a centipede once imprisoned in a hollow tree. Mr. Jones said that after his father, John Jones, settled on the flat of land on the east side of Big Buck Creek in the southeast part of Taney County, his father told him one day in the autumn of 1861, to split some rails to build a hog pen.

Going out across the Pond Hollow onto the flat of land, he felled a post oak tree one and one-half feet in diameter. There was a small cavity at the butt of the tree. After chopping off one rail cut he found that the hollow extended only four or five feet into the rail cut, and was perfectly sound above it. After splitting the log open he was astonished at finding a centipede eight inches in length, coiled in a knot in the upper part of the cavity. At first there appeared to be no life about it.

"I took two sticks," said he, "and unrolled it and found that it was alive. It was wrapped around numerous young centipedes, which were massed together in the shape of a little ball. The old centipede was almost white in color. After a thorough examination of the stump and the ground around it, I found no place where the centipede could have crawled in. Neither, in the log, was there any place where it could enter. How it got there I am not able to explain and how long it had been an inhabitant there is another mystery to me."[148]

Mr. Jones also related that one day himself and the writer's brother, James D. Turnbo, who is dead now, were together at the foot of the bluff near a spring on the north side of the river just above Bradley's Ferry. The spring runs out of the sloo bank. Jim was a lad of a boy, and had gone with Jones squirrel hunting. They had become separated a short distance when Jones heard Jim call out that something was trying to catch him. Jones thinking it was a panther or catamount, ran to him and was much surprised to see an enormous centipede pursuing the boy.

When Jones reached the spot, the centipede stopped and bowed its body up preparatory to jumping, and while it was in this position Jones shot it. He said it was twelve inches long and one inch wide.

Talking of centipedes of an unusual size, C. W. "Wilse" Griffin, who lives on Mountain Creek in the northeast corner of Marion County, Ark., related to me that on a certain occasion he and Woodrow Owen were together on Mountain Creek and saw a large centipede run into a hollow stump.

"Not knowing how else to rout it out with safety to ourselves, we set the stump on fire," said Mr. Griffin, "and compelled the centipede to run out at another hole in the stump and we killed it. It measured just twelve inches in length."

William Patton, who settled on Clear Creek in Marion County, Ark., in 1854, and became totally blind and is dead now, says that one day while his eyesight was good he was in the woods on foot stock hunting. When about one and one-half miles west of where the village of Powell now is, he noticed something a short distance from him crawl into a hollow tree at the ground.

"On approaching the tree to identify the object," remarked Mr. Patton, "I saw a monster centipede lying just on the inside of the hollow, which was the object I had just observed crawl into the tree. I placed the muzzle of my rifle near the opening and shot it nearly in twain, and taking a long stick I pulled it out of the hollow and finished killing it with stones. I had no way of measuring it accurately, but a close estimation proved that it was not less than fourteen inches long and over an inch wide."

The biggest centipede found in the Ozarks that I have a record of, was captured alive by Bent Music on Jimmie's Creek in Marion County in 1860. Henry Onstott, an uncle of the writer, and Harvey Laughlin, who was a cousin of mine, kept a drugstore in Yellville and collected rare specimens of lizards, serpents, spiders, horned frogs and centipedes and kept them in a large glass jar which sat on their counter. The jar was full of alcohol, and the collection was put in the jar for preservation as they were brought in. Amongst the collection was the monster centipede mentioned above.

It was of such unusual size that it made one almost shudder to look at it. Brice Milum, who was a merchant at Yellville when Mr. Music brought the centipede to town, says that he assisted in the measuring of it before it was put in the alcohol and its length was found to be eighteen inches. It attracted a great deal of attention and was the largest centipede the writer ever saw.

The jar with its contents was either destroyed or carried off during the heat of the war.[149]

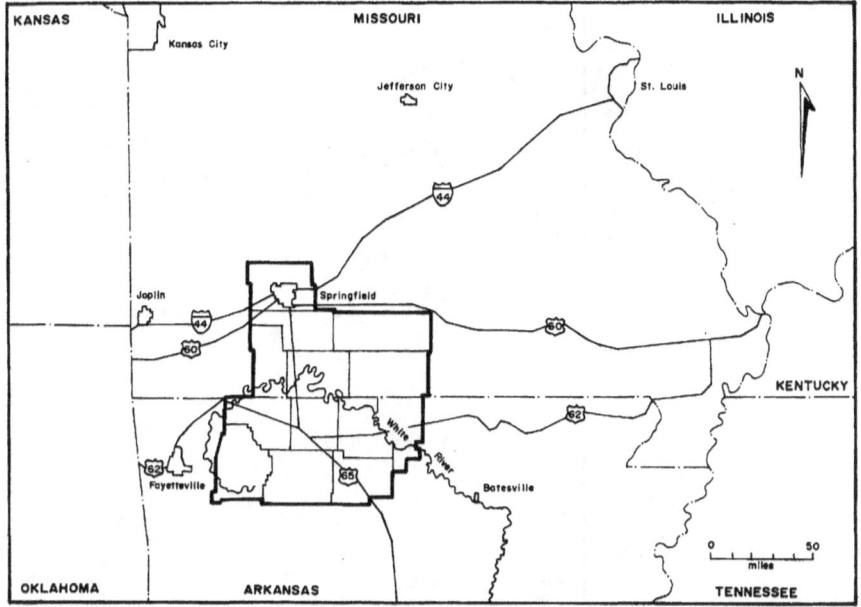

Modern highway access to Turnbo's major area of work. Regional maps by Larry Grantham.

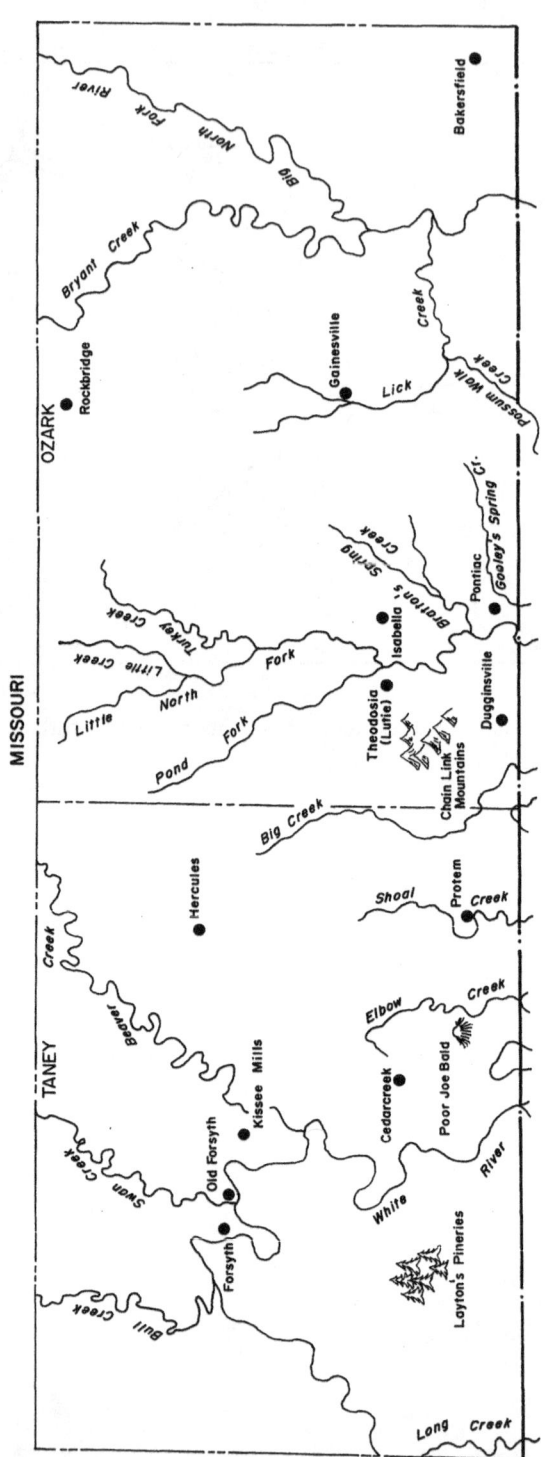

Major place-names used by Turnbo in Taney and Ozark counties, Missouri.

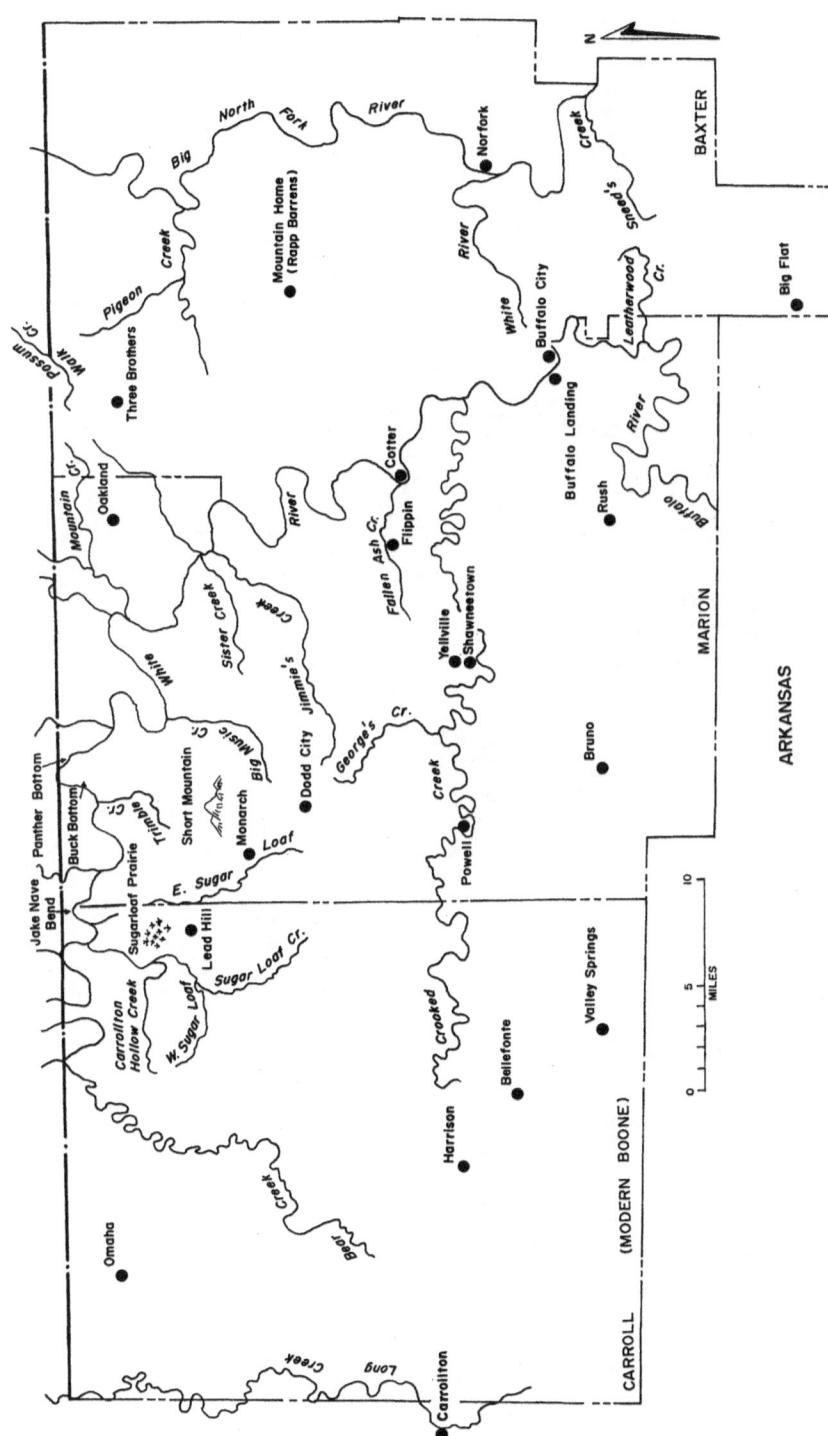

Major place-names used by Turnbo in Boone and Marion counties, Arkansas.

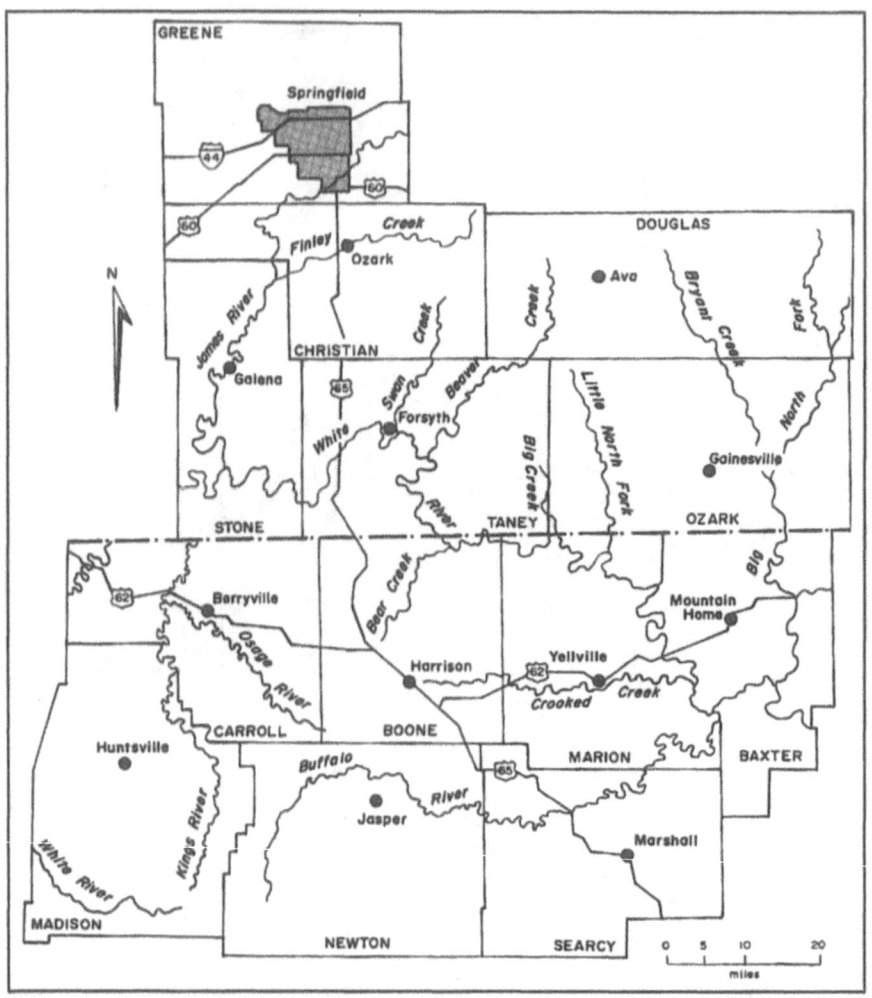

These counties in Missouri and Arkansas are the principal setting for Turnbo's history and folklore.

Ozarks couple in an ox-drawn wagon. *Robert Rains Collection, University of Central Arkansas Library Archives, Conway.*

Although Turnbo lamented the decline of game animals, this turn-of-the-century, ca. 1890s, hunting pair had a number of deer and wild turkeys. *Robert Rains Collection, University of Central Arkansas Library Archives, Conway.*

Furbearers like raccoons provided sport for both hunting and trapping. The raccoon population declined drastically in the early twentieth century but in the mid-forties began a dramatic comeback that continues to this day. *Robert Rains Collection, University of Central Arkansas Library Archives, Conway.*

Rowing a ferry across the White River, ca. 1890. *Special Collections, Mullins Library, University of Arkansas, Fayetteville.*

This turn-of-the-century hunter was typical of those in the White River country who used horses and dogs to pursue game. The meat was used by their families or sold with the furs or pelts for necessities. A lot of game had to be taken to feed a pack of dogs adequately. *Robert Rains Collection, University of Central Arkansas Library Archives, Conway.*

The boats that plied the waters of the White River during the late nineteenth century were work boats, not the gilded palaces we usually see illustrated. The *Myrtle Corey* was probably more typical of the steamboats of that time. *Robert Rains Collection, University of Central Arkansas Library Archives, Conway.*

Crossing the White River in Arkansas on a cable ferry at the turn of the century. *Arkansas History Commission, Little Rock.*

Large snakes figure prominently in folklore and in Turnbo's chronicles. This bull snake is unusual in that it ordinarily is found in prairie habitats, not in the White River country, ca. 1930. *Boone County Historical Photograph Collection, Northwest Arkansas Regional Library, Harrison.*

Veterans of the Blue and the Gray from the White River country met on Decoration Day in 1910 to honor fallen comrades. *Boone County Historical Photograph Collection, Northwest Arkansas Regional Library, Harrison.*

Lead Hill, Arkansas, which figures prominently in many of Turnbo's tales, looked like this in the 1890s. *Boone County Historical Photograph Collection, Northwest Arkansas Regional Library, Harrison.*

A cluster of single-pen buildings along the Arkansas-Missouri border, 1899. *Loyd Matthews Collection.*

An Ozarks family portrait, ca. 1910. *Missouri Department of Natural Resources, Division of Geology and Land Survey Archives, Rolla, Missouri.*

Neighbors from all over the area came together to help in a house raising. This group is at Hill Top, Arkansas, in 1913. *Boone County Historical Photograph Collection, Northwest Arkansas Regional Library, Harrison.*

The Jacob Wolf house in Norfolk, built ca. 1826, is the oldest house in Arkansas. *Jacob Wolf Memorial Committee.*

This panther, killed south of the White River country, ca. 1920s, was typical of those met by the pioneers. Although panthers were not aggressive, they were greatly feared by the White River settlers. *Special Collections, Mullins Library, University of Arkansas, Fayetteville.*

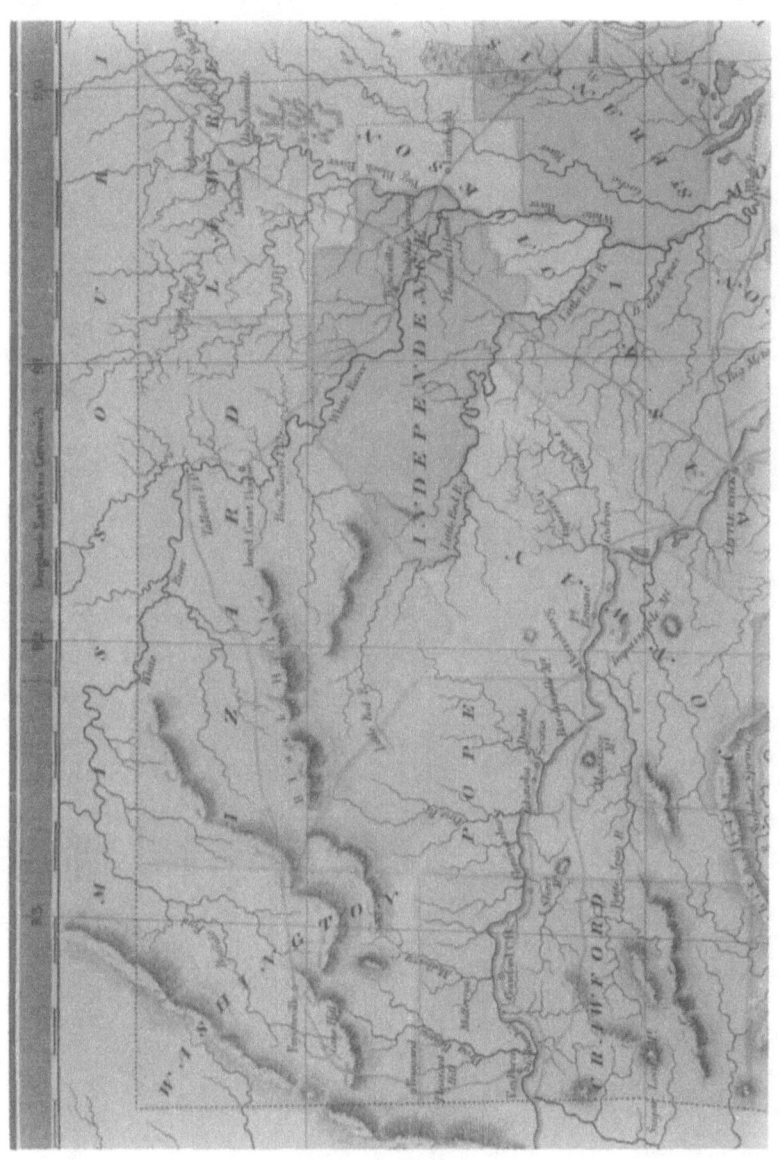

An 1835 map of the White River area showing the county alignment at that time. *Special Collections, Mullins Library, University of Arkansas, Fayetteville.*

> Montoya, New Mexico
> April 24, 1913.
>
> Mr. W. E. Connelley, Topeka, Kan
>
> Friend Sir and friend. Your favor of the 19 inst come due to hand. Many thanks for your letter.
>
> I have not the least idea what the material is worth. It might not be of any value — then it may be worth something. It is owing to what you could get out of it if put in book form. Of course I went to a great deal of trouble in collecting the material. I am not sorry that I gathered it together for if it was in readable shape and put in print some people would read it with some interest. I will say this that if you are willing to buy it I will be satisfied with a reasonable price. But if you do not want it I would not

Turnbo's letter (1913) to W. E. Connelley stating his willingness to accept any offer Connelly would make for his manuscript. *William Elsey Connelley–Silas C. Turnbo Correspondence, Springfield–Greene County Public Library, Springfield, Missouri.*

> 816 Lincoln Street,
>
> Topeka, Kansas, May 13, 1913.
>
> S. C. Turnbo, Esq.,
>
> Montoya, New Mexico,
>
> Dear Mr. Turnbo:
>
> I send you herewith Postoffice Money Order for $27.50, and hope it will come safe to hand.
>
> I send it with the understanding that the manuscripts are to be mine from this date. I understand your letter in that way. I was not in position to buy these manuscripts, but I could not deny an old-time friend in need, so I made extra effort and got the money.
>
> I take over these manuscripts knowing that it will be hard work to get any money out of them. It is getting harder every year to get publishers for books, and I may never get anything out of these, but I will take the risk. I know they have value, especially local value, and I will get them published if I can. But they will have to be re-written to put them in shape for publication, and it is a big job to re-write them. I have already spent about $250.00 in having them copied on a typewriter, and have not got them all copied yet. So, you see I am getting a good deal of money into them.
>
> I will assure you, though, my old friend, that if I ever

Copy of W. E. Connelley's letter to Turnbo notifying him of a money order for $27.50, which he paid for the manuscript in 1913. *William Elsey Connelley–Silas C. Turnbo Correspondence, Springfield–Greene County Public Library, Springfield, Missouri.*

> Montoya. New mexico
> May 21. 1913.
>
> 878
>
> Mr William E. Connelley.
> To Peka. Kansas.
>
> dear kind Sir and friend – I received the $27.50 you sent me for the manuscripts – yes, all the manuscripts I have sent to you is yours. I have no claim on it now, I was glad to get the money. the registered letter reached

Turnbo's letter to Connelley acknowledging sale of his manuscript for $27.50 and relinquishing all claim to it. *William Elsey Connelley–Silas C. Turnbo Correspondence, Springfield–Greene County Public Library, Springfield, Missouri.*

John Hodge, great-grandson of Jimmie Cook on Swan Creek, Taney County, Missouri, and informant of local tradition (1989). *Lynn Morrow photo.*

A 1989 photo of a slab-rock burial site in Ozark County, Missouri. Turnbo wrote of such sites in his letters. *Ben Harris photo.*

Silas Claiborne Turnbo, about 1920, seated on the steps of the school at Locust, Missouri, with Donnie Breeding Owens, Thana Breeding Mahan, Leslie E. Breeding, and Benton Breeding (on Thana's lap). The children are grandchildren of Elizabeth Turnbo Upton. *Stella Luna Collection.*

"Tilda" Turnbo (1849–1922) treating her cow, ca. 1910, for hollow tail, a calcium deficiency that was usually fatal. *Leslie Breeding Collection.*

"Turnbo General Store" in Three Brothers, Arkansas, 1989. *Ben Harris photo.*

Typical clearing and settlement of log structures on the open range in the Ozarks Highlands at the turn of the century. *Missouri Department of Natural Resources, Division of Geology and Land Survey Archives, Rolla, Missouri.*

Backwoods Ozarks house interior, early twentieth century. *Arkansas History Commission, Little Rock.*

Ozarks sawmill board house, ca. 1910, with board underpinning attached to pier foundations to keep range hogs from going underneath the house. *Center for Ozarks Studies, Southwest Missouri State University, Springfield.*

Sorghum making with a commercially built metal mill, ca. 1920. *Center for Ozarks Studies, Southwest Missouri State University, Springfield.*

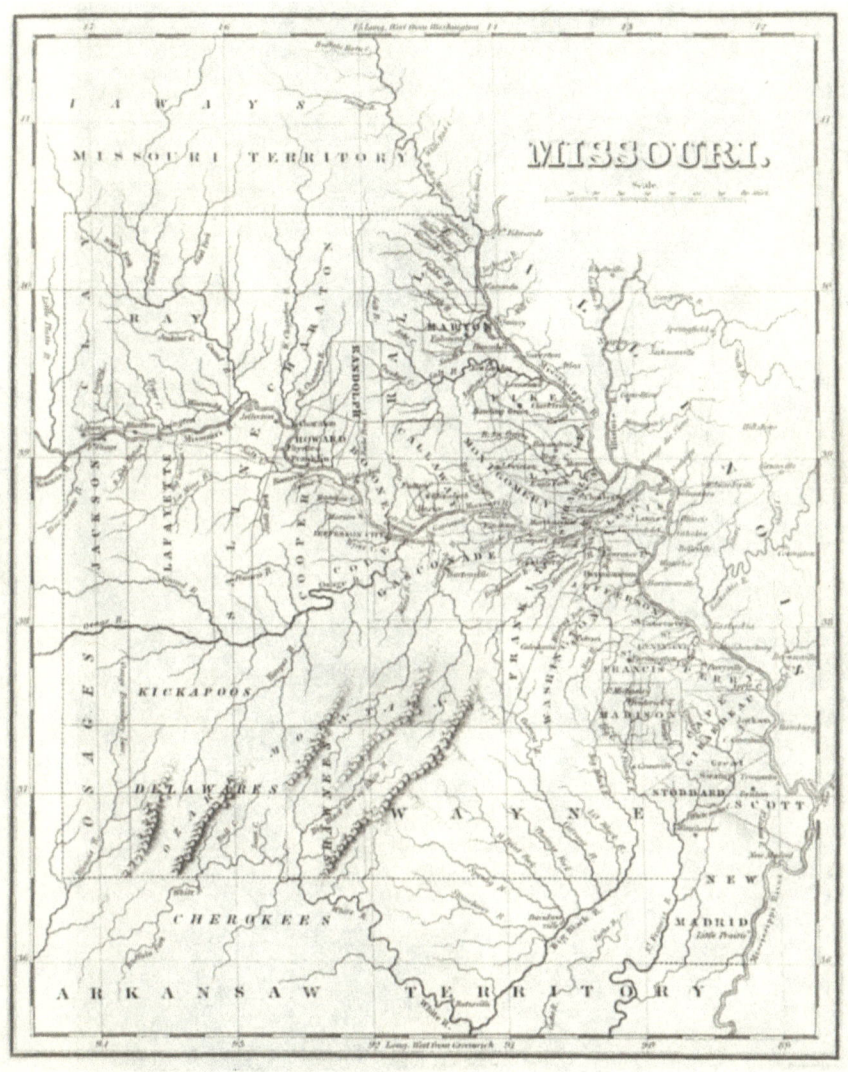

Missouri map shortly after statehood in 1821 shows the White River country allotted to various Indian tribes. There already was a considerable white squatter population in the area, however. *State Historical Society of Missouri, Columbia.*

Country store interior, ca. 1915. *Center for Ozarks Studies, Southwest Missouri State University, Springfield.*

These primitive bee hives, often made from the wood of gum trees, hence the name "bee gums," provided sweetening for the pioneer family, ca. 1928. Later, sorghum syrup, sometimes called "long sweetening," was added to the menu. *Vance Randolph Collection, College of the Ozarks, Point Lookout, Missouri.*

Country road and split-rail fencing in Carroll County, Arkansas, ca. 1900. *Carroll County Historical and Genealogical Society, Berryville, Arkansas.*

Tilling new ground in 1899. Note the girdled and deadened trees, the technique used by the pioneers to clear land for farming. The deadened trees later would be burned at a "log rolling." *Loyd Matthews Collection.*

Good view of an old snake-rail fence in Boone County, Arkansas, 1989. Fence rails typically were ten and twelve feet in length and stacked seven to nine rails high. Many Turnbo tales use fence rails as units of measurement. *Lynn Morrow photo.*

Cleared property often revealed seriously eroded land. Note the surface rocks and the remains of old tree stumps still visible on this Taney County upland, ca. 1895. *The History Museum for Springfield–Greene County, Missouri.*

Swine, allowed to run free feeding on oak and hickory mast, were a major form of livestock in the White River area, ca. 1935. Only in fairly recent times has the open range been closed to free-roaming livestock in Missouri and Arkansas. *Mark Twain National Forest, Rolla, Missouri.*

Silas Claiborne Turnbo, ca. 1905. *Leslie Breeding Collection.*

Keesee Church, Marion County, Arkansas, 1989. *Lynn Morrow photo.*

Ozark County, Missouri, in 1854. Note present county seat, Gainesville, did not yet exist. Rock Bridge was the principal settlement at this time. *Missouri Department of Natural Resources, Division of Geology and Land Survey Archives, Rolla, Missouri.*

Gainesville public square, ca. 1910. *Center for Ozarks Studies, Southwest Missouri State University, Springfield.*

Proud hunter poses with a black bear, apparently taken with the shotgun cradled in his arm, ca. 1890. *University of Arkansas at Little Rock, Archives and Special Collections.*

Ozark hunting party posing with a black bear, ca. 1890. The men are variously armed with both shotguns and rifles. *University of Arkansas at Little Rock, Archives and Special Collections.*

This hunting group poses with a dozen wild turkeys taken in the White River hills, ca. 1890. *University of Arkansas at Little Rock, Archives and Special Collections.*

Wild turkeys were hunted with both shotgun and rifle. Hunter in foreground holds a Model 94 Winchester rifle, the first sporting rifle constructed specifically for smokeless powder cartridges, ca. 1890. *University of Arkansas at Little Rock, Archives and Special Collections.*

Hunting party, ca. 1890, carrying a large buck deer. Note the blowing horns two of the men are wearing, which they used to communicate with each other or with their hounds. *University of Arkansas at Little Rock, Archives and Special Collections.*

Marvin Tong, culture broker for the sale of the Turnbo Collection from the Sender Book Shop to the Springfield Art Museum. Photo taken in 1955.
Ken Shuck photo, Kalen and Morrow Papers, Jefferson City, Missouri.

Dugout canoe, typical of those used by the early settlers. This canoe, which had sunk and had been covered by gravel deposits, was uncovered by flood waters of the White River near Shell Knob in 1965. It was hollowed from a single log and additional gunwale boards were added later. *Don Wooldridge photo, James F. Keefe Papers, Jefferson City, Missouri.*

V
"Hearts of Stone": The War at Home

Editors' note: Turnbo's accounts of the Civil War barely mention the great battles at Wilson's Creek or Pea Ridge. Instead, he wrote of his own experiences as a soldier and citizen of the Ozarks who witnessed the result of Confederate troop movements, Union scouts, provisioning of soldiers in the field, and guerrilla activities as the war totally disrupted civilian life and settlement.

In the Ozarks, and in much of Arkansas and Missouri, the war was between friends and neighbors; it was characterized by murder, arson, robbery, and ambush. Opposite sides called themselves Federals and Confederates, but as the war wore on, many pursued violence for their own personal gain or revenge. Small bands of unorganized individuals, who belonged to no formal authority, were called guerrillas, jayhawkers, and bushwhackers. When the regular armies captured these men they were often summarily executed.

The legitimate officers of both armies, however, were encouraged by what seemed to citizens to be lawless violence. For example, Brig. Gen. F. J. Herron wrote to Capt. Martin D. Hart that he sent soldiers to "White River to help clear that section... Don't take any of them prisoners... completely destroy the bands infesting that country, and... show no mercy to bushwhackers."[1] Additionally, Col. William Weer at Carrollton ordered his Unionists to "destroy every house and farm owned by seccessionists, together with their property that cannot be made available to the army; kill every bushwhacker you find."[2]

As the war continued, this kind of indiscriminate carnage increased, and it became difficult for locals to perceive just what force was responsible. As always in the theater of guerrilla warfare, civilians suffered the most, and it is that suffering that Silas Turnbo recorded.

The suffering of the Civil War was the nation's most traumatic time; it was no different with the White River families. The war was a terrible closure to the memory of youth, a "golden age," and the settlers' "easy life"—quick gains in possessions, large and small, where one's livelihood was free on a great open range—vanished. The hunting for subsistence continued, but men hunted one another, and instead of eating the richness of nature, hard times reduced them to eating wild onions, slippery elm bark, and cooked hides. Turnbo's war accounts focus upon those who maintained a commitment to survive and to continue a future life in their pioneer locale. Turnbo's own family fared relatively well, while the war decimated the Cokers.

Yellville in the Dark Days of Civil War [2:79]

THIS IS NOT written to stir up sectional strife or cause the old sores which have healed to break out afresh and again hear the moans of the dying and witness the devastation and destitution of the beautiful sunny land—far from it—but to give warning to future generations to look and reflect before they leap.[3]

Civil War should never be encouraged or tolerated in our land and country. If our great republic has to engage in war let it be against a foreign foe and never that unless it is compelled to save its honor and integrity. It is much better to keep out of war if we can avoid it in an honorable way than to plunge into it uncalled for. If war must come let it be against a foreign enemy, and not against ourselves. Just think of the hundreds and thousands of men who enlisted in the armies of the blue and gray from 1861 to 1865 who perished from exposure on the march and in camp and on the field of slaughter. Remember these men were from North and South. They were Americans. Yet they fell out over a matter that could have been set right without the force of arms. But the agitators of the north and south could not be satisfied until the people of the United States divided against themselves and the result was that a bitter war was stirred up and the men of north and south met each other on the battlefield and fought it to a finish. I shudder every time I think of it. In civil war, or war between nations, many individuals become speculators and grow rich through crookedness. While others have to stem the current of battle and the mass of people living in the territory involved are forced to bear the horrors of destitution and suffering imposed by the contending armies. What a grand thing it would be for all nations to be at peace with one another, and it ought to be that the people of every nation should live in peace with each other. But as long as one class of people or nation domineers over another there will be strife, contention, strained relations, rumors of war which may ultimately culminate in real war.

It should be the duty of rulers of the civilized nations to promote peace among their people by having them taught the principal of true Christianity and all those that would willingly accept the love of God would lay down their carnal weapons and put on the armor of God and do all they could to prevent war and its awful results. It should be the desire of every one from the highest official down to the humblest citizen to strive for a good government independent of some of the policies of political parties. There is too much craving and pulling for the almighty dollar. Money is all right in its place and it is all wrong when it is improperly used. In many cases the dollar is used to the advantage of one class of people and to the disadvantage of another. Too much politics and the hunger and greed for the accumulation of money creates dissatisfaction among the people which usually brings on bad results. Yellville was quite a little town when the civil war with its fiery darts struck the state of Arkansas during that awful strife, nearly every building in the town was reduced to ashes. To give an idea of the destruction of property in Yellville and neighborhood we will make a brief statement of the burning of the town as gleaned from a reliable source.

There is a hill south of Crooked Creek known in the pioneer days as Bald Jess which was named for Jess Everette who in time of the Everette and King war at Yellville would frequently ascend to the top of this hill and watch the village to note if there were any disturbance in town between the two factions. If there were any trouble in sight he would stay away from the village until quiet prevailed. But if the villagers seemed to be at peace with each other he would venture into town.

Mr. Brice Milum,[4] who was a resident of Yellville and who was a merchant there at the breaking out of hostilities, informed me that when part of the town was set on fire he was standing on the summit of this same hill and saw thirteen houses burn down at the same time. The beautiful little town, where once was life and activity, vanished in smoke and cinders. It was a sad day for the surviving residents to view the dense volumes of black smoke as it floated high above the burning town and drifted over the crests of the neighboring hills.[5]

I well remember being at Yellville one day in the month of July, 1861, when a call was made for volunteers to join the Confederate army. A company of men raised in Marion County and the southern part of Taney County, Missouri, were present.[6] Those patriotic citizens had volunteered their services to defend the southern cause. Their commanding officer was Captain William C. Mitchell, whose company afterward formed part of the 14th regiment of Arkansas Infantry.[7] Capt. Mitchell marched his company back and forth through the streets to the music of two violins in the hands of Dan Coker and "Yellville" Bill Coker who were members of the company. As the soldiers marched along with the colors flying at the head of the column, both officers and men extended invitations to the men present to enlist in their ranks. A number of those gallant young men responded to the call of their friends and fell in line to shed their blood for the sunny south. Most all of them gave up their lives on the battlefield or fell victims to exposure to the wintry weather and ravages of disease. In many cases their bones repose in unmarked graves. Oh, let us not forget to honor their names by remembering their patriotism in a cause they believed was right.

How I Was Befriended Once in War Times [1:59]

THE FIRST NIGHT after the arrival of our regiment[8] on Polk Bayou three miles above Batesville, Arkansas, which was on the 28th of July, 1862, I with ninety three other privates was used for a chain guard around our camp with instructions to halt everyone that approached in fifteen paces of us and allow no one to pass into camp or out of it without the countersign. We were ordered to pace our beats constantly.

Our camp was on the east bank of the Bayou just below Brickey's Mill and near the mouth of Miller's Creek. The place of this encampment was known as Camp Bragg.[9] The camp was just below a waste field where there was big timber and dense thickets in places.

The night was very dark and where they posted me was in a thick patch of brush where I could not walk to and fro without gouging my eyes out against the limbs and after the relief was gone I quietly sat down and waited for time to pass. When I grew drowsy I would get up and stamp around, then sit down again and would get up again when I became sleepy.

Finally I heard the relief guard go thrashing along in the thicket fifty yards or more outside of the guard line. They had missed their way and I was amused to hear them floundering about. I did not halt them nor reveal my place on the line for I was told to not halt anybody unless they got in fifteen paces of me and I wanted to obey my orders.

Finally, when they found the right direction again and approached in fifteen paces of me, I halted them and ordered the corporal of the guard to advance and give the countersign, which he did. The corporal was very angry because I did not halloo at them while they were hunting around in the brush to discover me and said he was going to report me to Colonel Shaler. I told him that I had no instructions to halt men forty and fifty yards distant off. He flew into a rage and said that I was asleep or I would have challenged them before they got in fifteen paces. I told him I had no orders to do that. The new-fledged corporal was so hot with anger and wanted to be promoted for doing an act of some kind charged me with going to sleep on post, neglect of duty and disobedience of orders.

I was not guilty, but I had to bear it all the same, and on the following morning, Colonel Shaler had me placed under guard. I was kept in close confinement for six days in an old log cabin that stood in the edge of the waste field. On the morning of the seventh day which was Monday, Colonel Shaler ordered the officer of the guard to send me to his quarters under the escort of two guards. On arriving at his tent, he told me to come in and after a short rough talk to me, he said, "I intend to have you shot," and ordered the guards to take me back to the guardhouse. I asked permission of the Colonel to explain my case to him, but with a haughty air he ordered me away.

While the guard was taking me through our company grounds, some of the boys asked me what Shaler said to me and I told them how it was. In two hours after I was put back into the guardhouse, Shaler come into the cabin and took me by the right hand and told me in a very kind way that I was released and to report to my company for duty. I was so disgusted at the way he abused me in his tent that I never thanked him and wondered why he set me at liberty so soon after treating me so harsh. But I soon learned the course of it as soon as I reached the men and officers of our company.

The officers had taken steps immediately to prevent Shaler from having me court martialled for they knew he had no authority to place me under arrest even. They informed me that as soon as I had gone back into the guardhouse, Lieutenant Curtis Rea[10] called on Shaler to intercede in my behalf, when the renowned Colonel ordered him back to his quarters. Then Captain Fred Wood[11] visited Shaler in his den and he treated him likewise. But they both promptly paid him another visit. Major John Methvin,[12] hearing of it, also paid the Colonel a visit. He was cut short as the others had been. He then consulted with Captain Wood, Lieutenant Rea, Lieutenant [A. S.] "Bud" Wood[13] and other officers and went back to Shaler and convinced him that if he undertook to have me shot it would cause more shooting. Each one of these officers informed me of the part he [had] taken in my behalf and a good number of the private soldiers said they had put their guns in good shape for use and intended to use them if Shaler made an attempt to have me put on trial for my life. If I had been guilty of the charge, the men and officers would not have taken it into their hands, but as it was, they were convinced that I was innocent and they were determined to defend me and thus by making a bold stroke, Shaler released me at once.

A man cannot realize the use of a true and faithful friend until he stands in need of one, and I felt very grateful to the men and officers who took part in my defense, and have never forgot the memory of any of them.

I recollect a week's stay at Yellville in war days. Our regiment the 27th of Arkansas with Colonels White and Shaver's[14] commands were on their way from Pocahontas, Arkansas, to join General Tom C. Hindman's division[15] at the mouth of Mulberry River, Ark. We arrived at Yellville on Wednesday evening at three o'clock on the 22nd of October, 1862, and pitched our tents in a field on the opposite of the creek from town where we rested a week and procured supplies. This camp was known to us as Camp Adams.

On the day of our arrival here we found the town crowded with Missouri confederates who were drawing their pay in "Clabe Jackson money"[16] and this sort of currency circulated plentiful among those warm hearted men. Their pay master occupied Isaac Wilson's hotel and this is where the soldiers were receiving their money. On the second night after we reached here a remarkable snowfall struck us which lasted until Friday morning the 24th. The snow was six inches deep and is the greatest snowfall on record so early in the fall in north central Arkansas. It went off quickly, however, and the weather turned off bright and warm again. The majority of the men in our company lived in Marion County and the camp was always full of relatives and friends bringing supplies of needed woolen clothing from the home spinning wheels and hand looms. 🌿

A Leader of a Southern Band of Men Attempts to Force a Union Man to Join His Forces [4:42]

THE GREAT WAR in the United States from 1861 to 1865 proved the domineering spirit and bad disposition of hundreds of men of both sides where they had an opportunity to show their authority. They were abusive and cruel to those they had in their power. It was not uncommon to meet these overbearing fellows in the armies of both the north and south, but it was usually the case these men did not belong to the regular army, but numbered among the guerrillas and outlaws who carried on an irregular warfare.

One day in the month of August, 1903, I received a letter from J. D. Row of Pruitt, Boone [Newton] County, Arkansas, dated July 30th giving a story of war days which runs as follows.

J. M. Booth come from near Jonesborrough, Tenn., in 1853. Being then thirteen years old he lived with his father Joseph Booth on the east side of White River at the mouth of Yocum Creek in Taney County, Mo. In 1860 J. M. Booth married Miss Agnes Russell whose parents lived near Springfield, Mo. They lived together thirty one years, raised a family of seven children, three sons and four daughters. Like numbers of other old timers of the White River Valley, Mr. Booth has passed through some very interesting and exciting scenes in the forest while hunting game and encountered serious trouble during war times. His father died before the war broke out and he was living on the old farm with his young wife when the bloody conflict began between the states.

In the summer of 1861 about twenty five men rode up where he was at work near the house and requested him in no polite terms to join their band. The men were in charge of a rough man.

"You must join my company," said the commander.

"I cannot accept your proposition," said Mr. Booth.

"Why not?" yelled the captain.

"Well," says Mr. Booth, "my reasons for not enlisting in your company is that you claim to be southern men and you are opposing the government of the United States and I believe in the union of states and cannot afford to go with a company of men who are warring against the stars and stripes."

The remarks were spoken in a mild way but the leader flew into a rage and without further interrogation, he rammed the muzzle of his gun against his breast and shouted, "Now, damn you, join us or I will put daylight through you in a moment."

To this Mr. Booth said, "Sir, you have the advantage of me now and you can pull the trigger when you get ready. I will die rather than join your company."

At this the enraged leader saw that he could not compel the man to enlist in the band through abuse and the influence of the gun and he cooled down for he found that bulldozing made matters worse and tried to reason the case with Mr. Booth and talked to him in a kind way and advised him like a father giving admonition to his son. When Booth would not give way to his pleadings he said, "We are going across the country, and shall be gone about two weeks. When we return if you do not come and join our company I will have my men shoot you on sight." And thus they left him.

Mr. Booth knew he had met desperate men and was convinced that they would carry their threats into action unless he joined the company, and he would face death rather than do it. He knew he could not remain at home in safety and he come to a decision at once. His beloved wife was at the house ignorant of what had passed between himself and the commander of the band of men and leaving his work he went to the house and told his wife what had happened and the noble and brave hearted woman was ever ready to protect him with her life if necessary. He informed her that they would have to get out of there for it was impossible for him to remain at home and they would go up north where she would be more safe [in Greene County, Missouri] and he would enlist in the Union army.

With their hurried conversation he told his wife to prepare provision enough to last three or four days, [and] get all the household goods in shape to load into the wagon as soon as dark come. They would take part [of their goods] if not all. He had a crib full of old corn and a fine crop of corn just in silk and tassel. To lose this would be a severe loss, but life was at stake and it was more dear to him than a crib of corn and a field of roasting ears. Then if he was killed his poor wife would be left alone to face all the misfortunes and afflictions that would be forced on her and he loved her too well to think of leaving her to battle with the sore trials she would be compelled to meet.

As soon as night spread its dark mantle over the hills and valleys they loaded their bedding, wearing apparel, and provision into the wagon, yoked a fine yoke of oxen and hitched them to it and soon left their home and what they left there to go to destruction. It was a sad night and a tearful leaving to them but such is war and its awful results. The weather was warm and cloudy. A heavy rain had fallen the night previous to their departure and the streams were swollen. The oxen moved along slow; it seemed to the anxious couple that the cattle traveled as slow as snails and as the wagon wheels run over the rough road it appeared that the jolts and resulting noise could be heard for miles and the man expected to be overtaken by a band of bushwhackers and killed and his dear wife would be left at the mercy of a heartless foe, but they were not molested.

Finally they passed the Miliken Bald Hill[17] then they reached Cedar Creek and crossed it in safety. It was daylight when they reached Beaver Creek at the Mat Laughlin Ford which they found past fording. They halted near the bank of the creek and waited until the following morning for the stream to run down and still it was not fordable. Mr. Booth and his wife were discouraged. They were satisfied they would be pursued and they decided that they must get away from there. They must either cross the creek or go another direction.

Just then they heard the clatter of horses feet on another road that lead down to the same ford where they were camped. It proved to be a lone rider and as he galloped up he never halted and rode into the creek and passed over.

The water at the deepest place run over the horses' back but it was only a few feet across the deepest part and Booth and his wife decided at once to attempt to cross over. They tied their clothing and bedding all into one bundle and Booth yoked the cattle and hitched them to the wagon and into the creek they went. The oxen were large and stout and they took the running gears of the wagon to the opposite shore. In the deepest part of the ford the wagon bed floated off the wagon and down it went in a rush with Booth and wife and their effects in it. The preservation of the life of his wife was uppermost in his mind. There was no time for consultation and he leaped into the water and took hold of one corner of the wagon box and attempted to swim to the shore with it. A few rods downstream the [Beaver] creek made a bend where a bunch of sycamore trees stood at the edge of the water from the limbs of which a cluster of grape vines hung down into the water. These vines were about fifteen feet from the shore. Then these vines turned from where they were hanging in the water and lead to the shore to where they were growing from the bank above the water.

It was evident that Booth could not reach the shore before the current carried him and his wife and the wagon box with its contents into the tangled mass of vines. When he saw this he told his wife to jump into the water close to him but she must not take hold of him. The brave and trusting woman instantly obeyed and as she struck the water her husband released the wagon box and he caught her and swam with her safely to the shore.

The water carried the wagon box swiftly against the cluster of grape vines and held it there until the bottom or floor of the box become detached and floated out. The side pieces of the box by some means closed around together and held the bundle of clothes and bedding securely between them and tore loose from the vines and lodged against a drift a few yards below the sycamore trees.

Booth and his wife landed on the same side [where] the oxen [had] taken the remainder of the wagon out [of the river and] where they had stopped in the road close to the creek. Man and wife were in sore distress and as they were not able to get their bed clothes and wearing apparel from the drift while the water was up they drove the oxen with what was left of the wagon to an acquaintance who lived only a few miles away and the family furnished them with food, dry clothes and bedding and lumber for a new wagon box.

As soon as the water subsided sufficiently, Mr. Booth and his friends fished the bedding and clothes out of the water and carried them to his friend's house and dried them. This was all they saved.

In a reasonable time they reached Mr. Russell's house where Mr. Booth left his wife and went on to Springfield where he enlisted in the federal army. At the close of the war he received an honorable discharge and is now living on Bee Creek, near the line between Boone County, Ark., and Taney County, Mo.

SIMPLY HORRIBLE [4:32]

ONE AMONG THE OLDEST citizens who lived on the right bank of White River in what is now Crockett Township, Marion County, Arkansas, when the war between the states broke out was Ned Coker. Mr. Coker was intelligent and was a good common sensed man, very prosperous and owned several slaves. The writer has enjoyed many pleasant hours with him for he took pains to give me many incidents that occurred on the upper White River in the long ago.

It was supposed by some that he possessed a big sum of gold and silver which was said to be concealed somewhere on his farm or in the near neighborhood,[18] from this cause he was treated very cruel by the bandits that infested the county during the war. Mr. R. S. Holt, whose father,

William Holt, owned the river farm on the opposite side of the river from the Ned Coker farm informed me that during the turbulent days of blood and death the bad men stole all of Coker's horses and cattle except one wild mare as they called her which he managed to keep out of the reach of the desperadoes.

One night a band of robbers paid him a personal visit in disguise and demanded his money which he flatly refused to give up. They threatened to do violence to him unless he revealed to them the place where he had hid his gold and silver, but he had a stout heart and a resolution made of iron almost and they found that threats were unavailing to compel their victim to give up his money.

And so they proceeded to torture him with fire and inflicted all the suffering and pain they were able to heap on him to force him to yield up his gold but he held out so strong against the awful tortures from their hands that they resorted to other means and they procured a rope and tied one end around the poor old man's neck and passed the other end of the rope over a beam or other object and pulled him up and tied the rope fast with the intention to leave him suspended until he was dead, but as the bandits turned away from him to take their departure one of the band stopped and stepped back to the hanging and struggling form and cut the rope and he fell to the floor.

After the robbers were gone and Mr. Coker had revived he called his faithful slave whose name was Jeff and who was a bow legged Negro to bring up the wild mare and they would make an effort to get into Missouri where there would be some show of receiving protection.[19] The Negro was not long in bringing the mare to his master's house. The thieves had stolen Mr. Coker's saddle but the now almost helpless old man by the assistance of his slave mounted the mare bareback and Jeff lead the mare. They traveled night and day and went part of the way where there was no road. Mr. Coker was able to ride only a few miles at a time when he was compelled to stop and rest and go on again. In this way he rode the mare all the way into Greene County, Mo., bareback and Jeff the Negro walked and lead the mare all that distance."

THE SCOUNDRELS WERE BAFFLED [3:20]

ONE OF THE EARLIEST settlers on Big Creek [Ozark County, Missouri] was Robert Casebolt. He settled on school land on the west side of the creek in Ozark County, Missouri. A fine spring of water run out of the hill one hundred fifty yards north of the house. He built a small hut for temporary use until he could build a better house which was eighteen feet square. Then he added another house sixteen by eighteen feet ten feet south of the first house (not the hut) with a hall between and made a porch on the west side of the last house built. Both buildings were constructed out of logs.[20]

Mr. Casebolt was born in the state of Tennessee in 1811. His wife was named Jemima Casebolt and was a daughter of Matthew and Lucinda Sims and was born in the state of Indiana in 1815. Her parents emigrated to Greene County, Missouri, when she was a little child and there was scarcely a settlement in that part of Missouri. Mr. Sims and his family camped a few days on the ground where a part of the old town of Springfield now stands. There was not an improvement of any sort there then and was the home of the deer and wild turkey. Robert went from Tennessee to Greene County later where as time went on he met his future wife, Miss Jemima Sims, on Sac River, a tributary of the Osage, and they were married on this stream in the early Thirties.

They lived in Missouri until in 1836 when they moved in Marion County, Arkansas, and lived on White River. They settled the bottom just below Bull Bottom which was afterward known as the John Terry place. Mr. Casebolt brought a fine yoke of steers with him and during the following winter after his arrival here, while he and wife were clearing some land in the bottom, a hackberry tree fell on one of the oxen and killed it.

After leaving this bottom they settled on Big Creek [Marion County] where they made their home until after the commencement of the civil war.

Mr. Casebolt and his wife reared a large family.[21] As we have already said, Mr. Casebolt and his family were true southerners, fearless and met all kinds of hardships and done their duty without wavering. Casebolt was captain of a small company of men a few months in 1862. The entire family suffered from the depredations of thieves during the war and they found it necessary to conceal as much of their provision and other things that were useful as could be done. Among the last named was an ox cart, the wheels of which were banded with heavy iron tire, and Mrs. Casebolt and her daughters pulled and pushed the cart to the top of the hill west of the house and hid it in a thicket of brush. By some means word got out where the cart was concealed and its whereabouts was soon known over the neighborhood.

One day three men rode up to the yard gate and stopped. Two of them dismounted and went into the house to plunder and select articles of the household to carry off. The other man rode on up the hill toward where the cart was hid and in a few minutes Mrs. Casebolt and her daughters heard him pounding on the wheels to get the tire off and Mrs. Casebolt remarked, "If that scoundrel ain't found the cart and is knocking the tire off, two of you girls go with me and we'll go see about it." And Jane and Lucinda stepped forward to go with her. Then turning to the other children she says, "The rest of you stay here and keep them other two rascals from stealing what is in the house."

But as Mrs. Casebolt and the two girls left the house the two men walked out of the house and mounted their horses and rode on by the women and hurried up the hill to where their comrade was at work on the cart, and the three women when they reached the spot where the cart was the three men were there. The man had one tire off and had given it to one of the men on horseback and he was holding it. One of the girls told him to give it up but he refused to do so. "I will take it away from you," said she, and she took hold of it and attempted to pull it away from him. But he held to it and the other girl went to her aid and with their combined strength they jerked the tire away from him which came near pulling him off of his horse.

The scene was exciting and degrading to the men for they cursed and abused the women and the latter called them thieves and robbers. The man on the ground tried to get the tire off of the other wheel and Mrs. Casebolt ordered him to quit and let the tire alone but he cursed her and went on trying to take it off. Then she snatched up a rock and threatened to knock him down with it but this did not daunt him.

At this moment he got the tire off and it fell to the ground. But as he stooped over to pick up the tire the women snatched it up first and hung both the tires on one of the standards of the cart, and Mrs. Casebolt says, "Girls, let us take the cart to the house," and the two girls darted to the end of the tongue and raised it and pulled it along while their mother walked just behind the cart to guard the tire.

While they were taking the cart and tire down the hill and into the house yard the men followed them on their horses and abused the women in a scandalous manner and threatened to burn their house. When the women had pulled and pushed the cart into the yard the three men halted at the yard fence and went on their abuse in such a rough way and swearing that they were going to burn the house until Mrs. Casebolt determined she would not bear it any longer and she snatched up a stout club of wood and Jane picked up the chopping axe.

Mrs. Casebolt says, "The first man that dismounts from his horse I will kill him," and Jane says, "The first man that crosses the fence into the yard I will chop him to pieces with this ax." The men now used the vilest language they could command with their tongues but they dared not get off their horses. They were baffled.

Directly two of them rode off, but the other man swore he was not ready to go until he burned the house. Mrs. Casebolt says to him, "If you do not leave here at once your dead body will be found in a hole of water in Big Creek," and the scoundrel finding that he was outdone by the brave and honest women who were defending their home started off and followed on after his companions. 🌿

How a Woman Put Two Robbers to Flight [3:13]

THE WRITER HAS MENTIONED the Bull Bottom in these sketches on several occasions. As is well known in Marion County, Arkansas, this bottom is situated on the left bank of White River in Cedar Creek township. I am informed that George Weaver made the first settlement here. Weaver sold the improvements on this land to old man John Terry the first settler on the Asa Yocum place and Mr. Terry gave the improvements to his sons Tom and Ron Terry. After Tom Terry's wife died and Wilshire Magness died, Mr. Terry and Wilshire's widow were married in 1860 and lived in this bottom until the ravages of cruel war forced them to abandon their home here.

When Mr. Terry enlisted in the Union army, his wife whose name was Elizabeth Terry, was left alone with the children to contend against the hardships, thieves and robbers. There were six children, Joe Magness and Bob Magness, children by her first man Wilshire Magness, and Joe Terry, Dump Terry, and Mary Terry, which were Tom Terry's children by Mr. Terry's first wife who was a sister to Wilshire Magness, and Tom Terry an offspring of the marriage between Mr. Terry and Mrs. Magness; the latter child was six months old.

Mr. Terry's wife in describing the hardships she encountered in this bottom while her and the children were staying there alone said that one day two men who were horseback and well armed approached the house and rode up to the yard gate and stopped and demanded to know if she knew where any rebels were. She told them that she did not know anything about them. After they had repeated the inquiry a few times they reversed the questions put to her and they wanted to know if she knew where any feds were and she answered in the negative. They were very inquisitive and continued to ask her questions until they found that they could not obtain any information from her. They then backed their horses from the gate and reining them around as if they were going to ride off and stopped and held a whispered conversation and then they started off down toward the lower part of the bottom.

"I was convinced [said Mrs. Terry] that they had gone off to procure help to rob the house and drive off the stock. I and Mr. Terry owned more than one hundred head of cattle which Terry kept on the range in the hills of Music Creek. This was just after we were married, but in 1862 the land pirates [had] taken all but a few of them and disposed of them. Mr. Isaiah Wilkerson who lived on Music Creek just above the mouth, noticing that the principal part of the cattle had been stolen, he gathered up the remainder which included a few milk cows and drove them across the river where we could find them. The cows were giving milk and the milk from the cows kept the children from starving.

"After the two men had left I went to work with a determination to save my stuff in the house and my milk cows if I had to fight for the property and with the help of the children that was old enough to do anything I went to work and carried all our household stuff into the house that had only one door. I forgot to mention that there were two houses with a hall between them. Then I armed myself and the oldest children with something to fight with such as the chopping axe, hatchet, butcher knives, clubs and so on. Then I and the children sit down and waited for the return of the bandits and in a little while I saw the same two men coming back driving the milk cows before them.

"I saw at once that it was their intention to steal all we had and I says, 'Children, let us not let them scoundrels have an easy job taking our stuff from us.' When they had reached near the cow lot gate with the cattle the calves began to bleat, and the children began to cry for the little innocent and helpless children depended on the cows for a living, and when they realized that the robbers intended to take the cattle from us we would all have to meet starvation and distress. My heart seemed to sink in despair for I knew they had the power to drive them off but I had set a resolution that I would fight to the last moment to save the cows and my household. But what could I do to help myself? They would take all we had in spite of all the efforts I could do to prevent it.

"The robbers were preparing to let the calves out to the cows to make ready to drive them off and about the moment I was ready to interfere with their thievish plans a thought come into my mind that I might get rid of them before they had time to ride roughshod over me and the children, and I put it into execution at once by snatching the dinner horn from where it was hanging on the wall in the hallway and blew a loud blast with it, then stopped a moment and blew it a second time and then I hallooed at the top of my voice and used these words, 'Here they are, come quick!' Then I repeated the blowing of the horn and yelled out the same words.

"The two marauders seemed to be awfully surprised and remounted their horses and urging them into a gallop and run to the river bank and down it to the water's edge and plunged into the river and swam across to the opposite shore and up the bank they went beyond my view. As they were getting away I blew the horn and kept repeating the same words as loud as the strength of my lungs would admit. I had succeeded in bluffing them and saving my property from the rascals so far. No doubt they were fully convinced that a body of federal soldiers were nearby ready to pounce on them.

"I learned afterward that these men never stopped until they reached the John Knight cabin in the range of the Short Mountain [Marion County] which was used as a gathering place of a number of southern men in war days. In a short time after this I moved out into Missouri where I received better protection from the unwelcome bandits and guerrillas."

Mrs. Elizabeth Terry, who after the death of Mr. Terry, married Henry Clark died at her old home in the southeast part of Taney County, Missouri, February 13, 1907, and was buried in the graveyard at Protem on the following day.[22]

BRUTAL TREATMENT OF A WOMAN AND HER SON BY BANDITS [4:27]

A LARGE NUMBER of people who lived on the Buffalo Fork of White River did not escape the ravages of war. Men, women and children underwent some of the worst tortures. A number of people concealed part of their household goods and provision in the secluded spots of the mountains. They did likewise with their money if they had any on hand worth taking pains to put it in a place of safety. Mrs. Sarah Drake, daughter of Marion and Sarah Fowler, and who was born in the valley of the Buffalo River, relates a blood curdling story of a band of brutal fiends who visited the house of a man of the name of Baker who lived on a stream called Bear Creek which runs into Buffalo from the south side. This is in Searcy County, Arkansas, and Mr. Baker lived below Lebanon and near where Mr. Neser Arnold's mill and [cotton] gin is.

Mrs. Drake said, "If I mistake not Mr. Baker's wife's name was Nan. She had two daughters named Josie and Bias and two sons named Jim and Calvin. These children except Jim were small when the war was going on.

"One night while Mr. Baker and Jim was away from home, the band of heartless men rode up to the yard gate and dismounted and walked into the house and with threats and oaths they attempted to compel Mrs. Baker and Calvin to tell of the whereabouts of their money and other valuables which they refused to do. They then proceeded to whip the faithful woman with a drawing chain and hung Calvin by the toes to a joist in the house. Mrs. Baker was beaten almost to death with the chains before the brutes let up and Calvin suffered intensely before they let him down.

"In the meantime one of the men filled a sack full of tobacco in the twist and took it out and tied it to his saddle on the horse. Others carried the beds out into the wood yard where their horses was hitched and after the boy Calvin was set free he crept out of doors and seeing a chance without being observed and with a small knife he ripped the bottom of the sack open that held the tobacco, and when the thieves had done all the injury in their power without entirely killing any of the members of the family, they tied the bed ticks to the horses' tails then ripped one end open and mounted their horses and started off in a gallop and strewed feathers and tobacco all along the road until the bed ticks were exhausted of their feathers and the sack was empty of tobacco.

"The bandits did not stop at this but finally killed Mr. Baker and his son Jim in a cruel manner. Mrs. Baker, who had partially recovered from the terrible ordeal of being whipped with the chain, had her husband and son buried under a large apple tree that stood in the corner of the orchard.

"After the close of the war she had the two graves and the apple tree enclosed with paling. Mrs. Baker bore ugly scars on her body, head and limbs to the day of her death and was subject to spasms that attacked her after she had underwent the brutal treatment inflicted on her by the bushwhackers and cutthroats. Mrs. Baker when her death occurred received interment in a graveyard on the bank of Bear Creek."

Saving Her House through Tears and Prayer [3:67]

A MAN OF THE NAME of Joe Allen lived on Shoal Creek in Taney County, Missouri. His cabin stood on the east bank of the creek near one fourth mile below Protem. When the war broke out Allen claimed to be a southern man but refused to enlist in the confederate army. As the war progressed Joe proved to be a bad man and kept the worst of company. Peter Keesee, who lived on Big Creek on what is now the Sam Holett place, was a union man and when the war warmed up to red heat Keesee took his family and sought safety among his friends who lived on Little North Fork.

"A few hours after I was compelled to desert my home on Big Creek," said Mr. Keesee, "Joe Allen and his clan come along and finding that we were gone set fire to my dwelling and reduced it to ashes. I went on and as soon as I had got my family in safe quarters I lost no time in making preparations to retaliate on the destroyer of my residence. Joe Allen had burned my home and I was determined to burn his hut. I ask a few of my intimate friends to assist me at the burning and they promised to aid me. It was war times and who cared for burning a house when the enemy burns yours? My heart was hardened and with those that had promised to help me we mounted our horses and rode off toward Shoal Creek.

"We went at a rapid gait and it did not take us many hours to reach Joe's cabin. Of course Joe was not there but his wife, whose name was Alwilda, and two or three little children were in the house. The wife and children were destitute. Their clothes were in tatters and they were nearly without food. It was shameful for a man to turn a mother and her little ragged children out of doors. But I cared nothing for that. I was wanting revenge for the loss of my house.[23]

"I informed Mrs. Allen at once what we had come for and as I did not desire to deprive her of what few household property she had in the house I ordered her in a peremptory way that she must carry her household effects out of doors. She protested in piteous words not to destroy their only place of shelter. It seemed that I possessed the heart of a savage and refused to listen to her tearful entreaties. In reply I told her to hurry or I would set the house on fire before she carried her things out. With loud sobs and her eyes bathed in tears she began to move out the few bed clothes and scant furniture. She saw that it was useless to plead with a barbarian and went on with the work. We waited in silence until the despairing woman had carried all her effects to a safe distance so that they would escape the flying sparks from the burning hut. We now began to make preparations to set the building on fire for I was anxious to see it go up in flames.

"At this moment the now nearly crazed woman renewed her pleading to me not to wipe out their only shelter. She prayed that I might repent of my wicked design of burning their cabin and that she could not help what Joe had done and begged me and my friends to return back home and leave her house to shelter herself and helpless children. She looked up toward heaven and I saw her tear stained cheeks, and as the tears were streaming down her face she implored the good Ruler of heaven and earth to soften our hearts that we might abandon our heartless work and go away without destroying her only place of abode. She stood and pleaded and prayed as if her heart was broken. Her little children were standing there with her holding to her dress and crying. It was a heart rending scene.

"A few minutes before this Satan had control of my heart. But as I listened at the poor helpless woman's piteous sobs of grief and heard her devoted prayers and saw her children huddled about her, my wicked thoughts of burning the house began to soften. The spirit of revenge was leaving me and an impression of pity was taking the place of my stony heart. Her prayers were too much for me and I yielded to the influence of her supplications.

"Turning to my companions I said, 'Men, we cannot afford to burn this house,' and I told the weeping woman that she was at liberty to carry her stuff back into the hut for it was safe as far as we were concerned for we had got out of the notion of putting fire to the building. The nearly distracted woman could hardly believe it until I assured her that it was true. Then she gladly put away her tears and sorrows and rejoiced that I had changed my mind. Though Joe Allen had wronged me and it was my desire and intention to treat him likewise but the tearful prayers of his helpless wife had turned my reckless heart into one of mercy and I thank God to this day that I did not burn that cabin."

A Novel Way to Hide Money [27:45]

BARBER'S CREEK in Christian County, Missouri, is a tributary branch of Swan Creek. Though the stream is small, the valley narrow and rough, yet the water is so clear that it resembles the water of a beautiful flowing spring. The creek bed is lined with gravel which makes a pretty sight to view the crystal waters as it flows along in the channel and enters Swan Creek. Near the mouth of this little water course lives George Adams whose residence stands on the east bank and a short distance above Garrison Post Office.[24] Mr. Adams has lived here a number of years and his wife was principally reared on Swan Creek, Christian County, and she furnished the writer with a few items of interest in the following way.

"My maiden name was Jane Nance. My father's given name was Samuel, my mother's maiden name was Susan Adams. I was born in Lawrence County, Mo., August the 2nd, 1845. My parents moved to Swan Creek in Christian County, Mo., when I was a small child.

"Soon after we came here a man by the name of Dick Pigg who lived on Swan Creek three quarters of a mile above the mouth of Barber's Creek made brandy from paw paw apples. His distillery was at a little spring and in paw paw time he distilled several gallons of paw paw brandy from this wild fruit. The creek bottoms along Swan Creek furnished an abundance of paw paws in the early days and it was small trouble to gather bushels of them and haul them to Pigg's distillery and have them manufactured into brandy and he sold this stuff to as many people that desired to use it for a beverage. This brandy made of paw paw did not taste like that made of peaches or apples and did not command as ready sale."

In giving a little war time incident of how a citizen concealed his gold she said that her uncle Mathias Adams, who lived on Swan Creek a few miles above Swansville,[25] was a well-to-do man and owned a fine bunch of stock when the war broke out and sold it all for cash in the nick of time or the marauders of one side or the other would have captured and made way with it. Though he was now rid of his stock the question now was with him what would he do with his money for the robbers were liable to come along and kill him and take the money. If he failed to find a hiding place to conceal the precious metal for it was all gold—he would be no better off than before he sold his stock.

Then he collected his wits together and planned a way to save his money which was a novel one. "I was living with my uncle and aunt at the time and he kept his plans no secret from the family and this is the way he went about it.

"One cold morning soon after day light he went out into the wood yard and selected a white oak stick of wood and brought it into the house. This piece of wood was 2½ or 3 feet in length and he sawed both ends off with a hand saw, leaving the stick the desired length to suit him, he used an auger with a long shank and the size he wanted and after fastening the stick so that it would not move he proceeded to bore a hole length ways through the stick as far as he thought would answer his purpose. Withdrawing the auger and after cleaning out the auger hole he held the stick up right and began to drop his gold pieces into the auger hole. The money was composed of $20, 10, 5 and one dollar gold pieces. He went on dropping in the money in piece after piece until the cavity in the stick was almost filled. Only leaving a little space to drive in a wooden pin which he sawed off at the end of the stick or close as he could, and then took some mud and rubbed it over the end of the stick where the pin was drove in, then he dried the mud by the fire and took a rag and rubbed over it which gave it the appearance of being perfectly solid.

"After he had completed the work of storing away his money in this peculiar fashion he dropped the stick down on the floor near the jam rock and remarked to my aunt, his wife, that his money would be as safe in that stick of wood as any where else. But his wife did not think so and said, 'No, Mathias, do not leave it on the floor for some one might come into the house during a cold day and pick up that wood and lay it on the fire and of course you would jump up and take the wood out of the fire which would arouse suspicion that there was something valuable in that stick of wood that you did not want exposed and so you had best go and conceal your money somewhere else.'

"At this my uncle changed his mind by agreeing with her and picking up the stick of wood he walked out of doors with it and went into the forest where I suppose he carefully put it in a safe place.

"I never heard him or my aunt mention it any more but I suppose he revealed the whereabouts of it to her. My uncle died before the war closed and lies buried in the graveyard at Swansville in Christian County, Mo."

Hardships and Starvation in the Turbulent Days of War [23:36]

AN OLD TIMER of Marion County, Ark., who has lived on Jimmie's Creek since the early Fifties has this to say of hard times at the close of the war between the states.

"I and my wife lived three weeks at the close of the war without the least bit of bread. We were compelled to live on anything that we could use at all that had any nourishment about it and was not poisonous; wild onions and wild salad were hunted for and gathered all over the woods.

"Sam Railsback's wife would hunt all the slippery elm trees she could find and take the bark off and scrape off the outside bark and save the inner bark and cut it into small bits with a knife and dry it in the sun or heat of the fire and when she had a sufficient quantity of this she put it into a sack and carried it to Adams' Mill on Mill Creek south of Yellville where it was ground into meal and used it for bread by moisten[ing] the ground bark with water and making it into pones or flat cakes and baking it in a skillet.

"The old man Bosier who lived on Newton's Flat [Marion County] below Jimmie's Creek was so nigh starved to death that he would hunt all the old dry hides he could find and cut them into small pieces and scorch them on the fire and eat them."[26]

THE SALT PETER CAVE BLUFF AND THE CAPTURE OF THE POWDER WORKS THERE [2:50]

ON THE SOUTH SIDE of White River in Marion County, Arkansas, and some six or seven miles below Oakland is a noted bluff that a few of the early pioneers along White River claimed that during the earliest settling up of Marion County that one night an explosion occurred in the face of this bluff. The detonation was said to have been heard for miles and resembled the bursting of a large meteor causing the earth to tremble. Whether this be true or not I have no way of confirming. But it is possible that such a report was heard and was in connection with the memorable earthquake in 1811.[27]

This bluff was made famous during the early part of the civil war. The confederate authorities kept a small force of men here awhile to protect the powder works and the employees while engaged in the manufacture of powder from salt peter that was found here. The powder was made for the use of the confederate soldiers.[28] The salt peter was taken from a cave in the bluff hence the name of the bluff. A brief account from several sources of the capture of the Confederate forces and the works here are given to show something of the soldiers employed here and the extent of the works.

We will first quote from the *Official Records of the War of the Rebellion*[29] that the writer examined in the confederate home library at Higginsville, Missouri, in the month of June, 1907. General Samuel R. Curtis,[30] a federal officer in reporting to General H. W. Halleck[31] under date of November 30, 1862, says that General Herron[32] said that the salt peter works were destroyed. Sixty prisoners were taken and over one hundred horses. The troops who took the works were the 1st Iowa, 10th Illinois, and 2nd Wisconsin. The commander of this combined force was Colonel D. Wickersham of the 10th Illinois. The southern men captured belonged to Burbridge's command. Five hundred shot guns were also captured.

In another report we read that Captain Milton Burch,[33] 14th Missouri state militia, with forty men destroyed the salt peter works which included five buildings, one engine, twenty-six large kettles, six tanks, blacksmith and carpenter shops and tools, $6,000 worth of salt peter, five hundred barrels of jerked beef, and forty-two prisoners. This last report is claimed to be a second destruction of the works and was reported by Brigadier General E. B. Brown,[34] Springfield, Missouri, December 18, 1862, to General Samuel R. Curtis.

Another report says that Milton Burch claimed that the force at the cave were twenty-three men who were captured, the shot guns and old rifles were destroyed, four mules, three horses and two wagons were captured. The wagons were destroyed [and] the salt peter works cost the confederate government $30,000. Captain McNar[35] was in command of the southern forces at the cave. The federal forces marched to this bluff from Ozark, Christian County, Missouri.[36]

We will now give a brief account of the capture of the Salt Peter Cave bluff works by "Mun" Treat a southern man and who was one of the party employed to assist in making powder. He says, "When the federals attacked the works there were thirteen men present who were in charge of Perry Tucker with Fate Moreland as cook and waiter. Our camp was on the summit of the bluff and consisted of a few log huts two of which was filled with dried beef. The men were paid sixty cents per day in Chattanooga money which was good currency at that time. We had got in a fair way of turning out powder when the federal forces put an end to the works. The strength of the federal forces that captured the works was one hundred fifty strong and was under the command of Captain Milton Burch.

"Soon after we were taken prisoners the Union forces burned our quarters and destroyed the other works except that if I mistake not they left a few of the large kettles uninjured. Among our party that were captured were Henry Ray, son of M. P. Ray who lived at the mouth of East Sugar Loaf Creek, and John Yandell who lived on Elbow Creek in Taney County, Missouri, and John Crawford who also lived in Taney County." Henry Ray died suddenly on the sidewalk in St. Louis while the prisoners were being marched through the city. It was supposed that he was overcome by heat. It was intimated by Mr. Treat that the southern forces who were ordered to guard and protect the men and works got too far away on the approach of the federals.

Some of the foregoing reports made by some of the federal officers to their superiors in rank were no doubt exaggerated and if there was any second capture of these works I was never reliably informed of it.[37]

Reading the Bible by the Reflection of Light from a Burning Town [1:44]

ONE THAT NEVER experienced the terrors and destruction of life and property in civil war days can hardly realize the awful damages done by either army. Cities, towns, villages, and dwellings were all liable to go down in smoke and ashes. Mr. Ben Hager, who was a young fellow during the civil war and who lived in Madison County, Arkansas, relates an account of the burning of Huntsville, the county seat of Madison.[38] He said that he did not see the town while it was burning down, but he saw the light of it. Here is how he told it.

"We were living on Holman's Creek two miles south of town. The destruction of the place occurred about the last of February, 1863, and was set on fire on account of three men being killed near there. The town burned in the night while the weather was calm, cloudy, and no moon. I stood in the dooryard at home and watched the light of the burning town several hours. A high hill lay between our house and the town. The reflection of the fire was so bright and distinct that my father took his family Bible out into the yard and read nearly a chapter in the Book by the reflection of light from the destruction of the town. The only business houses left were Sam Kenner's store house and Tom Berry's hotel and Even Polk's hotel with seven or eight dwellings, among them was a house that belonged to Mr. Polk and one that belonged to Dr. Sanders. There were estimated to be one hundred fifty buildings of the town destroyed by fire."

Horrible Incident of the War and Other Family History [23:73]

WILLIAM L. BROWN married Miss Lizzie B. Whitlock daughter of William C. Whitlock who lived three miles north of Yellville, Ark. One day in May, 1895, Mrs. Brown gave the writer a history of her father's death in war times which is a sad story.

She said that one night in 1863 a party of men on horseback came to their house near midnight and took her father out of the house. "They also made Jess Whitlock a twelve year old brother of mine go with them. The men claimed that they would not hurt them but after they had left the house some distance Jess heard the men tell father that he might prepare himself for death for they intended to kill him, and while father was begging the men not to kill him Jess made a dash for liberty and escaped, but he was so bad scared and had ran so far without stopping that he did not come back home till late the following day.

"My poor mother grieved and weeped until the break of day when she started out into the woods to search for father for she had good reason to believe that the cold hearted men who took him off had killed him and it might be that they had killed Jess too. I was too young to be of any advantage to mother in helping her hunt for father. Mother tramped the wild woods till twelve o'clock without finding any trace of him, she gave up in despair, she did not know what to do. But she went out again and hunted all around and come back crying and wearied down in trying to find him. She believed that he was dead, that he was lying somewhere in the woods with no one present to care for his body. It was hard to give him up in the way he had to go and maybe her poor boy was dead too. It seemed that her heart would break but after a while she grew more calm and she said she would make another search for him.

"At this moment Jess come but he was so badly frightened that he was almost crazy. But thank God he was alive. After his excitement began to subside he told us what he heard the men tell father and where the locality was they were at and how he ran away from them. My poor distracted mother could wait no longer and she started out alone again and following the directions that Jess gave her she succeeded in discovering the dead body of my father lying some distance from the house. He had been shot [three times]—one ball took effect in the temple, one entered his mouth, and the other in the shoulder; his head was terribly mangled and his face was all covered with blood. My dear, dear mother was a large woman and my father was a small man. Mother said that it seemed that she was not able to bear up under the terrible affliction and sorrow that had fell her lot and that the tears from her eyes were so free that it seemed that she could wade in them, it seemed as though she would sink into a great dark gulf.

"Then she thought she must not give up and she prayed to God for help and finishing her prayer she rose up off of her knees and felt more composed, and more able to face the distress and great calamity that had visited her home. She could not bear to leave the body to seek help and with a resolution born of the moment she raised the lifeless form in her arms and carried it toward the house until she was compelled to lay it down from exhaustion. But after a short rest she raised the body in her arms again and went on with it toward home until she was forced to stop and lay it down again and take another resting spell. This repeated until she was in sight of the house when she met Cinda Stinnette, a colored woman who belonged to Dave Stinnette, and the kind hearted black woman assisted mother to carry my dead father into the house and helped to prepare the remains for burial.

"It was impossible then in that neighborhood to procure a coffin and mother placed the body in a box, and we were all in such a stress for clothes that mother was compelled to enclose him in the box in the same suit he wore when he was shot to death. My mother and a few other women and we children buried him on Lee's Mountain one and one half miles from home." 🌿

Visiting the Grave of Her Affiance [3:55]

ACROSS THE HOLLOW west of the Hoodenpyle graveyard, the way the old road leads, is a low hill that was once covered with trees and undergrowth. The land is now in cultivation. Just south of this rise toward the [White] river is the site of the old Pete Hoodenpyle residence. Just west of this across the hollow is where the Mat Hoodenpyle houses stood. The graveyard is situated on a beautiful plot of ground one fourth mile from the river and is known now as the John Riddle cemetery. Between the graveyard and the bank of the river is a spring where an old cabin stood in which Elijah Barnes and his family lived when the civil war began. This is on the north side of White River in Keesee township, Marion County, Arkansas.

During the third year of the war a young man of the name of John King was living at Aunt Sally Hoodenpyle's, who with her married daughter Mrs. Sarah Jane Murphy, was living in the Pete Hoodenpyle house. John Jones and family was occupying the Mat Hoodenpyle dwelling. Mr. King had come across the river from East Sugar Loaf Creek where he was engaged to be married to Miss Pop Wilmoth,[39] a sister of George Wilmoth (not Preacher George). A young horse had run away with him and he got his face badly bruised and was swelled.

One morning while he was there a company of mounted men rode up to the yard fence and halted and questioned the young man very closely and threatened to kill him. But Mrs. Hoodenpyle and her daughter pleaded with the men not to kill him and the company rode on down the road by the graveyard and crossed the river at the ford where the head of the island lies against the upper end of the old Allen Trimble land.

But before the company reached the ford of the river two of the cavalry men dropped out of ranks and rode back to the house and demanded John King. When the two men rode up to the fence King was sitting before the fire eating a cake that had been sweetened with sorghum molasses. Throwing part of the cake in the fire he remarked, "They have come back to kill me," and got up and went out to the fence where the two men sat on their horses and they ordered him to get over the fence and go with them. He obeyed and passed on and they reined their horses around and followed him. He knew they were unmerciful men and intended to murder him and he said but little. But as they were leaving Aunt Sally Hoodenpyle ran and overtaken the two blue coats and begged them not to shoot the young man. One of the men halted and conversed with her while the other man went on with the helpless captive.

After they had passed on a short while the report of a gun was heard toward the graveyard followed by the distressing cry of, "Oh—oh." Then a second shot was heard followed by a piteous cry of, "Oh, Lordy." Then all was silent. The man who was talking with Mrs. Hoodenpyle spurred his horse forward and galloped on to overtake his comrade in blood.

At this moment Miss Adaline Jones, daughter of John Jones and now the wife of George Holt, in company with Mrs. Sarah Jane Murphy, who was fourteen years old and Adaline fifteen years of age, started to the murdered man. When they reached the spot where he lay he was lying on his face just over the rise toward the graveyard. His head was downhill. One shot had took effect in the back at the cross of the suspenders. The second ball had passed into his head between the left ear and the back of the head. The man was still alive but unconscious. Miss Adaline and Mrs. Murphy raised up the nearly lifeless form and turned the head up the hill and placed him on his back. Then Adaline broke off some small bushes and little limbs and putting them together placed them under the dying man's head for a pillow. Sarah Jane now started back to the house for assistance while Adaline remained with him.

But she soon met her mother and Mrs. Elizabeth Jones coming and she returned with them, and by the time they got there Mr. King was dead. It was decided that while some of the ladies remained with the dead body to guard it from molestation from the dogs and hogs the others would go and hunt for a wagon and yoke of oxen to haul the dead body to the graveyard which was done as soon as possible. When the wagon was brought to where the dead man lay the women lifted the body into the wagon box. A pool of blood had run out at the bullet holes and Adaline covered the blood from view with dirt and trash, and while the dead man was being hauled across the hollow to the graveyard, she walked behind the wagon and covered up the blood as it dripped through the openings in the bottom of the wagon box to the ground.

When they reached the graveyard some boards were placed on the ground and the body was taken out of the wagon and laid on the board. In a short time other help arrived. The women and children dug a grave and just before they commenced to dig the vault John Jones come and dug the vault for them. When the preparations were made for the burial the body was wrapped in a bed sheet that Mrs. Hoodenpyle had furnished and lowered into the grave and some pieces of plank that Mr. Jones had furnished was laid over the vault and the dirt filled in.

In a few days after the death of the young man, his betrothed learning of his death, come over from Sugar Loaf Creek to visit the grave and Adaline and Mrs. Hoodenpyle accompanied her to the graveyard where Mrs. Hoodenpyle gave the girl a finger ring, a pocket book, and a lock of hair which she had taken out of the dead man's pocket. The ring and lock of hair belonged to the girl which the young man was keeping as a token of love he cherished for the now poor weeping girl.

A Bold Robbery [4:62]

THIS DETAILED ACCOUNT of a bold robbery perpetrated at the writer's father's house in war times was given me by my sister, Mrs. Margarette [Turnbo] Jones of Protem, Mo.

"When the robbery was committed my father was living on the left bank of White River in Keesee Township, Marion County, Ark. My sister said that it was winter time with a cold rain falling. A light snow had fell in the forepart of the night. There were seven in the family at home when the robber came. My father, mother, and my brother [Jasper] Newton, Lafayette (Bubby), myself, and my sisters, Mary L. and Gracie (Cricket) Elmira.[40] Henry Wilson and his wife whose name was Peggie had come to our house the evening before and stayed all night and was there when the robbery took place. My father had a painful catarrh [inflammation] on his right hand which caused him to suffer a great deal.

"It was just after daylight when two men rode up to the yard fence and called for breakfast and their horses fed. We had just eat and the unwashed dishes were sitting on the table. The men would not permit their horses to be put in the lot but fed them on the ground in the wood yard without taking off the saddles. Both the men wore flop hats and when we prepared breakfast for them they did not take off their hats until after they had sit down at the table when each one took his hat off and laid it on his lap. After they had eat breakfast they rose from the table and picking up the chair they occupied while eating and placed them before the fire and sit down and began to talk. The fire was getting low and as father was not able to do anything on account of his sore hand he ask my two brothers, Newt and Bubby, to get some wood and put on the fire.

"When they both got into the house with the wood, the two men rose to their feet and each one drew a revolver and sprang to the doors and one stood at one door and the other [at] the other [door] and one of them told my father that if anyone attempted to leave the house they would shoot them down. And the other says to my father, "You are the man that robbed my house in Newton County, Mo." Which of course was not true. Then they both demanded money. My mother had $1300 dollars in confederate money on her person which my father had turned over to her for safety and it was all the money we had. Seeing that we had no chance to save the money or make any resistance father told mother to give the money up to them which she did and when the robbers saw that it was paper money they began to curse and say, "Damn the confederate money! We want hard money."

"And father said, 'Gentlemen, I could hand down the moon to you as soon as I could give you gold and silver.'

"The scoundrels threatened and swore to their hearts' content thinking they would compel my parents to produce a lot of gold, but the thieves were much mistaken and gave it up and took their departure and we were more than glad to get rid of their unwelcome presence. On reaching their horses they mounted them and rode up the river and stopped at the Mat Hoodenpyle farm and took two horses from Aunt Sally Hoodenpyle, one of which was a black horse and the other a gray one. We learned afterward that the name of one of the men was John Huff and the other was Morris."

A SET OF THIEVES [4:56]

THE FOLLOWING ACCOUNT of how the writer's father's house was ransacked by marauders while he lived on the old George Fritts' farm on the left bank of White River in Keesee Township, Marion County, Ark., during the terrible strife in the days of war was furnished me by my sister, Mrs. Sally [Turnbo] Treadway of Peel, Arkansas.

She said that one night in the month of January, 1865, two men rode up to the yard fence and dismounted.

"One of them stayed out at the fence to guard the horses and to keep a look out for the approach of friends or foes. The other one come into the house. He was disguised by having his face blacked with some kind of coloring matter which was more than likely pot black.[41] My father and my brothers, Newt and Bubby, was gone. John Payne, who was afflicted with chronic sore eyes, had come there to mend our shoes. Lizzie and Sarah Craton Hogan, daughters of Crayton and Sarah (Trimble) Hogan, were there also. A heavy rain was falling and the night was intensely dark. It was just the kind of a night for thieves and wolves to prowl around. The man when he come into the house cursed and threatened and drove John Payne out of doors and made him stand in the yard while the rain was falling.

"About the first thing he did toward laying his hands on in the house was to pick up a pint bottle filled with spirits of camphor which he at first supposed was whiskey and being disappointed he dashed the bottle down on the floor and broke it into pieces.[42] A box that was painted red which we called a chest was sitting near the wall of the house which was filled with shelled corn and the robber made we children empty the corn out of the box onto the floor. But changing his mind the thief made us pick the corn up again and put it in a sack to feed his horses on. Lizzie and Sarah Crayton helped us pick up the corn and we put all the pieces of glass we could find on the floor and put them in the sack with the corn. The robber now went up in the loft and filled a sack with dried apples and brought it down. Then he took a pillow slip from the bed and stuffed it full of lint cotton that the seed had been taken out by the use of a small roller hand gin.

"We had a half side of home tanned sole leather concealed under the house floor[43] that only two other persons besides our own family knew where it was and these were George Simmons and Bill Riddle. Our family and Aunt Katie Simmons, mother of George Simmons, had leather enough tanned in partnership for the two families in our large tan trough that lay on the bank of the river at the side of the upper field. The robber knew where our part of the leather was hid and took it out from under the floor. Then he made my two sisters, Margarette and Mary, go to the smokehouse and bring a shoulder of meat into the house and lay it down on the table. The meat was fresh for it had not been killed more than a day or two. The robber on examining the meat gouged his finger into the meat and says, 'Ah, it's as green as poison. I will not take it.'

"While all this was going on my brother Andy, who was the baby, got scared at the robber and was crying at the top of his voice which did not please the robber and he says, 'Some of you go out and get a corn cob and stick it in that child's mouth and choke his noise off.' The man now proceeded to examine the bed clothes and picking out three of the best quilts he folded them up and laid them down and called to his companion who was still on guard at the fence to come in and help him carry the things out and they took the quilts, cotton, corn, dried apples and sole leather and put the stolen booty on their horses and rode off." ✍

Shocking Scenes Enacted at Yellville [2:76]

YELLVILLE, ARKANSAS, was a scene of blood and carnage during the latter part of the civil war. There were a large number of men shot to death in town and their bodies left where they fell for the hogs and dogs to devour. I will mention a few cases in a brief way to show how far this cruel war was carried on in this town at its worst. These accounts were gathered from reliable sources.

Miss Martha Ann Taylor, a daughter of William Taylor, who lived on Water Creek near where the Flag Spring is, said that while they were moving from Water Creek to Dallas County, Missouri, in war times they had to stop a few days in Yellville and while they were there she saw two dead men lying in a ditch and the hogs were eating them. Miss Taylor said when this horrible scene met her eye she staggered with terror and her limbs seemed paralyzed for a moment and as soon as she could recover from the shock she fled from the spot. Martha married William Mahan in Dallas County, Missouri, and she would often repeat this story to her husband. She died near Pontiac, Missouri, in 1889, and was buried in the graveyard at the mouth of Bratton's Spring Creek.

Mr. Brice Milum, a former resident of Yellville, told me that a man of the name of William Busket was shot to death in Yellville one day one hundred yards from the Weast hotel.[44] The weather was cold with snow on the ground and the body lay there three days and the hogs mutilated it by eating the ears off. Mrs. Sally Woods, wife of Derl Woods, and a few other women dug a grave and buried the remains near where Mr. Busket was executed. They had no coffin but they wrapped the body in a blanket. The ladies were not allowed to bury the dead man east and west according [to] burial rites and customs but made them dig the grave north and south or crossways as they termed it.[45] Mrs. Woods was a sister of John Adams and was a daughter of Mr. Matthew Adams.

One day in the early autumn of 1865 I and Lewis R. Pumphrey while passing along the street where the lower part of Yellville now stands he pointed to a spot of ground near where we were and said, "There is where one brave man died." And Mr. Pumphrey and Mr. Brice Milum give me a history of the case in the following way.

The man's name was Tom Jobe and he lived in Missouri and was accused of being a southern "bushwhacker." It was said that he was a desperate man and had slain several men who wore the blue. The federals captured him at the mouth of the South Fork of East Sugar Loaf Creek just above where the town of Lead Hill now stands. Jobe and Blueff McGroove were together. The latter escaped. Jobe wore a pair of boots and the enemy in shooting at him, one of the balls hit his boot leg while he was running and split it open. The ball wounded him in the leg. After they captured him they took him to Yellville and kept him under guard a week and then executed him which was done in the following way.

After Tom Jobe was conducted to the designated place for execution and after being told that he must die he was asked by the commanding officer how many federals he had slain since the beginning of the war and the doomed man reflected a half a minute and then replied in a stoical way, "Well, about forty is as nigh as I can estimate the number on this short notice." And the answer to this was a volley of bullets shot into the man's body and he passed from life into eternity.

Mr. Brice Milum said that Jobe was executed one hundred yards in front of his door yard and that his wife, Mrs. Elizabeth Milum saw the execution from the house. Mr. Milum and Mr. Lewis R. Pumphrey both said that Jobe's body lay in a mud hole several days where the dogs eat on it. Some of the soldiers as they rode by would ride over the body as it lay in the mud and others would pass around it. Those that rode over him had hearts of stone and cared for nothing of a Christian nature and the ones that rode around him was either of a superstitious feeling or carried a soft heart in their breast.

Mr. Milum said that after the federals left the town he and "Ice" [I. C.] Stinnette cut cedar poles from the cedar grove nearby and built a pen around the remains of Jobe and filled the pen with stones.

Appendix: Selected Genealogies of the Coker and the Turnbo Families

Selected Genealogy of the Turnbo Family

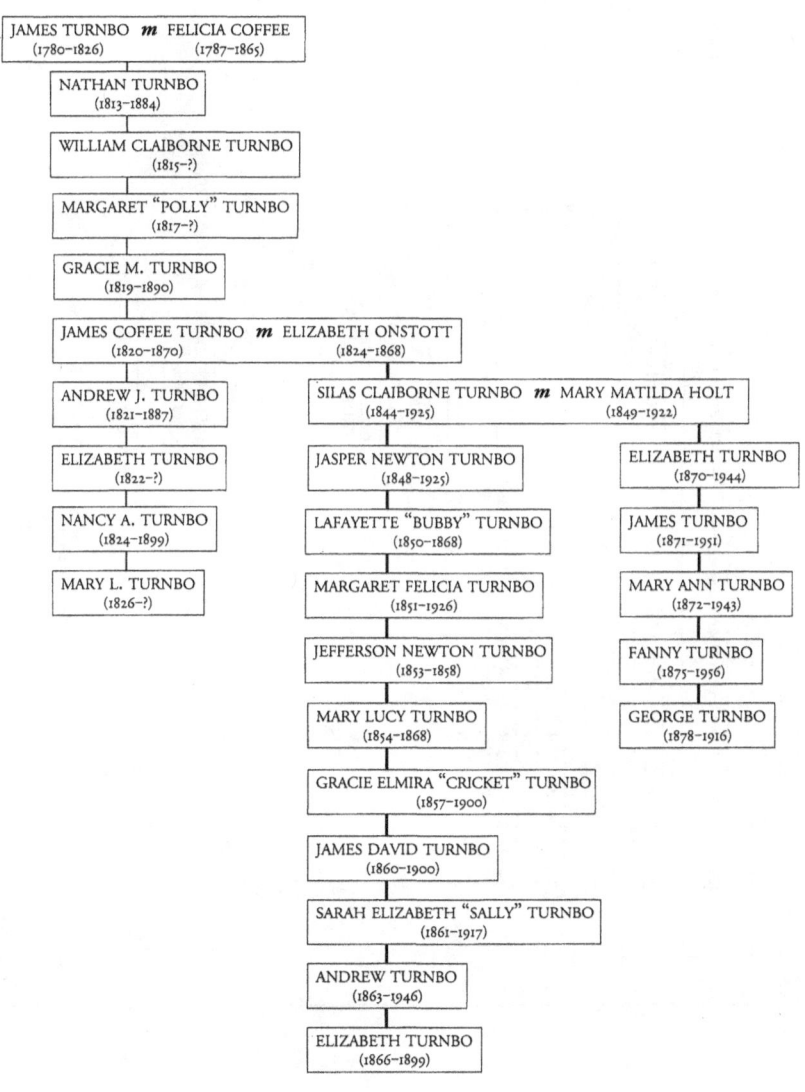

Selected Genealogy of the Coker Family

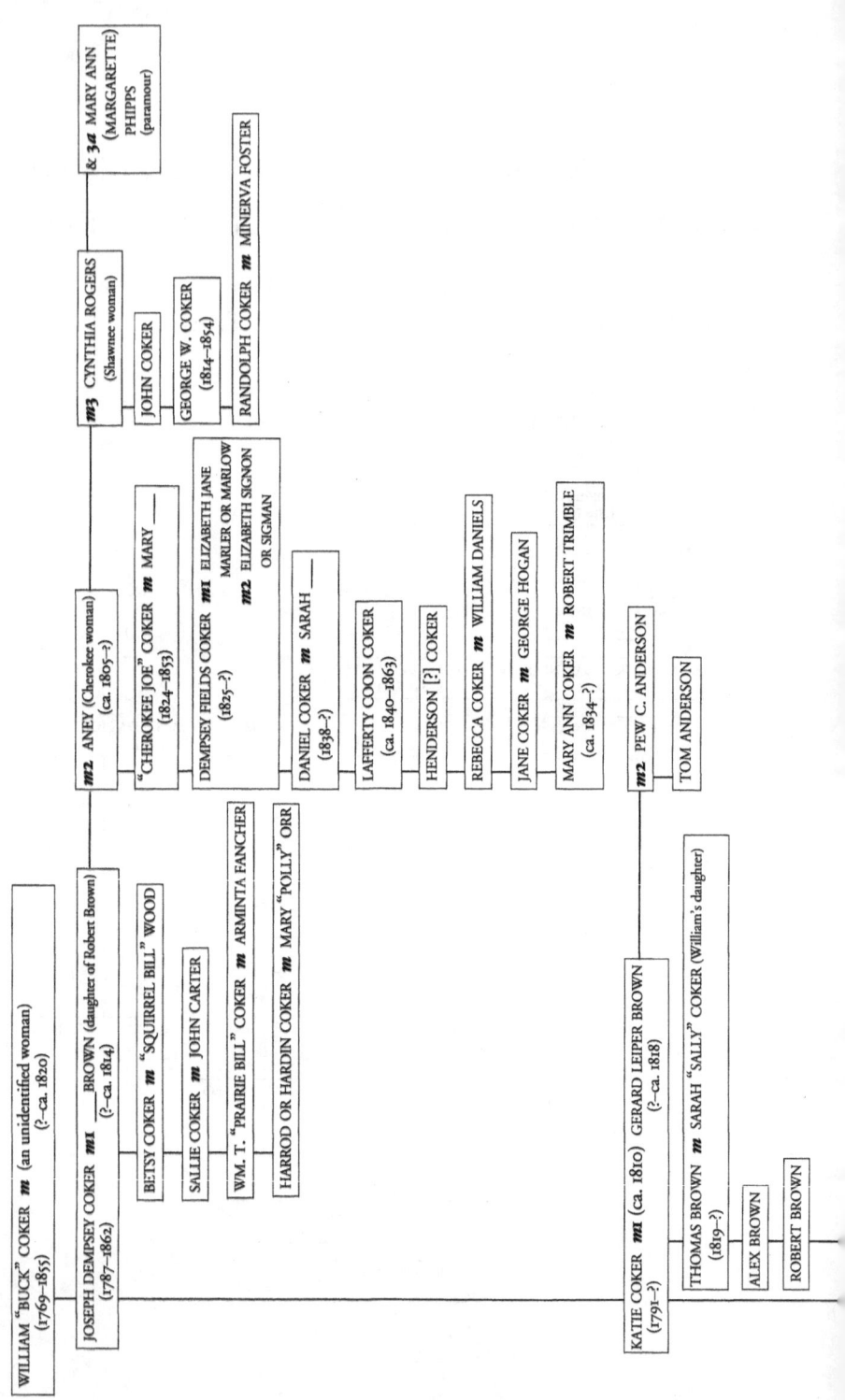

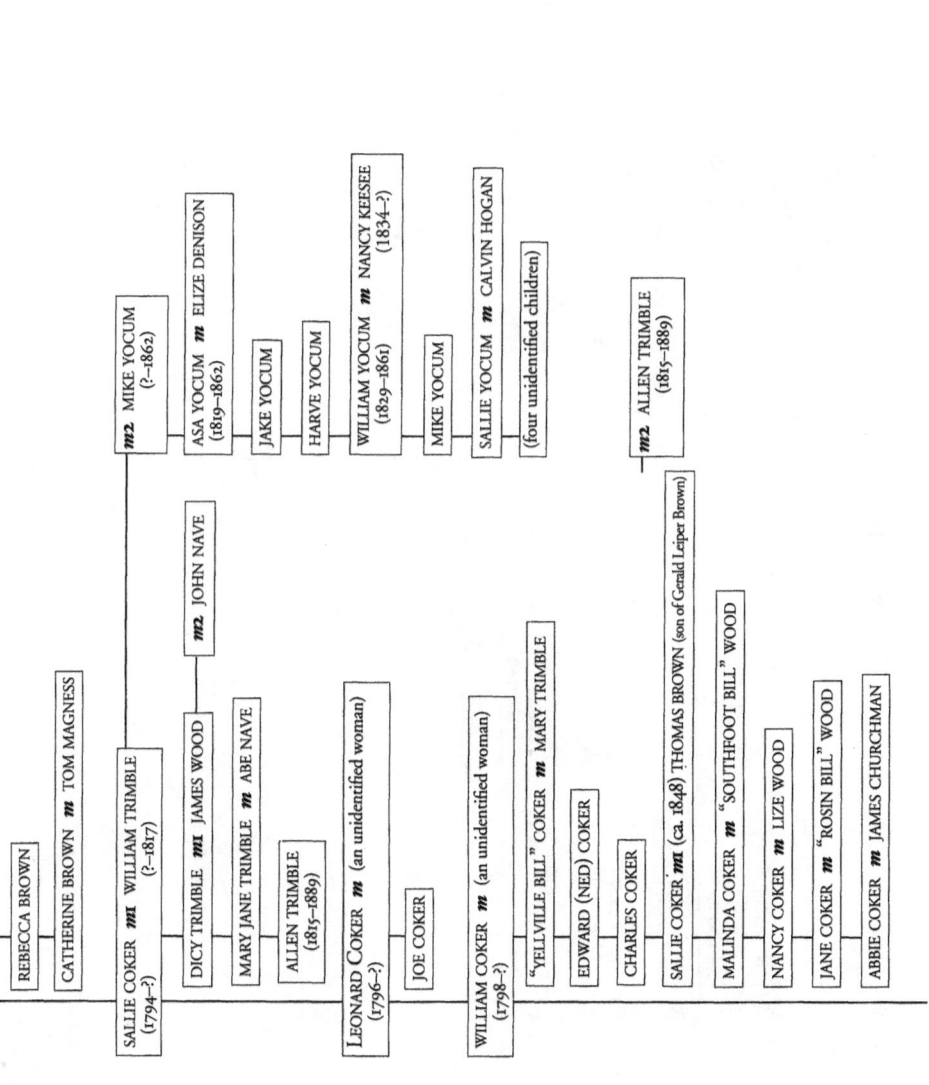

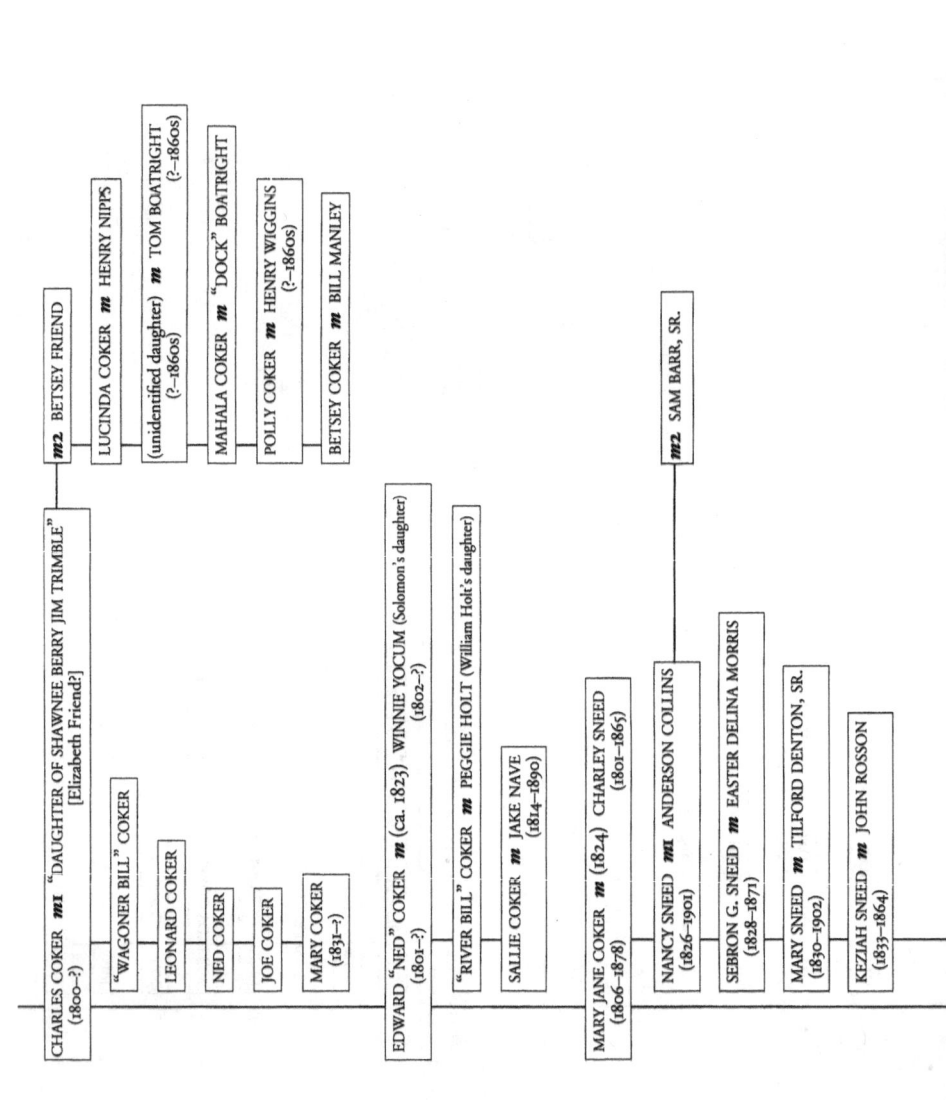

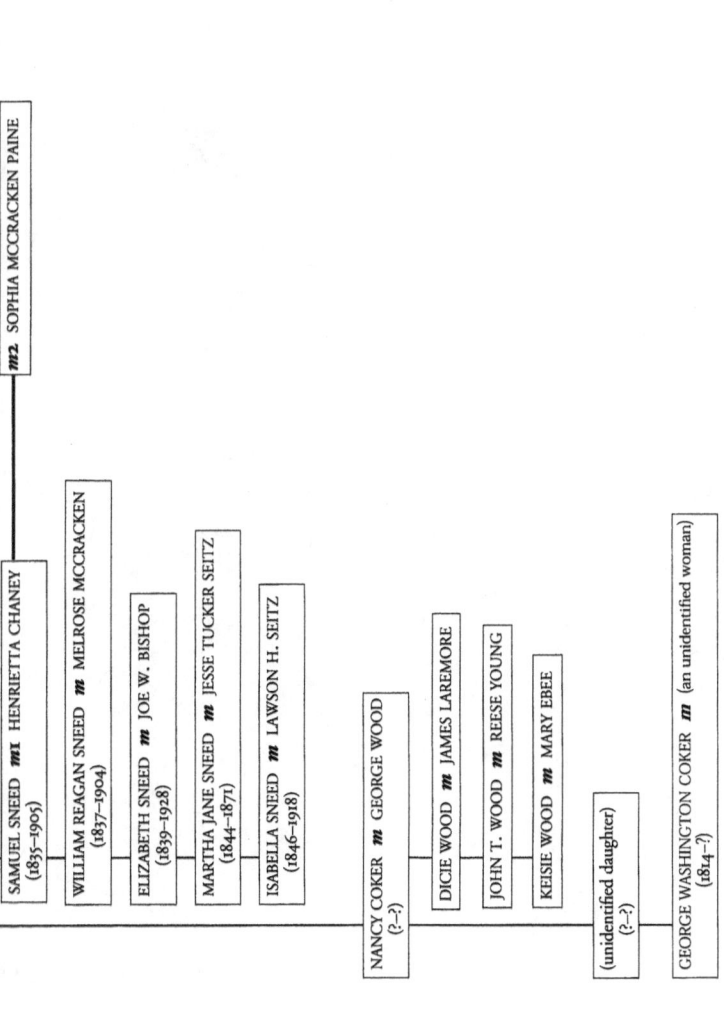

Notes

Introduction

1. This statement was made in a letter to William Elsey Connelley, 20 May 1907. The original letter and all of the rest of the Connelley-Turnbo correspondence cited here are in the William Elsey Connelley–Silas C. Turnbo Correspondence, Springfield–Greene County Public Library, Springfield, Missouri.
2. Harvey Wish, *The American Historian: A Social-Intellectual History of the Writing of the American Past* (New York: Oxford University Press, 1960), 133.
3. Ibid., 134.
4. Homer C. Hockett, *Introduction to Research in American History* (New York: Macmillan Company, 1938), 90.
5. Homer C. Hockett, *The Critical Method in Historical Research and Writing* (New York: Macmillan Company, 1955), 55.
6. Not all historians were as dogmatic as Hockett about the worthlessness of folk traditions for historical research, but even those who conceded that such material had some value still thought they should be used very cautiously. See, for example, the chapter "The Historian and the Historical Document" in Louis Gottschalk, Clyde Kluckhohn, and Robert Angell, *The Use of Personal Documents in History, Anthropology, and Sociology* (New York: Social Science Research Council, 1945), 26–27, in which Louis Gottschalk grants that folk traditions, fiction, song, and poetry in general, have some historical value but warns that "the historian does not dare to use the information" such sources contain "unless it is confirmed by other knowledge."
7. Hoffman published three articles, all with the title "Folklore of the Pennsylvania Germans," in the *Journal of American Folklore*. The first article appeared in 1 (1888): 123–35 and the others in 2 (1889): 23–35, 191–202.
8. Some references erroneously give the date 1842 (see, for example, Vance Randolph, *Ozark Folklore: A Bibliography* [Bloomington: Indiana University Center for Research in the Language Sciences, 1972], 211).
9. The information given in this essay concerning Turnbo's family is taken from Lynn Morrow, "'I Am Nothing but a Poor Scribbler': Silas Turnbo and His Writings," *White River Valley Historical Quarterly* 10 (Spring 1991): 3–9.
10. See Silas C. Turnbo Collection, 22:13, Springfield–Greene County Public Library, Springfield, Missouri.
11. This book was published as Silas C. Turnbo, *History of the Twenty-seventh*

Arkansas Confederate Infantry, ed. Desmond Walls Allen (Conway, Ark.: Arkansas Research, 1988).

12. Silas C. Turnbo, *Fireside Stories of Early Days in the Ozarks, Part Two* (Pontiac, Mo.: n.p., 1907), 10–14.

13. Ibid., 32–33.

14. William Elsey Connelley to Silas C. Turnbo, 9 June 1905, Connelley-Turnbo Correspondence.

15. Ethan Smith to Silas C. Turnbo, 14 June 1907, Connelley-Turnbo Correspondence.

16. William Elsey Connelley to Silas C. Turnbo, 16 February 1909, Connelley-Turnbo Correspondence.

17. William Elsey Connelley to Silas C. Turnbo, 19 April 1913, written in response to a letter of 10 April from Turnbo, Connelley-Turnbo Correspondence.

18. Silas C. Turnbo to William Elsey Connelley, 24 April 1913, Connelley-Turnbo Correspondence.

19. The books and the dates of their publication are as follows: Silas C. Turnbo, *Turnbo's Tales of the Ozarks: Schools, Indians, Hard Times and More Stories*, ed. Desmond Walls Allen (Conway, Ark.: D. W. Allen, 1987; rev. ed., Conway, Ark.: Arkansas Research, 1989); Silas C. Turnbo, *Turnbo's Tales of the Ozarks: War and Guerrilla Stories*, ed. Desmond Walls Allen (Conway, Ark.: Arkansas Research, 1987; rev. ed., Conway, Ark.: Arkansas Research, 1989); Silas C. Turnbo, *Turnbo's Tales of the Ozarks: Bear Stories*, ed. Desmond Walls Allen (Conway, Ark.: Arkansas Research, 1988); Silas C. Turnbo, *Turnbo's Tales of the Ozarks: Incidents, Mean Tricks and Fictitious Stories*, ed. Desmond Walls Allen (Conway, Ark.: Arkansas Research, 1988); and Silas C. Turnbo, *Turnbo's Tales of the Ozarks: Deer Hunting Stories*, ed. Desmond Walls Allen (Conway, Ark.: Arkansas Research, 1989).

20. Allen, "Editor's Note" in Turnbo, *Turnbo's Tales of the Ozarks: Incidents, Mean Tricks and Fictitious Stories*, 1.

21. For a brief summary of the hoop snake belief, see Richard M. Dorson, *Man and Beast in American Comic Legend* (Bloomington: Indiana University Press, 1982), 55–62. As Dorson's title suggests, many hoop snake yarns are told with humorous intent, but there are, or were until quite recently, persons who actually believed in the existence of such reptiles.

22. The version reported by Gerstäcker appears in Friedrich Gerstäcker, *In the Arkansas Backwoods: Tales and Sketches by Friedrich Gerstäcker*, ed. James William Miller (Columbia: University of Missouri Press, 1991), 56–61.

23. For a discussion of traditional Ozark fears concerning centipedes, see Vance Randolph, *Ozark Magic and Folklore* (originally *Ozark Superstitions*) (New York: Columbia University Press, 1947; reprint, New York: Dover Publications, 1964), 258–59.

24. See, for example, Richard M. Dorson, *American Folklore* (Chicago: The University of Chicago Press, 1959), 91.

25. For a list of folk motifs concerning prophecies, see Ernest W. Baughman,

Type and Motif—Index of the Folktales of England and North America (The Hague: Mouton and Company, 1966), motifs M300–M399, and for escape by making attacker believe there are many defenders, see motif K548.

26. See Baughman's type 1890 "The Lucky Shot" and motifs X1119.2 "Lie: remarkable bag of deer" and X1122.2 "Lie: person shoots many animals with one shot," in Baughman, *Type and Motif.*

27. Baughman's motif J1795 "Image in mirror mistaken for picture" applies here. See Baughman, *Type and Motif.*

28. See the album *Not Far from Here . . . : Traditional Tales and Songs Recorded in the Arkansas Ozarks* (Arkansas Traditions LP, no number) for the narrative "The Hudson That Killed the Panther," told by Dr. William Hudson, Jasper, Arkansas. Hudson (1891–1990) heard this story as a young child from his Uncle Sammy, who related it as a true story.

Chapter 1: Emigrant Indians and Plain Folk

1. For further discussion of the settlement context, see Ollie Orland Maxfield, "Geography of the Boston Mountains" (Ph.D. diss., Ohio State University, 1963), 85–102.

2. By 1806 Cherokees and Delawares, at the junction of the Black and White rivers (the future Jacksonport), traded with the government factor at Arkansas Post. By the 1810-19 decade Cherokees were trading thousands of skins and pelts with upper White River merchants and government factors at Ft. Smith and Spadre Bayou, near modern Clarksville. A large tract of land in northwestern Arkansas, which was never surveyed to its specific extent, but which included the Boston Mountains and parts of the White River Hills, was granted the Cherokee in 1817; in 1828 they receded it to the United States.

When the federal government established this reservation in 1817, they ordered white settlers who were in the general boundaries to move south of the Arkansas River. Perhaps some of the Cokers temporarily left, as did G. L. Brown, Buck Coker's son-in-law, who was killed on the Arkansas River. Joe Coker may never have left, since he brought a Cherokee wife to Arkansas. It appears from Turnbo's accounts, however, that the extended Coker relations and others generally roamed the White River region at will.

It was certainly common in Arkansas territorial and early statehood accounts to have Indians and whites hunting and socializing together. Friedrich Gerstäcker, for example, did not find it unusual to have Cherokee and Choctaw hunting companions in the Arkansas Ozarks in the years 1841–42. See Clarence Evans, "Gerstaecker and the Konwells of White River Valley," *Arkansas Historical Quarterly* 10 (Spring 1951): 1–36; Wayne Morris, "Traders and Factories on the Arkansas Frontier, 1805–1822," *Arkansas Historical Quarterly* 28 (Spring 1969): 44–45; and Aloysius Plaisance, "The Arkansas Factory, 1805–1810," *Arkansas Historical Quarterly* 11 (Autumn 1952): 193. Descriptions of the treaties may be found in Charles J. Kappler, comp. and ed., *Indian Affairs. Laws and Treaties*, vol. 2 (Washington, D.C.: Government Printing Office, 1904). For a general map of the region, see Gerald T. Hanson and Carl H. Moneyhon, *Historical Atlas of Arkansas* (Norman: University of Oklahoma Press, 1989), 18. The beginning of modern academic understandings and naming of Ozarks geographical divisions is the result of Carl Sauer's classic study, *The Geography of the Ozark Highland of Missouri* (Chicago: University of Chicago Press, 1920; reprint, New York: Greenwood Press, 1968); and studies on Cherokee migration include Grant Foreman, *Indian Removal* (Norman: University of Oklahoma Press, 1982), 229–312; and Grace Steele Woodward, *The Cherokees* (Norman: University of Oklahoma Press, 1963).

3. Jess Yocum was brother to Solomon, Jacob (1791–1850), and Mike. Turnbo said that Jess "has the credit for settling more than one bottom in White River." He opened the land that became River Bill Coker's farm and was the first claimant on the land that James Turnbo purchased in 1859. Jess married a Coker woman and was an uncle to Allen Trimble. Silas C. Turnbo Collection, 1:21, 5:83, 19:25, 25:22, Springfield–Greene County Public Library, Springfield. Missouri.

4. Pioneers encountered the Shawnee in the Upland South throughout the colonial and early statehood years; in fact, the Anglicized pronunciation *Shawnee* meant southerner. The Shawnee were a fragmented people and never united into a single society. They moved a great deal and have been associated with three-quarters of our eastern and southern states. The earliest record of them is on the Cumberland River in Tennessee, but by about 1730 they were on the north bank of the Ohio River where they were the most active and pertinacious foes of the whites in that section. By 1780 large numbers were crossing into the Trans-Mississippi, and in 1793 a considerable body moved to a Spanish land grant in the area of Cape Girardeau, Missouri. As they drifted throughout Missouri and Arkansas, bands of Delaware and Shawnee combined with them; a large group of Shawnee ultimately joined the Cherokees. The Shawnee belong to the Algonquian linguistic stock, their closest cultural relatives being the Delaware, Fox, Kickapoo, and Sauk. William C. Sturtevant, gen. ed., *Handbook of North American Indians*, vol. 15 (Washington, D.C.: Smithsonian Institution, 1978), and John R. Swanton, *The Indian Tribes of North America* (Washington, D.C.: Smithsonian Institutional Bulletin 145, Bureau of American Ethnology, 1952).

5. Batesville was and is the county seat of the new Independence County, formed in 1820. One of Arkansas's first government land offices was established there in 1818. Independence County later became the mother county of White River counties Baxter, Boone, Carroll, Fulton, Izard, Marion, Newton, Searcy, and Stone.

6. The 1817 Cherokee land grant in Arkansas was primarily negotiated by the western Cherokees and the U.S. government. The western Cherokees "were of course graciously compliant, since they had everything to gain and nothing to lose by an exchange. Its every clause revealed the influence of the emigrants, and it was they who were to profit by it." The Cherokees gave various Shawnee and

Delaware groups permission to settle on their lands in the White River country and were glad to have those groups above the mouth of the Buffalo River as their neighbors. By 1823, in addition to some six thousand Cherokees scattered in Arkansas Territory, there were some eight thousand Delaware, Shawnee, Kickapoo, and Illinois groups in the greater upper White River country. See the classic study by Annie Heloise Abel, "The History of Events Resulting in Indian Consolidation West of the Mississippi," in *Annual Report of the American Historical Association for the Year 1906*, vol. 1 (Washington, D.C.: Government Printing Office, 1908), 282; Henry Rowe Schoolcraft, *Information Respecting the History, Condition and Prospects of the Indian Tribes of the United States: Collected and Prepared under the Direction of the Bureau of Indian Affairs per Act of Congress of March 3rd, 1847*, vol. 3 (Philadelphia: Lippincott, Grambo & Company, 1853), 585, 596; Clarence Edwin Carter, comp. and ed., *The Territorial Papers of the United States*, vol. 21, *The Territory of Arkansas, 1829–1836* (Washington, D.C.: Government Printing Office, 1954), 270; and Clarence Edwin Carter, comp. and ed., *The Territorial Papers of the United States*, vol. 19, *The Territory of Arkansas, 1819–1825* (Washington, D.C.: Government Printing Office, 1953), 582, 615.

7. The Matthew Adams, Sr., family, Kentuckians, followed the Shawnee along the White River and to Marion County. Adams had several sons—Matthew Adams, Jr. (1799–1889); John (1796–1840); Robert (1808–?); and Peter (1806–?). Apparently, Matthew Adams, Jr., was brother-in-law to Jacob Wolf on the North Fork and trading partner with Menard and Valle of Sainte Genevieve, Missouri. The Shawnee had been affiliated with trader Louis Lorimier (1748–1812) in Cape Girardeau, Missouri, but after his death Pierre Menard in 1813 became the subagent for the Shawnee, Delaware, and Cherokee west of the Mississippi. The commercial alliance of the Valles and Pierre Menard in 1817 put the Ozarks Indian trade under their effective control until the 1830s.

Turnbo's stories about the Shawnees as desirable neighbors on the White River parallel the approving comments by whites toward Shawnees in southeastern Missouri. Mary Adams married Peter Cornstalk, descendant of the famous Cornstalk (1720–1777) of Lord Dunmore's War, who fought with Tecumseh in the War of 1812 and who was a leader among the Shawnees in Arkansas. The Cornstalk families lived on the White River several miles southeast of Shawneetown. Turnbo says Peter Cornstalk stayed until he left for the California gold fields. James J. Johnston, "Searcy County Indians in Tradition and History," *Mid-America Folklore* 12 (Spring 1984): 27–28; Turnbo Collection, 6:47; William E. Foley, *The Genesis of Missouri: From Wilderness Outpost to Statehood* (Columbia: University of Missouri Press, 1989), 120, 246; Mary Ann Messick, *History of Baxter County, 1873–1973* (Little Rock: International Graphics, 1973), 344–46; and Clarence Edwin Carter, comp. and ed., *The Territorial Papers of the United States*, vol. 14, *The Territory of Louisiana-Missouri* (Washington, D.C.: Government Printing Office, 1949), 632–33.

8. Top-sided saddle notching is the archaic pioneer form, due to the lesser amount of work it required. A builder cut this notch after the log was in place, up

on the wall, without measuring or refitting. Indian carpenters generally adopted and perpetuated the cruder pioneer carpentry, given the fact that their contact was with the backwoods pioneers. Terry Jordan, letter to Lynn Morrow, 22 May 1990.

9. The Green Corn Dance (Green Corn Ceremony or Busk) is a southeastern United States Indian ritual that originated in prehistoric times. It was the ceremony that climaxed the southeastern ceremonial year.

According to James H. Howard in *The Southeastern Ceremonial Complex and Its Interpretation,* Memoir No. 6 (Columbia: Missouri Archaeological Society, 1968), "Historic accounts attest to the importance of the Busk among most of the larger Southeastern groups in the early post-contact period. Today it remains the major ceremonial event of the year with those Creek, Seminole, and Yuchi who have not renounced the native religion for Christianity.

"The word 'busk' is a trader's corruption of the native Creek (Muskogi) word *puskita* meaning 'to fast.' This term was applied to many different kinds of fasts, but to two above all; first, the fast undergone by those who desired to become doctors or learned men, and the second, to the great annual ceremony ushering in the Creek new year. This latter is often called the Green Corn Ceremony, as it took place at the time when the maize had matured sufficiently to be eaten. In fact, the Busk is basically an agricultural rite, and one of its main functions was to prepare the people to eat this important food crop without disastrous effect."

Turnbo described a debased form of this important ritual.

10. The Black Bob band were Shawnee of Missouri who settled lands near Cape Girardeau. Black Bob was present throughout the early nineteenth-century experiences of Shawnees in Missouri, Arkansas, Kansas, and Oklahoma and participated in some of the treaty negotiations with the American government. For a survey of Shawnee, Delaware, and trader history in southeast Missouri, see Lynn Morrow, "New Madrid and Its Hinterland: 1783–1826," *Missouri Historical Society Bulletin* 36 (July 1980): 241–50.

11. Maj. Jacob Wolf (1786–1863) is a legendary figure in Arkansas history. Like the Yocums and Turnbos, Wolf descended from Palatinate Germans. He came to the White River country as part of a group migration of Adams and Wolf families. By the early 1820s Wolf and others had established a thriving agricultural and mercantile trade with Anglos and migrating Indians at the mouth of the Big North Fork River whose post office was Liberty. The first Izard County courthouse was placed in his home for five years, 1825–30. Wolf, a slaveholder, served Izard County for ten years in the Arkansas Territorial Council and in 1833 introduced the bill that created Carroll County. He became major of a territorial militia, became postmaster in 1826, and changed Liberty Post Office's name to North Fork (the modern Norfork). He and Robert Livingston built a saw and grist mill that was commonly patronized by many figures in the Turnbo Collection. Wolf was imprisoned at Batesville by the Federals early in the Civil War and died in 1863 leaving a large estate in the White River Valley. A nineteenth-century account concluded that Wolf had "perhaps the largest house-

hold of kindred and friends of any man on White River." Ironically, the location of his grave is unknown, but his ca. 1826 two-story dogtrot house remains as the oldest structure in Arkansas. See Russell P. Baker, "Jacob Wolf," *Arkansas Historical Quarterly* 37 (Summer 1978): 184–92; Bill D. Blevins, *Jacob Wolf, The Mansion and the Man* (Mountain Home, Ark.: Twin Lakes Printing & Publishing Company, 1982); and the serial *Wolf House Historian*, vol. 1 (January 1989–present).

Capt. Tom B. Stallings was a career steamboat captain on the White River. His father, John Stallings, had settled in Tucker Bottom, Marion County, by the late 1820s. In 1880 Tom and others built *The Lady Boone,* named for Boone County, Arkansas, and operated from Nave's Ferry Landing (old Dubuque) down to Jacksonport. Elmo Ingenthron, *Land of Taney: A History of an Ozark Commonwealth* (Point Lookout, Mo.: The School of the Ozarks Press, 1974), 63; and Earl Berry, *History of Marion County* (Little Rock: International Graphics Industries, 1977), 259.

Dearmond may be a descendant of Francois de Armond, who in 1766, established a trading post on the lower White River, later called Montgomery's (for William Montgomery) Landing, some 260 miles downstream from Batesville. Perhaps the de Armonds moved their business up White River, too. Robert L. Morris, "Three Arkansas Travelers," *Arkansas Historical Quarterly* 4 (Autumn 1945): 222.

12. James Adams, Jr. (1779–1855), a relative of John Quincy Adams, came to White River from Kentucky in the 1810–20 period. He brought slaves and a large family and built the first mill in the area on the south side of White River some five miles below the mouth of Buffalo Fork of White River, and later gave his name to "Adams Buffalo City Landing," an early steamboat stop. James Adams, Jr.'s, son George (1807–1854) and family were early settlers south of Yellville. Turnbo Collection, 10:74; *A Reminiscent History of the Ozark Region* (Chicago: Goodspeed Brothers, Publishers, 1894), 130–31; and Messick, *History of Baxter County,* 352.

13. The mills mentioned by Turnbo functioned to bolster the local subsistence economy rather than contribute to the market economy; that is, they were not commercial mills, but were an integral link in subsistence economy. See Larry Hasse, "Watermills in the South: Rural Institutions Working against Modernization," *Agricultural History* 58 (July 1984): 280–95.

14. Settlers reported bands of Indians, away from their western homes to hunt and fish, in southwest Missouri into the 1840s. One episode, known as the Sarcoxie or Osage War, created a sensation. Rumors mounted, militias were assembled, but the Osage were after game only, and there were no casualties on either side in southwest Missouri. Capt. Henry Fulbright, mentioned elsewhere in the Turnbo Collection, was one of the militia officers. R. S. Holcombe, *History of Greene County, Missouri* (St. Louis: Western Historical Company, 1883), 184–86; and Robert A. Glenn, "The Osage War," *Missouri Historical Review* 14 (March 1920): 201–10.

15. Turnbo referred to the hazelnut or filbert, *Corylus americana*, or *cornuta*, small trees or shrubs found in thickets or woods edges. Merritt L. Fernald, *Gray's Manual of Botany* (New York: American Book Company, 1950).

16. The frizzen, or battery, is the portion of the flintlock that covers the priming pan and is struck by the cock when the rifle is fired. It is hinged and the Indian wanted his father to use it as pliers.

17. The Ozark frontier was always short on salt, which had to be imported. Salt springs that yielded the mineral in commercial quantities were outside the region or too far west for the upper White River settlements. Stockmen needed salt for their animals and to preserve meat and hides. Like pelts, salt was used as a medium of exchange. Settlers on the upper James River during the 1820s bought cattle from the Delaware Indians with salt—one milch cow for a gallon, one three-year-old steer for a quart. During the Civil War, Unionists confiscated salt from southern merchants and farmers. Desperate homemakers had to resort to leaching salt from former drippings in the dirt on the floors of smokehouses. John Quincy Wolf, *Life in the Leatherwoods. An Ozark Boyhood Remembered*, (Memphis: Memphis State University Press, 1974, 1980; reprint, Little Rock, Ark.: August House, 1988), 22; Paul M. Robinett Collection, Joint Collection, University of Missouri–Columbia; Holcombe, *History of Greene County, Missouri*, 611; and Daniel F. Littlefield, Jr., "The Salt Industry in Arkansas Territory, 1819–1836," *Arkansas Historical Quarterly* 32 (Winter 1973): 312–36.

18. William Fulbright (1785–1843), descendant of Palatinate Germans, was one of five brothers, their families, and slaves who in 1829 settled on Kickapoo Prairie, which became the site of Springfield, Missouri; William remained in Greene County as a merchant and miller, while the others moved to Laclede County. Jonathan Fairbanks and Clyde Edwin Tuck, *Past and Present of Greene County, Missouri*, vol. 1 (Indianapolis: A. W. Bowen & Company, 1915), 740–44.

Joe Leeper was of the Hugh Leeper family from Tennessee that settled in Greene County in 1834. Fairbanks and Tuck, *Past and Present*, vol. 2, 1590–92.

19. By 1850 Springfield had a population of only 411; ten years later, it had grown to 2,500, including 140 slaves. Lynn Morrow, comp., "Greene County Demographic Profile, 1850–1910," Kalen and Morrow Papers, Forsyth, Missouri.

20. Another regional description of the great migration of Cherokees through southwest Missouri is the Dr. W. I. I. Morrow diary, Joint Collection, University of Missouri–Columbia.

21. Nettle is any one of several herbs, *Urtica spp.*, found in damp thickets, bottomlands, or richwoods. The leaves have stinging hairs which can cause pain when they prick the skin.

22. Maple Post Office (1889–1925) was about four miles east of Berryville. Russell Pierce Baker, *From Memdag to Norsk: A Historical Directory of Arkansas Post Offices, 1832–1971* (Hot Springs, Ark.: Arkansas Genealogical Society, 1988).

23. Precious ore legends have circulated in the Ozarks ever since the early eighteenth-century Mississippi Bubble land speculation scheme of John Law. An

early compilation of these legends is in "Legends of Lost Mines and Hidden Treasure," in Fred W. Allsopp's *Folklore of Romantic Arkansas,* vol. 1 (Little Rock: The Grolier Society, 1931), 282–98; general background and specific folklore drawn from the legend is explained by Lynn Morrow in "The Yocum Silver Dollar: Images, Realities and Traditions," in Howard Marshall and James Goodrich, eds., *The German-American Experience in Missouri: Essays in Commemoration of the Tricentennial German Immigration to America, 1683–1983* (Columbia: Missouri Cultural Heritage Center No. 2, University of Missouri, 1986), 159–75. Observing the Ozarks promotional hype for such phenomena, one Ozarker said, "It would be something to laugh about, were it not so closely related to tragedy . . . Actually the 'sucker' crop has been one of continuing profit for the stickers here for many years, and the end is not in sight." Jesse Lewis Russell, *Behind These Ozark Hills* (New York: The Hobson Book Press, 1947), 68–69.

Chapter 2: First Families

1. Coker Family Histories, Bessie J. Ingenthron Papers, Forsyth, Missouri, Public Library. The Turnbo Collection is a superb collective reminiscence of the "plain-folk" culture established by Frank Owsley in his famous *Plain Folk of the Old South* (Baton Rouge: Louisiana State University Press, 1949; reprint, Baton Rouge: Louisiana State University Press, 1982). These hunter/stockmen lived outside the plantation economy and formed the bulk of the South's free population. A brief summary that describes the antecedents of Turnbo's first families is John Solomon Otto's, "The Migration of the Southern Plain Folk: An Interdisciplinary Synthesis," *Journal of Southern History* 51 (1985): 183–200; and the most recent interpretation of the plain-folk school is Grady McWhiney's, *Cracker Culture: Celtic Ways in the Old South* (Tuscaloosa: University of Alabama Press, 1988).

The Coker Clan

2. The Union victories at Port Hudson, Louisiana, in May 1863 and at Vicksburg in July 1863 converted many Arkansawyers to the Unionist cause. Soon, the Confederate loss of Little Rock in September 1863 signaled a drastic blow to Confederate authority throughout Arkansas. Ruth Caroline Cowen, "Reorganization of Federal Arkansas, 1862–1865," *Arkansas Historical Quarterly* 18 (Summer 1959): 32–33.

3. Dubuque, a small river hamlet and steamboat landing during the 1850s, was entirely destroyed during the Civil War and was not rebuilt. It was a recruiting center for Confederates and was the primary White River crossing between Forsyth and Yellville. Nearby, southerners operated a smelter that provided lead for molding bullets for the Confederacy. Jacob Nave (1814–1890) married Buck Coker's granddaughter Sallie and had the highest dollar assessment in Marion

County real estate in 1850—five thousand dollars. Courtney and Gerlene York, comps. and eds., *Marion County Arkansas Census, 1850* (published by authors, n.d.); Earl Berry, *History of Marion County* (Little Rock: International Graphics Industries, 1977), 82–83; and for a map of Dubuque, see Elmo Ingenthron, *Borderland Rebellion: A History of the Civil War on the Missouri-Arkansas Border* (Branson, Mo.: The Ozarks Mountaineer, 1980), 241.

4. Solomon Yocum (1773–1850), reputed to be the first white settler in Stone County, Missouri, was a principal figure in the distillation of spirits and its illegal sale to immigrant Indians on the James Fork of White River. Solomon had three brothers—Mike, Jesse, and Jacob. The famous ethnographer, Henry Rowe Schoolcraft, during his 1818–19 tour in the Ozarks, stayed with Solomon and Jacob. In 1827 the land office at Batesville granted pre-emption rights to Solomon for public land he settled within land ceded to the Cherokees. See Clarence Edwin Carter, comp. and ed., *The Territorial Papers of the United States*, vol. 20, *The Territory of Arkansas, 1825–1829* (Washington, D.C.: Government Printing Office, 1954), 535–36; Levi Pettibone, "With Schoolcraft in Southwest Missouri," *Missouri Historical Society Collections* (January 1900): 50; Lynn Morrow, "Trader William Gilliss and Delaware Migration in Southern Missouri," *Missouri Historical Review* 75 (January 1981): 147–67; and Lynn Morrow and Dan Saults, "The Yocum Silver Dollar: Sorting out the Strands of an Ozarks Frontier Legend," *Gateway Heritage* 5 (Winter 1984–85): 8–15.

5. Silas Turnbo and the Allen Trimble family were longtime friends. William Trimble, who married Sallie Coker, settled on the White River in 1814, but died in 1817 when Allen (1815–1889) was a small child. Allen settled above the mouth of Trimble Creek, the location of Trimble cemetery, Marion County, in 1842, and later owned the claim on White River that became J. C. Turnbo's in 1859. During the 1850s, Allen Trimble's and James Turnbo's children went to school together, and the males of the two families hunted together. In 1873 Allen and the much younger Silas Turnbo went back to the old home places where Allen related several stories that Turnbo later recorded. Allen and his son, William Trimble, became sources for many of Turnbo's writings. Silas C. Turnbo Collection, 2:88, 9:24, 11:72, 17:36, 19:40, Springfield–Greene County Public Library, Springfield, Missouri.

6. What happened after this bloodletting is not clear. Coker family traditions imply that several Cokers, perhaps John and Randolph included, had to leave the area following conflicts with the law and migrated into the Indian nations.

7. Turnbo mentioned Bull Bottom often. Mike Yocum's son, Asa, bought an improvement here in 1842 and built a house. At his death in 1862, neighbors began the Asa Yocum graveyard opposite the Bull Bottom. Turnbo had informants from the Casebolt, Friend, Magness, and Terry families, all of whom lived in or adjacent to Bull Bottom. Most of the cemeteries mentioned in the Turnbo Collection were moved in the mid-twentieth century due to the construction of Bull Shoals and Table Rock reservoirs. The Bull Shoals project forced reinter-

ment of twenty-five cemeteries into eleven upland sites; Table Rock brought thirty-six cemeteries to eight locations. See Lois Stanley, Maryhelen Wilson, and George F. Wilson, comps., *Cemetery Relocations by the U.S. Army Corps of Engineers in Illinois, Iowa, Missouri, and Arkansas* (St. Louis: The St. Louis Genealogical Society, 1977); and Turnbo Collection, 6:56.

8. Panther Bottom figured prominently in Turnbo's stories. Hunters gave it the name after killing panther there—a mother and three cubs. During the 1850s, when the Turnbos lived in the southeast corner of Taney County, Panther Bottom was opposite their farm to the southeast, lying partly in Taney and Ozark counties and partly in Marion County, and the Missouri and Arkansas state line ran east and west through it. In 1857 Silas Turnbo and others attended a subscription school in Panther Bottom. Turnbo Collection, 16:62, 18:8–9, 19:32–34.

9. John Piland, who married Asa Yocum's daughter Sallie, became the first burial in the new Tommy Norris graveyard. His family were among the leading Unionists in Ozark County during the Civil War. John and three of his sons, Elisha, John Barnard, and Wesley, all perished in the Civil War—Elisha and Wesley were victims of bushwhackers. The Piland Camp, a camp meeting ground on Little Creek named for the family, now known as Mt. Lebanon Baptist Church, became the place of origin for the General Baptist denomination in Missouri. Lynn Morrow in Lynn Morrow and Robert Flanders, *An Overview of Seven Ozarks Counties for the Historic Preservation Program, Missouri Department of Natural Resources, Jefferson City, Missouri* (West Plains, Mo.: South Central Ozarks Council of Governments, June 1989), 73; Shirley Carter Piland, "'Big Billy' Piland of Ozark County," *The Old Mill Run* 4 (April 1990): 10; and Turnbo Collection, 15:63.

10. This form of symbolic sarcophagus built above ground is mentioned in the Turnbo Collection several times and can still be seen in many Ozarks cemeteries. It is a "permanent" continuation of the southern mortuary tradition of building mounds and false crypts. A rare earthen survivor of this mounded burial system may be observed at Mossville, Newton County, Arkansas. See Terry G. Jordan, *Texas Graveyards: A Cultural Legacy* (Austin: University of Texas Press, 1982), 16–19.

11. Buck Coker is the father of Joe Coker. Joe Coker and his life on Sugar Loaf Prairie, where Buck Coker spent his senior years, was a favorite subject for Silas Turnbo, and Joe was the "Mr. Coker" whom Schoolcraft mentioned several times.

After his introduction to Joe Coker, Schoolcraft (1793–1864) reflected upon the people and the area, writing, "Corn, and wild meats, chiefly bear's meat, are the staple of food. In manners, morals, customs, dress, contempt of [agricultural] labor and hospitality, the state of society is not essentially different from that which exists among the savages. Schools, religion, and learning, are alike unknown. Hunting is the principal, the most honourable, and the most profitable employment . . . They are, consequently, a hardy, brave, independent people, rude in appearance, frank and generous, travel without baggage, and can subsist any where in the woods, and would form the most efficient military corps in frontier warfare which can possibly exist . . . Their system of life is, in fact, one continued scene of camp-service." Henry Rowe Schoolcraft, *Journal of a Tour into the Interior of Missouri and Arkansas in 1818 and 1819,* ed. Hugh Park (London: Phillips & Company, 1821; reprint, Van Buren, Ark.: Press-Argus Printers, 1955), 86–87. Schoolcraft and other Yankees who wrote travelogues about their encounters with hunter/stockmen in the South, however, failed to balance their accounts with mention of the numerous squatters who, despite superficial appearances, were aggressive and shrewd capitalists in frontier economies.

12. Protem Post Office (1875–present) is in southeast Taney County. Robert G. Schultz, *Missouri Post Offices, 1804–1981* (St. Louis: The American Philatelic Society, St. Louis Branch No. 4, 1982), 44.

13. Pineries were areas of extensive pine stands within the Ozarks' essentially oak-hickory forest complex. The pines were southern shortleaf pines, *Pinus echinata,* and were the first forest trees to be exploited for commercial lumber in the Ozarks. A study of pine in the Missouri Ozarks by P. W. Fletcher and R. E. McDermott, *Influence of Geologic Parent Material and Climate on Distribution of Shortleaf Pine in Missouri* (Columbia: Agricultural Experiment Station, Research Bulletin 625, University of Missouri, 1957), stated that pine occurs in some frequency on 44 percent of Ozark forest lands; pure stands, however, are rare.

14. A normally remembered great flood of the twenties was in 1826; however, A. C. Jeffery also recorded a destructive 1824 flood as the "Pumpkin Freshet." Jeffery also listed 1826, 1844, and 1856 as years of great inundation. The 1819–20 report of Stephen Long's western expedition warned readers about "overwhelming freshets" and sudden floods of the White River that rose more than twenty feet in one night. Edwin James, *James's Account of S. H. Long's Expedition, 1819–1820* (Philadelphia: H. C. Carey & I. Lee, 1822–23: reprint, New York: AMS Press, Inc., 1966), 125; "Missouri Floods," *Missouri Historical Review* 37 (October 1942): 66–70; and A. C. Jeffery, *Historical and Biographical Sketches of the Early Settlement of the Valley of White River Together with a History of Izard County* (Melbourne, Ark.: *Melbourne Clipper,* 1877; Yellville, Ark.: Yellville *Mountain Echo,* 1895; reprint, Richmond, Va.: The Jeffery Historical Society, April 1973), 65.

15. The most famous of nineteenth-century floods in the region was the one in 1844. It was preceded by a particularly severe winter. See "The Great Flood of 1844," *Missouri Historical Review* 29 (April 1935): 206–11.

16. Honeydew is a sweet, sticky substance, excreted by aphids, found on the leaves and stems of trees and plants, formerly imagined to be akin to dew in origin. William Monks wrote, "Honeydew fell in such quantities as to completely kill the tops of the grass where it was open. I have known young turkeys, after they were large enough for use, to have their wings so gummed with honeydew that they could not fly out of the way of a dog—have known lots of them to be caught with dogs when they wanted to use them." William Monks, *A History of Southern Missouri and Northern Arkansas: Being an Account of the Early*

Settlements, the Civil War, the Ku-Klux, and Times of Peace (West Plains, Mo.: West Plains Journal Company, 1907), 9; and *Oxford English Dictionary*, 2d ed., s.v. "honey dew."

17. Early travelers always commented on the immense number of dogs among the hunters and frontiersmen. Schoolcraft wrote, "The hunter . . . is nevertheless a slave to his dog, the only object around him to which he appears really devoted . . . It is no easy task to provide a pack of hungry dogs, from six to twelve, the usual number owned by every hunter, with meat . . . " Schoolcraft, *Journal of a Tour into the Interior of Missouri and Arkansas in 1818 and 1819*, 99–100.

18. Unfortunately, Turnbo does not ever comment on how blacks really fared on the White River frontier. Inferences can be made, however, that support the traditional belief that slavery in the uplands was much less harsh than it was in the Deep South, a sentiment found throughout Missouri as well. Significantly, Marion County had the largest nonslave black population in Arkansas (21 percent in 1850), and in 1840 and 1850 it contained more free blacks than slaves—very unusual for an antebellum southern state. The 1850s growth in population led to a diminution of geographic and social space for everyone. By 1860 practically all of the free blacks were gone, perhaps influenced by secessionist and Know-Nothing nativist rhetoric of 1859. See Dwight Pitcaithley, "Settlement of the Arkansas Ozarks: The Buffalo River Valley," *Arkansas Historical Quarterly* 37 (Autumn 1978): 220–21; and Arvarh E. Strickland, "Aspects of Slavery in Missouri, 1821," *Missouri Historical Review* 65 (July 1971): 520ff.

19. Mike Yocum married Sally Coker Trimble, daughter of Buck Coker and widow of William Trimble, who was shot and killed on the White River in 1817. Mike and Sally settled during the early 1820s above the mouth of Shoal Creek in northeast Boone County. The Yocums moved later and rebuilt and operated an 1825 mill at the mouth of Little North Fork River with their children settling farms up the Little North Fork. Yocum's sawmill also supplied lumber that replaced puncheon floors in log houses and was used in other construction. In another story Turnbo credited Mike Yocum with finding a record thirteen bee trees in one day at the mouth of the James River. After the Civil War, the Hollingsworth brothers built a new mill near Yocum's old one. Turnbo Collection, 5:65, 12:32, 15:13, 23:24, 24:9–10, 25:45.

20. Mike Yocum's political opponent for state senator, representing Marion, Searcy, and Van Buren counties, was Col. Henry Maxwell. Turnbo was wrong about Yocum's victory, as Maxwell was elected in 1850 and 1852. See story on Maxwell in the Little Rock, Arkansas, *Arkansas Gazette*, 31 May 1850.

21. Federals arrested Mike Yocum in fall 1862 and imprisoned him at Springfield, Missouri, until December 1862. He was physically broken, but walked and crawled to the farm of his old friend Junius Campbell south of Springfield, where he soon died. Friends buried him on the Campbell farm. Turnbo Collection, 1:21–23.

The Turnbo Neighborhood

22. Terry Jordan, letter to Lynn Morrow, 30 July 1990.

23. Settlement from Tennessee dominated the interior Ozarks. As Turnbo related, many of these were part of group migrations. For example, in Newton County, 47 percent of the population in 1850 claimed Tennessee as their home state, and by 1860 Tennessee accounted for 50 percent of new arrivals to Marion and Searcy counties. Springfield, Missouri, has long been known for its Tennessee "first families." Thus, the pioneer immigrants often referred to customs as the "Tennessee style," echoing their former homeland, but the custom of corn shucking was generally universal throughout the southern uplands. Tennessee continued to rank first as a source of migration into Arkansas until 1880. Robert B. Walz, "Migration into Arkansas, 1820–1880: Incentive, and Means of Travel," *Arkansas Historical Quarterly* 17 (Winter 1958): 312; Russel L. Gerlach, *Settlement Patterns in Missouri* (Columbia: University of Missouri Press, 1986), 22–23; Pitcaithley, "Settlement of the Arkansas Ozarks," 215–16; and Ollie Orland Maxfield, "Geography of the Boston Mountains" (Ph.D. diss., Ohio State University, 1963), 113.

24. Cattle were the most highly valued commodity on Turnbo's frontier. They had the added advantage of being mobile and capable of being driven to distant markets. Monks wrote that cattle, age four years or older, were driven to Jacksonport and shipped to New Orleans. Horses and mules were driven to Mississippi, Louisiana, and southern Arkansas, with prices ranging from $75 to $150. In general, however, the farther north the market, e.g., Springfield, Rolla, and St. Louis, the higher the price received for cattle. As the California markets opened ca. 1850, cows could be purchased for five dollars in the Ozarks and sold for fifty in the western mining camps. Cattlemen in the Arkansas-Missouri border counties commonly bought stock as far south as the Arkansas River Valley and moved them north toward Springfield, and during the twentieth century, to railheads in Arkansas until World War II. The twentieth-century drives varied between fifty and two hundred head and Ozarkers continued to participate in small cattle drives into the 1950s. Rudolph Crouse, interview with Lynn Morrow, 11 January 1984, Boxley Valley Oral History Project, Center for Ozarks Studies, Southwest Missouri State University and Buffalo River National Park; J. H. Atkinson, "Cattle Drives From Arkansas to California Prior to The Civil War," *Arkansas Historical Quarterly* 28 (Autumn 1969): 276; and Monks, *A History of Southern Missouri and Northern Arkansas*, 31.

25. See the appendix for birth years of James and Felecia's children.

26. Early nineteenth-century doctors proscribed the intake of water during fevers. Ozarker Theodore Pease Russell saved his own life in Connecticut during the 1820s when he disobeyed the doctor and quenched his thirst. See Theodore Pease Russell, *A Connecticut Yankee in the Frontier Ozarks: The Writings of Theodore Pease Russell*, ed. James F. Keefe and Lynn Morrow (Columbia: University of Missouri Press, 1988), 36–39.

27. Counterfeit money was widespread on the Arkansas frontier. At the time of Turnbo's story, the country was suffering from a widespread depression, and banks commonly printed their own notes to supplement gold and silver specie. Counterfeiters imitated notes on distant banks affiliated with the Bank of the United States and on state banks in Arkansas and Missouri. See Waddy W. Moore, "Some Aspects of Crime and Punishment on the Arkansas Frontier," *Arkansas Historical Quarterly* 23 (Spring 1964): 50–64.

28. Nearly everyone honored the frontier tradition of buying and selling claims to government-owned lands. J. C. Turnbo's official entry of land in the 1840s was one of the earliest in the area. In fact, settlement in the upper White River country preceded land survey work. Thomas Nuttall (1786–1859) recorded in 1819 that the "hilly lands [Ozarks] have not been thought worthy of a survey." Land in the Cherokee reservation, during the period 1817–28, was closed to white land entries until after 1828 and one statistical summary in the Buffalo Fork of White River indicated that 74 percent of the settlers during the 1830s and 1840s did not secure title to their land. And on the Missouri side, the first land patent in modern Douglas County, Missouri, did not come until 1847. "First Homesteaders of Douglas County, Missouri," *The Old Mill Run* 4 (January 1990): 7; Pitcaithley, "Settlement of the Arkansas Ozarks," 217–18; and Thomas Nuttall, *A Journal of Travels into the Arkansas Territory During the Year 1819* (Philadelphia: T. H. Palmer, 1821; reprint, Norman: University of Oklahoma Press, 1980), 129.

29. Flatboats and keelboats were commonly used on all waters of the Mississippi River Valley during the nineteenth century. So many regional variations existed that it prompted Timothy Flint to say that "there are monstrous anomalies, reducible to no specific class of boats, and only illustrating the whimsical archetypes of things that have previously existed in the brain of inventive men, who reject the slavery of being obliged to build in any received form." The tradition of using these small craft lasted much longer on the inland waterways of the Ozarks that allowed only seasonal steamboat traffic or none at all. The famous twentieth-century descendant of the flatboat in the Ozarks is the johnboat, made popular by the craft of Charley Barnes on James and White river float trips. See Malcolm L. Comeaux, "Origin and Evolution of Mississippi River Fishing Craft," *Pioneer America* 10 (1 June 1978): 73–97; and Lynn Morrow and David Quick, "Transportation and Tourism in the Shepherd of the Hills Country: The Case of the Y-Bridge," *White River Valley Historical Quarterly* 10 (Fall 1989): 4–10; (Winter 1990): 4–10.

30. New Orleans served as a viable market for White River traders until the St. Louis and Iron Mountain Railroad founded Newport near Jacksonport in 1872. Practically all traders, like Majors, would not, however, have made the trip themselves to New Orleans, but would have met other traders at Batesville or Jacksonport, sold and transferred their goods, and returned home. Majors and a Mr. Maynard operated a mercantile at Dubuque, and R. S. Holt (1832–?), a Turnbo informant, clerked for them.

31. The long distance trader encountered perilous risks, but success—often just one trip—meant major financial rewards. Southern and western historian Lewis E. Atherton discussed several facets of this kind of frontier business in "The Santa Fe Trader as Mercantile Capitalist," *Missouri Historical Review* 77 (October 1982): 1–12. A few of Turnbo's stockmen fit the mercantile capitalist mode in their marketing ventures to New Orleans and later California; many preferred the closer St. Louis market. Pioneers to the Ozarks often had a knowledge and tradition of trading with New Orleans as they and their forebears had done so in Tennessee and Kentucky.

32. Forsyth was a trade destination in high water and represented a special challenge for steamboat pilots. As Turnbo and others have reported, pilots occasionally had to spend weeks or months in Forsyth because the water level fell before the steamer could leave.

33. In July 1844 the *Springfield Advertiser* began agitating for improvements on the White River for the commercial development of southwest Missouri. In March 1851 the Missouri legislature appropriated funds for river channeling and approved the charter for the White River Steamboat Company, founded by Springfield businessmen. James A. Holmes, "History of Ozark County, Missouri, to 1865" (master's thesis, University of Kansas, 1967), 116–17.

34. Harrison Snapp (1812–1863) was a descendant of Palatinate Germans who migrated to Philadelphia in 1733, later to Virginia, and after the War of 1812, to Tennessee; Harrison came to Missouri with three brothers in 1839. He had a large stock farm on the White River across from Forsyth and took the lead in early progressive causes. Three of his sons served the Confederacy while Federals destroyed his fences and outbuildings and killed his stock. The family fled to Cooper County, Missouri, where he died. The first term of Taney County circuit court after the war was held at Harrison Snapp's house in 1865, as few buildings of any description stood near the county seat, Forsyth. The Snapp cemetery, still used by the public, is located on the old farm. Elmo Ingenthron, *Land of Taney: A History of an Ozark Commonwealth* (Point Lookout, Mo.: The School of the Ozarks Press, 1974), 34; and Ruth Gillis Ryser, "The Snapp Family," *White River Valley Historical Quarterly* 4 (Spring 1971): 2–3.

35. Elmo Ingenthron recorded *Yohogony* as the proper name of this sixty-five ton steamer. Ingenthron, *Land of Taney*, 428, n. 14.

36. Heavily loaded boats had difficulty ascending the shallow White River. During the 1840s Missouri merchant Joseph McClurg bought salt in New Orleans, shipped it to Jacksonport, Arkansas, the head of year-round navigation for steamboats on White River, and hired teamsters to haul it to Hazelwood (in modern Webster County, Missouri). At another time McClurg tried to go further upriver, but had to unload at the mouth of the Big North Fork River, where he hired teamsters and a crew to open a new wagon road that became famous in the region as the Salt Road. See Turnbo Collection, 5:28, 22:36; and Lynn Morrow, "Joseph Washington McClurg: Entrepreneur, Politician, Citizen," *Missouri Historical Review* 78 (January 1984): 168–201.

37. By 1831 the first steamboat arrived in Batesville—a benchmark in the advance of the frontier—and they soon plied the waters of the upper White River from Batesville to Jacob Wolf's at the mouth of Big North Fork River. Within a year after steamers began to dock at Batesville, the price of groceries fell by half.

The life of a steamer averaged only three and a half years, and seven or eight years was a long time. Most were relatively small boats and often towed flatboats or keelboats that merchants loaded for downstream export. Historian Mary Ann Messick listed a number of White River steamers and their pilots that were not on Turnbo's list. Mooney and Pearson were partners in the *Thomas P. Ray*, a steamer that "in 1858 carried over 3,000 barrels of salt, not to mention whiskey, up White River this season." For a famous trip to the mouth of the James River, the owners decorated the boat with flags in honor of their feat. After the trip, they sold the engine, which was then used to operate a sawmill, which was later destroyed by Federals in the Civil War. The construction of the White River Railroad ended the regular steamboat traffic in 1903, the last one was the *Ozark Queen* which ran out of Batesville. Mary Ann Messick, *History of Baxter County, 1873–1973* (Little Rock: International Graphics, 1973), 55–59; Jeffery, *Historical and Biographical Sketches*, 66; Virgil H. Holder, "Historical Geography of the Lower White River," *Arkansas Historical Quarterly* 27 (Summer 1968): 135; and Mattie Brown, "River Transportation in Arkansas, 1819–1890," *Arkansas Historical Quarterly* 1 (December 1942): 343, 349.

38. About 1810 Jacob Mooney (?–1832) came with slaves to the modern Cotter area on the White River. He maintained homes on the White River and in Tennessee. He had five children, one of whom was Jesse (1818–1884), who migrated to his father's old trading post on the White River, ca. 1840. Jesse was Marion County sheriff, 1844–50, operated Mooney's Ferry, which replaced Talbert's Ferry, managed a cotton gin, and developed Mooney's Landing, a steamboat dock. He has the honor of having piloted a steamboat farther up the White River (to the mouth of the James River) than anyone else. He served the Confederacy with the rank of major. Messick, *History of Baxter County*, 6–10, 418–20.

39. Rockbridge Post Office (1842–62, 1869–80, and 1883–present), originally located near the junction of Spring and Bryant creeks, was the antebellum county seat of Ozark County; it was destroyed during the Civil War. After the war, Gainesville served as the county seat and citizens began a new Rockbridge further up Spring Creek. It became a grain-milling and saw-milling community, located in one of the large Ozark pineries, carried on significant trade with settlers in Arkansas, and remains today as the home of the Rainbow Trout Ranch resort and one of the most idyllic historic hamlets in the Ozarks. See Schultz, *Missouri Post Offices;* Claude R. Bruner, *The Rockbridge Story* (n.p., 5 June 1981); and Stephen F. Whitted, "Pioneer Rockbridge Road Connected Springfield with Arkansas," *Ozarks Mountaineer* 6 (July 1958): 15, 18.

40. Turnbo mentioned an Enoch, a John, and a Tom Fisher, all of whom lived up and down the upper White River. Perhaps they were kinsmen of the Mr.

Fisher whom Schoolcraft stayed with at the mouth of Beaver Creek. Enoch and John worked for James C. Turnbo on his farm during the 1850s. It is also worth mentioning that Schoolcraft's Mr. McGary, whom he met in 1819 opposite the mouth of Little North Fork River, is the same McGary who a few years later owned the claim upriver that Allen Trimble bought and that was later owned by James Turnbo. Further downriver Schoolcraft encountered Augustine Friend, a kinsman of Jake and Polly Friend, whose son Peter gave his name to Friend Bend above Bull Bottom Shoals. Two of Jake's grandsons, Steve and Jim, gave several stories to Turnbo. See Turnbo Collection 7:60, 12:58, 19:25.

41. Hides and skins provided basic barter for the frontiersman. The Jacob Wolf store ledger (1851–53) at Norfork has numerous entries for deer skins (the largest single entry is for six hundred), coon skins, and buffalo hides. Apparently some hunters continued to follow buffalo west of upper White River and brought buffalo hides to exchange for manufactured goods. At the same time, Monks said that good coon skins brought forty to fifty cents, fox, twenty-five to thirty cents, and mink, sixty-five to seventy-five cents. Monks, *A History of Southern Missouri and Northern Arkansas*, 11; and Bill D. Blevins, *Jacob Wolf, The Mansion and the Man* (Mountain Home, Ark.: Twin Lakes Printing & Publishing Company, 1982), 61–62.

42. Sorghum was introduced in the U.S. in 1854. In the Ozarks, farmers began experimental cultivation of sorghum during the late 1850s, but it did not become universal until after the Civil War. See John J. Winberry, "The Sorghum Syrup Industry, 1854–1975," *Agricultural History* 54 (April 1980): 343–52.

43. The principal craft material for everything from toys to houses in the upper White River country during antebellum decades was wood—the same was true for mechanical devices, such as sorghum mills, hydraulic water pumps, hinges, etc. Reputedly, the first metal sorghum mill was not introduced into Newton County until 1893. Billie Touchstone Hardaway, *These Hills, My Home* (Republic, Mo.: Western Printing Company, 1980), 55.

44. Named for Musick families who settled and gave their name to Big, Little, and Dry Music creeks in Marion County.

45. By the 1840s there was a primitive mill operation at the Kissee Mill site. The first successful miller was David Nelson, followed by David Clapp, who sold it early in the Civil War to William Fenex. Fenex, a Unionist, allowed the Federals to establish Camp Hawkins there. As a result, the mill survived the war and was one of the few in the entire upper White River country in 1865. A. C. Kissee's family acquired the mill after the war, leasing it to the Hollingsworth brothers. In 1883 when the railroad reached Chadwick in Christian County and after the Forsyth courthouse burned in 1885, Kissee Mill became an unsuccessful contender for the Taney County seat. The Kissees established a water-powered cotton gin, converted to a roller mill in the 1890s, and operated a licensed distillery. The Corps of Engineers razed the mill in the late 1940s. Turnbo Collection, 28; and Ingenthron, *Land of Taney*, 174–76, 320–21.

46. Nurseries began business in the Arkansas Ozarks during the late 1850s at

Batesville and Fayetteville, but a large-scale nursery business did not begin until after the Civil War. Many Civil War period orchards were ruined by soldiers who hitched their horses and mules to the trees. By 1860, however, Missouri was the leading southern state in orchard production. See Lewis Cecil Gray, *History of Agriculture in the Southern United States to 1860,* vol. 1 (Washington, D.C.: Carnegie Institution of Washington, 1933), 826; and C. Allan Brown, "Horticulture in Early Arkansas," *Arkansas Historical Quarterly* 43 (Summer 1984): 99–124.

47. This technique of planting cedar bushes was used in the White River country and throughout the Ozarks, but we do not know if it existed elsewhere. The placement of a flat rock was an Ozarker's attempt at outwitting the Grim Reaper and avoiding an early death. See explanation by Otto Ernest Rayburn in *Ozark Country* (New York: Duell, Sloan & Pearce, 1941), 273–74; and W. K. McNeil, letter to Lynn Morrow, 9 March 1990.

48. The late antebellum illiteracy rate in the Buffalo Fork of White River counties (Marion, Newton and Searcy), according to census records, was between forty and sixty per cent. Pitcaithley, "Settlement of the Arkansas Ozarks," 220.

49. Education in early U.S. history was a service purchased by the individual or family. Thus, neighborhoods on the frontier could band together and hire a teacher for a season that normally lasted three or, occasionally, six months in the Turnbo neighborhood.

50. The Laughlins migrated from Virginia to Kentucky, and arrived in Taney County, ca. 1830s, and first settled above the mouth of Beaver Creek. William was the father of the family and Mat and Henry were sons. The Laughlins became prosperous stockmen at Laughlin Ford, Beaver Creek. Mat Laughlin married Lucy Onstott, sister of Silas Turnbo's mother, and Silas attended his first school on Beaver Creek with cousins James Harvey, Margarette, and Elizabeth Laughlin. James Harvey Laughlin (1814–?), who served the Confederacy, and Silas's uncle, Henry Onstott, managed a drugstore in Yellville on the eve of the Civil War and Henry became one of the first Taney County judges following the war. Ingenthron, *Land of Taney,* 457; and Turnbo Collection, 16:75, 23:17, 39.

Chapter 3: The County Seats and Outlying Settlements

1. Col. Samuel W. Peel provided a couple of stories to Turnbo. His family immigrated from Ireland to Kentucky and, in a large group migration, to the Batesville area in 1815. S. W.'s family continued to migrate up the White River. He became a county politician, owned mercantiles in Berryville and Hindsville, Arkansas, and citizens elected him as a congressional representative in 1882, 1884, and 1886. The hamlet Peel, which is named for him, briefly had a post office in 1885, but did much more business due to the regional economies of cedar timber

(for pencils) and lead and zinc minerals in the early twentieth century. Ozarkers know the place-name because the Peel Ferry plies across Lake Bull Shoals, one of the few inland ferries left in the Midwest. Ernie Deane, *Arkansas Place Names* (Branson, Mo.: The Ozarks Mountaineer, 1988), 173; Fay Hempstead, *A Pictorial History of Arkansas from the Earliest Times to the Year 1890* (St. Louis and New York: N. D. Thompson Publishing Company, 1890), 1038; and *History of Benton, Washington, Carroll, Madison, Crawford, Franklin, and Sebastian Counties, Arkansas* (Chicago: Goodspeed Publishing, 1889; reprint Chicago: Goodspeed Publishers, 1978), 458, 879.

2. Carrollton Post Office (1834–1922) was the county seat, 1834–75; it is about seven miles southeast of Green Forest. The Carrollton Road was the primary east-west corridor through the upper White River country in antebellum Arkansas, following a path from Lawrence County west to Fayetteville. The townsite is significant in local history as it was to Carrollton that pioneers returned the surviving children of the 1857 Mountain Meadows Massacre in Utah. At the end of the civil war, the only buildings remaining were a spring house, which contained the county records, and a stable. Russell Pierce Baker, *From Memdag to Norsk: A Historical Directory of Arkansas Post Offices, 1832–1971* (Hot Springs, Ark.: Arkansas Genealogical Society, 1988); James J. Johnston, "Land of Anarchy, Land of Desolation: Buffalo River, 1861–1865," typescript, 15 February, 1978; and see map by Gerald T. Hanson and Carl H. Moneyhon, *Historical Atlas of Arkansas* (Norman: University of Oklahoma Press, 1989), 33.

3. The typical frontier image of hewed log houses dominating the landscape is erroneous, at least in earliest settlement years. The hunter/stockman log shelter was commonly built of round logs or poles, and settlers often used round log buildings for years as they frequently moved before they built the more permanent hewed log house. Moisture caused much more damage to the round log than it did to the hewed log structure.

The four or five tools carried by hunters and "first settlers" simply would not have built a good hewed log house. For example, the Lewis Russell family migrated to Carroll County in 1822, took refuge in Greene County, Mo., toward the end of the civil war, returned to the Carroll County homestead in 1868, and built a new log house "a little more elaborate than the first one in that the logs were hewn." A Texan crossing Arkansas in the Civil War remarked, "The houses are built of poles and are open and half of them [are] without covering" [i.e., without clapboards or siding].

The great majority of these houses were one room, called single-pen houses, and Tate Page wrote humorously that when a second pen was added to the original single-pen dwelling, "it was built because of the need for outside wall space on which to hang more curing pelts." These pole houses normally had stick and mud chimneys instead of stone. Conversion of these pioneer chimneys to stone chimneys continued into the late nineteenth century. Tate C. Page, *The Voices of Moccasin Creek* (Point Lookout, Mo.: The School of the Ozarks Press, 1979), 342; Jesse Lewis Russell, *Behind These Ozark Hills* (New York: The

Hobson Book Press, 1947), 7–9; the Texan's comment is in William L. Shea, "A Semi-Savage State: The Image of Arkansas in the Civil War," *Arkansas Historical Quarterly* 48 (Winter 1989), 328; and construction technology applicable in the Ozarks is addressed by folklorist Warren E. Roberts in "The Tools Used in Building Log Houses in Indiana," *Pioneer America* 9 (1 July, 1977): 32–61. An inventory of twenty-four thousand frontier tools may be examined in Naylor, Missouri, at The Center for the Study of Early American Industries, managed by anthropologist Dr. James E. Price.

 4. A puncheon is a half-log, roughly dressed on the flat side, used as flooring and as a framing timber in pioneer houses.

 5. William C. Mitchell was Carroll County clerk, 1836–40, served as Carrollton postmaster, 1837–43, commanded a Carroll County militia in the 1840s, and was state senator, 1840–53. He resigned from office in 1854 and moved to West Sugar Loaf Creek, Marion County. In mid-1861 Mitchell organized a company of men from Taney and Marion counties into the Fourteenth Arkansas Regiment. J. C. Turnbo, among many others, joined Mitchell's command. See the 1876 Centennial history by Bradley Bunch, "History of Carroll County," *Carroll County Historical Society Quarterly* 31 (Autumn 1985): 4–9; and Silas C. Turnbo, *History of the Twenty-seventh Arkansas Confederate Infantry*, ed. Desmond Walls Allen (Conway, Ark.: Arkansas Research, 1988), 20.

 6. Charles Sneed (1801–1865) is given credit for being the first permanent settler in modern Carroll County. He resided for several years on Bear Creek among the Coker clan, marrying Jane Coker (1806–1878), eldest daughter of Buck Coker, in 1824. Sneed built the wagon road from Dubuque to Carrollton, the first court session of Carroll County presided over by Archibald Yell was held in his house, he was county sheriff, 1836–42, and served as a local postmaster, 1848–56, and the Sneed cemetery, Carroll County, is named for his family. Tennesseans James M. Kenner and James Fancher (1790–?) settled in the upper Osage Creek valley during the 1830s, and Fancher assumed the role of legendary figure in Carroll County. He was a veteran of the War of 1812 and the Creek Indian wars of 1814. Citizens elected him to the Arkansas state legislature for a term, 1842–44, and he is considered the patriarch of several Fancher-related families that migrated to Arkansas. Capt. Alexander Fancher of Mountain Meadows fame was his first cousin. Jim Lair and O. Klute Braswell, *An Outlander's History of Carroll County, Arkansas, 1830–1983* (Marceline, Mo.: Walsworth Publishing Company, 1983), 92–94, 312–14.

 7. Prior to the passage of local-option fencing laws, which began to close the open range by township and by county, fences were used to keep free-ranging livestock out of yards and crop fields, but not to keep livestock contained. The ground inside the fence was typically swept clean with a broom. The evolution of Missouri fence legislation is discussed by John H. Calvert in "Fencing Laws in Missouri—Restraining Animals," *Missouri Law Review* 32 (Fall 1967): 519–42. In Arkansas, state tax policy encouraged squatting on the antebellum open range—settlers received a tax exemption for houses built on public land. In the

Arkansas uplands, squatting was the antebellum rule rather than the exception. The "farming" that Turnbo refered to is more properly termed open-range herding or, in modern terminology, slash-and-burn cultivation. Open-range economy and culture continued into the twentieth century, gradually closing as immigration increased, timber companies patented titles, and the National Forests cleared titles, ended indiscriminate fires, and promoted fencing. A cattleman in Newton County, Ark., remembering the transformation, said, "The woods was full of hogs and cattle and they done well. They cut Arkansas' throat when they passed the stock law . . . and the poor man took the brunt of it all." Rudolph Crouse, interview with Robert Flanders and Lynn Morrow, 8 June 1984, Boxley Valley Oral History Project, Center for Ozarks Studies, Southwest Missouri State University and Buffalo River National Park; John Solomon Otto and Augustus Marion Burns, "Traditional Agricultural Practices in the Arkansas Highlands," *Journal of American Folklore* 94 (April–June 1981): 177–78; and Robert B. Walz, "Migration into Arkansas, 1820–1880: Incentives and Means of Travel," *Arkansas Historical Quarterly* 17 (Winter 1958): 313–14.

8. In 1827 Americans from the Arkansas River Valley settled Cane Hill, twenty miles southwest of Fayetteville, as Cherokees vacated northwest Arkansas. The settlement's first name was Boonsboro. Deane, *Arkansas Place Names*, 140.

9. A farm sled was a vehicle on runners used for conveying loads short distances—it was simpler to construct than a wheeled vehicle. Studies about sleds exist for the British Isles and Appalachia, but not for the Ozarks. Ozarkers used sleds for work and play. Turnbo recorded in 20:12ff that sleds were used to haul stones for mortuary monuments, and W. B. Flippin in his "Early History," Yellville *Mountain Echo*, 1 September 1899, recorded that pioneers used sleds to haul filled barrels.

In the twentieth century, goats were harnessed to sleds to haul firewood or stave bolts, to haul fertilizer to the garden, children rode sleds off hillsides for play, and builders used mules and sleds to haul rocks for fireplaces. Remains of old "sled roads" still exist in some Ozark locales. Doy and Blanche Scroggins, interview with Lynn Morrow and Kay Murnan, 6 June 1983, Boxley Valley Oral History Project, Center for Ozarks Studies, Southwest Missouri State University and Buffalo River National Park; Bill Duty, interview with Lynn Morrow and Robert Flanders, 9 June 1983, Boxley Valley Oral History Project, Center for Ozarks Studies, Southwest Missouri State University and Buffalo River National Park; Gertrude Studyvin, interview with Robert Flanders and Lynn Morrow, 7 June 1984, Boxley Valley Oral History Project, Center for Ozarks Studies, Southwest Missouri State University and Buffalo River National Park; and Blanton Owen, "The Farm Sled of the Southern Appalachian Highlands: Its Construction, Use and Operation," *Pioneer America Society Transactions* 3 (1980): 25–44.

10. That is, the bed was in a corner and the bed railings were fitted into holes in the wall that had been bored with an augur. One of the finest descriptions of domestic arrangements in and around these single-pen, frontier cabins in the

Ozarks is Page, *The Voices of Moccasin Creek*, 24–42. A major chore in the care of this kind of wood furniture was "spring cleaning" to rid the house of bedbugs whose eggs were laid in the bed. As Page pointed out, the transition to lightweight iron beds significantly reduced the work of spring cleaning.

11. Scholars have given little attention to folk dancing and the play party. For a list and a bibliography of such common performances as "Barbara Allen," "Do-Se-Do," "Here We Go Round the Mulberry Bush," "Itisket Itasket," "Little Brown Jug," "London Bridge," "Old Dan Tucker," "Ring Around the Rosie," "Skip to My Lou," and dozens of others more common in the Ozarks, see Altha Lea McLendon, "A Finding List of Play-Party Games," *Southern Folklore Quarterly* 8 (September 1944): 201–34. Vance Randolph was the first collector of Ozarks play party culture. See Vance Randolph, "The Ozark Play-Party," *The Journal of American Folklore* 42 (July–September 1929): 201–32; and Vance Randolph and Nancy Clemens, "Ozark Mountain Party-Games," *The Journal of American Folklore* 49 (July–September 1936): 199–206.

12. The Tabor families are one of the largest networks of long-time residents in the Ozarks. By the mid-1830s they had settled in Taney, Ozark, Carroll, and Marion counties. Elijah (1790–?) and Sarah's son, John H. (1809–1902) married Elizabeth Magness. Some Tabors hunted the last of Ozarks buffalo with the Indians, intermarried with Indians, and one family member, Nimrod Teaf, who married Nancy Tabor, was a gunsmith who did a lot of business with Indians at Shawneetown. See William A. Yates, "The Taber Family of Big Creek, Taney County, Missouri," *White River Valley Historical Society* 4 (Summer 1972): 2–7; and Earl Berry, *History of Marion County* (Little Rock: International Graphics Industries, 1977), 259–60.

13. The longest elk antler in the Boone and Crockett Club records is 64 1/2 inches long, although there are no early records for elk in the Missouri-Arkansas region. Antler growth is a matter of genetics and nutrition, with the best-nourished animals growing the largest antlers. They are shed annually. William H. Nesbitt and Jack Reneau, eds., *Records of North American Big Game* (Dumfries, Va.: The Boone and Crockett Club, 1988).

14. Powell Post Office (1888–1904) succeeded Clear Creek (1855–88). Powell is about eight miles west of Yellville. Baker, *Arkansas Post Offices*.

15. Dr. James M. Cowdrey (1795–1866) is credited with establishing the first medical practice in the upper White River country in Arkansas. He spent a few years in Batesville, then Fayetteville, and in 1836 moved to Yellville, where he remained. He became surgeon for Col. William Mitchell's Fourteenth Arkansas Infantry. See *A Reminiscent History of the Ozark Region* (Chicago: Goodspeed Brothers, Publishers, 1894), 106–10.

16. John P. Houston was elected as the first Izard County clerk in 1825, served seven terms, and became a noted Arkansas character of a violent disposition. He sometimes worked in Jacob Wolf's house and served in office at the same time as Wolf's brothers-in-law, John Adams, sheriff, and Matthew Adams, county judge.

Russell P. Baker, "Jacob Wolf," *Arkansas Historical Quarterly* 37 (Summer 1978): 185–86.

17. Turnbo reported several instances of Indian harassment by whites. In 1830 Jacob Wolf, John Adams, and Matthew Adams (brothers-in-law to Wolf) brought an official complaint to the governor of Arkansas Territory against Alfred Musick, Daniel Griggs, and John and Samuel Wood for fraudulently supplanting Delaware Indians on lands in Izard County. Matthew Adams, as county judge and trading partner with Menard and Valle in Sainte Genevieve, Missouri, knew the official channels and was probably looking after his customers. James J. Johnston, "Searcy County Indians in Tradition and History," *Mid-America Folklore* 12 (Spring 1984): 24-31. and Bill D. Blevins, *Jacob Wolf, The Mansion and the Man* (Mountain Home, Ark.: Twin Lakes Printing & Publishing Company, 1982), 51.

18. The land became known as Magness Bottom and their many children married into the pioneer families of the upper White River. Silas Turnbo was related to them through the Onstotts who settled on Beaver Creek, Taney County.

19. The St. Louis and Iron Mountain Railroad completed the White River Railway in 1905. In 1917 Missouri Pacific acquired the line. See W. J. Burton, "The White River Railway" (St. Louis: Union Pacific Railroad, n.d.); and James R. Fair, Jr., *The North Arkansas Line: The Story of the Missouri and North Arkansas Railroads* (San Diego: Howell-North Books, 1969).

20. Modern physicians inform us that formerly patients with palsy used a device to maintain a certain amount of use of their limbs. It was a large wheel, with a handle, mounted *vertically*, which the patient turned. Turnbo's sounds as if it was mounted horizontally, and the patient walked *around* as it turned. It is no longer prescribed.

21. The great meteor shower of November 1833 was a national phenomenon. Churches and neighborhoods sponsored revivals and anticipated the approaching millennium.

22. In fall 1832 at Castor Hill, St. Louis, William Clark, representing the federal government, ratified with the chiefs of the Shawnees and Delawares another treaty for their removal farther west. See the particulars in Charles J. Kappler, comp. and ed., *Indian Affairs. Laws and Treaties,* vol. 2 (Washington, D.C.: Government Printing Office, 1904), 370–72.

23. Kingdom Springs Post Office (1902–33), an Ozarks mining camp in Marion County, was about eight miles north of Yellville. Baker, *Arkansas Post Offices.*

24. The Tutt and Everett families from Tennessee were among the very first whites to settle at Shawneetown. Both families did business in Yellville and members of both families ran for political office there. Hansford (or Hamp) was elected coroner in 1842 after his brother R. B. served as sheriff, 1836–38. Among the Everetts, Jesse was county surveyor, 1836–38, I. B. (Bart) was sheriff, 1838–42, and Thomas Ewell was county judge, 1836 and 1840–42. Supposedly tension and conflict arose between the families during the 1830s that erupted in the "June

fights of 1844," an election year. Name-calling and violence continued, the King family arrived and took the Tutt side, and on 4 July 1849 both sides met each other in Yellville, resulting in several deaths. Vengeance followed on both sides until two Carroll County militias, one commanded by Capt. W. C. Mitchell (referred to elsewhere by Turnbo), quelled the disturbance. Still, the combatants sought retribution until an assassin, named by W. B. Flippin as a Mr. Wickersham, killed Hansford Tutt. Jesse Everett, the mortal enemy of Tutt, died soon after of cholera during his exile in Louisiana. Versions of the conflict besides Turnbo's are in W. B. Flippin, "The Tutt and Everett War in Marion County," 1877 manuscript, reprinted in *Arkansas Historical Quarterly* 17 (Summer 1958): 155–63; A. C. Jeffery, *Historical and Biographical Sketches of the Early Settlement of the Valley of White River together with a History of Izard County* (Melbourne, Ark.: Melbourne Clipper, 1877; Yellville, Ark.: Yellville *Mountain Echo*, 1895; reprint, Richmond, Va.: The Jeffery Historical Society, April 1973); and William Monks, *A History of Southern Missouri and Northern Arkansas: Being an Account of the Early Settlement, the Civil War, the Ku-Klux, and Times of Peace* (West Plains, Mo.: West Plains Journal Company, 1907). Some of the Everetts and Tutts were involved in additional well-known regional episodes of violence. Jess fought the cantankerous John Houston, until onlookers pulled him off, at the mouth of the Big North Fork River. "Wild Bill" Hickok (1837–1876) killed David K. Tutt in a celebrated gunfight on the town square in Springfield, Missouri, 20 July 1865. Jim Everett, in 1883, was killed in his Forsyth mercantile-saloon, an event that triggered the formation of local vigilantes.

25. Dr. Augustus S. Layton (1813–1877), a Virginian, moved to Greene County, Missouri, in 1842 but soon established his practice in Forsyth. He also built a sawmill in a pinery in southwest Taney County that shipped lumber to Springfield and to as far away as Warsaw on the Osage River. He marketed cattle successfully to California during the 1850s, and Layton's Mill was a post office, 1860–63. Dr. Layton and his sons, siding with the Confederacy, moved to the deep South during the war, while his brother John sided with the Union. Dr. Layton returned later to Yellville and resumed his saw-milling ventures along the Missouri and Arkansas line and practiced medicine in Yellville. His son A. S. (1843–1903) became a leading merchant and banker in Yellville, establishing the Layton Building in the period 1903–06, now on the National Register of Historic Places. Robert G. Schultz, *Missouri Post Offices, 1804–1981* (St. Louis: The American Philatelic Society, St. Louis Branch No. 4, 1982); Elmo Ingenthron, *Land of Taney: A History of an Ozark Commonwealth* (Point Lookout, Mo.: The School of the Ozarks Press, 1974), 80; *A Reminiscent History of the Ozark Region*, 55–56; Berry, *History of Marion County*, 197–98; and the Layton Building, National Register of Historic Places nomination. Arkansas Historic Preservation Program, Little Rock, Arkansas.

26. The Lewis Pumphrey family migrated from Tennessee to Fulton County, Arkansas, in 1835. Son Franklin came to Shoal Creek, northeast Marion County, prior to the Civil War. Silas Turnbo went to a neighborhood subscription school

in the latter 1850s and in the years 1860–61 that was also attended by Frank's children. Silas C. Turnbo Collection, 17:85, 22:89–91, Springfield–Greene County Public Library, Springfield, Missouri.

27. Lewis Herron's family settled on Big Creek, Taney County, in 1843 and by 1845 were on Shoal Creek where they remained for many years. Sons Mort (1834–?) and Simon (1828–?) married sisters, the daughters of Henry and Ruth Tabor, and gave many stories to Silas Turnbo. Mort was a frequent horse racer at the track in Protem. Mort is sometimes rendered Mart in Turnbo's writings. Turnbo Collection, 18:51–52, 21:17.

28. Several generations of the Hollinsworth family built mills in Maryland, Indiana, and Arkansas. Robert (1845–1899) and Lemuel (1854–1935) homesteaded land and accumulated over a thousand acres on the Little North Fork River, Marion County. Their three-story mill was also the center for a sawmill, mercantile, and cotton gin at the Oakland hamlet. Berry, *History of Marion County*, 177–78.

29. The Kissee family came from Indiana to Christian County, Missouri, in 1846. Alexander C. Kissee was a Unionist soldier stationed at Ozark and came to Taney County in 1869. He acquired the mill seat at what became Kissee Mills, established a post office there and became a wealthy and influential merchant and stock dealer. He took a position of leadership in the Baldknobber vigilante group, published the *Taney County Times* to promote Kissee Mills for a new county seat following the burning of the Forsyth courthouse in 1885, and managed his gristmill, sawmill, and cotton gin on Beaver Creek. *A Reminiscent History of the Ozark Region*, 349–53.

Lt. Willis Kissee was a Unionist soldier who served under Capt. William Fenex, owner of the Beaver Creek mill seat that would later bear the Kissee Mill name. Fenex sent Kissee in command of the soldiers who killed Alph Cook and captured a number of Confederates in Marion County. Kissee achieved fame as an Ozarks guerrilla fighter, claiming to have killed thirty-two. After the war he was killed in a gunfight in Colorado. His name was honored in Taney County with the establishment of the Willis Kissee Camp, No. 48, G. A. R. Elmo Ingenthron, *Borderland Rebellion: A History of the Civil War on the Missouri–Arkansas Border* (Branson, Mo.: The Ozarks Mountaineer, 1980), 294–95.

30. James E. Everett is a descendant of the Marion County Everetts of the famed Everett-Tutt War. He and brother Barton Yellville Everett came to Forsyth in 1868. Although Jim did not go into the mill business with the Hollinsworth brothers, he and Yell Everett in the early 1880s built the Everett Mill near the Springfield-Harrison road on Bull Creek, Taney County. In September 1883 Al Layton killed Jim Everett in his Forsyth mercantile and saloon, which was the event that triggered the formation of the Baldknobber vigilantes. Ingenthron, *Land of Taney*, 167; and Lucile Morris Upton, *Bald Knobbers* (Caldwell, Idaho: The Caxton Printers, 1939), 48–51.

31. In the 1860s James Leffel published a monthly serial, *Leffel's Illustrated Milling and Mechanical News*, which he edited and revised into book form as *The*

Construction of Mill Dams: Comprising also The Building of Race and Reservoir Embankments and Head Gates, The Measurement of Streams, Gauging of Water Supply, Etc. (Springfield, Ohio: James Leffel and Company, 1874). The book advertised and promoted a state-of-the-art Leffel double turbine water wheel, pictured on page 330 of the book. The water wheel was an advance in durability, and a loss of working friction increased the power of the water wheel. Leffel boasted that over seven thousand were in use by 1874.

32. Barnett P. Parrish, born in Ohio, grew up in Polk County, Missouri. He enlisted in the Union army there and migrated to Forsyth in 1866. He was a farmer, sired many children, several of whom became prominent business people in Taney County, and established the Parrish Hotel in Forsyth. *A Reminiscent History of the Ozark Region*, 146–49.

33. John E. Williams lived on lower Beaver Creek. His son, Samuel J. Williams, built a dogtrot house in 1886 on the family farm. When the Corps of Engineers built Bull Shoals Lake in the late 1940s, the Williams house was removed to old Forsyth and reassembled where it stands today as Taney county's pioneer house icon.

34. Jacksonport, downriver from Batesville at the junction of the Black and White rivers, prospered from the trade of both river valleys and became an early point of transfer of boat cargoes, due to its being an all-season port. The town was laid out in 1833, the year of the first steamboat arrival, and had its heyday during the 1850s, serving as county seat, 1853–62. For example, in one year, 1859–60, there were 355 separate steamboat arrivals in Jacksonport from the upper White River. The construction of the St. Louis and Iron Mountain Railroad led to the founding of the nearby town of Newport in 1872—Newport then assumed the former commercial role of Jacksonport. See Virgil H. Holder, "Historical Geography of the Lower White River," *Arkansas Historical Quarterly* 27 (Summer 1968): 131–45; and Mabel West, "Jacksonport, Arkansas: Its Rise and Decline," *Arkansas Historical Quarterly* 9 (Autumn 1950): 231–39.

35. It is not surprising that Lemuel Hollinsworth had fears in 1872 about the KKK. During the late 1860s Arkansas was the scene of violent KKK nightriding, although most of it took place south of the Ozarks. Governor Powell Clayton proclaimed martial law in 1868 and the state spent tens of thousands of dollars quelling the conflict. Tales of violent KKK activity circulated in state newspapers, and south of the White River in Pope County a number of people were killed in Reconstruction violence. William Monks devoted a great deal of space in his *A History of Southern Missouri and Northern Arkansas*, 207ff., to record episodes of KKK disturbance in the north-central Arkansas Ozarks and in northeast Arkansas. See Margaret Ross, "Retaliation Against Arkansas Newspaper Editors During Reconstruction," *Arkansas Historical Quarterly* 31 (Summer 1972): 150–65; Earl Leroy Higgins, *Source Readings in Arkansas History* (Little Rock: Pioneer Press, 1964), 249–53; and Page, *The Voices of Moccasin Creek*, 55–56.

36. The first ferry on the White River, and the first in Arkansas, was located at Poke Bayou (Batesville) in 1818. The operation of ferries was controlled by law

and as such was often the focus of litigation. Arkansans passed ferry laws, and when a ferry was located on a public road, that ferry was open by permission of the county court. The ferry owner had to obtain a license, pay a special tax, and post a bond. Rates had to be posted and they could be challenged in court. After the Civil War, controversies arose over the right of a county to abolish an existing ferry and institute a free public ferry—in Arkansas, the Supreme Court upheld the county government view. The many legal issues concerning ferries are treated by Michael B. Dougan, "The Doctrine of Creative Destruction: Ferry and Bridge Law in Arkansas," *Arkansas Historical Quarterly* 39 (Summer 1980): 136–58.

37. A windlass is normally a device for raising or lowering something by use of a crank. The common image most people have is the windlass on a water well.

38. It is not clear if Turnbo is trying to cite verses from one or from two songs. Folklorist W. K. McNeil says, "The line about Jeff Davis is sometimes used as a verse of 'John Brown's Body' which is, of course, where the first line comes from. The line 'we'll free the niggers without the least doubt' is not usually run together with the one about the knapsack.

"'Glory Hallelujah!' was published late in 1861 although it was composed sometime before 1855 by one, William Steffe, a native of South Carolina. Prior to the Civil War it became a popular camp-meeting song, with the refrain, 'Say, brothers, will you meet us on Canaan's happy shore?' According to tradition, the Tiger company of the Twelfth Massachusetts Regiment used the tune to taunt a soldier named John Brown. This supposedly occurred early in the war while the regiment was stationed at Fort Warren in Boston Harbor. The song became the regiment's marching song and was known as 'The John Brown Song,' 'John Brown's Body,' and 'Glory Hallelujah!'

"Later, of course, Julia Ward Howe wrote some 'more dignified' words to the tune and it became known as 'The Battle Hymn of the Republic.' If the tradition is true, which I doubt, a transition was made from the Massachusetts John Brown to the Kansas abolitionist.

"'We'll hang Jeff Davis from a sour apple tree' is what folklorists call a 'floating verse' that appears in a number of songs, including 'John Brown's Body.' There were songs that used the idea in the title, such as James W. Porter's 'Hang Him on the Sour Apple Tree,' and J. W. Turner's 'The Sour Apple Tree' or, 'Jeff Davis' Last Ditch.' The point is that the 'sour apple tree' was, in the minds of many people, songwriters included, an appropriate way to deal with Davis."
W. K. McNeil, letter to Lynn Morrow, 9 March 1990.

39. Micajah and Etny Haworth, small Kentucky slaveholders, settled south of Forsyth in 1853. Micajah was a farmer and a wheelwright who developed a wagon yard and campsite for freighters near Pleasant Hill school and church. Like Dr. A. S. Layton, Haworth took his slaves south to weather the civil war, and his wife and children fled east to stay with relatives in Kentucky. Bushwhackers killed their son Jonas, but son Jordan became an active politician, minister, merchant, and booster of Forsyth. See Marie Eva Johnson, "Native of the Ozarks," typescript, n.d.

40. Merchant-doctors marketed dozens of homemade pills on the antebellum frontier. Though some were placebos, and others ineffective, many after 1840 had a quinine base that was an effective medicine for malaria. Defects in these medicines caused by a lack of quality control in their cottage manufacture, however, led to deafness in some people. A promoter and largest dispenser of such quinine-base pills was Dr. John Sappington of Saline County, Missouri. Sappington's family business extended throughout the Mississippi River Valley, including the Arkansas and Missouri Ozarks, the Deep South, and especially Texas. See Lynn Morrow, "Dr. John Sappington: Southern Patriarch in the New West," manuscript, 1988.

41. Jesse Jennings' (1802–1877) saddlebag house (a double-pen house with the chimney centrally placed) stood near what is now Cedar Point and was a temporary seat of Taney County in 1837. Jennings served as one of the first county judges and then was elected state representative eight times between 1840 and 1868. Ingenthron, *Land of Taney*, 22, 463.

J. P. Vance (?–1862) was one of three early merchants who lived at Forsyth in 1839 (town founder John Danforth and Dr. A. S. Layton being the other two). Vance's store was often the site for hunters' display of big game trophies. Vance moved to Yellville in the 1840s. He managed the J. P. Vance and Co. general mercantile in Yellville for some years before it became in 1854 the Vance and [J. H.] Berry store which continued until the Civil War. Vance died in Yellville. *A Reminiscent History of the Ozark Region*, 232; and Turnbo Collection, 15:42.

42. William C. Berry was Taney County clerk, 1858–60, was elected county school commissioner in 1860, and was postmaster in 1860. James H. Berry (1823–96) was a Forsyth merchant, ca. 1840–51, when he relocated in Yellville. He taught school during the Civil War and invested in sawmilling. The 1850s Berry house in Yellville (adjacent to the Cowdrey property and one of the few town buildings to survive the civil war) is now the oldest structure in town. Berry, *History of Marion County*, 135–36.

43. During the Missouri territorial period, the mouth of Swan Creek became a traders' rendezvous. Louis Lorimier (1748–1812), a Cape Girardeau trader, or another trader with the same surname, established a post there which was purchased by William Gilliss in 1822. The generic name for the area was "Three Forks of White River," meaning the center of the Bull, Swan, and Beaver creeks' drainages. Joseph Philibert managed this post and one on the upper James River for Gilliss. Traders from Batesville also ascended the White River and made their own deals with various groups of Indians near Swan Creek. The migrating Indians left their villages during the period 1829–31. See Lynn Morrow, "Trader William Gilliss and Delaware Migration in Southern Missouri," *Missouri Historical Review* 75 (January 1981): 147–67.

44. What Turnbo meant is that since 1840 there had been a locally significant number of whites residing in the area who imported and exported goods.

45. Farmers in the late nineteenth century endured a generation of falling

prices. Agricultural unrest took form in several movements including the Grangers, Greenbacks, Brothers of Freedom, Agricultural Wheel, Farmers' Alliance, and finally the Populists. All wanted to restore the prosperity to agriculture that speculators and capitalists had eroded. For a regional account, see Berton E. Hennington, Jr., "Northwest Arkansas and the Brothers of Freedom: The Roots of a Farmer Movement," *Arkansas Historical Quarterly* 34 (Winter 1975): 304–24; and the national standard is Lawrence Goodwyn, *The Populist Moment: A Short History of the Agrarian Revolt* (New York and Oxford: Oxford University Press, 1978).

46. The 1890 stone courthouse, the fourth in Taney County's history, was funded by a special legislative bill. Based upon the state auditor's statistics that Taney County had less real estate and personal property tax revenue than other Missouri counties and that the county suffered an indebtedness in excess of forty thousand dollars, the Missouri legislature appropriated five thousand dollars for the construction of a new county building. See Douglas Mahnkey, *Taney County Bench and Bar, The First 150 Years* (Branson, Mo.: The Ozarks Mountaineer, 1990). Details concerning the courthouses and nineteenth-century town plans of old Forsyth are found in W. J. Bennett, Jr., and Jeffrey A. Blakely, *Archeological and Historical Investigations, Old Forsyth Site (23TA41) Taney County, Missouri* (Little Rock: U.S. Army Corps of Engineers, 1987).

47. James Cook, Jr. (1806–1888) was the eldest of five sons and four daughters of James Cook (1772–1864). This large Kentucky family settled in Taney and Christian Counties in the late 1830s. James Cook, Jr.'s, youngest brother, Alfred (1820–1865), was the subject of a civil war incident at Alph Cook's Cave, Marion County, Arkansas, recorded in the Turnbo Collection, 1:4–7. In 1864 James Cook, Jr., became one of many area southerners to change sides in the war. He went to Springfield, enlisted in the Union army, and farmed for four years in Greene County following the war. While he was in the army, Unionists killed his brother in Marion County. In 1869 he returned to the family farm on Swan Creek, Taney County. The 1836 Jimmie Cook house is the oldest structure in Taney County. Cook Family Papers, Kalen and Morrow, Forsyth, Missouri; and Kristen Kalen Morrow, "The James Cook Jr. House," *Ozarks Watch* 2 (Summer 1988): 14–15.

48. Silas's father, James Turnbo, was a leader in the local company. In June 1846, Taney Countians elected James as first lieutenant of the militia company; Harrison Snapp was their captain. "Miscellaneous Records from the *Springfield Advertiser* Springfield, Missouri, 1844–46" (Springfield, Mo.: Rachel Donelson Chapter, Daughters of the American Revolution, 1980), 161.

49. Henry Bratton had a general mercantile located at Dick Martin Spring on Bratton's Spring Creek. The earlier name had been Brock's Spring Creek, and in the twentieth century the watercourse has been known as simply Spring Creek. Turnbo Collection, 24:32.

50. String halt is a nerve disorder in horses that causes exaggerated flexing movements in walking.

51. William Garrison was a farmer and blacksmith in Christian County, and John Hoover erected an early mill in Christian County, ca. 1840, on Finley Creek at Linden. He operated it until 1886, selling it to the firm of Tunnell, Stone, and Stapp. He also had the Hoover Mill in Ozark, Missouri. Jim Gardner operated the mill at Linden and later managed the Dave Walker Mill. Paul Johns, *Unto These Hills* (Ozark, Mo.: Bilyeu-Johns Enterprises, 1980), 47; and *A Reminiscent History of the Ozark Region*, 390–91.

52. The Friend family came from Scotland to America during the eighteenth century. By 1796 Charles Friend had received a Spanish land grant in the New Madrid District of Missouri, and Charles' sons migrated into the Ozarks along the White River. One, Augustine, hosted Henry Rowe Schoolcraft during his tour of the Ozarks, and brother William (1784–1855) was cofounder of Linden in Christian County, where Augustine joined him in 1835. See Dean Wallace, "Our Friend Family," *White River Valley Historical Quarterly* 3 (Summer 1969), 3.

53. The forks of the Finley and James rivers were the southern boundary of the Delaware Indian reservation during the 1820s. Just south of the forks, Solomon Yocum and others erected whiskey and brandy stills to continue an illegal liquor trade following their eviction from the reservation in 1825. Trader William Marshall had a mill at the forks, which Solomon's son, George W. Yocum (1800–1848), acquired after the Indians removed to Kansas and Oklahoma. George Yocum exported his flour down to James and White river settlements. In 1850 the value of his mill production was *twice* that of any other Taney County mill. George's son A. T. became a prominent late nineteenth-century businessman and financier in Ozark, Missouri. A. T. continued the Yocum tradition in the milling business by constructing a mill at Ozark and building a grain elevator in Springfield. See map of reservation in Morrow, "Trader William Gilliss and Delaware Migration in Southern Missouri," 154; *Products of Industry Census, 1850, Taney County*. U.S. Census. Manuscript Schedule; and *A Reminiscent History of the Ozark Region*, 383–84.

54. Brig. Gen. Colley B. Holland (1816–1901) came from Tennessee in 1841 and became a merchant on Springfield's town square, later building one of the few antebellum brick houses in Greene County. He became a successful land speculator and promoted the development of Springfield. During the Civil War, he was an officer with Phelps' Regiment and was second in command of the Unionists who repulsed Gen. J. S. Marmaduke and the Confederates in the Battle of Springfield, 8 January 1863. After the war, he was a prominent manufacturer at Springfield Cotton Mills and founder of the Holland Banking Company. Martin Hubble, *Personal Reminiscences and Fragments of the Early History of Springfield and Greene County, Missouri* (Springfield, Mo.: Museum of the Ozarks, Sesquicentennial Edition, 1979), 23, 69; and Jonathan Fairbanks and Clyde Edwin Tuck, *Past and Present of Greene County, Missouri*, vol. 2 (Indianapolis: A. W. Bowen & Company, 1915), 1744–48.

55. William McElhaney was a Unionist with the 2nd Arkansas Cavalry, organized in Springfield in March 1864 under the leadership of Col. John E. Phelps.

It was this company that enrolled the "Mountain Feds" from northwest Arkansas into Union service. Turnbo knew many who had served with this cavalry. R. S. Holcombe, *History of Greene County, Missouri* (St. Louis: Western Historical Company, 1883), 467–68.

56. Albert G. McCracken (1823–1878) was Greene County circuit clerk 1854–60. In 1855 he began an extensive regional nursery business that had branches in Arkansas and Kansas. He also was copartner in the Ingram milling business on the James River, 1859–78. Holcombe, *History of Greene County, Missouri*, 696.

Chapter 4: Man and Wildlife

Tales of Buffalo

1. Famous local bear hunter John Gaskins (1816–1901) wrote that when the 1844 flood influenced him to move from the White River in Marion County to Carroll County, all the buffalo were gone. His Unionist sympathies led him to seek refuge in Greene County, Missouri, during the Civil War. He returned to Carroll County in 1868, and the railroad whistle stop Gaskins Station was named for him. His pioneer exploits with bear and other game had become subjects for fireside chats in the region by the 1880s. John Gaskins, *The Life and Adventures of John Gaskins in the Early History of Northwest Arkansas* (Published by author, 1893; reprint, Eureka Springs, Ark.: Eureka Springs Historical Museum, n.d.), 10; and *History of Carroll County, Arkansas. Reprint of the Carroll County section of the Goodspeed Publishing Company's Northwest Arkansas history. Arranged by O. Klute Braswell* (Chicago: Goodspeed Publishing, 1889; reprint, Berryville, Ark.: Braswell Printing Company, n.d.), 1055–56; and Charles W. and Elizabeth R. Schwartz, *The Wild Mammals of Missouri* (Columbia: University of Missouri Press, 1981), 350.

2. See Victor Tixier, *Tixier's Travels on the Osage Prairies*, ed. John F. McDermott, trans. Albert J. Salvan (Norman: University of Oklahoma Press, 1968).

3. Southerners and frontiersmen commonly kept game animals as pets. As the game approached maturity and became too much to control, the owners killed them for food and their skins.

4. Scud clouds are loose vapory clouds driven swiftly by the wind.

5. An open-face camp could be two "Y" poles stuck in the ground holding a pole joist upon which brush leaned. Bark might cover the brush and the floor might be dressed with leaves or brush. After the Civil War destruction of Ozark towns, some settlers lived in this kind of shelter until better housing could be provided.

An open-face camp today is a tent or a brush structure closed on three sides and heated by a reflected fire on the open side of the tent or structure.

6. The Baughman family helped establish Baptist fellowships in Madison County, Missouri, during the 1830s and in Marion County during the 1840s; they were evangelicals in the Bethel Association of United Baptists spawned in Tennessee. Peter W. Baughman (1830–1904) became a skilled blacksmith and carpenter, building wagons, houses, chimneys, and the Bald Knob School in Taney County. He had an acreage in Taney County northwest of Horseshoe Bend on the White River, and gave several stories to Turnbo. See the excellent family history by J. Ross Baughman, *Some Ancestors of the Baughman Family in America; Tracing Back Twelve Generations from Switzerland through Virginia, etc.* (Edinburg, Va.: Shenandoah History, Publishers, 1989).

7. This is unlikely since the seeds of pine are wind disseminated. Their occurrence here was probably due to the bare soil around the lick, which pine seeds need to germinate.

8. The *Oxford English Dictionary* does not indicate use of the term *surly* to designate a bull or male animal. This must be of local origin, as some Ozarkers use the term *gip* or *gyp* to indicate a bitch. Rural women, maintaining their modesty, used the term *jersey* to indicate a bull; it was indelicate to use the term *bull*.

Tales of Bear

9. Mabel West, "Jacksonport, Arkansas: Its Rise and Decline," *Arkansas Historical Quarterly* 9 (Autumn 1950): 236.

10. For example, John Gaskins's bear-hunting career in Carroll County began in 1855 and lasted into the 1890s. Gaskins, *The Life and Adventures of John Gaskins*.

11. Otto Ernest Rayburn, "Arkansas Folklore: Its Preservation," *Arkansas Historical Quarterly* 10 (Summer 1951): 210; see the discussions of this important subject, including the fact that the legendary hunters on the American frontier are all southerners, in Katherine G. Simoneaux, "Symbolism in Thorpe's 'The Big Bear of Arkansas,'" *Arkansas Historical Quarterly* 25 (Autumn 1966): 240–47; Ted R. Worley, "An Early Arkansas Sportsman: C. F. M. Noland," *Arkansas Historical Quarterly* 11 (Spring 1952): 25–39; James R. Masterson, *Tall Tales of Arkansas* (Boston: Chapman & Grimes, Publishers, 1943), 55–75; "Davy Crockett Shoots Bears," in Clarence Gohdes, sel. and ed., *Hunting in the Old South: Original Narratives of the Hunters* (Baton Rouge: Louisiana State University Press, 1967), 153–54; and the book-length study by Norris W. Yates, *William T. Porter and the Spirit of the Times: A Study of the BIG BEAR School of Humor* (Baton Rouge: Louisiana State University Press, 1957).

12. Bur oak, also called mossycup oak, *Quercus macrocarpa*, is a tree of the bottomlands, rich woods, and fertile slopes; it grows to quite a large size.

13. Talbert's Ferry, named for brothers Frederick, "Wat" (Walter), "Sim" (Simean), and Bazzeel Talbert, was located just above modern Cotter; the ferry crossing was first known as Denton's Ferry and became Mooney's Ferry after it was Talbert's Ferry. It was the primary crossing of the White River on the old

east-west Carrollton Road, established ca. 1832, and according to W. B. Flippin, it was the only territorial period ferry above Batesville. The Talbert cemetery is just east of Mountain Home, where the name Talbert Barrens succeeded Rapp Barrens as an early place-name before the area became Mountain Home. Silas C. Turnbo Collection, 6:66, 7:35, 18:77, Springfield–Greene County Public Library, Springfield, Missouri; Mary Ann Messick, *History of Baxter County, 1873–1973* (Little Rock: International Graphics, 1973), 200, 444; and W. B. Flippin, "Early History," Yellville *Mountain Echo,* 5 May 1899.

14. That is, all the families were members of the Coker clan.

15. That is, he rejected the idea with contempt.

16. Alex and Betsy Duggins were the "first settlers" at the mouth of Big Creek, Marion County; they buried a son at the first burial in the graveyard on Joe Magness's farm in 1822. Dugginsville, Ozark County, is named for the family. Turnbo Collection, 17:99–100.

17. Bee bread is a bitter, yellowish-brown pollen stored in cells and mixed with honey by bees to be used as food.

The honey bee, *Apis mellifera,* was brought to the New World early, and in the great deciduous forests quickly went wild. The bee, noted by the Indians as the "white man's fly," preceded the European in his westward movement. The earliest settlers hunted bees for honey and wax, the honey satisfying their craving for sweets and the wax being used to make candles. Honey and wax also were traded for necessary goods. Coopers built hogsheads to hold and transport honey after it was separated from the beeswax.

Settlers kept hives of bees in bee gums, so called as species of the gum tree were used to house them. The gum was a trough or hive made from a hollowed gum log. In the southern United States the sweet gum is *Liquidambar Styraciflua*; sour or black gum or tupelo is *Nyssa Sylvatica.*

18. The giant cane, *Arundinaria gigantea,* is a bottomland plant, and is usually located in river banks and swamps; in moist soil or in water; in wet shores, shallow water, and borders of swamps. However, cane in the Ozarks can and does grow up hillsides. Merritt L. Fernald, *Gray's Manual of Botany* (New York: American Book Company, 1950), 96.

19. It is unusual to use shot pellets, which ordinarily are used in smoothbore guns, in a rifle. The rifling would deform and cause shot to behave erratically. The size pellet most commonly used in hunting squirrels is No. 6, with about 220 pellets to the ounce.

20. Turnbo and his informants tried to keep their bear-hunting stories in a traditionally humorous vein, common on the frontier. The serious view is seldom told, but one famous bear hunter in Arkansas, Friedrich Gerstäcker, did relate a story with a fatal ending on the upper White River in 1842. The eighteen months he spent on the upper White River became the setting for Gerstäcker's mythical *Germelshausen* village in subsequent writings. See Clarence Evans, "Gerstaecker and the Konwells of White River Valley," *Arkansas Historical Quarterly* 10 (Spring 1951):

26–29; and Clarence Evans, "A Cultural Link Between Nineteenth-Century Germany and the Arkansas Ozarks," *Modern Language Journal* 35 (1951): 523–30. For a summary of Gerstäcker's time in Arkansas and the Ozarks, see Evan Burr Bukey, "Frederick Gerstaecker in Arkansas," *Arkansas Historical Quarterly* 31 (Spring 1972): 3–14; and Friedrich Gerstäcker, *Wild Sports in the Far West* (London: G. Routledge, 1854; reprint, Durham: University of North Carolina Press, 1968).

21. Turnbo frequently makes the point that in settlement days the landscape was relatively clear of brush. A closed canopy would have had this effect, but frequent fires also accounted for the phenomenon. Joseph Brown, surveyor in the White River country in 1815 and 1823, remarked upon the diminution of game between the two dates as "The Indians, for the sake of hunting, have burnt nearly the whole country where the South boundary [Missouri and Arkansas] passed." Additionally, Friedrich Gerstäcker lamented the passing of the Arkansas wilderness he had known in the years 1838–42 when he traveled the state in 1867. Gone were the "open grassy hills" that were then dense with young growth as the land had been "neglected for years and never burned out . . . I could not see ten feet to the right or left of it. To think of hunting in this wilderness was impossible." Suppression of wildfires was a probable cause of brush, although concerted action to suppress wildfires did not come into the region until the 1930s with widespread governmental programs. See Anita Bukey and Evan Burr Bukey, trans. and eds., "Arkansas After the War: From the Journal of Frederick Gerstaecker," *Arkansas Historical Quarterly* 32 (Autumn 1973): 255–73; and Dwight Weaver, "Setting the Cornerstones of Missouri: 1815–1989," *Missouri Resource Review* 6 (Fall 1989): 9.

22. The huckleberry, *Vaccinium arboreum*, also called farkleberry and sparkleberry, is a relative of the blueberry.

23. That is, the priming of the flintlock flashed without setting off the main charge, called "a flash in the pan." At this late date (after 1845) it would have been unusual for hunters to have been using flintlock rifles. The percussion cap had been adopted prior to 1820, but on the frontier some clung to their flintlocks as being more "reliable." One could always find a piece of flint to fire one's rifle, but losing one's percussion caps could be tragic. Others simply couldn't afford to buy a newer firearm.

24. Tar Kiln Creeks and Tar Kiln Hollows are place-names throughout the Ozarks. However, little is known about the pioneer extractive industry of tar smelting mentioned by Turnbo. For example, only two such sites are known among the twenty-nine thousand archaeological sites on record at the Archaeological Survey of Missouri, University of Missouri–Columbia. In one description from the oral tradition in Ripley County, Missouri, they were described as "built on a large flat rock outcrop, preferably with a slight slant. A large pile of pineknots was made on the slab and covered with a layer of soil. The pineknots were ignited and given air through holes in the soil mantle. The pine tar was cooked out and ran out the bottom of the kiln into a ditch made with soil or stone from which it was collected and containerized." James E. Price, letter to

Lynn Morrow, 6 March 1990; and Tom L. Burge, letter to Lynn Morrow, 11 April 1990.

25. *Muley cow* is an old term for a hornless cow, now common in the U.S. The term is of Gaelic origin. *Oxford English Dictionary*, 2d ed., s.v. "muley."

26. *Rubus species,* of which there are many different forms, both native and introduced, is a small shrub with prickly canes and delicious black fruit.

27. Pioneer cellars, located beneath the cabin floor in front of the fireplace, could be entered by removing a puncheon or raising a trap door; sometimes they were located in the floor of the breezeway or trot of a dogtrot house, and the cellars varied considerably in size.

Well into the twentieth century, Ozarkers dug small ground cellars near the house or a dependency. They lined the earth with straw and sometimes sand or rock, placed potatoes, turnips, or fruit in it, and covered the top with boards or tin. The produce could be easily retrieved for a meal or a snack. The commonly recognized above-ground cellar may have evolved from the older pit cellars. For an Ozarks study, see Sarah Brown, "The Storm Cellar: A Compass on the Homesteads of Rural Arkansas," *Mid-America Folklore* 12 (Fall 1984): 1–16; and John Solomon Otto and G. D. Gilbert, "The Plain Folk of the American South: An Archeological Perspective," *Pioneer America* 14 (July 1982): 73.

28. Gooley's Spring Creek is shown on modern maps as Gulley Spring Creek. Charles S. Gooley was the first settler on this creek that now drains into Bull Shoals reservoir in the vicinity of Pontiac, Ozark County, Missouri. Turnbo Collection, 28:4.

29. He meant the gun's wooden stock. The actual breech of a muzzleloading rifle is the rear end of the barrel, which is stopped by the threaded breech plug.

30. Capt. James H. Sallee (1833–?) was the eldest of eleven children; the family were pioneers along Pond Fork Creek, Ozark County. Sallee, in 1861, joined the Home Guards and later served as sergeant in Company F, Phelps' regiment. His family was one of several Union and Republican supporters in Ozark County. James became supervisor of registration in Ozark County following the war and was a Methodist minister; his father had been a Baptist minister. *A Reminiscent History of the Ozark Region* (Chicago: Goodspeed Brothers, Publishers, 1894), 735–36.

31. Noah Mahan was a brother to Isaac Mahan (1823–?), who had preceded him in the family immigration to Ozark County. Isaac's son John (1843–?), who was imprisoned twice in the war by Confederates and who later married Mary Nave (1848–1905), gave several stories to Turnbo. Isaac Mahan's family settled on Bratton's Spring Creek in 1841, gave their name to Mahan Hollow, and later moved up to a location near Rome, Douglas County, and finally to a location near Rockbridge. Noah's family settled on Pond Fork, where descendants remain today. The Mahan families were some of the Ozark County Unionists during the war. Turnbo Collection, 1:46, 50; 19:51–53.

32. Reminiscences of Ozarks nineteenth-century life prior to the pervasive economic impact of railroad development and national marketing are filled with

recollections of the "easy life" afforded to settlers on the open range. Travel accounts sometimes referred to the domestic landscape as one of "carelessness and abundance." John Gaskins said of Carroll County, Arkansas, in 1855, "I had been very prosperous and was getting along well, which was an easy matter to do in those times"; merchant G. R. Kenamore described the Current River country of Missouri in the 1870s, "Why in those days of the long ago the one big drawback to Shannon County was that her people could make a living too easy within her borders"; and Ben Stults wrote about his years in Stone County, Missouri, 1883–1905, but viewed the new White River Railroad and his job as a timber worker and said, "But now them Easy days are gone." Ben T. Stults, "A Sketch of the Many Ups and Downs in Life of Ben T. Stults As a Boy to a Man as a Hunter," manuscript, Kalen and Morrow Collection, Forsyth, Missouri, 70; Eminence, Missouri, *Current Wave,* 1 October 1925; Gaskins, *The Life and Adventures of John Gaskins,* 16.

33. It was a miracle the gun didn't burst like a grenade. As it was, the recoil from the explosion must have knocked Keesee senseless. Double-loading a muzzleloading firearm when in an excited state is not uncommon. During the Civil War, soldiers, in the din and excitement of battle, were often unable to tell if their rifle had gone off. They frequently put charge after charge into their weapons, unaware that the first charge had failed to fire.

34. Fodder could be the leaves of corn pulled, bundled, and stored in barns or dependencies for local use; harvesting in this manner was very labor intensive. In Missouri and throughout the Ozarks the practice of cutting and shocking the entire stalk for storage was widely practiced. The agricultural tradition of using fodder in the United States lasted longer among small farmers of the South. See Lewis Cecil Gray, *History of Agriculture in the Southern United States to 1860,* vol. 2 (Washington, D.C.: Carnegie Institution of Washington, 1933), 814–15.

35. A steelyard is a weighing device composed of a balance in which the object to be weighed is suspended from the shorter arm of a lever and the weight of the object found by moving a counterpoise along the longer arm, which has been calibrated, to produce equilibrium. A relatively primitive device, it has been used for many centuries to obtain the weights of bulky objects.

36. This would be the upper limit for bear in the Ozarks.

Tales of Elk and Deer

37. Schwartz and Schwartz, *The Wild Mammals of Missouri,* 350. Turnbo recorded that in 1851 hunters killed six elk at Five Oak Bald Hill, the last in Taney County, Missouri. Turnbo Collection, 9:58.

38. *Bald* is a term much used in the Ozarks for the crests of hills largely bare of trees. *Glade* would be a more proper term for this type of environment. Balds were the result of fires on essentially dry sites with high transpiration and evaporation ratios. Certainly fire and grazing maintained such sites, and, with the cessation of wild fires and the control of grazing, many balds became covered with

trees. Henry Rowe Schoolcraft used the term regularly in his 1818–19 account and apparently used balds for landmarks in traveling, as did the hunters. John Mason Peck, in his 1831 geographic commentary, referred to them as *knobs* "elevated from one to three hundred feet above the neighboring bottoms . . . Considerable strips of the country . . . on the White river and its branches in Arkansas, are made up of knobs." A Turnbo informant remembered Sugar Loaf Knob, Marion County, Arkansas, "as this knob had been fresh burned over, it loomed up above the Sugar Loaf Prairie like a big black cone." Turnbo Collection, 5:76; and John Mason Peck, *A Guide for Emigrants* (Boston: Lincoln and Edmands, 1831; reprint, New York: Arno Press, 1975), 128–29.

39. The post oak, *Quercus stellata*, usually a small, shrubby oak, is common to dry, sterile soils in the Ozarks.

40. Fires have been a part of the Ozarks landscape since time immemorial. Antoine Simone Le Page du Pratz in his *History of Louisiana*, trans. Joseph G. Tregle, Jr. (Baton Rouge: Louisiana State University Press, 1975), 134, wrote that the Indians set fire to the landscape every fall to improve conditions for game, and Schoolcraft remarked that the sterile look of the Ozarks resulted from the effects of burning. "These fires," he said, "continued for ages by the natives, to clear the ground for hunting, have had the effect not only to curtail and destroy large vegetation, but all the carbonaceous particles of the top soil have been burned, leaving the surface in the autumn, rough, red, dry and hard." In the early 1830s in Phelps County, Missouri, it became a political issue as Maramec Iron investors called upon Governor John Miller to punish Indians who fired the woods near the ironworks. American pioneers, however, continued the same tradition in maintaining the hunting and herding economy of open range. Settlers also practiced spring burning in the belief that it improved grazing conditions and held down snakes, ticks, and chiggers. The major environmental and historical work is Stephen J. Pyne, *Fire in America: A Cultural History of Wildland and Rural Fire* (Princeton: Princeton University Press, 1982). Pyne suggests on page 80 that man has manipulated the forest environment so long that the "American forest may be more a product of settlement than a victim of it." Henry Rowe Schoolcraft, *The Indian in His Wigwam, or Characteristics of the Red Race of America* (New York: W. H. Graham, Tribune Building, 1848), 48; and James D. Norris, *The Story of the Maramec Iron Works, 1826–1876* (St. James, Mo.: The James Foundation and The State Historical Society of Wisconsin, 1972), 46.

41. Igo Post Office (1892–1914) was named for Harrison Igo. Capt. James H. Sallee (often mentioned in the Turnbo Collection) and others built the Igo school in 1897. It served families in the Pond Fork Creek valley in western Ozark County. When it closed, the post office was transferred to Thornfield. In 1837 Methodist preacher Leven T. Green and his five sons settled on Little North Fork, Ozark County. Turnbo wrote that all were "famed hunters" and recorded how Leven's son Phillip killed 114 deer in a twelve-month period. The Greens also killed the last of the elk in their area. Robert G. Schultz, *Missouri Post Offices, 1804–1981* (St. Louis: The American Philatelic Society, St. Louis Branch No. 4,

1982); Turnbo Collection, 9:65, 11:14; and "No 'Nockin' Off of Hats and No Sparkin' at Igo School District No. 5," *The Old Mill Run* 4 (January 1990): 11.

42. Saw briar is another name for cat brier or greenbrier, *Smilax spp.*, several species of which are found in the Missouri and Arkansas Ozarks.

43. Paul C. Phillips, *The Fur Trade*, vol. 1 (Norman: University of Oklahoma Press, 1967), 468.

44. Ibid., vol. 2, 148ff.

45. Henry Rowe Schoolcraft, *A View of the Lead Mines of Missouri* (New York: Charles Wiley & Company, 1819; reprint, New York: Arno Press, 1972), 250.

46. The transitional zone of timber and forest was also the preferred site of settlement for many pioneers and was often the site used to develop towns. Pioneers referred to the open areas as prairies, barrens, or flats, and they were important in shaping the pattern of initial settlement. Access to natural resources at the first effective settlement was maximized in these zones, and guides for western immigrants encouraged their readers to settle in these zones as early as 1817. For example, settlers established towns such as Springfield, Missouri, on the Kickapoo Prairie, and Mountain Home, Arkansas, on Talbert's or Rapp's Barrens. Ozark prairies were grazed before farmers began cultivation upon them. For a discussion of the many advantages at these settlement sites, see Terry G. Jordan, "Between the Forest and the Prairie," *Agricultural History* 38 (October 1964): 205–16; and Gray, *History of Agriculture*, 866.

47. That is, a squatter's claim on the open range.

48. The St. Louis game market, supported in great measure by the expansion of the St. Louis and Iron Mountain Railroad south of Pilot Knob, Missouri, into central Arkansas, was one of the largest in the country during the late nineteenth century.

49. To load a muzzleloading firearm, one pours a measured charge of black powder down the barrel, then pushes a lead ball, enclosed in a greased patch of cloth or thin buckskin, down on top of the powder with a hickory ramrod or gunstick. If the firearm is a percussion lock gun, one places a percussion cap on the tube or nipple; if the firearm is a flintlock, one puts a charge of priming powder in the pan and closes the frizzen. In an emergency a hunter might forego the cloth patch and push a "naked" ball down on top of the powder charge. Some accuracy is lost but at close range this is not important.

50. Fire-hunting was the use of a torch at night to illuminate the eyes of deer. Turnbo's fire-hunters used canoes, but Theodore Pease Russell describes fire-hunting from horseback in *A Connecticut Yankee in the Frontier Ozarks: The Writings of Theodore Pease Russell*, ed. James F. Keefe and Lynn Morrow (Columbia: University of Missouri Press, 1988). Ben Stults reported using "those old fashion Sulphur Matches" attached to his gun barrel in order to kill deer at night in Stone County, Missouri, during the 1880s. In today's Ozarks, fire-hunting is called spotlighting or jacklighting and is quite unlawful. Stults, "A Sketch," 42.

51. These animals were acting in an unusual manner, which is the point of the story. As long as the deer does not *scent* an odor it associates with danger, it

does not spook. Smart hunters can stop a running deer by giving a loud whistle. The deer often stops to ascertain where the sound comes from, but not always.

52. We are unsure exactly what the term in the original text is. It is written grans, and may be grams, but surely Turnbo meant grains. The proper terms, *dram* or *grain*, are units of measure applied to black powder. A *gram* is a metric unit. Since a dram is equivalent to 27.343 grains, three drams would be about 82 grains—far too much for priming a flintlock, where only a few grains are sufficient. Possibly he meant three grains, rather than three grams.

53. Herron traveled to Rolla to get a better price because Rolla was at the end of the railroad (1861–67) until after the Civil War, when promoters extended it to Springfield and the southwest. Rolla also received some of the "Arkansas trade" for a few years as freighters from the White River country traveled back and forth. Messick, *History of Baxter County*, 12.

54. Adult deer weigh from 100 to 300 pounds. The Missouri state record deer weighed 369 pounds. Females average lighter in weight than males, and north Missouri deer average heavier than those of the Ozarks. This would have been a fairly large deer for the Ozarks region, where buck deer probably would not average more than that live weight. Deer lose about 20 percent of their live weight when field dressed.

55. Turnbo's hunters get "bewildered" instead of lost.

56. A seasonal way of life built up around rafting logs; like freighters, rafters often moved around a great deal. Trees were cut and trimmed and pushed over log "chutes" into the river. One such chute can still be easily seen on the north side of the White River, downstream from the Peel Ferry. The timber was gathered into long rafts, which were floated down to a sawmill, often several days distant. The rafters then walked home to begin the round anew.

57. Abraham Cole (1821–1899), a Kentuckian and a Unionist in the Civil War, lived primarily on Big Creek (Taney County, 1858–99), where his log dogtrot house was razed in 1989. Following the war, he served on the first Taney County circuit court grand jury held at Harrison Snapp's house, near Forsyth. Turnbo Collection, 11:41, 12:83, 17:31.

58. Muzzleloading rifles had no standard, but a typical one was about five feet long, with a heavy octagonal barrel averaging forty inches in length. Such a rifle might weigh from eight to fifteen pounds. The gun stocks, usually of maple or walnut, were frail, especially in the wrist region, and easily broken with rough treatment.

59. John Mosely (ca. 1824–?) came from Illinois with his parents to Beaver Creek, Taney County, in 1840; many years before, his grandfather had preceded them to Beaver and had died there. John farmed and operated a sawmill, a gristmill, and a cotton gin. He became county judge, 1852–58, and sheriff, 1880–84. He was a small slaveholder, lost all his property during the Civil War, retreated to Christian County for safety during the war, and lived the rest of his life on Beaver Creek. *A Reminiscent History of the Ozark Region*, 615–16.

60. A cap box is a small, round tin box containing percussion caps. Loss or spillage of caps under hunting conditions was a common occurrence and hunters

resorted to all sorts of devices, from pieces of leather punched with holes to hold caps to elaborate metal containers that dispensed one cap at a time.

61. A calculus, or stony object, occasionally found in the stomachs of ruminants, was once believed to possess magical powers to detect or draw poisons. Almost always they are formed around some foreign object and are composed commonly of calcium, magnesium, phosphorus, or other minerals. Most highly prized was a madstone from an albino deer.

62. Oregon County, Missouri, is just east of the White River region, but we include this story as one example that Turnbo collected near the White River country.

63. Turnbo's story demonstrates that not everyone knew or participated in all aspects of folk culture, any more than everyone knew about the techniques of making and setting live traps—a circumstance often overlooked in hindsight by modern folklorists and historians.

64. This was probably the timber rattlesnake, *Crotalus horridus Linnaeus*. Ozarkers erroneously often call this a "diamond" or "diamondback" rattlesnake.

65. This was the black rat snake, *Elaphe obsoleta obsoleta*, a large, forest-dwelling species.

66. That is, it was rattling.

67. A whip saw is a narrow pit saw tapering from butt to point, having hooked teeth, and averaging from five to seven and one-half feet in length. It could be transported with little trouble on the frontier and was operated in an open pit or with a raised scaffold to hold the log. The term is sometimes used for a two-man crosscut saw, also, but since they were sawing lumber, this was probably a pit saw. The pit saw continued to be used in the twentieth century by ship-builders on the east coast and was exported to Russia for use in distant hinterlands. Charles E. Hanson, Jr., provides further description in "The Pit Saw," *Museum of the Fur Trade Quarterly* 11 (Winter 1975): 1–6.

Tales of Wolves

68. *Venison* is the flesh of any animal killed in the chase or by hunting and used as food. It formerly applied to any game animal, but is now almost entirely restricted to deer. *Jerked meat* is meat cut into strips and dried. *Jerky* comes from the Spanish *charqui*. *Oxford English Dictionary*, 2d ed., s.v. "venison," "jerked meat," and "jerky."

69. Pen traps are another little-studied aspect of folk culture. Turnbo reports only large live traps, built to catch bear, wolf, and panther; he does not report the use of any small live traps so common in the twentieth century for small game like rabbits. Perhaps the smaller live trap evolved as larger game disappeared. For a beginning study, see Gary S. Foster, "The Social Dimensions of Traditional Live Traps: Expanding Paths in Material Folklife," *Southern Folklore Quarterly* 45 (1981): 101–08. The Ozarks sinkhole might be considered a "natural trap" as dogs could run bear into them to be shot by the hunter.

70. The maximum life span of wolves in the wild has never been determined. Wolves in captivity have lived for sixteen years. A twenty-three-year-old wolf would be unusually long lived, but not impossible. L. David Mech, *The Wolf* (Garden City, N.Y.: The Natural History Press, 1970).

71. It was not unusual throughout the nineteenth century and well into the twentieth century for hunters from regions and towns northward to take a hunting trip in the White River country. Businessmen from the Tri-State mineral region also came. Ben Stults reported that during the 1880s, "They would bring lots of Beer & whiskey. Some wouldn't hunt at all, Just Stay in camp & drink. Some would hunt." Symbolic of wilderness safaris to the upper White River country was the establishment of the St. Louis Game Park in southeast Taney County in 1891. M. B. Skaggs, owner of Safeway Grocer Company, purchased the land in 1929. Skaggs added the Drury ranch and provided turkey and deer brood stock to the Missouri Department of Conservation. Part of the land today is owned by the MDC and part remains in private hands. See Douglas Mahnkey, "The Game Park at Mincy," *Ozarks Mountaineer* 31 (June 1983): 44–47; and Stults, "A Sketch," 52.

72. Both Missouri and Arkansas enacted bounty laws on certain wildlife at an early date. The hunter could collect a cash payment for "scalps" or get credit toward his taxes. For a chronology of bounty laws, see James F. Keefe, *The First 50 Years* (Jefferson City: Missouri Department of Conservation, 1987), 324ff.

73. Hunting small fur-bearing animals in this fashion continued over time in the Ozarks. Apparently, the technique had something of a revival in the hard times of the Great Depression in the twentieth century, as related in the documentary film, *Shannon County: Home,* executive producer Robert Flanders (Springfield: National Endowment for the Humanities and Southwest Missouri State University, 1981, film).

74. The culture and economics of the open-range lifestyle have received considerable attention in recent years, most notably by Forrest McDonald and Grady McWhiney in their articles, "The Antebellum Southern Herdsman: A Reinterpretation," *Journal of Southern History* 41 (May 1975): 147–66; and "The South from Self-Sufficiency to Peonage: An Interpretation," *American Historical Review* 85 (December 1980): 1095–118. See also Grady McWhiney and Forrest McDonald, "Celtic Origins of Southern Herding Practices," *Journal of Southern History* 51 (1985): 165–82; and Grady McWhiney, *Cracker Culture: Celtic Ways in the Old South* (Tuscaloosa: University of Alabama Press, 1988). One localized study that has application to Ozarks history is Matthew R. Walpole, "The Closing of the Open Range in Watauga County, N.C.," *Appalachian Journal* 16 (Summer 1989): 320–35. As was North Carolina, the Ozarks was a vast region of small landholders, and large pockets of open range survived until different decades in the twentieth century when the communal land-use system gave way to the dominance of private property and capitalism. It is significant that in the White River country, where the first man-made impoundment for recreation, Lake Taneycomo, was built, tourism

played a major role in politicizing the closing of the range in the twentieth century.

75. Turnbo's accounts of the numbers of turkeys killed are supported by other writings. Theodore Russell enjoyed hunting turkey more than he enjoyed hunting any other species. When Schoolcraft and Pettibone wanted turkey for Christmas dinner in 1818, their hunter hosts easily brought back fourteen.

Famous Arkansas hunter and author C. F. M. Noland killed fifty-four turkeys at the beginning of a season on the White River. Noland of Batesville and William Quesenbury of Fayetteville helped establish Arkansas's fame as a fishing state, and Quesenbury recorded the use of horses in gigging fish. Horses were commonly used with dogs in the pursuit of deer and to penetrate dense thickets during the chase. For a guide to Noland's exploits, see Worley, "An Early Arkansas Sportsman: C. F. M. Noland," 25–39. Quesenbury's story is quoted on page 33 of the same article.

76. Ordinarily, a hunter would use a measure made of horn or tin to charge his rifle with black powder and would use a cloth or thin buckskin patch around the bullet. In an emergency he might just guess at a powder charge and put the ball down "naked."

77. To prime, he would place a percussion cap on the nipple if the firearm was a percussion rifle; or he would place fine black powder in the lock pan if the firearm was a flintlock.

78. David Clapp apparently purchased the former Nelson mill and remodeled it during the 1850s. The Clapps were southerners and fortunately sold the mill, ca. 1862, to William Fenex, a Unionist. Fenex and Union soldiers developed a small garrison there known as Camp Hawkins. The result was that the mill was a rare survivor of the war. Elmo Ingenthron, *Land of Taney: A History of an Ozark Commonwealth* (Point Lookout, Mo.: The School of the Ozarks Press, 1974), 175.

79. That is, his ramrod, usually made of hickory.

80. Elixir Springs Post Office (1880–97) was some five miles southwest of Lead Hill. Russell Pierce Baker, *From Memdag to Norsk: A Historical Directory of Arkansas Post Offices, 1832–1971* (Hot Springs, Ark.: Arkansas Genealogical Society, 1988).

81. Thomas H. Flippin and his family moved from Kentucky to Marion County in 1837, giving their name to the Flippin Barrens, the Flippin graveyard, and the modern railroad town Flippin. Eldest son W. B. Flippin (1817–?) was county surveyor, 1838–48 and 1852–54; was justice of the peace many years; was elected state representative in 1854 and in 1874; raised a company of Confederate soldiers and served as quartermaster in Confederate general James H. McBride's brigade, active in Missouri-Arkansas border war; and was county judge, 1864–68. He was known for his many community promotions, and he gave a few stories to Silas Turnbo. He is also remembered for his celebration of the nation's centennial in his 1877 manuscript, "The Tutt and Everett War in Marion County," 1877 manuscript, in *Arkansas Historical Quarterly* 17 (Summer 1958): 155–63. See also *A Reminiscent History of the Ozark Region*, 507–8.

82. Early plows were made of wood with metal facing. The shovel plow was

faced with a blade fixed so as to slice, lift, and turn the soil. The bull tongue plow—the more primitive of the two types—was more or less arrow shaped and was used for breaking rough ground and for cultivating by forcing its wide blade through the soil. In the rocky Ozark ground the metal facing of either type of plow had to be repaired or replaced frequently.

83. That is, it "Weaned" her from such behavior. Another example of the usage is that the first house lived in by newlyweds was sometimes called a "weaning house," that is, a house, for weaning them emotionally and economically from their parents. These were normally single-pen or double-pen houses that owners used for hired hands or for temporary rent houses. The time spent in one by newlyweds varied according to individual family needs. Bill Duty, interview with Lynn Morrow and Robert Flanders, 9 June 1983, Boxley Valley Oral History Project, Center for Ozarks Studies, Southwest Missouri State University and Buffalo River National Park; and Gertrude Studyvin and Ruth Armer, interview with Robert Flanders and Lynn Morrow, 9 January 1984, Boxley Valley Oral History Project, Center for Ozarks Studies, Southwest Missouri State University and Buffalo River National Park.

Tales of Panther

84. Schwartz and Schwartz, *The Wild Mammals of Missouri*, 324–28. On rare occasions, hunters have sighted panther in the Ozarks in the late twentieth century. A Current River, Missouri, family reported killing one in 1978.

85. Dave McCord settled in West Sugar Loaf Creek, ca. 1840, and in the late nineteenth century owned the old Buck Coker farm in Jake Nave Bend on the White River.

86. Spicebush is either *Lindera benzoin* or *Lindera melissaefolium*, a member of the Laurel family along with sassafras. Both have spicy, fragrant stems and leaves and yellow flowers.

87. David Hall was a free black from North Carolina who migrated first to Tennessee and then to the White River with his wife, Sallie. They had several sons, including Absalom, Leonard, Willoughby, James, and Joseph (1820–1900). Joseph, who gave several stories to Turnbo near the end of his life, claimed that his father, David, brought the first whiskey still to Marion County. Turnbo Collection, 21:19–21.

88. Samuel (1810–?) and Andrew (1818–?) Hudson, brothers, came from Tennessee to Newton County in 1831. Panther Creek, Newton County, Arkansas, got its name from a Sam Hudson panther kill, and he is credited with the discovery of Diamond Cave. Sam operated a mill and cotton gin at Parthenon and served a term as state representative during the late 1850s. Legends of Hudson convinced Fred W. Allsopp to use him as his lead character in his "Hunting and Animal Stories" chapter in his classic *Folklore of Romantic Arkansas,* vol. 2 (Little Rock: The Grolier Society, 1931), 237ff.; Walter F. Lackey, *History of Newton*

County, Arkansas (Point Lookout, Mo.: The School of the Ozarks Press, 1971), 211–12, 232; and Billie Touchstone Hardaway, *These Hills, My Home* (Republic, Mo.: Westernn Printing Company, 1980), 85.

89. Bee hives were often made from hollow logs. Pioneers preferred the gum species, but commonly used Linn trees because of their "unpleasant taste to mice and other field rodents which would otherwise have chewed through the hives to get to the honey." Lynwood Montell, "The Upper South and the Case for Oral Folk History," *Proceedings of the Pioneer America Society* 1 (1972): 93.

90. It seems odd that the settler's children could not distinguish a panther from a wolf, but Turnbo relates other instances where children—and even adults—could not identify a wild animal. Ben Stults recorded how young neighbor Ben Garber in Stone County, Missouri, mistook three deer for three goats. Stults, "A Sketch," 55–56.

91. Turnbo uses the terms *wildcat* or *catamount* to distinguish the bobcat, *Lynx rufus,* from the panther. Both species of North American cat occupied the same range in Missouri and Arkansas.

92. Fire-hunting was done at night, using a torch to illuminate the eyes of deer.

As mentioned elsewhere in the Turnbo Collection, "mossing" meant the coming of deer to the streams or springs to eat the "moss" or algae that grew there. Mossing time was late summer when the rivers usually had lots of filamentous algae, commonly called moss, and deer were supposed to come to the river to feed on the moss. Modern biologists consulted are unaware of such activity in deer today.

93. By the period 1900–1910, the approximate time Turnbo conducted most of his interviews, the big-game populations had been decimated, a result of increasing population in the late nineteenth century, the construction of railroads, which offered a ready market for game, and the railroads' sponsorship of hunting and fishing guides—an important aspect of early tourism in the Ozarks.

There was, however, a strong commercial market for wild game of all species. Buyers collected fur and pelts at general mercantiles, and hunters could also mail their kill to St. Louis. Missouri newspapers during the 1880s began to report the great diminution of deer population that was supported by Ben Stults's reminiscences in southwest Missouri. One early twentieth-century account in Ozark County claimed that 90 percent of the hides consisted of possum and the rest were coons and skunks. "Catching 10 or 12 possums a night and selling them for an average of 25 cents was easy money as well as fun . . . I do not know whether there were any game laws or not; certainly if there were any game laws the people did not pay much attention to them," wrote Omer E. Brown in *Son of Pioneers: Recollections of an Ozarks Lawyer* (Point Lookout, Mo.: The School of the Ozarks Press, 1973), 101, 103. Tate Page wrote of his Uncle Joe in 1955 that "It was not deer season but that hadn't bothered him in the least. It is reasonable to assume he had never owned a hunting license. Man-made rules never bothered mountain men like Uncle Joe." Tate C. Page, *The Voices of Moccasin Creek* (Point

Lookout, Mo.: The School of the Ozarks Press, 1979), 410. In Shannon County, Missouri, the absence of large game and the market hunt for small game, including a listing of animals killed with different weapons, can be followed in the years 1906–26 in the William A. French Diaries, Joint Collection, University of Missouri–Rolla. See Stults, "A Sketch," 64; and see the discussion by Richard West Sellars about field sports and tourism in his "Early Promotion and Development of Missouri's Natural Resources" (Ph.D. diss., University of Missouri, 1972), 120–78.

94. During the antebellum decades, 1820–60, the upper White River country, especially counties in Missouri, did business along a north-south trade axis that led to Springfield, to towns on the Osage River (Warsaw and Linn Creek), and to Boonville on the Missouri River. The primary road north from Springfield was called the Boonville Road, and Boonville Street remains today.

95. There are three species of buffalo fish in Missouri. They are seldom caught on hook and line but are fine food fishes. According to William L. Pflieger, author of *The Fishes of Missouri* (Jefferson City: Missouri Department of Conservation, 1975), in a personal communication to James F. Keefe, records of any species of buffalo fish in the White River in modern times are scarce. There was an oral report of a bigmouth buffalo caught ten miles south of Reeds Spring, Stone County, Missouri, in 1940, but intensive sampling of the White River from 1946 to 1956 recorded sixty species of fish, but no buffalo fish. Pflieger says, "I have no reason to doubt the authenticity of the early report by Allen Lucas. Probably, White River was a very different stream with a somewhat different fauna at that time than it has been in the last fifty years . . . I would not rule out the probable occurrence of one or both of the other buffalo species." William L. Pflieger, letter to James F. Keefe, n.d.

96. *Fice* is a corruption of the term *feist,* meaning a small dog. It is used chiefly in the South.

Tales of Various Species

97. Schwartz and Schwartz, *The Wild Mammals of Missouri,* 328–32.

98. A log chute was where logs were pushed off the river bank into the water. There they were formed into rafts and floated down to a sawmill. A log chute may still be seen on the north side of the White River, a half mile downstream from Peel Ferry.

99. Turnbo's cedar is the eastern red cedar, *Juniperus virginiana,* although on some Ozark bluffs the Ash juniper, *J. mexicana,* is found.

100. The height of harvesting the upper White River's cedar was in the first decade of the twentieth century, although cedar rafting began in the 1880s. The Eagle Pencil Company of Danbury, Connecticut, had facilities at Branson, Missouri, and at Cotter, Arkansas, and hired hundreds of woodsmen to cut, haul, and float cedar logs. The huge Hanford Cedar Yard, Batesville, became a

significant market. After the Missouri and North Arkansas Railroad crossed the White River, one float, composed of some 185,000 logs, drifted for twenty-two days on the Buffalo River to the railhead at Gilbert. The construction of the M. N. A. Railroad from Seligman, Missouri, to Helena, Arkansas, created a boom in Arkansas Ozarks timber products, ca. 1903–20. Lawrence R. Handley, "Settlement Across Northern Arkansas as Influenced by the Missouri and North Arkansas Railroad," *Arkansas Historical Quarterly* 33 (Winter 1974): 273–92; Hardaway, *These Hills*, 89–93. For reminiscent accounts, see Daniel Boone Lackey, "Cutting and Floating Red Cedar Logs in North Arkansas," *Arkansas Historical Quarterly* 19 (Winter 1960): 361–70; and George Clinton Arthur, *Backwoodsmen: Daring Men of the Ozarks* (Boston: Christopher Publishing House, 1940), 84–85.

101. Water oak, *Quercus nigra*, common along streams.

102. The bung was the stopper in the whiskey barrel.

103. Turnbo's accounts conform to other local reports that claim that wildlife of all species made a dramatic comeback in the region during the Civil War. Because of the war, large areas were devoid of human population, a condition that favored wildlife.

104. The coon market, like others, fluctuates. The Davy Crockett craze in the 1950s, for example, created a great demand. The opening of the Ozarks coon season in recent years, however, has been important economically to coon hunters. They value their coon dogs highly, as a first night's hunt may net pelts worth several hundred dollars when sold. A hunter in the Buffalo Valley during the Depression said he could make as much as a regular month's wages by hunting coon. Hurchal, Mrs. Norma, and Eddie Fowler, interview with Lynn Morrow and Kay Murnan, 6 June 1983, Boxley Valley Oral History Project, Center for Ozarks Studies, Southwest Missouri State University and Buffalo River National Park.

105. Malaria was *the* United States disease of the late nineteenth century. Turnbo, unaware of recent medical discoveries, was not aware of the role of the mosquito in transmitting malaria and did not equate malaria with the old-time chills and fever. Malaria was not as common in the upland Ozarks as it was in the lowland regions, where early settlers often were plagued by the "ague."

Following its introduction into American medicine in the 1830s, quinine became one of several ingredients in compounds dispensed in pills. The widespread use of these pills by patent medicine entrepreneurs accounts, in part, for the success of some patent medicines in the treatment of malaria. Numerous spas sprang up around mineral springs, where people came to be treated for ague and other complaints. Hot Springs and Eureka Springs, Arkansas, and Excelsior Springs, Missouri, all had their origins in such spas. These represent towns, growing up around spas, that persisted; many others have disappeared. See Erwin H. Ackernecht, *The History and Geography of the Most Important Diseases* (New York: Hafner Publishing Company, 1965); and Melinda S. Meade, John W. Florin, and Wilbert M. Gesler, *Medical Geography* (New York: The Guilford Press, 1988).

106. Being entertained by viewing violence between animals or by inflicting violence upon various natural species has been a cultural factor for centuries. At Batesville on 4 July 1842, the celebration included a "bear-baiting contest," in which a two-year-old bear was pitted against all the dogs in town; the bear died of his wounds. The diffusion of bourgeois culture and manners throughout the Western world has tempered this impulse. Johnson's response that the activity was "sport" but "none to him" is a sentiment, for example, voiced today by commentators on cockfighting. For the national context of the latter, see Charles H. McCaghy and Arthur G. Neal, "The Fraternity of Cockfighters: Ethical Embellishments of an Illegal Sport," *Journal of Popular Culture* 8 (Winter 1974): 557–69; and Steven L. Del Sesto, "Roles, Rules, and Organization: A Descriptive Account of Cockfighting in Rural Louisiana," *Southern Folklore Quarterly* 39 (March 1975): 1–14. The bear story is from Malcolm J. Rohrbough, *The Trans-Appalachian Frontier: People, Societies, and Institutions, 1775–1850* (Belmont, Calif.: Wadsworth Publishing Company, 1990), 234.

107. A water turtle of this size probably was the alligator snapping turtle, *Macroclemys temminckii*. Their carapace length is from 15 to 26 inches and the record weight is 219 pounds, according to Tom R. Johnson, *The Amphibians and Reptiles of Missouri* (Jefferson City: Missouri Department of Conservation, 1987).

108. The fox squirrel, *Sciurus niger rufiventer*, is the larger of the two squirrel species found in the White River country, the other being the gray squirrel, *Sciurus carolinensis*. Although their ranges overlap, the fox squirrel seems to prefer more open woods.

109. Borrowers and lenders traded notes that were IOUs and legally binding. Any survey of county probate cases of the period contains numerous examples. Lenders sometimes carried these notes for many years, and it was not uncommon for the note never to be retired.

110. There are a number of early accounts of gray squirrels performing mass migrations, and this may be what McKinney observed. Such migrations seem to have been more common in the past and probably were in response to some environmental pressure, such as food shortage. The phenomenon was noted in the southeast Missouri Ozarks by Theodore Pease Russell in *A Connecticut Yankee in the Frontier Ozarks*, 250–51.

111. The Isabella post office operated in the years 1856–64 and from 1867 to the present. It was earlier called "Goober Spring" for the area's reputed inability to grow goober peas. Schultz, *Missouri Post Offices;* and Linnie J. Kyle, "Goober Spring Becomes Lake Resort," *The Old Mill Run* 3 (October 1988): 5.

112. Turnbo gave Lige Motley credit for being one of the great hunters of Marion County. Motley told of fire-hunting on the White River one night in a drifting canoe that passed among seventy-five deer and how interesting it was to "view their beautiful forms and shining eyeballs all around us" before he opened fire. In another account, Motley confirmed the great hunting years following the Civil War as he recounted his kill of thirty-five deer in August 1867 near Talbert's Ferry. Turnbo Collection, 9:63, 82.

113. Tennessean John "Jack" Haggard settled on Swan Creek, Taney County, in 1841. He enlisted in the Confederacy and moved to Arkansas during the war. He spent his later years at Peel, Arkansas, and gave several hunting stories to Turnbo. Turnbo Collection, 6:40, 10:32.

114. Benjamin F. McKinney (1838–?) came from Tennessee with his parents to Taney County in 1846. The family owned a few slaves, and in 1862 Ben joined the Confederacy in Yellville, served the duration of the war, and accompanied Gen. Sterling Price on his famous invasion of Missouri in 1864. In 1868 he and his new bride, Belveretta Casey, moved to the White River above Forsyth at modern Long Beach where the land is still known as McKinney Bend. They had no children of their own, but reared six orphans. Mrs. McKinney was known as the hunter of the family. E. J. and L. S. Hoenshel, *Stories of the Pioneers* (Branson, Mo.: *Branson White River Leader*, 1915; reprint, Forsyth, Mo.: Little Photo Gallery, 1985), 60–70; and *A Reminiscent History of the Ozark Region*, 276–77.

115. The Casey family migrated in 1726 from Tyrone County, Ireland, to Maryland. Descendants lived in Virginia, South Carolina, Georgia, and eastern Tennessee before coming to the Ozarks in 1834. Abner Casey was a millwright on the Buffalo River in Newton County, Arkansas, and his son Levi (1809–?), a small slaveholder, settled in 1848 on Swan Creek near Forsyth. He and two sons served the Confederacy, and in their absence guerrillas burned several houses in their neighborhood, including some Casey buildings. Levi's house, however, survived, and a descendant donated it to Silver Dollar City, where it was moved to become a principal pioneer icon in the theme park. Modern Casey Road in Swan Valley memorialized the family name. Margaret Casey, "Early History of the Casey Family," *White River Valley Historical Quarterly* 1 (Spring 1964): 3–5; and Hoenshel and Hoenshel, *Stories of the Pioneers*, 65, 68.

116. Turning squirrels is a hunting strategy whereby one person moves to one side of a tree, thus driving the squirrel to the side of the tree the gunner is on. Lone hunters sometimes frighten squirrels to move to their side of the tree by throwing a branch to the opposite side.

117. As is mentioned in the previous anecdote, Clark did fail, apparently purposefully, to deliver honey to Abe Cole.

118. Some bee hunters did have exceptional eyesight, which they could use to "course a bee." However, most bee hunters attracted bees with bait—honey or syrup or burning sections of honey comb—and then followed their flight to the tree hive. Of course, not all pioneers were adept at the many skills required for successful hunting. For details of bee hunting, see Douglas Mahnkey, *Hill and Holler Stories* (Point Lookout, Mo.: School of the Ozarks Press, 1975; reprint, Branson, Mo.: The Ozarks Mountaineer, 1984), 218–20.

119. Sumach, or sumac, is *Rhus spp.* There are several species of this small tree or large shrub in the region. The staghorn sumac is the common one.

120. This practice was apparently used throughout the country. A successful hunt for honey resulted in deer skins that were hung full of honey from a wagon's ridge pole for the trip home. These sacks were later hung in a smokehouse where

women separated the honey and the beeswax. Hunters like Friedrich Gerstäcker made sack-like cases from deer skins and filled them with gallons of bear grease in order to transport it on horseback. Craftsmen also made primitive bellows from tanned deer skins to operate small smelters. See William Monks' excellent account of deer sacks in his *A History of Southern Missouri and Northern Arkansas: Being an Account of the Early Settlements, the Civil War, the Ku-Klux, and Times of Peace* (West Plains, Mo.: West Plains Journal Company, 1907), 9–11.

121. The "punk" mentioned in old accounts, used to catch the spark from flint and steel, remains something of a mystery. Some accounts state that it was the rotted wood of certain trees, which are never identified. Russell, in his writings in the *Ironton Register*, refers to punk, also, as being the "dry fungus found on the inside of some kinds of old dead trees"; see Theodore Pease Russell, *A Connecticut Yankee in the Frontier Ozarks*, 232. George Clinton Arthur in his *Backwoodsmen*, writing about the Big Piney and Gasconade rivers, referred to it as *spunk*, which could be found in decayed logs and was "a soft velvet-like substance which burns easily." Thomas Jerome Estes, in his *Early Days and War Times in Northern Arkansas* (Lubbock, Tex.: privately printed, 1928), 13, said that spunk was "a soft dry substance that grew in oak trees." Charred cotton or linen cloth was the preferred medium in which to catch the sparks, but probably was not always available.

122. The ironic success of modern conservation practices in the Ozarks might be measured in Missouri, in part, by the fact that reported illegal killings of eagles is on the rise, reaching nine in 1989.

123. Turnbo's "grey eagle" is puzzling. He distinguishes bald eagles, so we must assume his grey eagle is an immature bald eagle (most likely, since bald eagles do not get the white tail and head until their fourth year) or a golden eagle. Both species are known from Missouri and Arkansas, but the bald eagle is more common. The golden eagle is believed to be somewhat more predatory than the bald eagle.

124. Miles Pease (?–1879) was a native of Vermont who superintended mills at Lowell, Massachusetts, and Burlington, Vermont, prior to his immigration in 1854 to Minnesota. In 1859 he came to Missouri and worked along the Missouri River Valley before locating in 1865 in Rolla, and in 1867 he built one of the very first postwar regional saw- and grist-milling concerns on the Big North Fork River in eastern Douglas County. His descendants continued significant milling concerns in Douglas and Ozark counties, and they also managed the large Enterprise Roller Mills at West Plains, Missouri. *A Reminiscent History of the Ozark Region*, 369–70.

125. This is surely an exaggeration.

126. The large Wood family had immigrated to the upper White River by the mid-1820s and some married into the Coker family. George Wood married Nancy Coker, the youngest daughter of Buck Coker, and George's Creek was named for him. In 1854 he built a water mill on East Sugar Loaf Creek at Big Spring near modern Monarch. One of George and Nancy's daughters, Jane,

married "Dud" Coker. Turnbo Collection, 7:28, 21:31; and Earl Berry, *History of Marion County* (Little Rock: International Graphics Industries, 1977), 273.

127. The bald-faced hornet, *Vespula maculata,* a social wasp, builds a large nest, covered with a papery substance, in tree limbs.

128. That is, the house was a round log house without pier foundations and no normal crawl space under the floor. No folk builder, intending to live in one place for some time, would have constructed a hewed log house and not built it on some kind of foundation.

129. The yellow jacket is a small, social wasp that nests in the ground. They are aggressive, and when they are attracted to areas where organic refuse accumulates, such as picnic areas, they can render such areas unusable with their vicious stings.

130. Cayenne pepper is a very pungent powder obtained from the dried and ground pods and seeds of various species of *Capsicum,* especially *C. annuum* and *C. frutescens,* used as a condiment in cookery and as a stimulant in medicine. It is named for Cayenne, French Guiana. *Oxford English Dictionary,* 2d ed., s.v. "cayenne pepper."

Tales of Snakes and Centipedes

131. The Cokers were premier bear hunters. By the late 1820s the mouth of Bear Creek was the site of a major market hunting industry that historically had moved up the White River from its eighteenth-century base at Arkansas Post to Oil Trough, to the mouth of the Big North Fork River, and to Bear Creek. Just prior to the War of 1812, three hunters descended from the upper White River with three hundred bear skins and eight hundred gallons of bear oil to sell. Schoolcraft noted that it was at the head of Bear Creek that hunters procured flints for their rifles. On lower Bear Creek, some thirty men worked at Dr. Alvah Jackson's bear-oil rendering plant: barrel makers, bear skinners, rendering operators, and boatmen who transported their product downstream. The fame of the Great Bend of the upper river encouraged such men as Kansas City merchant and frontiersman Alexander Majors to come to Taney County to hunt bear in 1839. See Alexander Majors, "Hunting Black Bear in Taney County," *White River Valley Historical Quarterly* 1 (October 1961): 10–11; Dwight Pitcaithley, "Settlement of the Arkansas Ozarks: The Buffalo River Valley," *Arkansas Historical Quarterly* 37 (Autumn 1978): 205; Steele T. Kennedy, "Bears Once Important to Life of Arkansas Hills," *Ozarks Mountaineer* 6 (May 1958): 3; and Henry Rowe Schoolcraft, *Journal of a Tour into the Interior of Missouri and Arkansas in 1818 and 1819,* ed. Hugh Park (London: Phillips & Company, 1821: reprint, Van Buren, Ark.: Press-Argus Printers, 1955), 133.

132. The first surveys in Arkansas resulted from promises given to veterans of the War of 1812. Surveyors conducted a baseline and principal meridian survey establishing a corner in eastern Arkansas in 1815. A new land office opened in St. Louis in 1818 that was to prepare lands for sale in the White River country and

elsewhere, and the Batesville Land District was created the same year. The land office business was a slow and controversial process that dragged on for years. Turnbo refers to the "first division line" that Joseph Brown (1784–1849) ran in 1823. The second line was run some twenty years later and is the survey in his story. Surveys for land entry in most of the upper White River country did not begin until ca. 1840 and afterward. Maps that depict the development of land districts and offices affecting the general area in 1819 and 1834 may be seen in Malcolm J. Rohrbough, *The Land Office Business: The Settlement and Administration of American Public Lands, 1789–1837* (Belmont, Calif.: Wadsworth Publishing Company, 1990), 104, 180. Two surveyors discovered the corner trees of the 1815 lines in 1921, and a granite marker commemorates the site for public viewing near Helena, Arkansas. See Carl Stamps, "Sally Hollow Historical Marker," *Carroll County Historical Society Quarterly* 32 (Winter 1986–1987): 11; Robert R. Logan, "Notes on the First Land Surveys in Arkansas," *Arkansas Historical Quarterly* 19 (Autumn 1960): 262–65; and Weaver, "Setting the Cornerstones of Missouri: 1815–1989," 4–9.

133. Turnbo's "diamond rattlesnake" must surely have been the timber rattlesnake, *Crotalus horridus*. Tom R. Johnson, in *The Amphibians and Reptiles of Missouri*, says there are no valid records of western diamondback rattlesnakes, *Crotalus atrox*, from Missouri, and that timber rattlesnakes were wrongly identified early as diamondbacks.

134. That is, it was rattling.

135. Hunting families, early on, may have had venison in their regular diet. The most common meat consumed in the nineteenth-century Ozarks, and throughout the South, however, was pork. See the classic study by Sam Bowers Hilliard, *Hog Meat and Hoecake: Food Supply in the Old South, 1840–1860* (Carbondale: Southern Illinois University Press, 1972).

136. The copperhead is *Agkistrodon contortrix contortrix*, the southern copperhead, or the Osage copperhead, *A. c. phaeogaster*. Populations of the species congregate at favorite wintering sites in autumn—usually south-facing, rocky ledges. It is the most commonly encountered venomous snake in the region, although there is no Missouri record of a human death caused by this species. Johnson, *The Amphibians and Reptiles of Missouri*, 306–08.

137. Some Ozarkers continue to hunt snakes in caves during the winter. One area in which such hunting occurs is the Sunklands, a large collapsed karst area in Shannon County, Missouri, where snake hunters search the caverns and kill as many snakes as possible before the snakes awake.

138. Commonly known as the "black snake," the black rat snake, *Elaphe obsoleta obsoleta*, is a forest-dwelling species. There is a record of a black rat snake measuring 101 inches, but the largest Missouri specimen measured 84 inches according to Johnson in *The Amphibians and Reptiles of Missouri*, 240–42.

139. The wahoo, *Euonymus atropurpureus*, also called burning bush, is a large shrub or small tree of open woods, banks of streams, and thickets. The winged elm, *Ulmus alata*, is sometimes called wahoo.

140. This plum tree was either the wild plum, *Prunus americana*, or the

Chickasaw plum, *P. angustifolia,* both shrubs or small trees of thickets or the woodland border.

141. Possibly the Cooper's hawk, *Accipiter cooperii,* or the sharp-shinned hawk, *Accipiter striatus,* both birds of the open woodlands.

142. The eastern coachwhip, *Masticophis flagellum flagellum,* a large, slender, fast moving snake of the Ozarks region. Adults range from 42 to 60 inches in length. It prefers dry, rocky, brushy, or wooded hillsides, especially cedar glades. It is considered Missouri's fastest snake. See Johnson, *The Amphibians and Reptiles of Missouri,* 259–60.

143. Mr. McCollough was relating an old fable in snake lore as a personal incident. Turnbo relates it uncritically, but surely must have had reservations about its authenticity. There is no such thing as a hoop snake. The claims for hoop snakes are related to other such exaggerations collected by Vance Randolph in "Fabulous Monsters in the Ozarks," *Arkansas Historical Quarterly* 9 (Spring 1950): 65–75.

144. Large Missouri centipedes are usually *Scolopendra viridus,* whose habitat is dry, rocky bluffs and glades.

145. Centipedes bite with jaws; they do not sting. Very large centipedes may inflict a painful bite. Glands at the base of the jaw produce poison, which causes the area about the bite to become swollen, feverish, and painful. The swelling and tenderness may persist for several weeks.

146. It is reported that centipede bites sometimes suppurate and are slow to heal. However, the description of the course of this child's illness is more reminiscent of a brown recluse spider's bite than of a centipede's. Gerstäcker, in 1867, had reported the same conclusion: "An American quack told him a centipede had crawled over it [an arm], but the fool didn't know that, at most, such bugs cause only temporary infections." Bukey and Bukey, trans. and eds., "Arkansas After the War," 264.

147. The tip of each leg does indeed have a sharp claw, but it is not a stinger, though simple observation might lead one to think that it is. The three "pointers" are incredibly strong grasping hooks but contain no stingers.

148. Centipedes do take care of their young. Despite this excellent observation by Mr. Jones, he had to have overlooked some small crack or opening for the centipede to have entered.

149. Wildlife ecologist Dennis E. Figg of the Missouri Department of Conservation observes that today a twelve-inch centipede is barely believable and an eighteen-inch specimen would be incredible. He believes the giant centipede has declined in numbers because of altered habitat, the loss of glades in Missouri.

Chapter 5: "Hearts of Stone": The War at Home

1. Leo E. Huff, "Confederate Arkansas: A History of Arkansas During the Civil War" (master's thesis, University of Arkansas, May 1964), 182–83. The most

recent account concerning bushwhackers is Michael Fellman, *Inside War: The Guerrilla Conflict in Missouri During the American Civil War* (New York: Oxford University Press, 1989).

2. Huff, "Confederate Arkansas," 185–86. For a summary of guerrilla war in the White River country, see Leo E. Huff, "Guerrillas, Jayhawkers, and Bushwhackers in Northern Arkansas During the Civil War," *Arkansas Historical Quarterly* 24 (Summer 1965): 127–48.

3. Occasionally, Turnbo wrote about healing the emotional wounds of the war in forgiveness and honoring the soldiers of both sides. By the time he wrote these sentiments, he surely must have attended the numerous turn-of-the-century encampments held for veterans of both sides. Turnbo's sentiments sound as though he listened carefully to the orators who were popular at the encampments.

4. The Samuel Milum family left Tennessee to come to Marion County in 1844. Brice (1823–?), one of Samuel's sons, was a Yellville merchant when the Civil War began. Brice's son Thomas served with Turnbo in the Twenty-seventh Arkansas Confederate Infantry. Brice subsequently occupied the old Joe Coker house in Lead Hill, owned a small mill there, and became the source of several stories for Silas Turnbo. The Milum cemetery is located on Crooked Creek several miles below Harrison, and Milum Spring was just south of Harrison. Silas C. Turnbo Collection, 12:20, 24:12, Springfield–Greene County Public Library, Springfield, Missouri.

5. Yellville was burned three times during the war. Federal troops burned the business section early in the war. The second burning, by Gen. F. J. Herron from the Federal garrison at Ozark, Missouri, apparently took place in fall 1862. The third burning, by Capt. Jonas Webb's bushwhacker forces, was the most severe—some thirty buildings, including two hotels, were torched. Near the end of the war, local men trapped Webb and most of his comrades near Shipp's Ferry below the mouth of the Buffalo River on the White River and killed them. Adding to Yellville's housing problems, Federals dismantled log houses to construct a breastworks in anticipation of a Confederate assault. Thomas Jerome Estes, *Early Days and War Times in Northern Arkansas* (Lubbock, Tex.: privately printed, 1928), 10; Earl Berry, *History of Marion County* (Little Rock: International Graphics Industries, 1977), 75–80; and Elmo Ingenthron, *Borderland Rebellion: A History of the Civil War on the Missouri-Arkansas Border* (Branson, Mo.: The Ozarks Mountaineer, 1980), 302–03.

6. Territory south of the Great Bend of the White River in Taney County was known as secessionist country during the Civil War. These southern men who signed up with Confederate troops did so in Arkansas. Later in the war, Confederates ordered Union sympathizers to leave the country and "not stop south of White River on penalty of death." Mount Pleasant, Iowa, *Home Journal*, 4 April 1863.

7. The Fourteenth Regiment was the one joined by Silas's father, James C. Turnbo.

8. Silas Turnbo served in the Twenty-seventh Arkansas Confederate

Infantry from June 1862 to June 1865. It was organized in Yellville and manned by soldiers from the upper White River neighborhoods in modern Boone, Carroll, Marion, Madison, Newton, Searcy, and Fulton counties, Arkansas, and Taney County, Missouri. Turnbo himself wrote the regimental history, *History of the Twenty-seventh Arkansas Confederate Infantry*, ed. Desmond Walls Allen (Conway:, Ark.: Arkansas Research, 1988). Turnbo identified himself as the author of "A Private of Company A of Said Regiment—An Honest Man and a Good Soldier," although he claimed to have been a fourth sergeant, too. Turnbo, *History of the Twenty-seventh Arkansas Confederate Infantry*, 72, 160.

9. Camp Bragg, located at modern Prescott, Arkansas, was named for Gen. Braxton Bragg (1817–1876), a national hero at the Battle of Buena Vista in the Mexican War, a favorite of Jefferson Davis, and a controversial military leader. Turnbo remembered his stay at Camp Bragg well as it was the location where the hated Col. James R. Shaler was relieved of his command. Turnbo blamed Shaler's harsh discipline for numerous desertions from the Twenty-seventhth Infantry. Turnbo, *History of the Twenty-seventh Arkansas Confederate Infantry*, 169–70; and Ezra J. Warner, *Generals in Gray: Lives of the Confederate Commanders* (Baton Rouge: Louisiana State University Press, 1959), 30–31.

10. Lt. (later Capt.) John Curtis Rea (1837–1907), born in Illinois, came with his father to Marion County in 1846. He had half-brothers who served on both sides during the Civil War. Rea Valley below Yellville is named for the family. Lieutenant Rea, who intervened for Silas with Colonel Shaler, also figured in other conflicts with Shaler. Turnbo wrote, "Capt. Rea always stood for the rights of his men and would give his aid and protection to any of the boys when they deserved it." See Turnbo Collection, 1:29–31, 1:42–43, 19:8–9.

11. Captain Wood was apparently a member of the large Wood family in Marion County.

12. Maj. John W. Methvin (?–1863) lived at Cowan Barrens, Marion County. He was circuit clerk of the county, 1858–62, enlisting in the Twenty-seventh Arkansas Infantry in 1862. The federals captured him at Talbert Barrens, Baxter County, in October 1862 and took him as a prisoner of war to Rolla, Missouri, where he died. His daughter married J. W. Coker. Turnbo Collection, 13:46; and *A Reminiscent History of the Ozark Region* (Chicago: Goodspeed Brothers, Publishers, 1894), 670.

13. Lt. (later Capt.) A. S. "Bud" Wood gave several stories to Turnbo. He was a member of the Abram Wood family, which migrated from South Carolina to Tennessee to the mouth of the Big North Fork River in 1825. The next year they took residence near Shawneetown, where they did some trading with the Indians. His father, William, was county judge in Marion during the period 1838–40. A. S. was a witness to the King and Everett War at Yellville in the late 1840s. Turnbo Collection, 18:75, 26:81, 83.

14. Probably Col. J. D. White, the officer in charge of the Ninth Infantry Regiment of the Missouri Confederate State Guard at Helena, Arkansas. Elmo Ingenthron, *Borderland Rebellion*, 55.

Col. Robert Glenn Shaver organized the Seventh Arkansas Infantry in 1861; in 1862 he organized the Thirty-eighth Arkansas Infantry and in 1864 was elected colonel of the Twenty-seventh. Known as "Fighting Bob," he led men from Independence, Jackson, and Howard counties. His surrender at Jacksonport on 20 June 1865 is considered the last formal surrender of an organized Confederate force.

15. The dictatorial and volatile Thomas Carmichael Hindman (1818–1868), lawyer, congressman, and hero at the Battle of Shiloh, assumed control of the Trans-Mississippi District at Little Rock on 30 May 1862. He strove to rebuild the Confederate capacity in Arkansas, especially in support of southern units operating in the Ozarks, and enacted severe disciplinary commands. Desertion of southern troops became a major problem as Hindman overstepped his authority (for example, his declaration of martial law); his regional command lasted only sixty days as he lost the Battle of Prairie Grove. He fled to Mexico after the war, but returned to Arkansas, where he was assassinated in 1868. See Bobby L. Roberts, "General T. C. Hindman and the Trans-Mississippi District," *Arkansas Historical Quarterly* 32 (Winter 1973): 297–311; and Thomas E. Wright, ed., "The Capture of Van Buren, Arkansas, During the Civil War: From the Diary of a Union Horse Soldier," *Arkansas Historical Quarterly* 38 (Spring 1979): 75–76.

16. Several reminiscences of the war written by Federals in the Army of the Frontier recalled that the natives preferred rebel scrip to U.S. currency in northwest Arkansas and southwest Missouri. The soldiers bought counterfeit Confederate scrip at job printing rates in St. Louis, which Ozarkers honored and, in some cases, gave change for! This "down South money" circulated freely as Turnbo says, but its value decreased as the war progressed, and it was worth nothing at the end. John Bradbury, letter to Lynn Morrow, 27 March 1990.

17. Miliken Bald was a prairie hill in Taney County named for Charley Miliken, a hunter who built an early hut there. The hamlet Cedar Creek is just to the northwest, and the Bald Knob schoolhouse/church was built here in the late nineteenth century. Turnbo Collection, 6:76, 11:60.

18. Bushwhacking stories that involve hidden gold or silver are common in the Turnbo Collection. James J. Johnston in "Jayhawker Stories: Historical Lore in the Arkansas Ozarks," *Mid-South Folklore* 4 (Spring 1976), 3–9, recounted several examples, including a citation from Turnbo claiming that *jayhawking* was the common term for bushwhacking; however, the term *jayhawker* is rarely used in the Turnbo Collection, although it is common in other Arkansas sources, including John Quincy Wolf's famous *Life in the Leatherwoods: An Ozark Boyhood Remembered* (Memphis: Memphis State University Press, 1974, 1980: reprint, Little Rock: August House, 1988). *Jayhawker* became common usage in Searcy County because of a significant neighborhood Unionist "Peace Society" formed for the protection of lives and property. This famous "jayhawking society" spread to Newton, Marion, Carroll, and Izard counties, and other mountain regions. *Jayhawker* is sometimes used in the southeast Missouri Ozarks (e.g., Howell, Oregon, and Shannon counties), where Gen. James H. McBride led significant

regional activity and support for the Confederacy. Turnbo used *bushwhacker* or *guerrilla*, and he does identify several of the attackers. For the Peace Society see Huff, "Confederate Arkansas," 193–200.

19. Civil War refugees fled to Union garrison towns in and around the Ozarks; the upper White River folks commonly chose Springfield. Turnbo and other regional accounts frequently mention the war exodus to Springfield, for example, the Russell and Gaskin families of Carroll County survived the war there. One Union source who recruited men hiding out in the Ozarks woods wrote, "We proceeded to Springfield with the soldiers and refugees, who when in the line of march formed a column fully three miles in extent of crying children, men swearing, women scolding, dogs barking, mules braying, cattle bellowing and sheep bleating, which formed a babel of unearthly sounds unparalleled by anything that has been upon the boards since." The refugee population in Springfield toward the end of the war was particularly large—one Union report recorded "an unending stream . . . pouring in from Arkansas." For specific examples of many refugees who went to Springfield, see James J. Johnston, "Land of Anarchy, Land of Desolation: Buffalo River, 1861–1865," typescript, 15 February 1978; Lyman G. Bennett, "Recruiting in Dixie," *Christian County Historian* 3 (Spring 1990): 58; Michael A. Hughes, "Wartime Gristmill Destruction in Northwest Arkansas and Military-Farm Colonies," *Arkansas Historical Quarterly* 46 (Summer 1987): 178; John Gaskins, *The Life and Adventures of John Gaskins in the Early History of Northwest Arkansas* (Published by author, 1893; reprint, Eureka Springs, Ark.: Eureka Springs Historical Museum, n.d.), 2; and Jesse Lewis Russell, *Behind These Ozark Hills* (New York: The Hobson Book Press, 1947), 7.

20. The Casebolt house was a dogtrot house, a distinctive frontier model. A generation ago, geographer Martin Wright assembled data concerning the obscure origins of this popular house. Recently, geographers Terry Jordan and Matti Kaups argued that the house was a part of successful woodland pioneering culture initiated by back-country Finns during the seventeenth century in the Delaware Valley. The Scotch-Irish, arriving in the early eighteenth century, adopted and diffused this house form throughout the American frontier. It was common in the Ozarks and persisted longer in Arkansas than in Missouri. It has become a frontier icon in public preservation for visitors in many Upland South communities, such as Forsyth, Missouri. Terry Jordan and Matti Kaups published a case study of the dogtrot house in its broadest cultural terms in "Folk Architecture in Cultural and Ecological Context," *Geographical Review* 77 (January 1987): 52–75. See also Terry G. Jordan and Matti Kaups, *The American Backwoods Frontier* (Baltimore and London: The Johns Hopkins University Press, 1989), 179–210; and Martin Wright, "The Antecedents of the Double–pen House Type," *Annals, Association of American Geographers* 48 (1958): 109–17.

21. Turnbo said elsewhere that "The Casebolts were strictly southern and the old folks, including their children, were true and faithful to the South." Robert Casebolt, a justice of the peace on Big Creek, was killed during the war on the Buffalo River. Turnbo Collection, 2:46, 61; 26:56.

22. Families on upper Big Creek and upper Little North Fork were known for Unionist support during the Civil War. Indeed, the Turnbos sought refuge among them in 1865. Protem became the location for the Green Hampton Post of the G. A. R. in the 1880s. Celebrations were attended by citizens from Taney, Ozark, Boone, and Marion counties. Elmo Ingenthron, *Land of Taney: A History of an Ozark Commonwealth* (Point Lookout, Mo.: The School of the Ozarks Press, 1974), 411–12.

23. Allen and Keesee were near neighbors, only twelve houses apart on the 1860 census list. At that time, Joe Allen was twenty-six years of age, Alwilda nineteen, and Peter Keesee thirty. Janice Soutee Looney, comp., *Taney Co., Mo., 1860 Fed. Census* (Walnut Grove, Mo.: Janice Soutee Looney, 1987), 42–43.

24. Garrison Post Office (1884–present) is located on upper Swan Creek in southeast Christian County. Schultz, *Missouri Post Offices, 1804–1981* (St. Louis: The American Philatelic Society, St. Louis Branch No. 4, 1982).

25. Swan Post Office (1841–44, 1860–64, 1880–1957) lies on the banks of the creek in north-central Taney County. Robert G. Schultz, *Missouri Post Offices.*

26. Thomas Estes wrote that some people did starve to death. One tradition related that the Abee family lived two weeks on the inside part of slippery elm bark. Estes said that these destitute families did not have guns to hunt game. Others rubbed wheat into a dough and made a soup from it, and others had meals consisting of skunk. Estes, *Early Days and War Times in Northern Arkansas,* 8–9.

27. The standard work on this great natural phenomenon is James L. Penick, *The New Madrid Earthquakes* (Columbia: University of Missouri Press, 1981).

28. Black powder is an explosive propellant made from saltpeter (potassium nitrate), sulphur, and charcoal. The saltpeter mentioned in Turnbo was leached from bat guano deposits in the cave. These deposits in caves were one of the mineral attractions of the greater Missouri Territory "which ought not to be passed over unnoticed," wrote botanist John Bradbury in his *Travels in the Interior of America in the Years 1809, 1810, and 1811* (London: Sherwood, Neely and Jones, 1819; reprint, Lincoln: University of Nebraska Press, 1986), 247. Several locations are discussed by William Clark Breckenridge, "Early Gunpowder Making in Missouri," *Missouri Historical Review* 20 (October 1925): 85–95; and the strategic importance of the saltpeter deposits during the Civil War is discussed by James J. Johnston, "Bullets for Johnny Reb: Confederate Nitre and Mining Bureau in Arkansas," *Arkansas Historical Quarterly* 49 (Summer 1990): 124–67.

29. Turnbo was using *The War of the Rebellion: A Compilation of the Official Records of the Union and Confederate Armies,* ser. 1, vol. 22, pt. 1 (Washington, D.C.: Government Printing Office, 1880–1901). Reports of Union raids on the regional saltpeter works are in *The War of the Rebellion,* 159–60, 213–14.

30. Gen. Samuel Ryan Curtis (1805–1866) was a West Point graduate in 1831, a civil engineer, a lawyer, and a congressman from Iowa in the late 1850s. He commanded the Department of Missouri, 1862–63, the Unionists at Pea Ridge, and was appointed major general for his success. He later commanded the

Department of Kansas, 1863–65, negotiated treaties with Plains Indians after the war, and died while examining construction of the Union Pacific Railroad. Ezra J. Warner, *Generals in Blue: Lives of the Union Commanders* (Baton Rouge: Louisiana State University Press, 1964), 107–08.

31. Gen. Henry Wager Halleck (1815–1872) graduated from West Point in 1839 and later authored a popular book on military science. He was instrumental in California governmental affairs, including the formulation of the constitution, following the Mexican War. In 1854 he headed the leading legal firm in California, but turned his talents to writing, business, and the California militia. He acquired a fortune in publishing, especially in the fields of mining and international law. Marriage and social connections helped him to attain an appointment as major general in August 1861. He brought discipline and order to the Department of Missouri, but floundered in his own military attempts in the field. He spent most of the war in Washington, D.C., offices and continued in military appointments after the war at San Francisco and Louisville until his death. Warner, *Generals in Blue*, 195–97; and see Stephen E. Ambrose, *Halleck: Lincoln's Chief of Staff* (Baton Rouge: Louisiana State University Press, 1962).

32. Francis J. Herron (1837–1902) was an Iowa businessman and Union volunteer. He was a veteran of the First Iowa and Wilson's Creek. He became lieutenant colonel of the Ninth Iowa Infantry and was with the unit at the Battle of Pea Ridge. Although he was captured at Pea Ridge, Herron won a commission as brigadier general for heroism and many years later was awarded a Medal of Honor. He led part of the Army of the Frontier at the Battle of Prairie Grove and was made army commander in 1863. At various times with the Army of the Frontier, Herron's headquarters were at Springfield, Missouri, and at Fayetteville, Arkansas. See Warner, *Generals in Blue*, 228–29; and S. H. M. Byers, *Iowa in War Times* (Des Moines: W. D. Condit and Company, 1888), 438–39.

33. Capt. Milton Burch commanded the Fourteenth Missouri Militia at Ozark, Missouri. On 1 August 1862 he met and repulsed a Confederate attack, following up three days later in pursuit of the Confederates in Taney County. A skirmish occurred at Harrison Snapp's farm near Forsyth, where he captured stock and equipment. In the fall of 1862, he retreated north in the face of Gen. John S. Marmaduke's attack on small garrisons in the area and warned Springfield of Marmaduke's approach. See Howard V. Canan, "Milton Burch: Anti-Guerrilla Fighter," *Missouri Historical Review* 59 (1965): 223–42.

34. Gen. Egbert Benson Brown commanded Federal troops in the loss to Confederate forces at the Battle of Newtonia, near Neosho, Missouri, in September 1862. He was later in charge of Union forces at the Battle of Springfield, Missouri, at the time of Gen. John S. Marmaduke's assault upon the town in January 1863. Apparently, a southern sympathizer in Springfield, hiding along the road, shot Brown—he recovered, living until 1902. Unionists held Springfield, but Missouri Federals were made very uneasy by the Confederates' penetration into southwest Missouri. Ingenthron, *Borderland Rebellion*, 220–35, 262–66.

35. This was probably Capt. Evander McNair (1820–1902), who was appointed brigadier general in November 1862. He was a veteran of battles at Wilson's Creek, Pea Ridge, Vicksburg, Jackson, and Chickamauga. Mark Mayo Boatner, *The Civil War Dictionary* (New York: David McKay Company, 1959).

36. In the spring of 1862, Capt. Milton Burch commanded the Fourteenth Missouri Militia at Ozark; by fall, Maj. John C. Wilber, under the orders of Gen. Francis Herron, was in charge. Ingenthron, *Borderland Rebellion*, 216, 237.

37. Federals made successful raids on several saltpeter works. In late 1862 and early 1863, the Unionists attacked works in western Newton County and in Marion County near Yellville and Dubuque; in 1864 saltpeter works in Searcy County were destroyed. The Confederates exported the mineral to Arkadelphia, where the gunpowder was manufactured. See details in Johnston, "Land of Anarchy, Land of Desolation: Buffalo River, 1861–1865," 42–44.

38. Huntsville had residential and commercial buildings destroyed more than once during the war. The 1850 town had a population of 255, including 43 blacks, and that population had grown to only 312 by 1880. Some Confederates were particularly incensed over Huntsville because the Union's First Regiment, Arkansas Infantry Volunteers, had leaders from Huntsville. Isaac Murphy, Arkansas's first Republican and first Reconstruction governor (1864–68), was one of the Unionists. *History of Benton, Washington, Carroll, Madison, Crawford, Franklin, and Sebastian Counties, Arkansas* (Chicago: Goodspeed Publishing Company, 1889; reprint, Chicago: Goodspeed Publishers, 1978), 455, 466.

39. The Wilmoths came from Tennessee to Madison County in 1853 and to the Sugar Loaf Creek area of northeast Boone County in 1856. Turnbo Collection, 15:36.

40. Turnbo is apparently giving his sister Margaret a chance to participate in his endeavor by telling one of the stories from their family tradition, but apparently Silas himself was present at the robbery while his sister Margaret was not.

41. That is, it was probably soot from a pot that had been sitting in the fireplace.

42. It was common for families to have home remedies in whiskey bottles resting on the fireplace mantle—commonly the content was alcoholic. Consumers purchased blocks of camphor that were taken home and heated over a fire until they melted into a liquid. The melted camphor and a mixture of other elements were then poured into a bottle and placed on the mantle. During respiratory ailments, family members rubbed the contents on their chests or drank some of the liquid. John Hodge (great-grandson of Jimmie Cook, mentioned elsewhere), interview with Lynn Morrow, 4 April 1990.

43. That is, it was concealed in the cellar under the floor.

44. Adam (?–ca. 1864) and Sophronia (?–1890) Weast and family migrated from North Carolina to Yellville in 1850. Their log hotel stood at the west end of Main Street. They were slaveholders, and five sons served the Confederacy. Berry, *History of Marion County*, 264–65.

45. A traditional western view is that Christ will appear in the east on the day

of resurrection. Evidence of the continuing east-west burial orientation (facing Jerusalem) has been observed by geographer Thomas J. Hannon, Jr., in "Nineteenth Century Cemeteries in Central-West Pennsylvania," *Proceedings of the Pioneer America Society* 2 (1973): 23–38. Archaeologists working in southeast Missouri have observed the same custom in cemeteries ca. 1800–1860, and scholars in eastern Kentucky have reported the same. See James E. Price and Cynthia R. Price, *An Investigation of Settlement Patterns and Subsistence on the Ozark Escarpment in Southeast Missouri During the First Half of the Nineteenth Century* (Columbia: Department of Anthropology, University of Missouri, 28 February 1978). Geographer Terry Jordan cited the common practice in Great Britain, including the punitive north-south alignment for evil men. Terry G. Jordan, *Texas Graveyards: A Cultural Legacy* (Austin: University of Texas Press, 1982), 30–33. The most recent scholarly inquiry into the east-west alignment and other diagnostic characteristics of pioneer cemeteries—D. Gregory Jeane, "The Upland South Folk Cemetery Complex," in Richard E. Meyer, ed., *Cemeteries and Gravemarkers: Voices of American Culture,* (Ann Arbor, Mich.: UMI Research Press, 1989)—concludes that this model is distinctive in the landscape from North Carolina to Texas.

WORKS CITED

Books

Ackernecht, Erwin, H. *The History and Geography of the Most Important Diseases.* New York: Hafner Publishing Company, 1965.

Allsopp, Fred W. *Folklore of Romantic Arkansas.* Vols. 1 and 2. Little Rock: The Grolier Society, 1931.

Ambrose, Stephen E. *Halleck: Lincoln's Chief of Staff.* Baton Rouge: Louisiana State University Press, 1962.

Arthur, George Clinton. *Backwoodsmen: Daring Men of the Ozarks.* Boston: Christopher Publishing House, 1940.

Baker, Russell Pierce. *From Memdag to Norsk: A Historical Directory of Arkansas Post Offices, 1832–1971.* Hot Springs, Ark.: Arkansas Genealogical Society, 1988.

Baughman, Ernest W. *Type and Motif—Index of the Folktales of England and North America.* The Hague: Mouton and Company, 1966.

Baughman, J. Ross. *Some Ancestors of the Baughman Family in America; Tracing Back Twelve Generations from Switzerland through Virginia, etc.* Edinburg, Va.: Shenandoah History, Publishers, 1989.

Beringer, Richard E., Herman Hattaway, Archer Jones, and William N. Still, Jr. *Why the South Lost the Civil War.* Athens: University of Georgia Press, 1986.

Berry, Earl. *History of Marion County.* Little Rock: International Graphics Industries, 1977.

Boatner, Mark Mayo. *The Civil War Dictionary.* New York: David McKay Company, 1959.

Bradbury, John. *Travels in the Interior of America in the Years 1809, 1810, and 1811.* London: Sherwood, Neely and Jones, 1819; reprint, Lincoln: University of Nebraska Press, 1986.

Brown, Omer E. *Son of Pioneers: Recollections of an Ozarks Lawyer.* Point Lookout, Mo.: The School of the Ozarks Press, 1973.

Byers, S. H. M. *Iowa in War Times.* Des Moines: W. D. Condit and Company, 1888.

Carter, Clarence Edwin, comp. and ed. *The Territorial Papers of the United States.* Vol. 14, *The Territory of Louisiana-Missouri, 1806–1814.* Washington, D.C.: Government Printing Office, 1949.

Carter, Clarence Edwin, comp. and ed. *The Territorial Papers of the United States.* Vol. 19, *The Territory of Arkansas, 1819–1825.* Washington, D.C.: Government Printing Office, 1953.

Carter, Clarence Edwin, comp. and ed. *The Territorial Papers of the United States.* Vol. 20, *The Territory of Arkansas, 1825–1829.* Washington, D.C.: Government Printing Office, 1954.

Carter, Clarence Edwin, comp. and ed. *The Territorial Papers of the United States.* Vol. 21, *The Territory of Arkansas, 1829–1836.* Washington, D.C.: Government Printing Office, 1954.

Deane, Ernie. *Arkansas Place Names.* Branson, Mo.: The Ozarks Mountaineer, 1988.

Dillahunty, Albert. *Shiloh.* Washington, D.C.: National Park Service Historical Handbook, no. 10, 1955.

Dorson, Richard M. *American Folklore.* Chicago: The University of Chicago Press, 1959.

———. *Man and Beast in American Comic Legend.* Bloomington: Indiana University Press, 1982.

Du Bois, W. E. B. *Black Reconstruction in America.* New York: Russell & Russell, 1935. Reprint, New York: Atheneum, 1983.

du Pratz, Antoine Simon Le Page. *History of Louisiana.* Trans. Joseph G. Tregle, Jr. Baton Rouge: Louisiana State University Press, 1975.

Fair, James R., Jr. *The North Arkansas Line: The Story of the Missouri and North Arkansas Railroads.* San Diego: Howell-North Books, 1969.

Fairbanks, Jonathan, and Clyde Edwin Tuck. *Past and Present of Greene County, Missouri.* Vols. 1 and 2. Indianapolis: A. W. Bowen & Company, 1915.

Fellman, Michael. *Inside War: The Guerrilla Conflict in Missouri During the American Civil War.* New York: Oxford University Press, 1989.

Fernald, Merritt L. *Gray's Manual of Botany.* New York: American Book Company, 1950.

Firearms Assembly I: The NRA Guidebook to Shoulder Arms. Washington, D.C.: National Rifle Association, 1978.

Foley, William E. *The Genesis of Missouri: From Wilderness Outpost to Statehood.* Columbia: University of Missouri Press, 1989.

Foreman, Grant. *Indian Removal.* Norman: University of Oklahoma Press, 1982.

Gerlach, Russel L. *Settlement Patterns in Missouri.* Columbia: University of Missouri Press, 1986.

Gerstäcker, Friedrich. *In the Arkansas Backwoods: Tales and Sketches by Friedrich Gerstäcker.* Ed. James William Miller. Columbia: University of Missouri Press, 1991.

———. *Wild Sports in the Far West.* London: G. Routledge, 1854. Reprint, Durham: University of North Carolina Press, 1968.

Gohdes, Clarence, sel. and ed. *Hunting in the Old South: Original Narratives of the Hunters.* Baton Rouge: Louisiana State University Press, 1967.

Goodwyn, Lawrence. *The Populist Moment: A Short History of the Agrarian Revolt.* New York and Oxford: Oxford University Press, 1978.

Gottschalk, Louis, Clyde Kluckholn, and Robert Angell. *The Use of Personal Documents in History, Anthropology, and Sociology.* New York: Social Science Research Council, 1945.

Gray, Lewis Cecil. *History of Agriculture in the Southern United States to 1860.* Vols. 1 and 2. Washington, D.C.: Carnegie Institution of Washington, 1933.

Hanson, Gerald T., and Carl H. Moneyhon. *Historical Atlas of Arkansas.* Norman: University of Oklahoma Press, 1989.

Hardaway, Billie Touchstone. *These Hills, My Home.* Republic, Mo.: Western Printing Company, 1980.

Hempstead, Fay. *A Pictorial History of Arkansas From Earliest Times to the Year 1890.* St. Louis and New York: N. D. Thompson Publishing Company, 1890.

Higgins, Earl Leroy. *Source Readings in Arkansas History.* Little Rock: Pioneer Press, 1964.

Hilliard, Sam Bowers. *Hog Meat and Hoecake: Food Supply in the Old South, 1840–1860.* Carbondale: Southern Illinois University Press, 1972.

History of Benton, Washington, Carroll, Madison, Crawford, Franklin, and Sebastian Counties, Arkansas. Reprint, Chicago: Goodspeed Publishing, 1889. Chicago: Goodspeed Publishers, 1978.

History of Carroll County, Arkansas. Reprint of the Carroll County section of the Goodspeed Publishing Company's Northwest Arkansas history. Arranged by O. Klute Braswell. Chicago: Goodspeed Publishing, 1889. Reprint, Berryville, Ark.: Braswell Printing Company, n.d.

Hockett, Homer C. *The Critical Method in Historical Research and Writing.* New York: Macmillan Company, 1955.

———. *Introduction to Research in American History.* New York: Macmillan Company, 1938.

Holcombe, R. S. *History of Greene County, Missouri.* St. Louis: Western Historical Company, 1883.

Houck, Louis. *A History of Missouri.* Vol. 2. Chicago: R. R. Connelley and Sons Company, 1908.

Ingenthron, Elmo. *Borderland Rebellion: A History of the Civil War on the Missouri-Arkansas Border.* Branson, Mo.: The Ozarks Mountaineer, 1980.

———. *Land of Taney: A History of an Ozark Commonwealth.* Point Lookout, Mo.: The School of the Ozarks Press, 1974.

James, Edwin. *James's Account of S. H. Long's Expedition, 1819–1820.* Philadelphia: H. C. Carey & I. Lea, 1822–23. Reprint, New York: AMS Press, 1966.

Johns, Paul. *Unto These Hills.* Ozark, Mo.: Bilyeu-Johns Enterprises, 1980.

Johnson, Tom R. *The Amphibians and Reptiles of Missouri.* Jefferson City: Missouri Department of Conservation, 1987.

Jordan, Terry G. *Texas Graveyards: A Cultural Legacy.* Austin: University of Texas Press, 1982.

Jordan, Terry G., and Matti Kaups. *The American Backwoods Frontier.* Baltimore and London: The Johns Hopkins University Press, 1989.

Kappler, Charles J., comp. and ed. *Indian Affairs. Laws and Treaties.* Vol 2. Washington, D.C.: Government Printing Office, 1904.

Keefe, James F. *The First 50 Years.* Jefferson City: Missouri Department of Conservation, 1987.

Lackey, Walter F. *History of Newton County, Arkansas.* Point Lookout, Mo.: The School of the Ozarks Press, 1971.
Lair, Jim, and O. Klute Braswell. *An Outlander's History of Carroll County, Arkansas, 1830–1983.* Marceline, Mo.: Walsworth Publishing Company, 1983.
Leffel, James. *The Construction of Mill Dams: Comprising also The Building of Race and Reservoir Embankments and Head Gates, The Measurement of Streams, Gauging of Water Supply, Etc.* Springfield, Ohio: James Leffel and Company, 1874.
Mahnkey, Douglas. *Hill and Holler Stories.* Point Lookout, Mo.: School of the Ozarks Press, 1975. Reprint, Branson, Mo.: The Ozarks Mountaineer, 1984.
Masterson, James R. *Tall Tales of Arkansas.* Boston: Chapman & Grimes, Publishers, 1943.
McWhiney, Grady. *Cracker Culture: Celtic Ways in the Old South.* Tuscaloosa: University of Alabama Press, 1988.
Meade, Melinda S., John W. Florin, and Wilbert M. Gesler. *Medical Geography.* New York: The Guilford Press, 1988.
Mech, L. David. *The Wolf.* Garden City, N.Y.: The Natural History Press, 1970.
Messick, Mary Ann. *History of Baxter County, 1873–1973.* Little Rock: International Graphics, 1973.
Meyer, Richard E., ed. *Cemeteries and Gravemarkers: Voices of American Culture.* Ann Arbor, Mich.: UMI Research Press, 1989.
Monks, William. *A History of Southern Missouri and Northern Arkansas: Being an Account of the Early Settlements, the Civil War, the Ku-Klux, and Times of Peace.* West Plains, Mo.: West Plains Journal Company, 1907.
Nesbitt, William H., and Jack Reneau, eds. *Records of North American Big Game.* Dumfries, Va.: The Boone and Crockett Club, 1988.
Norris, James D. *The Story of The Maramec Iron Works, 1826–1876.* St. James, Mo.: The James Foundation and The State Historical Society of Wisconsin, 1972.
Nuttall, Thomas. *A Journal of Travels into the Arkansas Territory During the Year 1819.* Philadelphia: T. H. Palmer, 1821. Reprint, Norman: University of Oklahoma Press, 1980.
Oxford English Dictionary. Second Edition. Prepared by J. A. Simpson and E. S. C. Weiner. Oxford: Clarendon Press, 1989.
Owsley, Frank. *Plain Folk of the Old South.* Baton Rouge: Louisiana State University Press, 1949. Reprint, Baton Rouge: Louisiana State University Press, 1982.
Page, Tate C. *The Voices of Moccasin Creek.* Point Lookout, Mo.: The School of the Ozarks Press, 1979.
Peck, John Mason. *A Guide for Emigrants.* Boston: Lincoln and Edmands, 1831. Reprint, New York: Arno Press, 1975.
Penick, James L. *The New Madrid Earthquakes.* Columbia: University of Missouri Press, 1981.
Pflieger, William L. *The Fishes of Missouri.* Jefferson City: Missouri Department of Conservation, 1975.

Phillips, Paul C. *The Fur Trade*. Vols. 1 and 2. Norman: University of Oklahoma Press, 1967.

Pyne, Stephen J. *Fire in America: A Cultural History of Wildland and Rural Fire*. Princeton: Princeton University Press, 1982.

Randolph, Vance. *Ozark Folklore: A Bibliography*. Bloomington: Indiana University Center for Research in the Language Sciences, 1972.

———. *Ozark Magic and Folklore*. (Originally *Ozark Superstitions*.) New York: Columbia University Press, 1947. Reprint, New York: Dover Publications, Inc., 1964.

Rayburn, Otto Ernest. *Ozark Country*. New York: Duell, Sloan & Pearce, 1941.

A Reminiscent History of the Ozark Region. Chicago: Goodspeed Brothers, Publishers, 1894.

Rohrbough, Malcolm J. *The Land Office Business: The Settlement and Administration of American Public Lands, 1789–1837*. Belmont, Calif.: Wadsworth Publishing Company, 1990.

———. *The Trans-Appalachian Frontier: People, Societies, and Institutions, 1775–1850*. Belmont, Calif.: Wadsworth Publishing Company, 1990.

Russell, Jesse Lewis. *Behind These Ozark Hills*. New York: The Hobson Book Press, 1947.

Russell, Theodore Pease. *A Connecticut Yankee in the Frontier Ozarks: The Writings of Theodore Pease Russell*. Ed. James F. Keefe and Lynn Morrow. Columbia: University of Missouri Press, 1988.

Sauer, Carl. *The Geography of the Ozark Highland of Missouri*. Chicago: University of Chicago Press, 1920. Reprint, New York: Greenwood Press, 1968.

Schoolcraft, Henry Rowe. *The Indian in His Wigwam, or Characteristics of the Red Race of America*. New York: W. H. Graham, Tribune Building, 1848.

———. *Information Respecting the History, Condition and Prospects of the Indian Tribes of the United States: Collected and Prepared under the Direction of the Bureau of Indian Affairs per act of Congress of March 3rd, 1847*. Vol. 3. Philadelphia: Lippincott, Grambo & Company, 1853.

———. *Journal of a Tour into the Interior of Missouri and Arkansas in 1818 and 1819*. Ed. Hugh Park. London: Phillips & Company, 1821. Reprint, Van Buren, Ark.: Press-Argus Printers, 1955.

———. *A View of the Lead Mines of Missouri*. New York: Charles Wiley & Company, 1819. Reprint, New York: Arno Press, 1972.

Schultz, Robert G. *Missouri Post Offices, 1804–1981*. St. Louis: The American Philatelic Society, St. Louis Branch No. 4, 1982.

Schwartz, Charles W. and Elizabeth R. *The Wild Mammals of Missouri*. Columbia: University of Missouri Press, 1981.

Solomon, Jack and Olivia. *Cracklin Bread and Asfidity: Folk Recipes and Remedies*. Montgomery: University of Alabama Press, 1979.

Sturtevant, William C., gen. ed. *Handbook of North American Indians*. Vol. 15. Washington, D.C.: Smithsonian Institution, 1978.

Swanton, John R. *The Indian Tribes of North America*. Washington, D.C.: Smithsonian Institutional Bulletin 145, Bureau of American Ethnology, 1952.

Tixier, Victor. *Tixier's Travels on the Osage Prairies.* Ed. John F. McDermott, trans. Albert J. Salvan. Norman: University of Oklahoma Press, 1968.
Turnbo, Silas C. *Fireside Stories of Early Days in the Ozarks, Part One.* Pontiac, Mo.: n.p., 1905.
———. *Fireside Stories of Early Days in the Ozarks, Part Two.* Pontiac, Mo.: n.p., 1907.
———. *History of the Twenty-seventh Arkansas Confederate Infantry.* Ed. Desmond Walls Allen. Conway, Ark.: Arkansas Research, 1988.
———. *Turnbo's Tales of the Ozarks: Bear Stories.* Ed. Desmond Walls Allen. Conway, Ark.: Arkansas Research, 1988.
———. *Turnbo's Tales of the Ozarks: Deer Hunting Stories.* Ed. Desmond Walls Allen. Conway, Ark.: Arkansas Research, 1989.
———. *Turnbo's Tales of the Ozarks: Incidents, Mean Tricks and Fictitious Stories.* Ed. Desmond Walls Allen. Conway, Ark.: Arkansas Research, 1988.
———. *Turnbo's Tales of the Ozarks: Schools, Indians, Hard Times and More Stories.* Ed. Desmond Walls Allen. Conway, Ark.: D. W. Allen, 1987. Rev. ed., Conway, Ark.: Arkansas Research, 1989.
———. *Turnbo's Tales of the Ozarks: War and Guerrilla Stories.* Ed. Desmond Walls Allen. Conway, Ark.: Arkansas Research, 1987. Rev. ed., Conway, Ark.: Arkansas Research, 1989.
Upton, Lucile Morris. *Bald Knobbers.* Caldwell, Idaho: The Caxton Printers, 1939.
Warner, Ezra J. *Generals in Blue: Lives of the Union Commanders.* Baton Rouge: Louisiana State University Press, 1964.
———. *Generals in Gray: Lives of the Confederate Commanders.* Baton Rouge: Louisiana State University Press, 1959.
Wish, Harvey. *The American Historian: A Social-Intellectual History of the Writing of the American Past.* New York: Oxford University Press, 1960.
Wolf, John Quincy. *Life in the Leatherwoods. An Ozark Boyhood Remembered.* Memphis: Memphis State University Press, 1974, 1980. Reprint, Little Rock: August House, 1988.
Woodward, Grace Steele. *The Cherokees.* Norman: University of Oklahoma Press, 1963.
Yates, Norris W. *William T. Porter and the Spirit of the Times: A Study of the BIG BEAR School of Humor.* Baton Rouge: Louisiana State University Press, 1957.

Articles

Abel, Annie Heloise. "The History of Events Resulting in Indian Consolidation West of the Mississippi." In *Annual Report of the American Historical Association for the Year 1906.* Vol. I. Washington, D.C.: Government Printing Office, 1908.
Atherton, Lewis E. "The Santa Fe Trader as Mercantile Capitalist." *Missouri Historical Review* 77 (October 1982): 1–12.

Atkinson, J. H. "Cattle Drives From Arkansas To California Prior to The Civil War." *Arkansas Historical Quarterly* 28 (Autumn 1969): 275–81.
Baker, Russell P. "Jacob Wolf." *Arkansas Historical Quarterly* 37 (Summer 1978): 184–92.
Bennett, Lyman G. "Recruiting in Dixie." *Christian County Historian* 3 (Spring 1990): 57–61.
Breckenridge, William Clark. "Early Gunpowder Making in Missouri." *Missouri Historical Review* 20 (October 1925): 85–95.
Brown, C. Allan. "Horticulture in Early Arkansas." *Arkansas Historical Quarterly* 43 (Summer 1984): 99–124.
Brown, Mattie. "River Transportation in Arkansas, 1819–1890." *Arkansas Historical Quarterly* 1 (December 1942): 342–54.
Brown, Sarah. "The Storm Cellar: A Compass on the Homesteads of Rural Arkansas." *Mid-American Folklore* 12 (Fall 1984): 1–16.
Bukey, Anita, and Evan Burr Bukey, trans. and eds. "Arkansas After the War: From the Journal of Frederick Gerstaecker." *Arkansas Historical Quarterly* 32 (Autumn 1973): 255–73.
Bukey, Evan Burr. "Frederick Gerstaecker in Arkansas." *Arkansas Historical Quarterly* 31 (Spring 1972): 3–14.
Bunch, Bradley. "History of Carroll County." *Carroll County Historical Society Quarterly* 31 (Autumn 1985): 4–9.
Calvert, John H. "Fencing Laws in Missouri—Restraining Animals." *Missouri Law Review* 32 (Fall 1967): 519–42.
Canan, Howard V. "Milton Burch: Anti-Guerrilla Fighter." *Missouri Historical Review* 59 (1965): 223–42.
Casey, Margaret. "Early History of the Casey Family." *White River Valley Historical Quarterly* 1 (Spring 1964): 3–8, 21.
Comeaux, Malcolm L. "Origin and Evolution of Mississippi River Fishing Craft." *Pioneer America* 10 (1 June 1978): 73–97.
Cowen, Ruth Caroline. "Reorganization of Federal Arkansas, 1862–1865." *Arkansas Historical Quarterly* 18 (Summer 1959): 32–57.
Del Sesto, Steven L. "Roles, Rules, and Organization: A Descriptive Account of Cockfighting in Rural Louisiana." *Southern Folklore Quarterly* 39 (March 1975): 1–14.
Dougan, Michael B. "The Doctrine of Creative Destruction: Ferry and Bridge Law in Arkansas." *Arkansas Historical Quarterly* 39 (Summer 1980): 136–58.
Evans, Clarence. "A Cultural Link Between Nineteenth-Century Germany and the Arkansas Ozarks." *Modern Language Journal* 35 (1951): 523–30.
———. "Gerstaecker and the Konwells of White River Valley." *Arkansas Historical Quarterly* 10 (Spring 1951): 1–36.
"First Homesteaders of Douglas County, Missouri." *The Old Mill Run* 4 (January 1990): 7.
Flanders, Robert, and Lynn Morrow. "Springfield and its Hinterland: Greene County and the White River Country." *White River Valley Historical*

Quarterly 10 (Fall 1988): 4–12; (Winter 1989): 4–9; (Spring 1989): 4–10; (Summer 1989): 4–11.

Flippin, W. B. "The Tutt and Everett War in Marion County." 1877 manuscript, in *Arkansas Historical Quarterly* 17 (Summer 1958): 155–63.

———. "Early History." Yellville *Mountain Echo*, 5 May 1899; 1 September 1899.

Foster, Gary S. "The Social Dimensions of Traditional Live Traps: Expanding Paths in Material Folklife." *Southern Folklore Quarterly* 45 (1981): 101–08.

Glenn, Robert A. "The Osage War." *Missouri Historical Review* 14 (March 1920): 201–10.

"The Great Flood of 1844." *Missouri Historical Review* 29 (April 1935): 206–11.

Handley, Lawrence R. "Settlement Across Northern Arkansas as Influenced by the Missouri and North Arkansas Railroad." *Arkansas Historical Quarterly* 33 (Winter 1974): 273–92.

Hannon, Thomas J., Jr. "Nineteenth-Century Cemeteries in Central-West Pennsylvania." *Proceedings of the Pioneer America Society* 2 (1973): 23–38.

Hanson, Charles E., Jr. "The Pit Saw." *Museum of the Fur Trade Quarterly* 11 (Winter 1975): 1–6.

Hasse, Larry. "Watermills in the South: Rural Institutions Working Against Modernization." *Agricultural History* 58 (July 1984): 280–95.

Hennington, Berton E., Jr. "Northwest Arkansas and the Brothers of Freedom: The Roots of a Farmer Movement." *Arkansas Historical Quarterly* 34 (Winter 1975): 304–24.

Hoffman, Walter James. "Folklore of the Pennsylvania Germans." *Journal of American Folklore* 1 (1888): 123–135; 2 (1889): 23–35, 191–202.

Holder, Virgil H. "Historical Geography of the Lower White River." *Arkansas Historical Quarterly* 27 (Summer 1968): 131–45.

Huff, Leo E. "Guerrillas, Jayhawkers, and Bushwhackers in Northern Arkansas During the Civil War." *Arkansas Historical Quarterly* 24 (Summer 1965): 127–48.

Hughes, Michael A. "Wartime Gristmill Destruction in Northwest Arkansas and Military-Farm Colonies." *Arkansas Historical Quarterly* 46 (Summer 1987): 167–86.

Jeane, D. Gregory. "The Upland South Folk Cemetery Complex." In Richard E. Meyer, ed. *Cemeteries and Gravemarkers: Voices of American Culture*. Ann Arbor, Mich.: UMI Research Press, 1989.

"John Adams, 1796–1840." *Wolf House Historian* 1 (January 1989): 1–10.

Johnston, James J. "Bullets for Johnny Reb: Confederate Nitre and Mining Bureau in Arkansas." *Arkansas Historical Quarterly* 49 (Summer 1990): 124–67.

———. "Jayhawker Stories: Historical Lore in the Arkansas Ozarks." *Mid-South Folklore* 4 (Spring 1976): 3–9.

———. "Searcy County Indians in Tradition and History." *Mid-America Folklore* 12 (Spring 1984): 24–31.

Jordan, Terry G. "Between the Forest and the Prairie." *Agricultural History* 38 (October 1964): 205–16.

Jordan, Terry G., and Matti Kaups. "Folk Architecture in Cultural and Ecological Context." *Geographical Review* 77 (January 1987): 52–75.
Kennedy, Steele T. "Bears Once Important to Life of Arkansas Hills." *Ozarks Mountaineer* 6 (May 1958): 3.
Kyle, Linnie J. "Goober Spring Becomes Lake Resort." *The Old Mill Run* 3 (October 1988): 5.
Lackey, Daniel Boone. "Cutting and Floating Red Cedar Logs in North Arkansas." *Arkansas Historical Quarterly* 19 (Winter 1960): 361–70.
Lair, Jim. "The Historic Coker Family of Northwest Arkansas." *Carroll County Historical Society Quarterly* 26 (Autumn 1990): 11–13, 26; (Winter 1990–1991): 14–17.
Littlefield, Daniel F., Jr. "The Salt Industry in Arkansas Territory, 1819–1836." *Arkansas Historical Quarterly* 32 (Winter 1973): 312–36.
Logan, Robert R. "Notes on the First Land Surveys in Arkansas." *Arkansas Historical Quarterly* 19 (Autumn 1960): 259–70.
McCaghy, Charles H., and Arthur G. Neal. "The Fraternity of Cockfighters: Ethical Embellishments of an Illegal Sport." *Journal of Popular Culture* 8 (Winter 1974): 557–69.
McDonald, Forrest, and Grady McWhiney. "The Antebellum Southern Herdsman: A Reinterpretation." *Journal of Southern History* 41 (May 1975): 147–66.
―――. "The South from Self-Sufficiency to Peonage: An Interpretation." *American Historical Review* 85 (December 1980): 1095–1118.
McLendon, Altha Lea. "A Finding List of Play-Party Games." *Southern Folklore Quarterly* 8 (September 1944): 201–34.
McWhiney, Grady, and Forrest McDonald. "Celtic Origins of Southern Herding Practices." *Journal of Southern History* 51 (1985): 165–82.
Mahnkey, Douglas. "The Game Park at Mincy." *Ozarks Mountaineer* 31 (June 1983): 44–47.
Majors, Alexander. "Hunting Bear in Taney County." *White River Valley Historical Society Quarterly* 1 (October 1961): 10–11.
"Missouri Floods." *Missouri Historical Review* 37 (October 1942): 66–70.
Montell, Lynwood. "The Upper South and the Case for Oral Folk History." *Proceedings of the Pioneer America Society* 1 (1972): 74–95.
Moore, Waddy W. "Some Aspects of Crime and Punishment on the Arkansas Frontier." *Arkansas Historical Quarterly* 23 (Spring 1964): 50–64.
Morris, Robert L. "Three Arkansas Travelers." *Arkansas Historical Quarterly* 4 (Autumn 1945): 215–30.
Morris, Wayne. "Traders and Factories on the Arkansas Frontier, 1805–1822." *Arkansas Historical Quarterly* 28 (Spring 1969): 28–48.
Morrow, Kristen Kalen. "The James C. Cook Jr. House." *Ozarks Watch* 2 (Summer 1988): 14–15.
Morrow, Lynn. "'I Am Nothing But a Poor Scribbler': Silas Turnbo and His Writings." *White River Valley Historical Quarterly* 10 (Spring 1991): 3–9.

———. "Joseph Washington McClurg: Entrepreneur, Politician, Citizen." *Missouri Historical Review* 78 (January 1984): 168–201.

———. "New Madrid and Its Hinterland: 1783–1826." Missouri Historical Society *Bulletin* 36 (July 1980): 241–50.

———. "Trader William Gilliss and Delaware Migration in Southern Missouri." *Missouri Historical Review* 75 (January 1981): 147–67.

———. "The Yocum Silver Dollar: Images, Realities and Traditions." In Howard Marshall and James Goodrich, eds. *The German-American Experience in Missouri: Essays in Commemoration of the Tricentennial German Immigration to America, 1683–1983*. Columbia: Missouri Cultural Heritage Center No. 2, University of Missouri, 1986.

Morrow, Lynn, and David Quick. "Transportation and Tourism in the Shepherd of the Hills Country: The Case of the Y-Bridge." *White River Valley Historical Quarterly* 10 (Fall 1989): 4–10; (Winter 1990): 4–10.

Morrow, Lynn, and Dan Saults. "The Yocum Silver Dollar: Sorting out the Strands of an Ozarks Frontier Legend." *Gateway Heritage* 5 (Winter 1984–85): 8–15.

"No 'Nockin' Off of Hats and No Sparkin' at Igo School District No. 5." *The Old Mill Run* 4 (January 1990): 11.

Otto, John Solomon. "The Migration of the Southern Plain Folk: An Interdisciplinary Synthesis." *Journal of Southern History* 51 (1985): 183–200.

Otto, John Solomon, and Augustus Marion Burns. "Traditional Agricultural Practices in the Arkansas Highlands." *Journal of American Folklore* 94 (April–June 1981): 166–87.

Otto, John Solomon, and G. D. Gilbert. "The Plain Folk of the American South: An Archeological Perspective." *Pioneer America* 14 (July 1982): 67–80.

Owen, Blanton. "The Farm Sled of the Southern Appalachian Highlands: Its Construction, Use and Operation." *Pioneer America Society Transactions* 3 (1980): 25–44.

Pettibone, Levi. "With Schoolcraft in Southwest Missouri." *Missouri Historical Society Collections* (January 1900): 46–51.

Piland, Shirley Carter. "'Big Billy' Piland of Ozark County." *The Old Mill Run* 4 (April 1990): 10.

Pitcaithley, Dwight. "Settlement of the Arkansas Ozarks: The Buffalo River Valley." *Arkansas Historical Quarterly* 37 (Autumn 1978): 203–22.

Plaisance, Aloysius. "The Arkansas Factory, 1805–1810." *Arkansas Historical Quarterly* 11 (Autumn 1952): 184–200.

Randolph, Vance. "Fabulous Monsters in the Ozarks." *Arkansas Historical Quarterly* 9 (Spring 1950): 65–75.

———. "The Ozark Play-Party." *The Journal of American Folklore* 42 (July–September 1929): 201–32.

Randolph, Vance, and Nancy Clemens. "Ozark Mountain Party-Games." *The Journal of American Folklore* 49 (July–September 1936): 199–206.

Rayburn, Otto Ernest. "Arkansas Folklore: Its Preservation." *Arkansas Historical Quarterly* 10 (Summer 1951): 210–20.

Roberts, Bobby L. "General T. C. Hindman and the Trans-Mississippi District." *Arkansas Historical Quarterly* 32 (Winter 1973): 297–311.

Roberts, Warren E. "The Tools Used in Building Log Houses in Indiana." *Pioneer America* 9 (1 July 1977): 32–61.

Ross, Margaret. "Retaliation Against Arkansas Newspaper Editors During Reconstruction." *Arkansas Historical Quarterly* 31 (Summer 1972): 150–65.

Ryser, Ruth Gillis. "The Snapp Family." *White River Valley Historical Quarterly* 4 (Spring 1971): 2–3.

Sanchez, Alison B., and S. Charles Bolton. "Gerstäcker's Arkansas: An Experiment in Museum-Scholar Cooperation." *Journal of American Culture* 12 (Summer 1989): 55–60.

Shea, William L. "A Semi-Savage State: The Image of Arkansas During the Civil War." *Arkansas Historical Quarterly* 48 (Winter 1989): 309–28.

Simoneaux, Katherine G. "Symbolism in Thorpe's 'The Big Bear of Arkansas.'" *Arkansas Historical Quarterly* 25 (Autumn 1966): 240–47.

Stamps, Carl. "Sally Hollow Historical Marker." *Carroll County Historical Society Quarterly* 32 (Winter 1986–1987): 11–13.

Strickland, Arvarh E. "Aspects of Slavery in Missouri, 1821." *Missouri Historical Review* 65 (July 1971): 505–26.

Wallace, Dean. "Our Friend Family." *White River Valley Historical Quarterly* 3 (Summer 1969): 3–5.

Walpole, Matthew R. "The Closing of the Open Range in Watauga County, N.C." *Appalachian Journal* 16 (Summer 1989): 320–35.

Walz, Robert B. "Migration into Arkansas, 1820–1880: Incentives and Means of Travel." *Arkansas Historical Quarterly* 17 (Winter 1958): 309–24.

Weaver, Dwight. "Setting the Cornerstones of Missouri: 1815–1989." *Missouri Resource Review* 6 (Fall 1989): 4–9.

West, Mabel. "Jacksonport, Arkansas: Its Rise and Decline." *Arkansas Historical Quarterly* 9 (Autumn 1950): 231–39.

Whitted, Stephen F. "Pioneer Rockbridge Road Connected Springfield with Arkansas." *Ozarks Mountaineer* 6 (July 1958): 15, 18.

Winberry, John J. "The Sorghum Syrup Industry, 1854–1975." *Agricultural History* 54 (April 1980): 343–52.

Worley, Ted R. "An Early Arkansas Sportsman: C. F. M. Noland." *Arkansas Historical Quarterly* 11 (Spring 1952): 25–39.

———. "Glimpses of an Old Southwestern Town." *Arkansas Historical Quarterly* 8 (Summer 1949): 133–59.

Wright, Martin. "The Antecedents of the Double-pen House Type." *Annals, Association of American Geographers* 48 (1958): 109–17.

Wright, Thomas E., ed. "The Capture of Van Buren, Arkansas, During the Civil War: From the Diary of a Union Horse Soldier." *Arkansas Historical Quarterly* 38 (Spring 1979): 72–89.

Wyatt-Brown, Bertram. "The Antimission Movement in the Jacksonian South: A Study in Regional Folk Culture." *Journal of Southern History* 36 (November 1970): 501–29.

Yates, William A. "The Taber Family of Big Creek, Taney County, Missouri." *White River Valley Historical Quarterly* 4 (Summer 1972): 2–7.

Pamphlets, Magazines, and Reports

Bennett, W. J., Jr., and Jeffrey A. Blakely. *Archeological and Historical Investigations, Old Forsyth Site (23 TA41), Taney County, Missouri.* Little Rock: U.S. Army Corps of Engineers, 1987.

Blevins, Bill D. *Jacob Wolf, The Mansion and the Man.* Mountain Home, Ark.: Twin Lakes Printing & Publishing Company, 1982.

Bruner, Claude R. *The Rockbridge Story.* N.p., 5 June 1981.

Estes, Thomas Jerome. *Early Days and War Times in Northern Arkansas.* Lubbock, Tex.: privately printed, 1928.

Fletcher, P. W., and R. E. McDermott. *Influence of Geologic Parent Material and Climate on Distribution of Shortleaf Pine in Missouri.* Columbia: Agricultural Experiment Station, Research Bulletin 625, University of Missouri, 1957.

Gaskins, John. *The Life and Adventures of John Gaskins in the Early History of Northwest Arkansas.* Published by author, 1893. Reprint, Eureka Springs, Ark.: Eureka Springs Historical Museum, n.d.

Hoenshel, E. J. and L. S. *Stories of the Pioneers.* Branson, Mo.: *Branson White River Leader,* 1915. Reprint, Forsyth, Mo.: Little Photo Gallery, 1985.

Howard, James H. *The Southeastern Ceremonial Complex and its Interpretaion.* Memoir No. 6. Columbia: Missouri Archaeological Society, 1968.

Hubble, Martin. *Personal Reminiscenses and Fragments of the Early History of Springfield and Greene County, Missouri.* Springfield, Mo.: Museum of the Ozarks, Sesquicentennial Edition, 1979.

Jeffery, A. C. *Historical and Biographical Sketches of the Early Settlement of the Valley of White River together with a History of Izard County.* Melbourne, Ark.: *Melbourne Clipper,* 1877. Yellville, Ark.: Yellville *Mountain Echo,* 1895. Reprint, Richmond, Va.: The Jeffery Historical Society, April 1973.

Mahnkey, Douglas. *Taney County Bench and Bar, The First 150 Years.* Branson, Mo.: The Ozarks Mountaineer, 1990.

Morrow, Lynn, and Robert Flanders. *An Overview of Seven Ozarks Counties for the Historic Preservation Program, Missouri Department of Natural Resources, Jefferson City, Missouri.* West Plains, Mo.: South Central Ozarks Council of Governments, June 1989.

Price, James E., and Cynthia R. Price. *An Investigation of Settlement Patterns and Subsistence on the Ozark Escarpment in Southeast Missouri During the First Half of the Nineteenth Century.* Columbia: Department of Anthropology, University of Missouri, 28 February 1978.

Stanley, Lois, Maryhelen Wilson, and George F. Wilson, comps. *Cemetery Relocations by the U.S. Army Corps of Engineers in Illinois, Iowa, Missouri, and Arkansas.* St. Louis, Mo.: The St. Louis Genealogical Society, 1977.

Wolf House Historian. Norfork, Ark. Vol. 1 (January 1989–present).
York, Courtney and Gerlene, comps. and eds. *Marion County Arkansas Census, 1850.* Published by authors, n.d.

Collections and Papers

Coker Family Histories. Bessie J. Ingenthron Papers, Forsyth, Missouri, Public Library.
Connelley, William Elsey–Silas C. Turnbo Correspondence. Springfield–Greene County Public Library, Springfield, Missouri.
Cook Family Papers. Kalen and Morrow, Forsyth, Missouri.
French, William A. Diaries. Joint Collection, University of Missouri–Rolla.
Lynn Morrow, comp. "Greene County Demographic Profile, 1850–1910." Kalen and Morrow Papers, Forsyth, Missouri.
"Miscellaneous Records from the *Springfield Advertiser* Springfield, Missouri, 1844–46." Springfield, Mo.: Rachel Donelson Chapter, Daughters of the American Revolution, 1980.
Morrow, Dr. W. I. I. Diary. Joint Collection, University of Missouri–Columbia.
Robinett, Paul M. Collection. Joint Collection, University of Missouri–Columbia.
Stults, Ben T. "A Sketch of the Many Ups and Downs in Life of Ben T. Stults As a Boy to a Man as a Hunter." Manuscript, Kalen and Morrow Collection, Forsyth, Missouri.
Turnbo, Silas C. Collection. Springfield–Greene County Public Library, Springfield, Missouri.

Government Records

Layton Building. National Register of Historic Places nomination. Arkansas Historic Preservation Program, Little Rock, Arkansas.
Looney, Janice Soutee, comp. *Taney Co., Mo., 1860 Fed. Census.* Walnut Grove, Mo.: Janice Soutee Looney, 1987.
Products of Industry Census, Taney County, 1850. U.S. Census. Manuscript Schedule.
U.S. Bureau of the Census. *U.S. Census of Population, 1870.* Washinton, D.C.: Government Printing Office, 1872.
The War of the Rebellion: A Compilation of the Official Records of the Union and Confederate Armies. Ser 1, vol. 22, pt. 1. Washington, D.C.: Government Printing Office, 1880–1901.

Newspapers

Eminence, Missouri, *Current Wave*, 1 October 1925.
Little Rock, Arkansas, *Arkansas Gazette*, 31 May 1850.
Mount Pleasant, Iowa, *Home Journal*, 4 April 1863.

Theses and Dissertations

Holmes, James A. "History of Ozark County, Missouri, to 1865." Master's thesis, University of Kansas, 1967.
Huff, Leo E. "Confederate Arkansas: A History of Arkansas During the Civil War." Master's thesis, University of Arkansas, May, 1964.
Maxfield, Ollie Orland. "Geography of the Boston Mountains." Ph.D. diss., Ohio State University, 1963.
Sellars, Richard West. "Early Promotion and Development of Missouri's Natural Resources." Ph.D. diss., University of Missouri, 1972.

Other Materials

Bradbury, John. Letter to Lynn Morrow, 27 March 1990.
Burge, Tom L. Letter to Lynn Morrow, 11 April 1990.
Burton, W. J. "The White River Railway." St. Louis: Union Pacific Railroad, n.d.
Crouse, Rudolph. Interview with Lynn Morrow, 11 January 1984. Boxley Valley Oral History Project, Center for Ozarks Studies, Southwest Missouri State University and Buffalo River National Park.
Crouse, Rudolph. Interview with Robert Flanders and Lynn Morrow, 8 June 1984. Boxley Valley Oral History Project, Center for Ozarks Studies, Southwest Missouri State University and Buffalo River National Park.
Duty, Bill. Interview with Lynn Morrow and Robert Flanders, 9 June 1983. Boxley Valley Oral History Project, Center for Ozarks Studies, Southwest Missouri State University and Buffalo River National Park.
Fowler, Hurchal, Mrs. Norma, and Eddie. Interview with Lynn Morrow and Kay Murnan, 6 June 1983. Boxley Valley Oral History Project, Center for Ozarks Studies, Southwest Missouri State University and Buffalo River National Park.
Fowler, Troy, and Dixie. Interview with Lynn Morrow and Kay Murnan, 7 June 1983. Boxley Valley Oral History Project, Center for Ozarks Studies, Southwest Missouri State University and Buffalo River National Park.
Hodge, John. Interview with Lynn Morrow, 4 April 1990.
Johnson, Marie Eva. "Native of the Ozarks." Typescript, n.d.

Johnston, James J. "Land of Anarchy, Land of Desolation: Buffalo River, 1861–1865." Typescript, 15 February 1978.
Jordan, Terry. Letters to Lynn Morrow, 22 May 1990; 30 July 1990.
Keefe, James F., and Lynn Morrow. "Turnbo Collection: Placename and Surname Index." Typescript, 1989.
McNeil, W. K. Letter to Lynn Morrow, 9 March 1990.
Morrow, Lynn. "Dr. John Sappington: Southern Patriarch in the New West." Manuscript, 1988.
Not Far From Here . . . : Traditional Tales and Songs Recorded in the Arkansas Ozarks. Arkansas Traditions LP, no number.
Pflieger, William L. Letter to James F. Keefe, n.d.
Price, James E. Letter to Lynn Morrow, 6 March 1990.
Scroggins, Doy and Blanche. Interview with Lynn Morrow and Kay Murnan, 6 June 1983. Boxley Valley Oral History Project, Center for Ozarks Studies, Southwest Missouri State University and Buffalo River National Park.
Shannon County: Home. Executive producer, Robert Flanders. Springfield: National Endowment for the Humanities and Southwest Missouri State University, 1981. Film.
Smith, Ethan Letter to Silas C. Turnbo, 14 June 1907.
Studyvin, Gertrude. Interview with Robert Flanders and Lynn Morrow, 7 June 1984. Boxley Valley Oral History Project, Center for Ozarks Studies, Southwest Missouri State University and Buffalo River National Park.
Studyvin, Gertrude, and Ruth Armer. Interview with Robert Flanders and Lynn Morrow, 9 January 1984. Boxley Valley Oral History Project, Center for Ozarks Studies, Southwest Missouri State University and Buffalo River National Park.

Index

Abbotte, Lafayette, 152
Abbotte, Matilda, 152
Abbotte, William, 152
Abel, Annie H., 265n
Accipiter cooperii, 313n
Accipiter striatus, 313n
Ackernecht, Erwin H., 307n
Adair, Bill, 64
Adair, Carroll, 64–66
Adair, Dick, 64
Adair, Jim, 64
Adair, Mary, 64
Adair, William, 64
Adams, George, 241, 267n
Adams, James, Jr., 267n
Adams, Jimmie, 8
Adams, John, 254
Adams, Mathias, 242
Adams, Matthew, 8, 254
Adams, Matthew, Sr., 265n
Adams, Susan, 242
Adams' Mill, Ark., 8, 243
Agkistrodon contortrix contortrix, 312n
Agkistrodon contortrix phaeogaster, 312n
ague, 307n
Ainey, 16
Alabama Indians, 113–14
Allen, Desmond Walls, xxiv, 262n
Allen, Joe, 239–41
Allsopp, Fred, 269n, 304n
Ambrose, Stephen E., 319n
Anderson, Arch, 17, 162, 189–90
Anderson, Elias, 182
Anderson, John, 36
Anderson, Pew C., 18, 19, 134
Anderson, Sallie, 162–63
Anderson, Tom, 61
Anderson, Tommy, 18
Aney, 2
animals as pets, 292n
Apis mellifera, 294n
Arkadelphia, Ark., 320n

Arkansas History Commission, xxiv
Arkansas Post, Ark., 79, 311n
Arkansas River, 206
Armer, Ruth, 304n
Arnold, Dr., 218
Arnold, Neser, 238
Arnold's Mill, 238
Arthur, George Clinton, 307n, 310n
Arundinaria gigantea, 294n
ash juniper, 306n
Astor, John Jacob, 114
Atherton, Lewis, 276n
Augusta, Ark., 61
Austin, Raleigh, 9

Baily, John, 26
Baker, Bias, 239
Baker, Caleb, 77–78
Baker, Calvin, 78, 239
Baker, Jim, 239
Baker, Jonathan, 182
Baker, Joshua, 77–78
Baker, Josie, 239
Baker, Mr., 238–39
Baker, Nan, 239
Baker, Russell Pierce, 267n, 268n, 280n, 284n, 303n
bald, 2, 297n
bald eagle, 199, 310n
bald-faced hornet, 311n
Bald Hills, Mo. 129
Bald Jess, Ark., 225
Bald Jess, Mo., 107
Bald Knob, Mo., 153
Bald Mountain, Mo., 148, 208
Barber's Creek, Mo., 241–42
Barnes, Charley, 275n
Barnes, Elijah, 248
Barnes, George W., 13
Barnes, Jasper, 13
Barnette, Jim, 133–34, 199
Barnette, Thomas, 199

Barnum, Gus, 188
Barren Fork, Mo., 103, 139, 142, 146
Barrett, 181
Bateman, Morgan, 32
Batesville, Ark., 5, 47, 59, 226, 264n, 270n, 275n, 287n, 306–07n, 308n, 312n
Batesville Land District, 312n
Baty, Newel, 132
Baty, Sam, 131–32
Baughman, Charity, 78
Baughman, Ernest W., 262–63n
Baughman, Henry, 78
Baughman, J. Ross, 293n
Baughman, Peter W., 78, 117, 122–23, 127, 157–59, 293n
Baughman family, 293n
Baxter County, Ark., 38
Bayles, Jess, 12
bear, 22, 76, 79–111, 163–65, 199
bearbaiting, 308n
Bear Creek, Ark., 79, 175, 205, 238
Bear Creek, Mo., 99, 109, 205, 311n
Bear Hollow, Mo., 208
Beaver Creek, Mo., 10, 37, 39, 56–58, 110, 129, 155, 231, 300n
Beaver Creek Mill, Mo., 56–58
Becca's Branch, Ark., 5, 16
bee bread, 87, 294n
bee coursing, 309n
Bee Creek, Mo., 13, 177, 182, 209, 232
bee gums, 294n
bee hives, 305n
bee hunter, 192
Bellfonte, Ark., 158
Ben, 23
Bennett, Lyman G., 317n
Bennett, W. J., Jr., 290n
Benton Barracks, Mo., 36
Benton County, Mo., 179
Berry, Earl, 267n, 270n, 283n, 285n, 286n, 289n, 311n, 314n, 320n
Berry, James H., 61, 289n
Berry, Tom, 246
Berry, William C., 61, 289n
Berryville, Ark., 279n
Bevins, Hester, 36
Bevins, Sam, 67–68
Bias, Hiram, 182, 188
Bias, John, 182, 218
Big Beach Hollow, Ark., 117, 184, 195
Big Buck Creek, Mo., 187, 192, 219
Big Creek, Ark., 84, 165, 234

Big Creek, Mo., 36, 64, 84, 121, 124, 125, 133, 134, 143, 155, 181, 183, 186, 194, 218, 233, 300n, 318n
Big Creek Mill, Mo., 64
bigmouth buffalo fish, 306n
Big North Fork River, Ark., 5, 7, 46–47, 72, 79, 160, 311n
Big North Fork River, Mo., 310n
Big Piney River, Mo., 310n
Big Spring, Ark., 310n
Bill, the negro, 143
Billings, George, 128–29
Billingsly, John, 198–99
Bison bison, 71
black bear, 71, 79–111
black bear releases, 80
blackberry, 100
Black Bob, 10, 266n
black gum tree, 294n
black oak tree, 205
black rat snake, 301n, 312n
blacks, 58, 273n
blacksmith shop, 49
black snakes, 133, 215–16, 301n, 312n
Blakely, Jeffrey A., 290n
Blevins, Bill D., 267n, 278n, 284n
blizzard, 33–34
Boatright, Dick, 18
Boatright, Tom, 18
Bob, 7
bobcat, 183, 305n
Boiler Spring, Ark., 31
Boone County, Ark., 13, 17, 22, 55, 73, 78, 79, 91, 99, 122, 174, 191
Boonsboro, Ark., 282n
Boonville, Mo., 306n
Booth, J. M., 229
Boothe, Mat, 13
Bosier, Mr., 243
bounty laws, 302n
Bradbury, John, 316n, 318n
Bradley's Ferry, Ark., 154, 185, 187, 197, 220
Bragg, Gen. Braxton, 315n
Branson, Mo., 306n
Braswell, O. Klute, 281n
Bratton, Henry, 199, 290n
Bratton's Spring Creek, Mo., 102, 107, 187, 197, 199, 208
Breckenridge, William C., 318n
Brickey's Mill, Ark., 226
Bridges, Bill, 115
Brock's Spring Creek, Mo., 290n

Brown, Alex, 18
Brown, Andrew, 207
Brown, Austin "Uncle Auss," 177, 206, 209
Brown, Baxter, 34
Brown, Becca, 18
Brown, Billy, 48
Brown, Bob, 2
Brown, C. Allan, 279n
Brown, Catherine, 18
Brown, Daniel, 207
Brown, Gen. Egbert Benson, 245, 319n
Brown, Gid, 162
Brown, Girard Leiper, 15, 81, 99, 206
Brown, John, 60, 288n
Brown, Joseph, 295n, 312n
Brown, Lizzie, 246–48
Brown, Martin, 207
Brown, Mattie, 277n
Brown, Omer E., 305n
Brown, Robert, 18
Brown, Sallie, 17
Brown, Sarah, 296n
Brown, Tom, 4, 17, 18
Brown, William, 118, 184
Brown, William L., 246
Brown, William M., 207, 209
brown recluse spider, 313n
Brummer, John, 191
Bruner, Claude R., 277n
Bruno, Ark., 87
brush, 295n
Bryant, John, 110
Bryant's Fork, Mo., 57, 105, 139
Buck Shoals Ford, 117, 189
buffalo, 47, 71–79, 163
Buffalo City, Ark., 38, 47
buffalo fish, 306n
Buffalo Fork, Ark., 87, 216, 238
Buffalo Lick, Ark., 78
Buffalo River, Ark., 162, 165, 238, 265n, 307n, 309n
Buffalo Valley, Ark., 307n
buffalo wool, 72
Bukey, Anita, 295n, 313n
Bukey, Evan Burr, 295n, 313n
bull, 293n
Bull Bottom, Ark., 18, 32, 34, 119, 236, 270n
Bull Bottom Shoals, 278n
Bull Creek, Mo., 9, 109
Bull Shoals, Ark., 59
Bull Shoals Reservoir, 280n
Bunch, Bradley, 281n

bung, 186, 307n
bur oak tree, 80, 293n
Burch, Capt. Milton, 244, 319n
Burdon, Ron, 68
Burge, Tom L., 296n
Burns, Sam, 51
Burton, W. J., 284n
bushwhackers, 223–24, 314n, 316–17n
Bushy Knob, 102
Busket, William, 253
Byers, S. H. M., 319n

calculus (madstone), 301n
Calf Creek, Ark., 165
California, 27
Calvert, John H., 281n
Camp Adams, Ark., 228
Camp Bragg, Ark., 226, 315n
Camp Hawkins, Mo., 278n, 303n
camp hunting, 94
Campbell, Junius, 273n
Canan, Howard V., 319n
Cane Hill, Ark., 45
Caney Creek, Mo., 105, 183
Canis latrans, 135
Canis lupus, 135
Canis rufus, 135
Cantrel, Dr., 131–32
Cape Girardeau, Mo., 264n
Cardwell, John, 149
Carpenter, Sam, 79, 122, 123, 149
Carroll, Tom, 181
Carroll County, Ark., 13, 42, 45, 59, 175, 191
Carrollton, Ark., 28, 42, 78, 164
Carrollton Road, 280n
Carter, Clarence E., 265n, 270n
Carter, Isaac, 122, 165
Carter, John, 17
Casebolt, Jemima, 234
Casebolt, Robert, 181, 233–35, 317n
Casey, Abner, 309n
Casey, Belveretta, 309n
Casey, Jasper, 216
Casey, Jesse, 216
Casey, Levi, 191, 309n
Casey, Margaret, 309n
Casey family, 309n
Casey Road, Mo., 309n
catamount, 161, 183, 305n
cattle, 274n
Cayenne annuum, 311n
Cayenne frutescens, 311n

342   INDEX

cayenne pepper, 311n
cedar, 185, 279n, 306n
Cedar Creek, Mo., 127–28, 134, 153, 231
Cedar Creek Post Office, Mo., 149
Cedar Point, Mo., 289n
cellars, 100, 296n
cemeteries (see also graveyards), 18, 27, 36, 47–48, 239, 243, 248, 253, 270–71n, 276n, 281n, 314n, 320–21n
centipedes, 205, 218–21, 262n, 313n
Cervus elaphus, 71, 111
Chapman, Anderson, 57
Chapman Mill, Ark., 57
Charley Smith Mill, Mo., 186
Chenoworth, Ben, 40
Cherokee Grant, 5
Cherokee Indians, 2, 5, 11, 13, 70, 263–64n, 264–65n, 268n
Chickasaw Indians, 113–14
Chickasaw plum, 312–13n
Child, Francis, xvi
chills and fevers, 187
Choctaw Indians, 113–14, 263n
Christian County, Mo., 69, 152, 200, 241, 245, 291n, 300n
Churchman, Jake, 94
Churchman, Jim, 17
Churchman, John, 94–95
Cinda, 248
Civil War, xxvi–xxvii, 13, 223–54
Clapp, David, 153, 278n, 303n
Clapp, Irving, 153
Clapp, Patterson, 153
Clapp family, 152–53
Clark (surveyor), 206
Clark, Bill, 64, 97, 155, 192
Clark, Calvin, 194
Clark, Ed, 214
Clark, Elizabeth, 208–09
Clark, Henry, 238
Clark, John, 97–99
Clarkstone, Jim, 31
Clarkstone, Lewis, 31, 62
Clarkstone, Tom, 31
Clarksville, Ark., 263n
Clay, John, 210–11
Clear Creek, Ark., 216, 220
Clemens, Nancy, 283n
Clifton, Bill, 6
clothing, dyed, 64
coachwhip snake, 216–17, 313n
Coiner, Dave, 125, 218

Coker, Abbie, 17
Coker, Betsey, 16, 17, 18
Coker, Buck, 2, 15, 17, 19, 20, 81, 101, 163, 271n, 304n, 310n
Coker, Charles, 2, 17–18
Coker, Dan[iel], 16–17, 226
Coker, "Dud," 311n
Coker, George, 17
Coker, Herrod, 2, 16, 20
Coker, J. W., 315n
Coker, Jane, 17, 163
Coker, Joe, 2, 15, 17, 81, 163, 263n, 271n
Coker, John, 17, 270n
Coker, Katie, 18, 99
Coker, Laferty Coon, 17
Coker, Lenard, 17, 206
Coker, Little Joe, 16
Coker, Lucinda, 18
Coker, Mahala, 18
Coker, Malinda, 17
Coker, Mary Ann, 17
Coker, Nancy, 17, 310n
Coker, Ned, 17–18, 20, 22, 154, 232
Coker, Nina, 17
Coker, Polly, 18
Coker, "Prairie Bill," 2, 16, 20, 154
Coker, Randolph, 17, 270n
Coker, Rebecca, 17
Coker, Sally, 17, 18, 270n
Coker, "Wagoner Bill," 17, 154
Coker, William, 17
Coker, William "River Bill," 20, 38, 54, 154
Coker, Winnie, 17
Coker, "Yellville Bill," 17, 154, 226
Coker family, 16–19, 79, 152, 310n
Cole, Abraham, 125–26, 142–44, 192, 300n, 309n
Cole County, Mo., xiii
Collier, Ellen, 109–10
Collier, Hiram, 109
Comeaux, Malcolm L., 275n
Confederate Soldiers Home, Mo., xii, xxii, xxiv, 244
Connelley, William Elsey, xii, xxi–xxiii, xxiv–xxv, 261n, 262n
Cook, Alfred, 290n
Cook, James, 63, 290n
Cook, James, Jr., 290n
Cooper County, Mo., 276n
Cooper's hawk, 313n
Copelin, Isaac, 189
Copelin, John, 189

Copelin, Steve, 84
Copelin, Tyne, 189
copperhead snake, 312n
Cornstalk, Peter, 265n
Corylus americana, 268n
Corylus cornuta, 268n
Cotter, Ark., 293n, 306n
cotton gin, 49, 238, 278n, 286n
cougar, 161
counterfeit money, 275n
Cowan, Bill, 65–66
Cowan, Silas, 51
Cowan Barrens, Ark., 315n
Cowdrey, Dr. James, 47, 283n
Cowen, Ruth Caroline, 269n
Cowpen Hollow, Mo., 115–16, 148
coyote, 135
Crawford, John, 245
Creek Indians, 266n
Crockett, Davy, 80
Crockett Township , Ark., 184, 197
Crooked Creek, Ark., 47, 73, 78, 89, 91, 93, 95, 117–18, 126–27, 157, 165, 198
Crooks, Ramsey, 114
Crotalus atrox, 312n
Crotalus horridus Linnaeus, 301n, 312n
Crouse, Rudolph, 274n, 282n
Curtis, Gen. Samuel R., 244, 318–19n
Cynthia, 2, 17

Dale, Edward Everett, xxiii
Dallas County, Mo., 253
Dama virginiana, 113
dance, 8, 46, 67–69
dance, Indian, 11
Danforth, John, 289n
Daniels, Bill, 17
Daves, Goodman, 147
Davis, Ira J., 131, 200
Davis, Jefferson, 60, 288n
Davis, Jobe, 182
Dean, Jim, 185
Deane, Ernie, 282n, 280n
Dearman, Ozz D., 96
Dearmond, Mr., 7
Decatur County, Tenn., 35
deer, 71, 111–34, 163
deer skins, 278n
Delaware Indians, 69, 263n, 264n, 284n, 291n
Delilah, 154–55
Del Sesto, Steven L., 308n
Denison, Elize, 19

Denton, Rube, 34
Denton's Ferry, 293–94n
Denver, Ark., 191
Dial, Bill, 34
Dial, Ms., 67
Diamond Cave, Ark., 304n
distilleries, 242, 278n, 291n
Dodd City, Ark., 162, 212
dogs, 22, 273n
dogtrot house, 317n
Dorson, Richard, 262n
Dougan, Michael B., 288n
Douglas County, Mo., 9, 187, 201, 217, 275n, 310n
Drake, Sarah, 238
drouth, 8
Drury ranch, 302n
Dry Caney Creek, Mo., 110
Dry Creek, Ark., 175
Dubuque, Ark., 17, 30, 54, 55, 269n, 275n
Duggins, Alex, 67, 84–85. 294n
Duggins, Betsy, 294n
Duggins, Cage, 67
Duggins, Moriah, 67
Dugginsville, Mo., 128, 208, 134, 148, 208, 218
dugout canoes, 29
du Pratz, Antoine Simone Le Page, 298n
Duty, Bill, 282n, 304n

eagles, 199, 310n
Eagle Pencil Company, 306n
East Sugar Loaf Creek, Ark., 46, 49, 57, 154, 163, 168, 202, 212, 248, 254, 310n
East Sugar Loaf Creek Mill, Ark., 49
Edward, Amos, 62
Edwards, John, 62
Eggleston, Edward, xvi
Elaphe obsoleta obsoleta, 301n, 312n
Elbow Creek, Mo., 2, 27, 31, 65, 81, 121, 122, 148, 155, 193, 209, 245
Elbow Shoals, 81
Eleven Points Creek, Mo., 131
Elixir Springs, Ark., 158
Elixir Springs Post Office, Ark., 303n
elk, 71, 111–34, 163
Ellison, Tom, 110
Enterprise Roller Mills, 310n
Eslick, Art, 9–11
Eslick, Beden, 11–12
Eslick, John, 11
Eslick, Sam, 11
Eslick, Zeke, 9–11

Essex, Isaac, 180–81
Estes, Thomas Jerome, 310n, 314n, 318n
Euonymus atropurpureus, 312n
Eureka Springs, Mo., 307n
Evans, Clarence, 263n, 294–95n
Everett, Barton Yellville, 51, 286n
Everett, Ewell, 51
Everett, Francis, 52
Everett, James E., 57, 286n
Everett, Jess, 8, 49, 225
Everett, John, 51
Everett, Matilda, 48
Everett, Simmon, 51
Everett Mill, Ark., 8, 286n
Excelsior Springs, Mo., 307n

Fair, James R., 284n
Fairbanks, Jonathan, 268n, 291n
Fallen Ash Creek, Ark., 160
Fancher, James, 45, 281n
farkleberry, 295n
feist dog, 182, 306n
Felis concolor, 161
Fellman, Michael, 314n
Fellows, Tersey, 159
Fenex, Capt. William, 278n, 286n, 303n
Fernald, Merritt L., 294n
ferries, 287–88n; Bradley's, 154, 185, 187, 197, 220; Denton's, 293–94n; Jones', 36; Long's, 27, 121; Mooney's, 277n, 293n; Pace, xxii; Peel, 280n, 300n; Roller's, 60; Shipp's, 314n; Talbert's, 81, 159, 277n, 293–94n, 308n
fice dog, 182, 306n
Figg, Dennis E., 313n
Filpot, Martha, 147
Finley Creek, Mo., 69–70, 291n
fire-hunting, 117, 177, 299n, 305n
Fisher, Enoch, 33, 277–78n
Fisher, John, 33, 277–78n
Fisher, Tom, 277–78n
Fish Trap Shoals, Ark., 154
Five Oak Bald Hill, Mo., 113, 187
Flag Spring, Ark., 253
Flanders, Robert, 302n, 304n
flash in the pan, 295n
flat boats, 28, 275n
flax, 46
Fletcher, P. W., 272n
Flippin, Allen, 160
Flippin, Ark., 160
Flippin, Thomas H., 159–61, 303n

Flippin, W. B., 159, 282n, 285n, 294n 303n
Flippin Barrens, Ark., 50, 159, 303n
floods, 20–21, 272n
Florin, John W., 307n
fodder, 109, 297n
Foley, William E., 265n
Ford, Elijah, 85–87
Ford, John, 85–87
Foreman, Grant, 264n
forest fires, 32, 112, 298n
Forrest, Bob, 138–39
Forrest, Jimmie, 138, 146
Forsyth, Mo., 29, 31, 40, 58, 60–64, 109, 153, 155, 178, 191, 219, 276n, 290n, 300n, 309n
Foster, Gary S. 301n
Fowler, Eddie, 307n
Fowler, Hurchal, 307n
Fowler, Marion, 238
Fowler, Mrs. Norma, 307n
Fowler, Sarah, 238
fox squirrel, 308n
Franklin Township, Ark., 184
Frazier, James, 95
Frazier, Taylor, 95–97
Freeman, Bill, 91
French, William A., 306n
Friend, Augustine, 278n
Friend, Betsey, 18
Friend, Billy, 69
Friend, Charles, 291n
Friend, Jake, 18, 278n
Friend, Jane, 124
Friend, Jimmie, 124–25, 127–31
Friend, Peter, 18, 127, 278n
Friend, Polly, 278n
Friend, Steve, 127–31
Friend Bend, 278n
Fritts, George, 5, 34
frizzen, 268n
frontier claims, 275n
fruit trees, 37–38
Fulbright, Henry, 267n
Fulbright, William, 12, 268n
Fulton County, Ark., 209

Gainesville, Mo., 201, 215, 218
Gaither Post Office, Ark., 174
gambling, 5
game, chuckaluck, 5
Garber, Ben, 305n
Gardener, Bill, 69
Garrison, Mo., 241

Garrison, William, 69, 291n
Gar Shoals, 82
Gasconade River, Mo., 310n
Gaskins, John, 292n, 293n, 297n, 317n
George's Creek, Ark., 17, 48, 95, 133, 310n
Gerlach, Russel L., 274n
Gerstäcker, Friedrich, xxvi, 262n, 263n, 294–95n, 310n, 313n
Gesler, Wilbert M., 307n
giant cane, 294n
gigging, 28–29
Gilbert, Ark., 307n
Gilbert, G. D., 296n
Gilbert Hollow, Mo., 113
Gilliss, William, 289n
Ginch, Ben, 181
gip, 293n
glade, 297–98n
Glenn, Robert A., 267n
Gohdes, Clarence, 293n
gold coins, 13, 27, 30, 232, 242–43
Goodwyn, Lawrence, 290n
Gooley, Charles S., 296n
Gooley's Spring Creek, Mo., 102, 296n
Gottschalk, Louis, 261n
Gourd, Eaph, 214
government claim, 115
Grace, Henry, 134
Graham, Levi, 145
Gratiot, Charles, 114
graveyards: Bear Creek, 239; Bratton's Spring Creek, 18, 253; Crooked and Clear Creeks, 47–48; George's Creek, 48; Hoodenpyle, 248; John Riddle, 248; Milum, 314n; Norris, 271n; Panther Bottom, 18, 36; Snapp, 276n; Sneed, 281n; Swansville, 243; Talbert, 294n; Trimble, 270n; Turnbo, 27; Yocum, 18, 270n
Gray, Lewis Cecil, 279n, 297n, 299n
gray squirrel, 308n
gray wolf, 135
Green, Ben, 135, 136, 298–99n
Green, George, 135, 136, 298–99n
Green, Jesse, 135, 136, 298–99n
Green, Leven T., 62–63, 113, 135–38, 145–46, 298–99n
Green, Phillip (son of Leven T. Green), 135, 145–46, 298–99n
Green, Phillip (grandson of Leven T. Green), 136–38
Green, Sarah, 46

Green, Tom "Pleasant Thomas," 135, 145–46
Green Corn Dance, 7, 266n
Greene County, Mo., 12, 87, 154, 188, 230, 233, 234
grey eagle, 200, 310n
Grider, Jake, 61
Griffin, C. W. "Wilse," 220
Griffy, Dr., 131–32
guerrillas, xiii, 13, 223–24, 316–17n
gyp, 293n

Hacket, Jesse, 190
Haddon, John, 28,
Hager, Ben, 210–11, 214–15, 246
Haggard, John "Jack," 191., 309n
Hall, Absalom, 304n
Hall, David, 171–72, 304n
Hall, Henderson, 212
Hall, James, 304n
Hall, Joe, 212
Hall, Joel, 62
Hall, Joseph, 171, 304n
Hall, Leonard, 304n
Hall, Sallie, 304n
Hall, Willoughby, 304n
Halleck, Gen. Henry Wager, 244, 319n
Hampton, Alf, 133
Hampton, Dave, 133
Hampton, Zeke, 133
Hampton Creek, Ark., 134
Handley, Lawrence R., 307n
Haney, 146
Hanford cedar yard, 306–07n
Hannon, Thomas J., Jr., 321n
Hanson, Charles E., Jr., 301n
Hanson, Gerald T., 264n, 280n
Hardaway, Billie Touchstone, 278n, 305n, 307n
Harrison, Ark., 168, 174
Hart, Capt. Martin D., 223
Hart, John, 79
Haskins, Joe Glass, 36–37
Hasse, Larry, 267n
Hassell, Charley, 57
Haworth, Absalom, 40
Haworth, Etny, 288n
Haworth, Jim, 40
Haworth, Jordan, 288n
Haworth, Micajah, 61, 288n
Hayden, Beeze, 12
hazelnut, 268n

346 INDEX

Hazelwood, Mo., 276n
Heiskell, J. N., xxiii
Helena, Ark., 307n, 312n
Helms, James, 97–99
Hempstead, Fay, 280n
Henderson, Bill, 45
Henderson, Chris, 187
Henderson, Jim, 187
Henderson, Wes, 183–84
Hennington, Berton E., Jr., 290n
Henry, Captain, 23
Hercules, Mo., 183
Herd, Eliza, xx
Herd, Jess, xx
Herron, Gen. Francis J., 223, 244, 314n, 319n
Herron, John, 64, 132
Herron, Lewis, 64, 286n
Herron, Mort, 55–56, 64–66, 155–57
Herron, Simon, 65–66, 121–22, 155
Hetherly, Jack, 187
Hetherly, Jake, 187
Heywood, 53
Hickok, "Wild Bill," 285n
Higgins, Earl Leroy, 287n
Higginsville, Mo., 244
Hilliard, Sam Bowers, 312n
Hindman, Gen. Thomas Carmichael, 228, 316n
Hindsville, Ark., 279n
Hockett, Homer C., xvi, 261n
Hodge, John, 320n
Hoenshel, E. J., 309n
Hoenshel, L. S., 309n
Hogan, Cage, 24, 33, 36
Hogan, Calvin, 19, 23
Hogan, Crayton, 252
Hogan, Ewing, 23
Hogan, George, 17
Hogan, Lizzie, 252
Hogan, Sarah, 252
Holcombe, R. S., 267n, 268n
Holder, Virgil H., 277n, 287n
Holett, Sam, 240
Holland, Gen. Colley B., 70, 291n
Hollinsworth, Lemuel, 56–60
Hollinsworth, Robert, 56
Hollinsworth family, 286n
Hollinsworth Mill, Ark., 56–60
Holman's Creek, Ark., 210, 246
Holmes, James A., 276n
Holmes, Mac, 68
Holmes, Mike, 147

Holt, Elizabeth, 54
Holt, Fielden, 54
Holt, George, 249
Holt, Mary A., 8–9
Holt, Mary L. "Polly," 20
Holt, Peggie, 17
Holt, R. S., 232–33
Holt, William, 17, 20, 232–33
honey bees, 85–87, 192–99, 294n
honeycase, 197
honey dew, 21–22, 272–73n
Hoodenpyle, Mat, 154, 187, 248, 251
Hoodenpyle, Pete, 248
Hoodenpyle, Sally, 248, 251
hoop snake, 217, 262n
Hoover, John, 69, 291n
Hoover Mill, Mo., 291n
hornets, 202–04
Horseshoe Bend, 123
Hot Springs, Ark., 307n
Houston, John P., 47, 283–84n
Howard, Billy, 33
Howard, James H., 266n
Howard, Sam, 96
Howell County, Mo., 175
Hubble, Martin, 291n
huckleberry, 93, 295n
Huddlestone, Jim, 61
Hudson, Agnes, 48
Hudson, Andrew, 304–05n
Hudson, Jesse, 48, 49
Hudson, John, 48
Hudson, John B., 48–49
Hudson, Johnnie, 173–74
Hudson, Capt. Lewis, 25
Hudson, Matilda, 48–49
Hudson, Samuel, 172–74, 304–05n
Hudson, Dr. William, 263n
Huff, John, 251
Huff, Leo E., 313n, 314n
Huffman, Alex, 105–07
Hughes, Michael A., 317n
hunger, 243–44, 318n
Hunt, Jerry, 133
hunting injury, 10
Huntsville, Ark., 164, 214, 246, 320n
Hurst, Jack, 47
Hutchison, George, 190
Hutchison, Jerry, 190, 208

Igo, Harrison, 298n
Igo Post Office, Mo., 113, 298n

Illinoise Creek, Ark., 77
illiteracy, 279n
Independence Day, 63–64
Indian carpenters, 266n
Indian burials, 47, 48
Indian dance, 7, 266n
Indians, xvii, 1–13, 23, 47, 48, 50, 61, 69, 71, 284n; Alabama, 113–14; Cherokee, 2, 5, 11, 13, 70, 263–64n, 264–65n, 268n; Chickasaw, 113–14; Choctaw, 113–14, 263n; Creek, 266n; Delaware, 69, 263n, 264n, 284n, 291n; Osage, 71, 267n; Shawnee, 264n, 265n, 266n
Indian wives, 1
Ingenthron, Elmo, 267n, 270n, 276n, 278n, 285n, 286n, 303n, 314n, 315n, 318n, 319n, 320n
Ingram, John, 187
Ingram, William M., 187
Iron County, Mo., 78
Ironton Register, 310n
Isabella Post Office, Mo., 145, 190, 308n

Jackson, Dr. Alvah, 311n
Jackson, Tom, 45
Jackson, Will, 45
Jacksonport, Ark., 59, 287n, 316n
Jacobs, Ben, 53–54
Jake Nave Bend, White River, 2, 16, 17, 19, 22, 101, 163, 304n
James, Edwin, 272n
James River, Mo., 12, 28, 69, 219, 277n
Jasper, Ark., 173
jayhawker, 316n
Jeane, D. Gregory, 321n
Jeff, 233
Jefferson City, Mo., 175
Jeffery, A. C., 272n, 285n
Jennings, Jesse, 61, 289n
Jennings and Goslin Mill, Mo., 57
jerked meat, 301n
jersey, 293n
Jew's Harp Hollow, Ark., 164
Jimmie's Creek, Ark., 221, 243
Jobe, Tom, 254
johnboats, 275n
Johns, Paul, 291n
Johnson, Calvin, 70
Johnson, Cornelius, 56
Johnson, Marie Eva, 288n
Johnson, Jane, 67, 68–69
Johnson, Joe, 181

Johnson, John, 181
Johnson, Martin, 26, 33, 34, 134
Johnson, Sam, 67
Johnson, Tom R., 308n, 312n, 313n
Johnson, W. C., 67, 188
Johnston, James J., 265n, 280n, 284n, 316n, 317n, 318, 320n
Jones, Adaline, 249–50
Jones, Dave, 103
Jones, Elizabeth, 154
Jones, Fate, 185, 186–87
Jones, Frank, 186–87
Jones, Hester, 36
Jones, Hugh, 36
Jones, James, 36
Jones, Jimmie, 103–04
Jones, John, 154, 185, 186, 219, 248
Jones, Margaret, 250–51, 320n
Jones, Pete, 68
Jones, R. M., 219–20
Jones, "Sugar," 103
Jones, Tom, 115
Jones' Ferry, Ark., 36
Jones' Mill, Mo., 36–37
Jordan, Terry G., 266n, 271n, 274n, 299n, 317n
Journagan, Jess, 33
Juniperus mexicana, 306n
Juniperus virginiana, 306n
Justus, Bob, 175–77
Justus, Ives, 175–77
Justus, Mary, 175–77

Kansas State Historical Society, xxiii
Kappler, Charles J., 263–64n, 284n
Katie's Prairie, Mo., 16, 66
Kaups, Matti, 317n
Keefe, James F., 299n, 302n, 306n
keelboats, 275n
Keesee, Capt. A. C., 56, 58, 278n
Keesee, Dick, 68
Keesee, Elias, 73–77, 81–83, 102–03, 107–08, 145 163, 197
Keesee, Gennie, 68
Keesee, Nancy, 19
Keesee, Paton, 15, 67, 72, 73–77, 80–83, 102, 107–08, 145, 163, 197
Keesee, Peter, 67–69, 73–77, 240
Keesee, Tyne, 189
Keesee, Willis, 56, 286n
Keesee Mill, Mo., 37, 56, 155, 278n, 286n
Keesee Township, Ark., 185, 190

348 INDEX

Keeton, Dula, 204
Keeton, George, 202–04
Keeton, John, 202–04
Keeton, Tom, 202
Kelly, Eph, 17
Kenamore, G. R., 297n
Kennedy, Steele T., 311n
Kenner, James M., 281n
Kenner, Mr., 45
Kenner, Sam, 246
Kersey, Mrs. Owen, 140–42
Kersey, Owen, 140–42
Kickapoo Prairie, 268n
King, Billie, 51, 53
King, Hosea, 51
King, Jack, 52, 53
King, James, 51
King, John, 248
King, Loomis, 53
King, Richard, 53
King, Solomon, 51, 53
King, Tom, 53
Kingdom Springs, Ark., 51
Kings River, Ark., 214
Kirbyville Road, Mo., 61
Kissee family (*see also* Keesee), 286n
Kissee Mills, Mo., 37, 56, 155, 278n, 286n
Knight, James, 87–89
Knight, John, 238
Knight, Jonathan, 87
Ku Klux Klan, 59–60, 287n
Kyle, Linnie J., 308n

Lackey, Daniel Boone, 307n
Lackey, Walter F., 304–05n
Lair, Jim, 281n
Lake Taneycomo, 302–03n
Lantz, Mose, 107–08, 197
Lathrop, Mose, 219
Laughlin, Elizabeth, 39, 279n
Laughlin Ford, 279n
Laughlin, Harvey, 221
Laughlin, James Harvey, 39, 279n
Laughlin, Lucy, 279n
Laughlin, Margarette, 39, 279n
Laughlin, Mat, 279n
Lawrence District, Ark., 114
Layton, Dr. Augustus S., 24, 179–80, 285n, 289n
Layton, Al, 286n
Layton pineries, Mo., 178

Layton's hotel, 53
Layton's Mill, Mo., 285n
Lead Hill, Ark., 17, 163, 168, 216, 303n
Lead Mine Hollow, Ark., 164
leather, 252
Lebanon, Ark., 238
Ledbetter, Harve, 214
Ledbetter, Hugh, 214
Leeper, Joe, 12, 268n
Leeper Prairie, Mo., 12
Lee's Mountain, Ark., 160, 248
Lick Creek, Mo., 115, 215, 218
Linden, Mo., 291n
Lindera benzoin, 304n
Lindera melissaefolium, 304n
Linn Creek, Mo., 306n
Liquidambar Styraciflua, 294n
Little Beach Hollow, Ark., 185
Little Buffalo Creek, Ark., 173
Little Cedar Creek, 85
Little Cedar Hollow, 84
Little Creek, Mo., 19, 135, 209, 271n
Littlefield, Daniel, Jr., 268n
Little North Fork River, Ark., 20, 56
Little North Fork River, Mo., 58, 67, 72, 82, 104, 115, 121, 133, 135, 163, 197, 199, 200, 208, 318n
Little North Fork River Mill, 57
Little Rock, Ark., 159
Livingston, Robert, 266n
Livingston's Creek, Ark., 5
Locust Hollow, Ark., 202
Loftis, Jim, 208
log chute, 184, 306n
log houses, 280–81n
log rafts, 20
logrolling, 68
Logan, Robert R., 312n
Long Beach, Mo., 309n
Long Creek, Ark., 78, 175, 191
Long's Ferry, Ark., 27, 121
Lorants, Dr., 131–32
Lord, Bill, 140
Lorimier, Louis, 265n, 289n
Lost Hollow, Mo., 62
Lower Caney Creek, 122
Lucas, Allen, 181, 306n
Lucas, Jesse, 181
Lucas, Jim, 181
Lucas, Lizzie, 181
Lutie, Mo., 103, 216
Lynx rufus, 183, 305n

INDEX 349

McBride, Gen. James H., 303n, 316–17n
McCaghy, Charles H., 308n
McClurg, Joseph, 276n
McCollough, Mr., 313n
McCollough, Pleasant, 199, 217
McCollough, Tom, 217
McCord, Dave, 61–62, 164–65, 179–81, 304n
McCord, John, 165
McCoy, Mr., 6
McCracken, Mr., 70
McDermott, R. E., 272n
McDonald, Forrest, 302n
McDonald, Mr., 39–40
McDowell, George, 61
McElhaney, Henry, 45
McElhaney, William, 70, 291–92n
McGary, Mr., 278n
McGroove, Blueff, 254
McGroove, Jobe, 254
McKinney, Benjamin F., 190, 191, 309n
McKinney, Catherine, 191
McKinney Bend, Mo., 309n
McLendon, Altha Lea, 283n
McMaster, John Bach, xv–xvi
McNair, Capt. Evander, 245, 320n
McNeil, W. K., 279n, 288n
Macroclemys temminckii, 308n
McVey Hollow, Mo., 216
McVey's Bald Hill, 121, 186
McWhiney, Grady, 269n, 302n
Madison County, Ark., 210, 246
madstone, 131–32, 301n
Magness, Betsey, 47
Magness, Bill, 17, 33
Magness, Bob, 236
Magness, Elizabeth, 236–38
Magness, Hugh, 48
Magness, Jimmie, 47, 48
Magness, Joe, 18, 33, 48, 84–85, 236, 294n
Magness, Nina, 17
Magness, Patsey, 84–85
Magness, Sam, 17
Magness, Tom, 18
Magness, Wilshire, 84, 236
Magness Bottom, Ark., 284n
Mahan, Isaac, 103, 115, 148, 200–01, 208, 296n
Mahan, John, 115–16, 148, 200, 296n
Mahan, Noah, 103–04, 135, 296n
Mahan, William, 253
Mahan Hollow, 200
Mahan Pine Branch Hollow, Mo., 148
Mahnkey, Douglas, 290n, 302n, 309n

Majors, Alexander, 311n
Majors, Ben, 28, 149
Majors, Lige, 149
malaria, 307n
Mangrum, Ok., 26
Manley, Bill, 18
Marion County, Ark., 4, 8, 18, 22, 37, 53, 56, 67, 73, 84, 85, 87, 89, 94, 95, 97, 116, 119, 171, 177, 184, 185, 187, 189, 190, 197, 198, 212, 216, 226, 234, 238, 243, 244, 248, 303n, 308n
Marsh, Peter, 132
Marshall, William, 291n
Martin, Dick, 199
Martin, John, 45
Masters, Mr., 195–97
Masterson, James R., 293n
Masticophis flagellum flagellum, 313n
Mathis, Jane, 27
Maury County, Tenn., 35
Maxfield, Ollie O., 263n, 274n
Maxwell, Col. Henry, 273n
May, Tom, 218–19
Meade, Melinda S., 307n
Mears, Mr., 52–53
Mech, L. David, 302n
Menard, Pierre, 265n
Messick, Mary Ann, 265n, 267n, 277n, 294n, 300n
meteors, 50–51
Methvin, Maj. John, 228, 315n
Miliken, Charley, 316n
Miliken, John, 154
Miliken's Bald Hill, Mo., 153, 231, 316n
militia, 290n
Mill Creek, Ark., 8
Miller, John, 143, 298n
Miller's Creek, Ark., 226
milling, 45
mills, 267n; Adams', 8, 243; Arnold's, 238; Beaver Creek, 56–58; Big Creek, 64; Brickey's, 226; Chapman, 57; Charley Smith, 186; East Sugar Loaf Creek, 49; Everett, 8, 286n; Hollinsworth, 56–60; Hoover, 291n; Jennings and Goslin, 57; Jones', 36–37; Kissee, 37, 56, 155, 278n, 286n; Layton's, 285n; Little North Fork River, 57; Nelson, 303n; Pease's, 201, 310n; Roberts, 12; sorghum, 36; Van Winkle's, 59; Wo'mack's, 37; Woods, 17; Yocum, 291n
Milum, Brice, 225, 253–54

Milum, Elizabeth, 254
Milum, Samuel, 314n
Milum cemetery, 314n
Milum Spring, Ark., 314n
mirror, 67
Missouri and North Arkansas Railroad, 307n
Missouri Department of Conservation, 302n
Missouri River, 306n
Mitchell, John, 40
Mitchell, Col. William C., 43, 226, 281n, 285n
M. N. A. Railroad, 307n
Monarch, Ark., 310n
Moneyhon, Carl H., 264n, 280n
Monks, William, 272n, 274n, 278n, 285n, 287n, 310n
Monroe County, Mo., 97
Montell, Lynwood, 305n
Montgomery's Landing, Ark., 267n
Mooney, Jacob, 277n
Mooney, Jesse, 31, 277n
Mooney's Ferry, Ark., 277n, 293n
Moore, Waddy, 275n
Moore, Dick, 61
Moore, Z. P., 40
Moreland, Fate, 245
Morgan, Lewis Henry, xvii
Morris, John, 64, 125, 133
Morris, Mr., 251
Morris, Robert L., 267n
Morris, Wayne, 263n
Morrow, Kristen Kaylen, 290n
Morrow, Lynn, 261n, 266n, 268n, 269n, 270n, 271n, 275n, 276n, 289n, 291n, 296n, 299n, 304n, 307n
Morrow, Tom, 123
Mosely, Joe, 131
Mosely, John, 129, 300n
mossing, 305n
Mossville, Ark., 271n
Motley, Elizabeth, 190
Motley, Lige, 190, 308n
Mountain Creek, Ark., 220
Mountain Home, Ark., 294n
mountain lion, 161
Mount Olive, Ark., 6
Mugginhead, 154–55
muley cow, 98, 296n
Murnan, Kay, 307n
Murphy, Isaac, 320n
Murphy, Sarah Jane, 248
Music, Bent, 221

Music Creek, Ark., 36, 94, 96, 97, 119, 237
Muzzleloading firearm, 299n

naked ball, 299n
Nance, Jack, 56, 64
Nance, Jane, 242
Nance, Samuel, 242
Napier, Mr., 122–23
Nave, Abe, 18
Nave, Jake, 17, 20, 21, 61, 269n
Nave, John, 18
Nave, Mary, 296n
Neal, Arthur G., 308n
Nelse, 53
Nelson, David, 278n
Nelson Mill, Mo., 303n
Neosho, Mo., 319n
Nesbitt, William H., 283n
nettles, 12, 268n
New Orleans, La., 28, 80, 274n, 275n, 276n
Newport, Ark., 59, 275n
Newton County, Ark., 168, 172, 274n, 304n, 309n
Newton County, Mo., 251
Newton's Flat, Ark., 243
Nipps, Henry, 18
Noland, C. F. M., 80, 293n, 303n
Norfolk, Ark., 278n
Norris, James D., 298n
North Fork Township, Ark., 119
nurseries, 278–79n
Nuttall, Thomas, 275n
Nyssa Sylvatica, 294n

Oakland, Ark., xxii, 244, 286n
Odocoileus virginianus, 71, 113
Ogle, Harkness, 40
Oil Trough, Ark., 79, 311n
Onstott, Eliza, 24
Onstott, Henry, 221, 279n
Onstott, Lucy, 279n
open-face camp, 292n
open range, 41, 281n, 302n
orchards, 279n
Oregon County, Mo., 131, 301n
Oregon Flat, Ark., 158
Orr, Polly, 17
Osage copperhead snake, 312n
Osage Creek, Ark., 45, 164
Osage Indians, 71, 267n
Osage River, Mo., 306n

Osage War, 267n
Otter Creek, Mo., 140
Otto, John Solomon, 269n, 296n
Overcan, John, 48
Owen, Blanton, 282n
Owen, Woodrow, 220
Owsley, Frank, 269n
Ozark, Mo., 245, 291n
Ozark County, Mo., 19, 67, 102, 103, 107, 115, 121, 124, 128, 134, 135, 181, 186, 187, 188, 190, 197, 206, 208, 233, 310n
Ozarks Mountaineer, xxiv

Pace, Joe, 171
Pace Ferry, Ark., xxii
Page, Tate C., 280n, 283n, 287n, 305n
Page, Uncle Joe, 305n
palsy, 49, 284n
Pangle Hollow, 96
Panther Bottom, Ark. and Mo., 18, 24, 32, 36, 128, 134, 181–82, 188, 206, 271n
Panther Creek, Ark., 304n
panthers, 71, 120–21, 161–82, 304–06n
Parks, Sam, 87
Parrish, Barnett P., 57, 287n
Parrish Hotel, 287n
Parthenon, Ark., 304n
patent medicine, 61, 289n
Patterson, Tom, 202
Patton, William C., 134, 220
Paxton, Mr., 96
Payne, John, 252
Peace, Elbert, 200
Pearce, Ben, 182
Pearson, George, 31
Pease, Miles, 310n
Pease's Mill, Mo., 201, 310n
Peck, John Mason, 298n
Peel, Ark., 19, 206, 251, 279–80n, 309n
Peel, Col. Samuel W., 42, 279n
Peel Ferry, Ark., 280n, 300n
Pelham, Jim, 216
Pelham, John, 36, 62
Pelham, Sam, 216
Penick, James L., 318n
pen traps, 136, 148, 301n
percussion cap, 295n
Perkins, Abe, 119
Perkins, H. H., 19
Pettibone, Levi, 270n, 303n
Pettigrew, Mrs., 64
Pflieger, William L., 306n

Phelps, John, 214
Phelps, Col. John E., 291–92n
Philibert, Joseph, 289n
Phillips, Jim, 40
Phillips, Paul C., 299n
Pigg, Dick, 242
Pigg's distillery, 242
Piland, Elisha, 271n
Piland, Joe, 143, 147
Piland, John, 19, 271n
Piland, Sallie, 271n
Piland, Sam, 147
Piland, Shirley Carter, 271n
Piland, Wesley, 271n
Piland, William, 143, 147
Pine Bayou, Ark., 5
Pine Branch, Mo., 182
Pine Creek, Mo., 105, 138–39
Pine Hollow, Ark., 20
Pine Hollow, Mo., 134
pineries, 272n
Pinus echinata, 272n
Pitcaithley, Dwight, 273n, 274n, 275n, 279n, 311n
pit traps, 71
Plaisance, Aloysius, 263n
play party, 46, 283n
plows, 303–04n
plum tree, 312–13n
Poke Bayou, Ark., 226, 287n
Polk, Mr., 246
Pond Fork, Mo., 113, 124, 133, 145, 183
Pond Hollow, Mo., 219
Pontiac, Mo., xx, xxii, 102, 134
Poor Joe Bald, Mo., 2–4, 16
Port Hudson, La., 269n
post oak tree, 112, 298n
Potts, John, 42
Powell, Ark., 47, 48, 89, 220
Powell, John Wesley, xvii
Price, Cynthia R., 321n
Price, James E., 295n, 321n
Price, Joe, 12
Price, Gen. Sterling, 309n
Protem, Mo., xxii, 20, 64, 121, 142, 183, 219, 238, 318n
Prunus americana, 312n
Prunus angustifolia, 312–13n
puma, 161
Pumphrey, Frank, 53
Pumphrey, Lewis, 254, 285n
puncheon floor, 46

punk, 310n
Pyne, Stephen J., 298n

Quercus nigra, 307n
Quercus stellata, 298n
Quesenbury, William, 303n
Quick, Aaron, 216
Quick, David, 275n
quinine, 307n

raccoon, 186–87
raccoon market, 307n
rafting logs, 300n
Railey's Creek, Mo., 219
Railsback, Sam, 243
Rainbow Trout Ranch, 277n
Rains, Bob, 28, 149
Randolph, Vance, xxviii–xxix, 261n, 262n, 283n, 313n
Rapp Barrens, Ark., 294n
rattlesnakes, 205–08, 214–15, 301n, 312n
Ray, Henry, 245
Ray, M. P., 38, 245
Rayburn, Otto Ernest, 80, 293n
Rea, Lt. John C., 228, 315n
Rea Valley, Ark., 315n
rebel scrip, 316n
red wolf, 135
Reeds Spring, Mo., 306n
refugees, 317n
Reneau, Jack, 283n,
Rhus spp., 309n
Rice, Rhoda, 115
Rice, Thomas, 115, 201
Richland Post Office, Mo., 201
Richmond, Nat, 148, 208
Riddle, John, 248
Riddle, William, 191, 252
Riddle cemetery, 248
Ridinger, George, 118
Risley, Ben, 145
river improvements, 30
Roberts, Bobby L., 316n
Roberts, John, 12
Roberts, Warren E., 281n
Roberts Mill, Mo., 12
Rock Bridge, Mo., 142, 148, 277n
Rocky Branch, Mo., 102
Rohrbough, Malcolm J., 308n, 312n
Rolla, Mo., 121, 274n, 300n, 310n
Roller, Wash, 60
Roller's Ferry, 60

Roselle, Jim, 38, 195
Ross, Dora, 168
Ross, John C., 168, 174
Ross, Margaret, 287n
Row, J. D., 13, 229–32
Rubus species, 296n
Rush, Loranzo, 158
Rush, Joe, 158–59
Russell, Agnes, 229, 230–32
Russell, Dave, 214
Russell, Jesse Lewis, 269n, 280–81n, 317n
Russell, Theodore Pease, 274n, 299n, 303n, 308n, 310n
Russellville, Mo., xiii
Ryser, Ruth Gillis, 276n

Sac River, Mo., 234
Safeway Grocer Company, 302n
St. Clair County, Mo., 146
St. Louis, Mo., 28, 115, 245, 274n, 276n
St. Louis Game Park, 302n
Sallee, "Chat," 103–04
Sallee, Captain James H., 103, 296n, 298n
saloon, 42–44
salt, 31, 114, 268n
Salt Bald, 102
saltpeter, 244–45, 318n, 320n
Sambo, 154–55
Sanders, Allen, 115
Sanders, Dr., 246
Sanders, Henry, 115, 201
Sanders, Rhoda, 201
Sappington, Dr. John, 289n
sarcophagus, 271n
Sauer, Carl, 264n
Saults, Dan, 270n
saw briars, 113, 299n
sawmills, 57; Boiler Springs, Ark., 31; Taney County, Mo., 285n; Yocum, 20, 273n
scalps, animal, 35
school, 38–40, 64
Schoolcraft, Henry R., xvii, 71, 265n, 271–72n, 273n, 278n, 291n, 298n, 299n, 303n, 311n
School of the Ozarks, Mo., xxiv
Schultz, Robert G., 272n, 277n, 285n, 298–99n, 308n
Schwartz, Charles W., 71, 162, 297n, 304n, 306n
Schwartz, Elizabeth R., 71, 162, 297n, 304n, 306n

Sciurus carolinensis, 308n
Sciurus niger rufiventer, 308n
Scolopendra viridus, 313n
Scott, Tom, 123
Scott, Walter, xxii
scud clouds, 73–74, 292n
Scroggins, Blanche, 282n
Scroggins, Doy, 282n
Seligman, Mo., 307n
Shaler, Col. James R., 227–28, 315n
Shannon, David, 62
Shannon County, Mo., 312n
sharp-shinned hawk, 313n
Shaver, Col. Robert, 228, 316n
Shawnee Indians, 5, 264–65n, 266n, 284n
Shawneetown, Ark., 6–7, 50, 93, 265n, 283n, 284n, 315n
Shea, William L., 281n
Shields (surveyor), 206
Shields, E. J., 110–11
Shipman, John, 69–70
Shipman, Nathaniel, 69
Shipp's Ferry, Ark., 314n
Shoal Creek, Ark., 54, 132, 154, 190
Shoal Creek, Mo., 34, 65, 187, 239
Short Mountain, Ark., 238
Shriver, Matthew, 115
Shuck, Ken, xxiii–xxiv
silver coins, 13, 27, 30, 232–33
Silver Dollar City, Mo., 309n
silver ore, 268–69n
Simmons, George, 252
Simmons, Katie, 252
Simoneaux, Katherine G., 293n
Sims, Jemima, 234
Sims, Lucinda, 234
Sims, Matthew, 234
Sinclair, Martin, 52
sink hole, 13
Sister Creek, Ark., 128, 212
Skaggs, M. B., 302n
slaves, 2, 8–9, 20, 22, 25, 63, 154–55, 232–33; Ben, 23; Cinda, 248; Heywood, 53; Jeff, 233; Nelse, 53
sleds, 45, 282n
Smilax spp., 299n
Smiley, Cain, 192
Smith, Charley, 186
Smith, Gum, 209
Smith, Harve, 188
Smith, John I., 187
snakes, 133, 205, 207–17, 301n, 312n

Snapp, Harrison, 30, 40, 61, 276n, 290n, 300n
Snapp, Peter, 33
Snapp cemetery, 276n
snapping turtle, 308n
Sneed, Charley, 19, 45, 163–64, 281n
Sneed cemetery, 281n
Snow, "Fie," 138–40, 146–47
sorghum mill, 36
sorghum seed, 35–36
Southworth, Nelson, 132
Spain, Sarah, 26
sparkleberry, 295n
Sparta, Mo., 153
spas, 307n
spicebush, 304n
Spring Creek, Mo., 290n
Springfield, Mo., 70, 122, 154, 174, 232, 268n, 274n, 300n, 306n, 319n
Springfield Art Museum, Mo., xii, xxiii
Springfield Cotton Mills, Mo., 291n
Springfield-Greene County Library, Mo., xii, xxiv, xxv
spunk, 310n
squatter's claim, 299n
squirrel hawk, 216–17
squirrel migrations, 308n
squirrels, 90, 189–91
squirrel shot, 90, 294n
Stacy, Campbell, 116
Stacy, Dr. Silas, 12, 70
Stacy, William, 12, 62, 70
staghorn sumac, 309n
Stallings, John, 267n
Stallings, Capt. Tom B., 7, 267n
Stamps, Carl, 312n
starvation, 243–44, 318n
steamboat fire, 32
steamboats, 29–32, 277n
steel traps, 136, 138–40
steelyard, 111, 297n
Stephens, Mr., 27–28
Stewart, Roscoe, xxiv
Stillhouse Hollow, Mo., 148
stills, 242, 278n, 291n
Stinnette, Cinda, 248
Stinnette, Dave, 248
Stinnette, I. C., 254
Stone, Martha (Filpot), 147
Stone, Sammy, 147, 209
Stone, William, 147
Stone County, Mo., 218, 299n, 305n, 306n

354 INDEX

Stover, Ward, 40
Strickland, Arvah E., 273n
Studyvin, Gertrude, 282n, 304n
Stults, Ben T., 297n, 299n, 302n, 305n
Sturtevant, William C., 264n
Sugar Camp Bottom, Mo., 65
Sugar Loaf area, Ark., 17
Sugar Loaf Knob, Ark., 163
Sugar Loaf Prairie, Ark., 2, 78–79, 163
Sugar Orchard Creek, Ark., 122, 158
sumac, 196–97, 309n
Sunday school, 56
Sunklands, Mo., 312n
surly, 293n
Sutton, Charity, 78
Sutton, John, 78, 122
Swan Creek, Mo., 61, 200, 241–42, 309n
Swansville, Mo., 242, 243
Swanton, John R., 264n
Swan Valley, Mo., 309n
sweet gum tree, 294n

Taber, Henry, 286n
Taber, Ruth, 286n
Table Rock Reservoir, 270–71n
Tabor, Arch, 64, 113
Tabor, Bennette, 188
Tabor, Elijah, 46, 283n
Tabor, Isaac, 121–22, 132
Tabor, Jim, 68
Tabor, Jimmie, 64, 124–25
Tabor, John H., 7, 46–48, 50–51, 64, 89, 198–99, 283n
Tabor, Nancy, 283n
Tabor, Russell, 64
Tabor, Sarah, 46, 283n
Tabor, Smith, 50
Tabor, Tom, 64
Tabor families, 283n
Taffer, Oliver, 87
Talbert, Bazzeel, 293n
Talbert, Frederick, 293n
Talbert, Simeon "Sim," 293n
Talbert, Walter "Wat," 293n
Talbert Barrens, Ark., 294n, 315n
Talbert Cemetery, 294n
Talbert's Ferry, Ark., 81, 159, 277n, 293–94n, 308n
tall tales, xxvii
Taney County, Mo., 2, 30, 32–33, 34, 35, 61, 63, 64, 66, 99, 109, 110, 113, 121, 124, 129, 133, 135, 149, 153–54, 155, 177, 179, 181, 182, 183, 187, 189, 192, 194, 206–07, 209, 218, 219, 226, 229, 239, 300n, 309n, 311n
tar smelting, 97, 295n
Taylor, Dave, 64
Taylor, Martha Ann, 253
Taylor, William, 253
Teaf, Nimrod, 50, 283n
Teague, Bill, 129–31
Tennison Hollow, Mo., 56
Terrapin Creek, Ark., 78
Terry, Dump, 236
Terry, Elizabeth, 236–38
Terry, Joe, 236
Terry, John, 236
Terry, Mary, 236
Terry, Ron, 236
Terry, Tom, 236
Teverball, Jess, 115
Thomasville, Mo., 131
Thompson Hollow, Mo., 147
Thornfield, Mo., 135, 140, 209
Thorpe, Thomas Bangs, 80
Thurman, Bob, 39, 215
Thurman, Elisha, 40
Thurman, G. W., 215, 219
Thurman, Granville, 215
Thurman, Jane, 215
Thurman, Martha, 215
Thurman, Tom, 215
Thurman, William, 40
Thurman, Willie, 215
Tixier, Victor, 292n
Tom Young Hollow, 127
Tong, Marvin, xxiii
tools, 280–81n
Trace Hollow, 102
trade, local, 43
Trammel, George, 91–92
Treadway, Bill, 18
Treadway, Sally, 251
Treat, Mun, 245
Trimble, Allen, 5, 7, 16–17, 20, 116–17, 118, 184, 194–97, 264n, 270n, 278n
Trimble, Bob, 17, 55
Trimble, Dicy, 18
Trimble, Jim, 17
Trimble, John, 202
Trimble, Mary Jane, 18
Trimble, Sally, 16, 273n
Trimble, Sarah, 252
Trimble, William, 5, 15, 16, 18, 20, 81, 116, 270n, 273n

Trimble cemetery, 270n
Trimble's Creek, Ark., 4–5, 16, 116
Tuck, Clyde Edwin, 268n, 291n
Tucker, Perry, 245
Tucker Bottom, Ark., 267n
Tulsa, Indian Territory, 206
tupelo tree, 294n
Turkey Creek, Mo., 25, 147
Turnbo, Andrew, xx, 26, 253
Turnbo, Clabe, 26–27
Turnbo, Elizabeth, xxii, 26
Turnbo, Gracie Elmira, 250–51
Turnbo, Gracie M., 26
Turnbo, James, 24, 26
Turnbo, James Coffee, xviii–xix, 24–25, 34, 38, 250–51, 264n, 275n, 278n, 281n, 290n
Turnbo, James D., 220
Turnbo, Jane Mathis, 27
Turnbo, Jasper Newton, 250–51
Turnbo, Lafayette, 250–51
Turnbo, Margaret, 26, 250
Turnbo, Mary L., 26, 250–51
Turnbo, Mary Matilda, xx
Turnbo, Nancy A., 26
Turnbo, Nathan, 26
Turnbo, Sally, 251–53
Turnbo, Sarah Spain, 26
Turnbo, Silas Claiborne, 250, 261n, 262n, 270n, 315n; books, xx; collecting material, xix–xx; failing health, xxii; manuscript, xxiii–xxiv; newspaper articles, xx; significance of, xxv
Turnbo, William Claiborne, 26
Turnbo family, xviii–xix, 25–27
Turnbo graveyard, Tenn., 27
Turnbo name origin, 24,
turning squirrels, 191, 309n
turtles, 187–89
Tutt, David K., 285n
Tutt, Davis Casey, 51
Tutt, Hansford, 51, 53, 284–85n
Tutt, Jefferson, 51
Tutt, R. B., 284n
Tutt family, 284–85

Ulmus alata, 312n
Upton, H. E., 105–07
Upton, J. M., 44–46
Upton, Jesse, 105–07
Upton, Lucile Morris, 286n
Upton, Ned, 105, 215–16

Upton, Tom, 105
Ursus americanus, 71, 79

Vaccinium arboreum, 295n
Vance, Calvin, 109
Vance, John P., 61, 179, 180, 289n
Vance, Lucy, 109–10
Van Winkle's Mill, Ark., 59
Vaughn, Enock, 167
venison, 301n
Vespula maculata, 311n
Vicksburg, Miss., 269n
von Ranke, Leopold, xv

Wagoner sheep ranch, Mo., 189
wahoo, 215, 312n
Walker, Dave, 291n
Walker Mill, Mo., 291n
Wallace, Dean, 291n
Walpole, Matthew R., 302n
Walz, Robert B., 274n, 282n
War Eagle River, Ark., 46, 210
Warner, Ezra J., 315n, 319n
Warsaw, Mo., 179, 285n, 306n
Washington County, Ark., 77
Water Creek, Ark., 253
water oak tree, 185, 307n
weaner, 161
weaning, 304n
weaning house, 304n
Weast, Adam, 320n
Weast, Sophronia, 320n
Weast Hotel, 253, 320n
Weaver, George, 236
Weaver, Dwight, 295n, 312n
Weer, Col. William, 223
Welch, Eli, 128
West, Mabel, 287n, 293n
Western Grove, Ark., 168
West Plains, Mo., 310n
West Sugar Loaf Creek, Ark., 21, 164, 304n
Wheeler, Bill, 39
Whetstone, Pete, 80
whipping, 64–66
whip saw, 301n
whiskey, 6, 37, 43–44, 186, 242, 291n
White, Col. J. D., 228, 315n
White River, 81, 205
White River Railroad, 277n
White River Steamboat Company, 276n
white-tail deer, 113
Whitlock, Jess, 246–48

Whitlock, Lizzie, 246–48
Whitlock, William, 246–48
Whitted, Stephen F., 277n
Wickersham, Col. D., 244
Wickersham, Daniel, 8
Wiggins, Billie, 18
Wiggins, Henry, 18
Wiggins, Joe, 18
Wiggins, Polly, 18
Wiggins, Robert, 18
wildcat, 305n
wild turkey, 184–85
Wilkerson, Isaiah, 237
Wilkerson, John, 12
Williams, Bob, 31
Williams, John E., 58, 287n
Wilmoth, George, 248
Wilmoth, Pop, 248
Wilmoth, Preacher George, 248
Wilson, Dr., 61
Wilson, Henry, 250
Wilson, Peggie, 250
Winberry, John J., 278n
winged elm, 312n
Wish, Harvey, 261n
Wolf, Maj. Jacob, 7, 67, 72, 266n
Wolf, John Quincy, 268n
wolves, 71, 135–60, 301n; life span, 302n
Womack's Mill, Mo., 37
Wood, Capt. A. S. "Bud," 51, 228, 315n
Wood, Ben, 8
Wood, Berry, 96
Wood, "Dancin'" Bill, 8, 48
Wood, Dave, 40
Wood, Derl, 253
Wood, Frank, 93–94
Wood, Capt. Fred, 228
Wood, George, 49, 202, 310n
Wood, Jane, 310–11n
Wood, Jim, 18, 218
Wood, John, 48
Wood, John B., 206
Wood, Lize, 17
Wood, Nancy, 310n

Wood, "Rosin Bill," 17
Wood, Sally, 253–54
Wood, "Snappin' Bill," 47
Wood, "Southfoot Bill," 17
Wood, "Squirrel Bill," 17
Wood, Tol, 188
Wood family, 310–11n
woods, open, 3
Woods Mill, Ark., 17
Woodward, Grace Steele, 264n
Worley, Ted R., 293n, 303n
Wright, Harold Bell, xxi
Wright, Martin, 317n
Wright, Thomas E., 316n

Yandell, Bob, 59
Yandell, Charley, 59
Yandell, John, 27, 155, 245
Yates, Norris W., 293n
Yates, William A., 283n
yellow jackets, 204, 311n
Yellville, Ark., 5, 47, 49, 50, 53, 78, 81, 93, 133, 155, 170, 221, 225, 246, 253–54, 279n, 285n, 309n, 314n
Yocum, A. T., 291n
Yocum, Asa, 18, 128, 270n
Yocum, George, 291n
Yocum, Harve, 18, 19
Yocum, Jacob, 264n
Yocum, Jake, 18, 23
Yocum, Jess, 5, 20, 23, 264n
Yocum, John, 19
Yocum, Mike, 18, 19, 22–23, 57, 128, 264n, 273n
Yocum, Nancy, 19
Yocum, "River Bill," 17
Yocum, Sally, 17, 18, 19, 273n
Yocum, Solomon, 17, 23, 264n, 270n
Yocum, "Thresher" Bill, 206, 212
Yocum, William, 18, 19
Yocum, Winnie, 17
Yocum Creek, Mo., 229
Yocum Mill, Mo., 291n
Young, John, 70

www.ingramcontent.com/pod-product-compliance
Lightning Source LLC
Chambersburg PA
CBHW021847230426
43671CB00006B/296